WAKE TECHNICAL ~~ LIBRARY
9101 ~~
~~ RALEIGH ~~ ~03

D0148138

Builder's Guide to Landscaping

Other volumes in the Builder's Guide Series

Builder's Guide to Landscaping

Jonathan Hutchings

McGraw-Hill

New York San Francisco Washington, D.C. Auckland Bogotá
Caracas Lisbon London Madrid Mexico City Milan
Montreal New Delhi San Juan Singapore
Sydney Tokyo Toronto

McGraw-Hill

A Division of The **McGraw·Hill** Companies

Copyright ©1997 by Jonathan Hutchings. All rights reserved. Printed in the United States of America. Except as permitted under the United States Copyright Act of 1976, no part of this publication may be reproduced or distributed in any form or by any means, or stored in a data base or retrieval system, without the prior written permission of the publisher.

1 2 3 4 5 6 7 8 9 0 DOC/DOC 9 0 1 0 9 8 7 6

ISBN 0-07-031809-3 (HC)
      0-07-031830-1 (PBK)

The sponsoring editor for this book was Zoe G. Foundotos, the editing supervisor was Sally Glover, and the production supervisor was Claire Stanley. It was set in Garamond by McGraw-Hill's Professional Book Group Composition Unit, Hightstown, N.J.

Printed and bound by R.R. Donnelley & Sons Company..

This book is printed on recycled, acid-free paper containing a minimum of 50% recycled, de-inked fiber.

McGraw-Hill books are available at special quantity discounts to use as premiums and sales promotions, or for use in corporate training programs. For more information, please write to the Director of Special Sales, McGraw-Hill, 11 West 19th Street, New York, NY 10011. Or contact your local bookstore.

Information contained in this work has been obtained by the McGraw-Hill Companies, Inc. ("McGraw-Hill") from sources believed to be reliable. However, neither McGraw-Hill nor its authors guarantee the accuracy or completeness of any information published herein and neither McGraw-Hill nor its authors shall be responsible for any errors, omissions, or damages arising out of use of this information. This work is published with the understanding that McGraw-Hill and its authors are supplying information, but are not attempting to render engineering or other professional services. If such services are required, the assistance of an appropriate professional should be sought.

Contents

Acknowledgments

I would like to take this opportunity to thank the individuals and companies that contributed to the production of this book and give them their deserved moment of your attention. These professionals are competent and caring people. We should all be proud that folks like these are continuing to build the American Dream.

National Landscaping Standards Committee, Washington, D.C.

National Safety Council, Itasca, Illinois

Fran Giknis, manager, Georgia-Pacific Timber Corp., Atlanta, Georgia

Mary Robinson, Toro Landscaping Equipment Corp., Riverside, California

Robert Davison, owner, Emerald Cut Graphics, Oak Harbor, Washington

Alice Haynes, American Timber Association, Seattle, Washington

Robert Cados, director, Construction Management Institute, Soquel, California

Chad Simmons, director, Construction Management Institute, Soquel, California

Special thanks and a tip of the hat to April D. Nolan, my former editor, whose continuing help, support, and professional expertise were pivotal factors in making this reference book available in the extensive McGraw-Hill *Builder's Guide Series*. Without her, this book would have never made the long journey to your hands, your eyes, your computer, and your business. She and all the folks I have dealt with over the years at McGraw-Hill have been outstanding individuals and very competent professionals.

For you, the builder, it all boils down to the fact that the American builder is in a transition period that may never cease. Probably won't. This generation will see a faster rate of change yet to come. The next generation will see an even faster one. So all that technology stuff you thought was way off in the future and could be dealt with later is here today. And you'd better deal with it pronto, because I can guarantee you that your competition is. In the coming weeks and the coming years, tomorrow's business (or lack of) and your business's reputation will ride on the trail that you leave today. Education and learning is a lifelong process, and the construction industry is evolving rapidly. If you ever reach the point in your career as a builder where you think you know it all, look down . . .

You've got one foot in the bear trap.

Foreword

I've known the author of this book for two decades now, and even though he's about as sophisticated as 10 miles of timber haul road, he's right about one thing. Times have sure changed in the construction industry. Used to be a builder learned the trade and applied it that way the rest of his or her days. Nowadays change is a daily part of any builder's business. It seems that any spare time I have these days is spent trying to catch up on the industry periodicals and magazines piling up on my desk. I can't avoid reading them as new technologies are in use everywhere in modern construction techniques, my customers ask about them, and every builder must master them to remain competitive in the long run.

I say this because you, the builder interested enough to pick up this book and check it out, must realize that the entire construction industry has changed drastically from the old days and the old ways, just as all businesses must, to survive the new age of the twenty-first century. This book can help you learn how to make the new technologies in project landscaping work for you now and in the coming years. What you will learn from this landscaping reference manual today is real-world application stuff that you can use on the job tomorrow. Builders these days know that to improve their business sales and remain competitive, they must learn to apply their skills by using the new technologies rushing at them at breakneck speed. In commercial construction projects today, I typically see that about 10 percent of landscaping components installed are new technology that I've never seen before or a new twist on an old component. The image of landscapers working out of the back of an old pickup has evolved to contractors using modern computerized irrigation and energy-saving water systems. Without these new, modern landscaping technologies, no commercial project would be economically feasible in terms of operational maintenance. The costs would simply be prohibitive, and that phase of the project would be unprofitable for the owner. The landscaping options at that point would be tumbleweeds and gravel.

Talk to any local builder nowadays and chances are he or she will tell you that one of the biggest areas of project profit concern is landscaping. The plants and irrigation must be cost-effective to install and take the first time for any profit to be made. Any callbacks for dead plants or lawn areas come right out of your pocket—forget breaking even. Builders also know that large companies have greater buying power when buying materials, so the only competitive edge the builder may have in landscaping is being up on new, cost-effective systems and techniques.

Building has always been a competitive business, but the structure of the building industry is fairly stable, despite the financial success of some large companies and the failure of small-volume companies in times of recession. Small-volume builders (those starting 25 units or fewer a year) accounted for 30 percent of all residential builders in 1995, a share that has remained relatively constant for the last two decades. Large companies (those starting 100 units or more a year) account for 70 percent of all builders. Their share of housing starts has edged up steadily during the past five years of the 1990s. The small builder has no choice anymore. To turn a profit in the landscaping portion of the job, today's builder must be savvy in the options of modern techniques if he or she is to survive.

For a construction project to have profitability, modern landscaping techniques can mean the difference between your company's healthy income this year or being history next year. Modern landscaping techniques are one way we builders manage to get a competitive leg up on project profit. And one of the best construction management professionals I've ever known is the author of this book. This edition will definitely be on my shelf, and if you're serious about carving out a successful career as tomorrow's American builder, my advice to you is to grab this very special book in a hurry before they sell out.

Chad Simmons
CA Lic 444986
President, Simmons Construction Company
Santa Clara, California

Introduction

We professional builders are not confused about our purpose. We are not here to leave some esoteric architectural legacy. We leave that stuff to the architects. We builders are here to make a profit. That's the truth, pure and simple (although the truth is rarely pure and never simple). No profit equals no business: It's a simple enough equation even we contractors can understand. My objective in this book is to help you make a profit in the landscaping phases of your projects by understanding the basic materials and procedures used today in modern building project landscaping and by making use of the new benefits of computerized layouts and takeoffs.

New landscaping components, systems, and techniques are rolling across residential and commercial job sites nationwide like tumbleweeds blowing across the high-plains desert. Even the old trade of site landscaping is evolving at a rapid pace as the age of technology advances the entire construction industry's rate of change. Builders are looking to modern landscaping systems for innovative and cost-effective ground cover. The modern age of technology has brought in new types of irrigation systems that use less energy and less water and provide better coverage than older, more expensive systems. Fertilization methods have improved, and botanical species of varying kinds can be grown right in among the indigenous plant life. Today's business facilities, developers, and home buyers are more sophisticated than ever before and are doing their homework. They want lush landscaping with a minimum of maintenance. They also want the monthly maintenance bill to be cheap. They are expecting these modern, low-maintenance, cost-effective landscaping systems from you, their potential builder.

The new age of technology has also brought in new types of geotextile materials and powerful new computer systems using dedicated software programs, opening the way for the average small-volume builder to easily design a complete, custom landscaping project for any job's requirements. In a world of constantly changing market environments, the small builder's survival strategy includes employing the most efficient and profit-effective new landscaping techniques that will actually be used in the next century.

According to a survey done by *Builder Magazine*, today's small-volume American builder is a business entrepreneur who builds fewer than 25 houses a year, has an average annual volume of less than $1 million, builds primarily single-family move-up houses of 1801 to 2500 square feet, employs one to three full-time staffers, dabbles in remodeling when things are slow, and has been in the business for more than 10 years. These small-business owners must constantly upgrade their skills to take advantage of the new technologies in construction techniques and remain competitive with the "big boys." This typical American builder is conservative, leans to the right in voting, and runs a local hometown business that is lean and mean with few full-time employees. Six out of ten build in one market only, but many have diversified into other businesses: Ninety percent do some remodeling, one in three develops land, and one in four does commercial work on the side. And builders, like people everywhere who work too hard, are always reassessing their priorities. When asked about their most important personal goal between now and the end of the century, most builders replied that it was spending more time with family. A close second was staying in business. Sound familiar? Well, that's my objective from here on out—to help you save time and money on the job in your project's landscaping needs.

This book is unique in that it addresses the field of small-volume builder needs in project landscaping as it has never been addressed before. The products and techniques learned from this book can be applied by any builder of residential or commercial construction projects. In today's fiercely competitive business world, there just isn't room any longer for mediocre procedures that are not cost-effective. Costs of materials and labor must be bid tight, and there's not much margin for error. Accordingly, today's profits in construction projects are being made by superior builders using updated construction production systems, including modern landscaping construction techniques. In modern residential and commercial construction, it is the cost savings of installing new-technology construction systems like the ones we'll explore in this book that are pivotal in bringing the project into existence on or under budget.

But the traditional ways that brought us function with quality, by proud craftsmen, will not be overlooked. I'm a definite advocate of technological change. I used to fear it because, as a small businessman, I couldn't control it, but time has gone by and I've used computers for so many years that now I realize computers are just dumb recording boxes that do calculations fast. The *real* technological change exists between our ears. But the one thing missing from the "better living through technology" theory is old-fashioned pride in craftsmanship. In the tradition of pride in quality of workmanship of the American builder, we start from square one with the traditional tools and methods and run the whole course.

I have earned my living in the construction industry for more than 20 years now, from apprentice to journeyman, foreman to contractor, in management roles from estimator to project manager. In those two decades, I have seen many changes that foreshadow even bigger changes in the future as the new century accelerates us into a new world. Of all the things we use today, 75 percent have been invented within the past 50 years. Of those, 80 percent have been invented in the past 10 years. It is estimated that, of all the things we will be building with by the year 2025, 90 percent *haven't even been invented yet.* Trick stuff like graphite-composite plastics that are stronger than steel, air-entrained lightweight concrete, and ultralight metal alloys are all space-age technology being used in modular construction today. And even as you read this, the clock on their obsolescence is ticking.

Paradigm means the currently accepted parameters of any specific thing, such as an industry. And the construction industry's paradigm is changing as fast as the clouds above your head. More importantly, as Alvin Toffler so correctly stated in his prescient book, *Future Shock*, the *rate* of that change is also accelerating exponentially. Change is happening faster to us than it did to our parents. Change is happening faster to our children than it did to us. Change is happening faster today than it did yesterday. Tomorrow it will be twice as fast. The winners of tomorrow will be those people who take advantage of change and use that change to their benefit.

Worldwide, in residential construction, American Western Platform Framing is the accepted standard of excellence in home-building. The Western Wood Products Association in the United States has grading rules for lumber that are among the most stringent in the world, and the European construction industry uses its products as building standards. After serving as an estimator and consultant for the insurance industry's reconstruction efforts in both the 7.8-Richter-scale Loma Prieta earthquake of 1989 and the 7.3-Richter-scale Northridge-Los Angeles earthquake of 1993 and having witnessed the devastation firsthand, I now understand why the rest of the world sends building officials and industry representatives to America to learn our methods of construction. When one stops and reflects, the reason the world looks to us for leadership in construction is quite clear . . . we build the best.

That is not just my opinion; it is documented fact. The statistics tell the story: 61 casualties in Northridge, Los Angeles, compared to 5000 in Kobe, Japan. Kobe registered 5.8 on the Richter scale, L.A. measured 7.3. Yet we had fewer casualties in the stronger quake. The difference was due, in part, to our highly evolved standards of construction techniques and superior materials. In residential and commercial construction, our methods of modern construction are unequaled in history. Construction is the last proud American industry still retaining global leadership and justifiably so. Modern landscaping construction is part of the next step in this proud industry, and you were wise to have picked up this book. A solid answer to your project's landscaping materials, cost, and systems selection lies here in your hands.

Remember, in matters of the real-world applications of construction contracts, always research the contract's general conditions and specifications thoroughly, make sure your cost estimates are as up-to-date as possible, and consult an attorney in all matters of contractual obligation. Further, please be informed that the subjects, theories, and opinions contained herein are for general information purposes only and are not to be construed as legal advice. Both the publisher and the author assume no liability whatsoever, either expressed or implied, for business applications or any other usage of this instructional reference manual. The entire contents of this product are protected from any form of physical or electronic copying, storage, or duplication, worldwide, by United States copyright law and are intended for instructional purposes only.

1

Safety

We begin at the fundamental start of any building-trades lesson, with operator safety. Your safety is *your* responsibility at all times in construction work. You can kill yourself with ignorance of the tools, chemicals, or working conditions in a construction project, and everyone will be sorry the accident occurred, but you'll be the one who's dead. Never for a moment forget how inherently dangerous your business is. And the landscaping aspect of your project is no place for you or your workers to be daydreaming. If your employees are working while looking for another station on their FM headphones, I suggest they do so in the unemployment line. Chemicals used in modern landscaping can injure or kill a careless operator. If he or she is your employee and it happens on the job, the Occupational Safety and Health Administration (OSHA) will see to it that you lose your license and your business.

Using pesticides

You are required by OSHA law to maintain material safety data sheets (MSDSs) on all hazardous chemicals used in your operations. Standard practical operating procedures for safety in using chemicals and pesticides in landscaping begin by always reading the label and MSDS and following the directions and stated precautions each time. That sentence sounds mundane, canned, and easily forgotten, but it is the first commandment of handling toxic chemicals. If you remember nothing else in this chapter, remember that. It will serve you well. And always insist your workers take the time to read the manual. Always read the manufacturer's label and instructions for warnings *before* opening the container. Never let your workers open something they are not trained and equipped to handle. OSHA mandates their training, and if your employee is injured or dies from your negligence in safety at work, you'll lose your business and may be incarcerated as well. Make sure a proper accident report is recorded (Figure 1-1).

Accident Report

(Please Print or Type All Entries)

Accident With Injury ☐   Accident With Property Damage ☐   Near Miss ☐

1. Dept.: _____   2. Date of Accident: _____   3. Time _____   a.m.   (Circle
   p.m.   One)

4. Name of Injured: _____   5. SSN: _____   6. Age: _____   7. Sex _____

8. Title/Occupation: _____   9. Time Employed in Present Position: _____

10. Employee is: Full Time   /   Part Time   /   Student   (Circle all that apply)

11. Location of Accident: (Be Specific) _____

12. Witnesses: _____

13. Severity of Injury: First Aid Only ☐   Medical Treatment Required ☐

14. Treatment was obtained at: ISU Health Center ☐   Personal Physician ☐
    Ames Medical Center ☐   Other ☐

15. a.   Accident may result in lost time from work?   Yes   /   No   /   Unknown   (Circle One)
    b.   Probable loss time: _____
    c.   Physician released injured to: Normal Duty ☐   Limited ☐
    If not released to duty or assigned to limited duty, estimate return to normal duty
    Date: _____
    d.   If property damage occurred, estimate dollar amount: _____

16. Kind of Injury: _____

17. Part of Body Involved: _____

18. Act or operation being performed at the time of injury: _____

19. Prior training or safety instruction for this job has been given?   Yes   /   No   /   Unknown   (Circle One)

20. What was the victim doing that may have contributed to the accident? _____

21. What personal factors may have contributed to the accident? _____

22. What conditions existed that may have contributed to the accident? _____

23. How could this accident have been prevented? _____

24. Report filed by: _____   Date: _____

FILE REPORT WITHIN 24 HOURS OF NOTIFICATION
The statements and facts included in this form shall not constitute nor be construed to constitute any admission or evidence of liability.

1-1 *Accident report.*

Always identify a plant's pest first and then determine if control is needed. If so, select the right pesticide for the crop, animal, or site and the associated pest problem. No shortcuts are acceptable here. Pesticides that require special protective clothing or equipment should be used only by trained, experienced applicators. Most states require that such a person be licensed. Store pesticides under lock and key in acceptable areas in the original container with proper labels affixed. Store feed or seed separately from pesticides. Keep herbicides separate from other types of pesticides to prevent contamination. Never transfer a pesticide to a container that would attract children, such as a food or soft-drink container. Keep pesticides in their original labeled container. Check the expiration date on the pesticide label. Do not use outdated chemicals. Do not save or reuse empty pesticide containers. Dispose of containers promptly as follows:

- Do not puncture or burn pressurized containers.
- Rinse empty containers that hold liquid pesticides three times before disposal.
- Dispose of the rinse water in a proper manner.
- Crush or puncture metal and plastic containers.
- Break glass containers and take them to a state-approved sanitary landfill.

Check your application equipment before each use for leaks and clogged lines, nozzles, and strainers. Calibrate your equipment frequently for proper output. Check gloves, respirators, and other protective clothing for holes and cleanliness before each use. Check respirators for clean filters and good fit. Make sure people have been warned and livestock and pets that may be exposed have been removed from the treated area. Do not open any hazardous chemical or pesticide without first reading the MSDS, and apply the exact amount of pesticide that the label recommends. When opening a container of liquid pesticide, keep your face away from and to one side of the cap or lid. Mix or prepare dusts or sprays only while wearing a respirator outdoors or in a well-ventilated area. And never smoke, eat, or drink while handling a pesticide. (Sounds like common sense, but you'd be surprised at the number of workers who sit down and eat their lunches without washing their hands.)

After finishing the work, wash exposed skin surfaces with soap and water. If you spill pesticide on your skin or clothing, remove the contaminated clothing quickly, and wash the exposed skin surfaces with soap and water. Launder the clothing before wearing again. If pesticide gets into your eyes, flush with water for 10 minutes, and get immediate medical attention. If you swallow or splash pesticide in your mouth, check the label to see if vomiting should be induced. If you become ill during or shortly after using a pesticide, call a physician or poison-control center immediately. Read the medical personnel the names of the active chemical ingredients from the label on the container. Follow their instructions for first-aid treatment. If you go to a physician or control center for treatment, take the label with you or as much information as possible about the pesticide, such as the names of the active ingredients, antidote statements, or statement of practical treatment. Check the label for recommended time intervals between the date of application and re-entry or harvest. If no re-entry time is given on the label, keep people, pets, etc., out of treated areas until sprays have dried and dusts have settled.

It is a violation of federal and state laws to misuse any pesticide. Always use any chemical product in a manner consistent with its labeling.

The types of pesticide exposures are

- *Dermal* (through the skin). Different parts of the body absorb the pesticide at different rates. The facial area absorbs three to four times faster than the hand or arm area.
- *Oral* (through the mouth).
- *Inhalation* (through the mouth or nose into the lungs).

Exposure to toxic pesticides can make you ill, and some pesticides are so poisonous that they can kill you. Some pesticides seem less harmful, so the applicator might not be as cautious around them. However, over a length of time, repeated exposures can build up in the applicator's body and cause serious illness or irreversible damage.

Pesticides carry one or more active ingredients in a liquid, powder, or granular form. Their availability is constantly shifting. New products continue to be developed and marketed. Existing products may be withdrawn from sale if research reveals hazards to health or the environment. On the label of each product is a list of plants and pests on which the control is registered for use. It is illegal to apply the control to a plant or pest that is not listed on the label.

You can use the best pesticides in the world, but they still can't make your pest-control program effective and responsible. That won't happen until you do three things:

1. Choose the right equipment.
2. Calibrate your equipment properly.
3. Calculate the proper pesticide amounts. Pesticides work only as well as your equipment.

Choose from the many different types of equipment to suit your preferences and needs.

Sprayers

Lawn spray guns are ideal for applying pesticides on lawn areas. These sprayers feature nozzle tips with a 45-degree full cone to provide a "showerhead" spray pattern. Guns also have a convenient trigger lock for continuous spraying. The maximum operating pressure is 150 pounds per square inch (psi). Extension wands are also available for low-volume and spot-spray applications. Lawn spray guns are economical and easy to use, clean, and store. Boom-type sprayers are designed to spray larger turfgrass areas fairly quickly and may be mounted on a vehicle or a walk-behind.

Nozzles

The spray nozzle is perhaps the least expensive but most important part of your sprayer. It directs the flow rate, breaks up the mixture into droplets, and disperses the droplets in a specific pattern. No single nozzle can meet all your spraying needs, so it pays to choose the right one, mount it at the correct height, spacing, and angle, and operate it at the right pressure range. You can choose from four popular nozzles with different angles and spray rates: whirl chamber nozzle, flat fan nozzle, wide-angle full cone nozzle, and flood nozzle.

Flood nozzles produce a wide, flat spray pattern for reduced spray drift. Use them for soil-applied herbicides. The wide spray angle (110 to 130 degrees) allows wider nozzle spacing and lower boom heights. Tests show a higher concentration of spray on the outer edges of the spray pattern, so each nozzle must be set at a spacing, height, and orientation to give at least double coverage (100-percent overlap). *Whirl chamber nozzles* form a hollow cone, saddle-shaped pattern with fan angles of up to 120 degrees. Lower concentrations of the spray appear in the center, while higher concentrations are on the outer edges of the pattern. That's why you should set each nozzle at the right angle, spacing, and height to overlap spray by 100 percent for uniform spray coverage.

Flat fan nozzles form a fan-shaped pattern and are typically used for postemergent herbicides. Many angles are available, but 80-degree tips are most common. The edges of this pattern have lower spray volumes than the center, so you should adjust the spray height and angle to overlap patterns by about 30 percent to get a consistent spray pattern without hot spots or skips.

Wide-angle full cone nozzles produce excellent spray distribution and large droplets to minimize spray drift. It's important to set your spray boom at the proper height and your nozzles at the correct spacing to prevent possible gaps in your pattern. Set both to achieve about a 15- to 20-percent overlap on each edge of the pattern, and your coverage will be uniform.

Granular applicators

Granular applicators include walk-behind drop and rotary-type spreaders, hand-carried knapsack and spinning-disk spreaders for broadcast application of granular pesticides, mounted equipment for band application, and tractor-mounted equipment for broadcast coverage. Their advantages are no mixing, low cost, and little drift.

Guidelines for applying pesticides

Obey all label instructions and precautions. Avoid working directly in drift, spray, or runoff, and always wear protective clothing. Do not wipe your gloves on your clothing. Never eat, drink, smoke, or chew when handling or applying pesticides. If you feel ill, seek help right away. Do not apply pesticides during or just before expected high winds or heavy rains. Check all equipment for leaking hoses, pumps, or connections, as well as for plugged, worn, or dripping nozzles, to prevent spillage. Never let children, pets, or unauthorized persons touch application equipment or enter storage areas. Use any leftover pesticide for labeled uses. Before applying, clear the area of all unprotected persons.

Turf spray guns

To properly calibrate these sprayers and train your applicators, you need to know these four important factors: application rate, swath width, walking speed, and calibration and flow rate.

The standard *application rate* is measured in the amount of liquid applied per unit area, usually in gallons per 1000 square feet.

Nozzle Styles and Pressure Ranges.

Nozzle type	Suggested uses	Pressure ranges (psi)	Overlap required
Flood	Preemergence and postemergence herbicides where drift may be hazardous	10–25	100%
Whirl chamber	Foliar applications of insecticides and fungicides	5–20	100%
Flat fan	Preemergence and postemergence weed control	15–60	30%
Wide-angle full cone	Preemergence and postemergence herbicides where drift control is needed	15–30	15–20%

Several factors can affect this rate: equipment, spray delivery system, product, target, growing conditions, and operational considerations. Your goal is to apply the proper rate consistently in a uniform practice.

For lawns, *swath width* ranges from 3 to 10 feet. You can use a series of collection cups or a spray tray to measure the swath width you want. A standardized height (and movement with certain handheld spray delivery systems) ensures that a constant swath width is maintained. An effective swath is the total swath width minus the amount of swath overlap, which can vary by spray delivery system.

Once you've established the dimensions of your calibration course, here's how to find out the right *walking speed* for application. Just time your trainee while he or she covers the course with the effective spray width. Or if you need to find out the speed in miles per hour, use the following formula:

Distance (feet)/time (seconds) × 60/88 = Walking speed (mph)

Calibration is the process of measuring and adjusting the amount of liquid mixture applied to an area. Use this basic formula:

Calibration course × flow = gallons/1000 square feet flow rate coverage time.

For example,

30 seconds/1000 square feet × 1 gallon/60 seconds = 1/2 gallon/1000
square feet

You can easily adapt this formula to any application rate, method, and coverage time. For example, if you have established an application rate of 3 gallons per 1000 square feet, and the spray method, overlap practice, and walking speed result in a coverage time of 45 seconds, you can find out the required nozzle flow rate for calibration by using the previous formula:

45 seconds/1000 square feet × ?/60 seconds = 3 gallons/1000 square feet

45 seconds × ? = 60 seconds × 3 gallons, or 180

? = 180/45 = 4

The flow rate should be adjusted to 4 gallons per minute.

Boom-type sprayers

For large turfgrass areas, follow these instructions to calibrate your boom-type sprayer.

Find an area that best represents the average topography for the area to be sprayed. Measure it and mark off the calibration distance that coincides with your nozzle spacing or band width. Walk or drive across the area, maintaining an even speed. If you are using a vehicle-mounted sprayer, notice what the engine rpm is and what gear it is in, and write it down so that you use the same speed during calibration and application. Record the number of seconds it takes to travel the calibration distance and write it down. Fill your sprayer with water, engage the pump, and adjust the pressure regulator to the boom pressure you want (between 15 and 50 psi for pesticides). Collect all the water from one nozzle for the same number of seconds you've recorded. For example, with a 20-inch nozzle spacing, if it took 35 seconds to travel 204 feet, collect the discharge of one nozzle for 35 seconds. The number of fluid ounces collected equals the gallons per acre (GPA) of output of that nozzle. For example, 20 ounces collected equals 20 GPA.

Repeat the previous step two more times, collecting water from a different nozzle each time. The average number of ounces collected from each of the three nozzles is equal to the gallons of water applied per acre for that boom. Also remember to maintain the same pressure and travel speed when spraying. Divide the capacity of the tank by the number of gallons of water applied per acre (GPA) to find out the area (in acres) you can cover with a tankful of spray. For example, 200 gallons per tank divided by 20 GPA equals 10 acres covered per tank. To find out how much pesticide you need to add to the spray tank, multiply the application rate of the product per acre by the acres covered per tank. Then add that amount of pesticide to your sprayer tank. For example, 2 quarts per acre times 10 acres per tank equals 20 quarts, or 5 gallons of pesticide per tank.

Granular applicators

Granular applicators can be calibrated in turf or other areas off the application site. You can also use plain fertilizers of the same type that you'll use in fertilizer/pesticide combination products. For manually operated spreaders, the person who does the actual application should be the one who calibrates the equipment. Just follow these simple steps:

Mark out a test strip of 440 square feet (approximately 1/100th of an acre). Weigh your granular pesticide before and after you apply.

Subtract the difference to get the amount applied, then multiply by 100 to get the amount you need per acre. Adjust your equipment and repeat the test until you have the correct setting for the required amount per acre. Different pesticides may have granules of different sizes. Also, a pesticide may change the size of its granules from one year to the next. You should repeat your calibration procedure each time you apply a different granular pesticide.

Fungicide products that can be applied through sprinkler irrigation systems (including center pivot) should not be applied through any other type of irrigation system. For spray preparation, remove scale, pesticide residues, and other foreign matter from the chemical tank and entire injector system. Flush with clean water. Prepare a suspension of the product in a mix tank. Fill the tank with three quarters the desired amount of water. Start mechanical or hydraulic agitation. Add the required amount of fungicide, and then the remaining volume of water. (Suspension concentrations are calculated using the appropriate dosage per acre recommended on the label.) Then set the sprinkler to deliver 0.1 to 0.3 inch of water per acre. Station sprinklers uniformly inject the suspension of fungicide into the irrigation water line so as to deliver the desired rate per acre. The suspension of fungicide should be injected with a positive displacement pump into the main line ahead of a right-angle turn to ensure adequate mixing. When treatment with the fungicide has been completed, further field irrigation over the treated area should be avoided for 24 to 48 hours to prevent washing the chemical off the crop. If you should have any other questions about calibration, you should contact your state extension service specialists, equipment manufacturers, or other experts.

General precautions for applications through sprinkler irrigation systems begin by maintaining continuous agitation in the mix tank during mixing and application to ensure a uniform suspension. Greater accuracy in calibration and distribution can be achieved by injecting a larger volume of a more dilute solution per unit time. The system must contain a functional check valve, vacuum relief valve, and low-pressure drain appropriately located on the irrigation pipeline to prevent water-source contamination from backflow. The pesticide injection pipeline must contain a functional, automatic, quick-closing check valve to prevent the flow of fluid back toward the injection pump. The pesticide injection pipeline must also contain a functional, normally closed, solenoid-operated valve located on the intake side of the injection pump and connected to the system interlock to prevent fluid from being withdrawn from the supply tank when the irrigation system is either automatically or manually shut down.

The system must contain functional interlocking controls to automatically shut off the pesticide injection pump when the water pump motor stops. The irrigation line or water pump must include a functional pressure switch that stops the water pump motor when the water pressure decreases to the point where pesticide distribution is adversely affected. Systems must use a metering pump, such as a positive displacement injection pump (e.g., a diaphragm pump), effectively designed and constructed of materials that are compatible with pesticides and capable of being fined with a system interlock. Do not apply when wind speed favors drift, when system connection or fittings leak, when nozzles do not provide uniform distribution, or when lines containing the product must be dismantled and drained. Allow sufficient time for the pesticide to be flushed through all lines and all nozzles before turning off irrigation water. A person certified as an applicator who is knowledgeable of the chemical and irrigation system and is responsible for its operation must shut down the system and make necessary adjustments should the need arise. Crop injury, lack of effectiveness, or illegal pesticide residues in the landscape may result from nonuniform distribution of treated water. Do not connect an irrigation system (including greenhouse systems) used for pesticide application to a public water system unless the label-prescribed safety devices for public water supplies are in place.

The applicator should wear clean cotton (or cloth) coveralls that cover all parts of the body except the head, hands, and feet. The coveralls must be worn over a long-sleeve shirt and long pants. Wear clean nitrile gloves, a chemical-resistant apron, goggles or a face shield, and chemical-resistant shoes, shoe coverings, or boots. When applying any product from a tractor (unless it has a completely enclosed cab) or when repairing or cleaning equipment used with the product, the applicator must wear clean nitrile gloves and clean cotton (or cloth) coveralls that cover all parts of the body except the head, hands, and feet. Coveralls must be worn over a long-sleeve shirt and long pants. All applicators (except for pilots) and all persons repairing or cleaning equipment used with this product must wear chemical-resistant shoes, shoe coverings, or boots. Application from a tractor with a completely enclosed cab or aerial application is required whenever a product is applied to 360 or more acres in a day. To avoid contamination, coveralls and gloves worn when handling the concentrate must be removed prior to entering an enclosed cab or cockpit. When applying the product from a tractor with an enclosed cab, clean coveralls and clean nitrile gloves must be kept inside the cab and must be worn when exiting the cab to perform in-field maintenance or repair. To reduce exposure to residues, wash the spray rig, tractor, and all other equipment used to handle or apply the product with clean water daily or before using the equipment for any other purpose. Before removing gloves or starting a new work operation, rinse the outside of the gloves thoroughly with water. Always remove gloves and wash your hands and face with soap and water before smoking, eating, drinking, or using the restroom.

When applying any product from aerial application, human flaggers are prohibited unless in enclosed vehicles. Aerial application is prohibited within 300 feet of residential areas (e.g., homes, schools, hospitals, shopping areas, etc.). If tank mixing, a compatibility test is recommended to ensure satisfactory spray preparation. To test for compatibility, use a small container and mix a small amount (0.5 to 1 quart) of spray, combining all ingredients in the same ratio as the anticipated use. If any indications of physical incompatibility develop, do not use this mixture for spraying. Indications of incompatibility usually appear within 5 to 15 minutes after mixing. To ensure maximum crop safety and weed control, follow all cautions and limitations on the labels of products used in the tank mixture. Maintain sufficient agitation while mixing and during application to ensure a uniform spray mixture. If the spray mixture is allowed to remain without agitation for short periods of time, be sure to agitate until uniformly mixed before application.

Fertilizers and spray additives can increase foliage leaf burn when applied with pesticides. Do not apply fertilizers or spray additives with pesticides if leaf burn is a major concern due to environmental conditions, crop, or variety sensitivity. Do not apply pesticides in combination with fertilizer or spray additive if restricted under the individual crop-use directions.

Terms and definitions

acre An area of land equal to 43,560 square feet.
acute toxicity The sudden onset of chemical poisoning symptoms from one exposure to a harmful chemical.
antidote A remedy to counteract the effects of poison.
application rate Amount of chemical applied per acre.
articulated equipment Tractors and/or implements that are connected with joints. These machines roll easily and can crush you. Extreme care must be used when operating them, especially on slopes.
boom A long pipe or tubing with several nozzles used to apply chemicals over a wide area at one time.
calibrate To determine the application rate of a sprayer or spreader.
chronic toxicity The gradual onset of chemical poisoning symptoms from frequent exposures to a harmful pesticide over a long time.

contaminate To accidentally poison desirable plants, animals, people, food, supplies, or the environment with harmful chemicals.
exposure Direct or indirect contact with a harmful chemical.
ground-driven Attachments that are operated by being pulled or pushed by a tractor.
hydraulic Operated or moved by means of water or other liquid in motion.
pest A plant or animal that annoys or is harmful to humans (weeds, insects, diseases).
pneumatic Operated or moved by means of air or other gas under pressure. Pneumatic pressure lines, if leaking, can inject the substance into your skin because of the high pressure.
poison A substance that through its chemical action can kill or injure an organism.

Storing hazardous chemicals

Improper storage and handling of chemicals and flammable liquids are the leading causes of industrial fires in the nation's construction-industry workplaces, causing millions of dollars of damage annually. Storing potentially dangerous chemicals on a job site properly can help eliminate the often avoidable damages suffered by construction companies and their employees. Standards have been developed by the National Fire Prevention Association (NFPA) and OSHA to ensure that storage cabinets for dangerous chemicals and flammable liquids meet specific legal requirements, which reduces the risk of danger to employees. NFPA and OSHA construction standards are listed, along with points to consider before choosing your safety cabinet. Remember that a cabinet's product life also depends on vapor types and concentrations present. Fire-rated cabinets must have a two-hour burn-through rate on the walls and one and a half-hour burn-through rate on the doors.

Metal cabinet requirements

Chapter 4, Sections 4-3.2 and 4-3.2.1 of NFPA Code 30 and OSHA 1910.106(d)(3) state:

Bottom, top, door and sides of cabinet shall be at least No. 18-gauge sheet steel.
Walls must be double walled with 1½" airspace.
Joints shall be riveted, welded or made tight by some equally effective means.
Door shall have a three-point latch.

Door sill shall be raised at least 2" above cabinet bottom to retain spilled liquid within cabinet; this 2" bottom well for spill containment must be liquid-tight.

Single or dual 2" flame arrestor vents with removable 2" steel plugs with integral perforated steel fire baffles covering each vent.

"FLAMMABLE — KEEP FIRE AWAY" legend sign must be on door.

Wood cabinet requirements

Chapter 4, Sections 4-3.2 and 4-3.2.2 of NFPA Code 30 and OSHA 29 CFR 1910.106(d)(3) state:

Bottom, sides and top shall be constructed of exterior grade plywood at least 1" thick.

Plywood shall be minimum 1" thick 9-ply high-density that will not break down or delaminate under fire conditions and interior must be laminated with a chemical resistant material such as Chemsurf™ [the same nonporous material used on lab countertops].

Joints shall be rabbeted and fastened in two directions with wood screws.

When more than one door is used, they should have rabbeted overlap of not less than 1".

Doors shall be equipped with latching and hinges that are mounted to not lose their holding capacity when subjected to fire.

Raised sill or pan capable of containing 2" depth of liquid shall be provided at the bottom of the cabinet; this 2" bottom well for spill containment must also be liquid-tight.

"FLAMMABLE—KEEP FIRE AWAY" legend sign must be on door.

The Uniform Fire Code 79.202 requires the same specifications as the NFPA Code 30 and OSHA 29 CFR 1910.106, plus self-closing doors. The other considerations the builder should use in comparing hazardous chemicals storage cabinets include

1. *What are you storing?* Determine the class of flammable or combustible liquids you need to safely house. OSHA divides liquids into classes depending on their characteristics. Refer to this chart for a breakdown of liquid classes. The class of a liquid can change due to contamination, and the volatility of liquids increases when heated. Classifications do not apply to mixtures. These classifications are based on information from OSHA 29 CFR 1910.106(a)(18).

Flammable and Combustible Liquid Classes.

Class	Flash point	Boiling point
Flammables		
IA	< 73½°F	< 100½°F
IB	< 73½°F	> 100½°F
IC	> 73½°F	< 100½°F
Combustibles		
II	> 100½°F	< 140½°F
IIIA	> 140½°F	< 200½°F
IIIB	> 200½°F	—

2. *How much will you store?* The answer helps you determine your cabinet capacity. This chart outlines the maximum storage capacities for various liquid classes.

Maximum Storage Quantities for Cabinets.

Liquid class	Maximum storage capacity (gallons)
Flammable/Class I	60
Combustible/Class II	60
Combustible/Class III	120
Combination of classes	120*

* Not more than 60 gallons may be Class I and Class II liquids, nor more than 120 gallons of Class III liquids may be stored in a storage cabinet as per OSHA 29 CFR 1910.106(d)(3) and NFPA 30 Section 4-3.1. Not more than three such cabinets may be located in a single fire area, according to NFPA 30 Section 4-3.1. Standard storage capacities are 16-, 30-, 45-, 60-, and 90-gallon cabinets.

3. *Which construction material is better?* In my mind, steel is the obvious choice for fire containment and maximum burn-through rate. However, since metal is not used in the interior of wood cabinets, you won't have rust or corrosion problems. Both metal or wood meet code requirements if the cabinet meets the described specifications. But always make sure that the liquids being stored are compatible with the cabinet construction. Specially designed cabinets are also available for storing acids and corrosives. Although they may look similar to flammable cabinets, acid cabinets are treated with special coatings to prevent rapid deterioration caused by corrosive liquids and vapors. These coatings are achieved by full or partial lining with a 0.125″ or thicker polypropylene lining. Polypropylene or polyethylene lining helps protect the acid-rated cabinet against aggressive and highly corrosive acids, including nitric, sulfuric, and hydrofluoric acids,

dichlorics, and phenols. Acids and corrosives, according to code, specifically require these special cabinets for storage. Since these substances can corrode metal safety cabinets, proper selection is important. Cabinets specifically manufactured for acids or corrosive storage should only be used for these chemicals.

4. *What are the necessary minimum requirements?* Sliding, self-closing or two-door, self-closing cabinets are regulation standards. Local codes may dictate door style, so check out all local regulations for flammable, combustible, and acid storage containers before choosing a cabinet. Fusible links (used to latch the door open) are available on sliding, self-closing cabinet and two-door self-closing cabinets. Fusible links melt at a prespecified temperature of 165½° F, automatically closing the door (if latched open) to keep fire away from cabinet contents. Fusible links must be UL-rated. An adjustable hydraulic cylinder controls door closure at a safe speed and shuts doors automatically, then self-latches to protect and contain contents.

5. *Is your storage cabinet located at the job site in the open environment?* If so, you need to protect your storage cabinet from the elements. Storing hazardous materials outside opens up valuable space inside the building, creates a safer work environment, and reduces worker exposure and emergencies such as spills and fires. It also poses less of a risk to personnel and property. So, in considering factors for exterior-located cabinets, add a sloped roof to encourage run-off and prevent corrosion, angled legs for raising the cabinet off the ground, a plastic flap to protect the handle, a steel overlap to cover the gap between the doors, and a clear epoxy spray to protect the exterior finish. These are factory-installed options that must be ordered at the same time as the cabinet, referred to as a cabinet protection package. Replacement and additional shelves are also available from the manufacturers.

Premium cabinets offer features such as a 2-inch insulated air-space between walls, giving greater thermal insulation than the standard 1½-inch airspace. Walls that are 16-gauge are 20 percent heavier than 18-gauge walls. Containment wells of 3½ inches hold 75 percent more spill than a standard 2-inch well. Corners with a 2-inch radius can be added with internally braced walls. Double-offset rabbeted doors are used for reduced heat transmission to the inside of cabinet, and explosion venting relieves internal pressure for extra safety in chemical storage. Forklift pockets are attached for easier relocation of cabinet. Vapor-absorbent cartridges can be added inside the cabinet for trapping noxious and harmful vapors, reducing health risks associated with vapor buildup inside the cabinet. Vapor-absorbent cartridges use specially treated activated carbon that absorbs flammable, combustible, and noxious vapors. An optional, additional, perforated 24-gauge zinc dichromate-plated steel exterior provides a large surface area for even, effective heat absorption. Inner door labels should also be used to date when product usage began.

Some landscape chemicals are Class III combustible liquids and need the storage safety of a Class III cabinet. The flashpoint of Class III combustible liquids is less than 140°F. These cabinets can store up to 120 one-gallon cans. Some also offer grounding attachments to prevent electrically generated fires. These static-ground connectors add an extra measure of safety by dissipating static electricity and reducing explosion hazards while transferring flammable liquids. An explosion-proof ventilation package can be installed that efficiently removes cabinet vapors, thus preventing dangerous vapor buildup. These packages have blower-motor assemblies with an aluminum flywheel and housing with 4-inch, inlet/outlet, galvanized, flexible metal ducting for forced ventilation. They deliver 343 cfm at 1-inch sp and 3450 rpms. Typically rated at ¾ hp, their 115/230-volt motors are rated for Class I, Group D, and Class II, Groups F and G use.

OSHA

OSHA is given the responsibility to make sure all American employers provide healthful and safe working conditions for their workers. It pays special attention to the construction industry because ours is such an inherently dangerous business. To carry out its mandate, OSHA is authorized by law to enforce effective standards, to assist and encourage employers to maintain safe and healthful working conditions, and to provide research, information, education, training, and enforcement in the field of occupational safety and health. All builders involved in landscaping must understand how OSHA affects their business and how to avoid costly errors in code compliance. OSHA is regulated by the Department of Industrial Relations. There are four divisions of OSHA:

1. The *Standards Board* is the legislative branch of OSHA, which makes the laws (sets the standards) that pertain to safety in the workplace. It can be compared to the legislative branch of government.

2. The *Department of Safety and Health* (DOSH) enforces the standards that are set by the Standards Board. Inspectors, incident investigators, and complaint investigators from OSHA are from this division. They can be thought of as the cops who enforce the laws and issue the citations for violations of safety and health laws.

3. The *Appeals Board* hears appeals to the citations issued by DOSH. It can be thought of as the court for dispute resolution between companies cited and DOSH. Appeals to citations issued by DOSH must be submitted within 15 days of issuance of that citation.

4. The *Consultation Board* issues safety posters and advice. It is an excellent resource for you, the professional builder. These people are extremely helpful and will tell you right over the phone what your project needs to have to be within code compliance. Forewarned is forearmed.

The law says that whenever OSHA learns or has reason to believe that any place within your project is not safe or is harmful to the welfare of any employee, it may investigate the place of employment with or without notice. When OSHA receives a complaint from an employee that his or her place of work is not safe, it is mandated to investigate within three days for serious violations and within 14 days for nonserious violations. OSHA is empowered to investigate and prosecute the causes of a project site accident that is fatal to an employee or that results in serious injuries to five or more employees. To make an investigation or inspection, OSHA has free legal access to any place of employment to investigate and inspect during regular working hours and any other reasonable times when necessary for the protection of employees' safety and health. If permission to investigate or inspect is refused, OSHA may obtain an inspection warrant. And that's just what they mean. The inspectors return, accompanied by two police officers.

The abridged version of what requirements are relative to you, the builder with employees, is as follows: The penalty for an employer's demoting or firing of an employee for notifying OSHA of a safety violation is that said employer will be forced to rehire or repromote the employee with all back pay. No employee can be laid off or discharged for refusing to work in an unsafe or unhealthful atmosphere. Any employee of any project has the right to discuss safety violations or safety problems with an OSHA inspector. If, upon inspection or investigation, OSHA believes that an employer has violated any health and safety order, it issues a citation to that employer.

The citation gives a time limit within which the violation must be fixed. Each citation must be prominently posted at or near each place within the project that a violation occurred, not in your files back at the office. All such postings must be maintained for three days or until unsafe conditions have been fixed, whichever is longer. The employer is given 15 days to appeal the citation. If the condition of any employment constitutes a serious menace to the lives or safety of persons, OSHA may apply to the superior court for an injunction restraining use or operation until such unsafe condition is corrected. This injunction causes immediate cessation of project production.

Notices placed in conspicuous places within the project must not be removed. Anyone using or operating any such operation or machinery before it is made safe or who defaces, destroys, or removes such notice without the authority of OSHA is guilty of a misdemeanor. Any authorized representative of OSHA may prohibit the use of a device, machine, or piece of equipment in the project for 24 hours on his or her finding that an imminent hazard exists. When, in the opinion of the regional manager, it is necessary to preserve the safety and health of workers, he or she may prohibit further use for not more than 72 hours. All employers must provide opportunity for every employee to observe "exposure-to-hazard" reports provided to employers identifying safety hazards. (See OSHA "Right To Know" regulations.) Any employer who willfully or repeatedly violates any occupational safety or health standard may be assessed a civil penalty of not more than $10,000 for each violation. Any employer who fails to correct a violation within the period permitted for its correction may be assessed a civil penalty of not more than $1000 for each day during which such failure exists. The following types of construction work involve historical risk of injury and require special permits from OSHA:

- The construction of trenches or excavation that are 5 feet deep into which a person is required to descend.
- The erection of scaffolding more than three stories high (jack scaffolds, or lean-to scaffolds, are now illegal).
- The demolition of any building or structure more than three stories high.
- Working more than 15 feet above ground level. (Safety lines and body harnesses that must be provided for workers under such conditions.)

Regularly scheduled safety conferences are required by OSHA. The safety conference must include a discussion of the employer's safety program and methods intended to be used in providing safe employment on the project construction site. "Tailgate" safety meetings with employees are required at least every 10 days. Employers must also hold monthly meetings with forepersons and management to discuss safety measures. These, as well as the tailgate meetings, must be documented and a copy must be given to the project's site supervisor, who in turn should record these on the field reports forwarded to the contract records.

Required safety gear
Ergonomics

Your construction business is required by law to have an ongoing safety program. This program begins by carrying the mandated first-aid kit to all work sites and goes as far as developing ways to improve safety training in all aspects of your daily work. By reducing the number of injuries related to tasks and movement, your ergonomics aspect of employee training can quickly improve the performance of your entire safety program. Conducting a task-by-task ergonomic analysis for every task in your workers' jobs is the best way to ensure your program is on track.

We'll start here with required back supports to prevent lifting injuries. These supports are designed to be worn outside the clothing for lifting, bending, reaching, and twisting support. To keep your worker's comp costs down, train your workers to always use proper body mechanics when lifting, bending, and carrying heavy loads. Several different types of back support belts are available:

- Rigid support belts provide abdominal and lower back muscles with firm support. Some have a foam core that enhances support and insulates muscles to keep them warm and flexible. These belts are best for lifting.
- Elastic support belts apply expandable compression around the back and abdomen. These are made from breathable nylon mesh fabric with adjustable monofilament side panels. You can adjust the amount of support received by clinching the belt tighter. They're also lightweight and highly flexible, so they don't restrict activity. These are ideal for general landscaping applications.
- Contoured support belts curve to fit the natural shape of the human body. These contours keep the support belt from digging into your rib cage and increase the support given to your lumbosacral region (the lower area of your spine known as the lumbar vertebrae). According to the folks at OSHA, this area is the most common spot of back injuries due to lifting.

Other elements to look for in support belts include shoulder straps that help keep the belt in place during nonuse, special lumbar support inserts that tuck into the small of your back for extra lifting support, and built-in stays for uniform pressure around the back and abdomen.

You can reduce the risk of hand and wrist injury by reducing sensitivity to impact and vibration. New-technology impact and antivibration gloves use a polyneoprene padding that lessens shocks that limit a worker's ability to hold and operate power tools. Use of power tools and constant stress on workers' forearms from common landscaping tasks can also lead to elbow injuries. Neoprene elbow supports use a principle of compression of muscles and cartilage that helps prevent and reduce pain and also aid in recovery from tendonitis and other elbow injuries. Use of foam knee pads relieve the pressure of kneeling so workers can proceed in comfort and concentrate on the job. They protect knees against bumps, abrasions, bruises, and other minor injuries. These pads are ergonomically designed to provide comfort when kneeling and ease of movement when walking. They are made from nonbinding molded foam pads reinforced with a second layer of rubber and held securely in place with cotton or elastic straps. Kneeling without protection is no joke: An old Japanese landscaper told me he didn't get his flat knees from praying, but if he had, he'd have prayed for new knees.

Eyewear

Protective eyewear is a must for landscapers because mowers and line trimmers throw rocks and debris unmercifully. Modern, economical, reusable safety glasses serve as ANSI/OSHA-accepted high-impact protective eyewear for you and your workers. Here you're looking for safety glasses that meet ANSI Z87.1-1989 compliance. They are made with scratch-resistant polycarbonate lenses, and some have an impact-resistant wraparound frame that protects the temples as well. They are designed to be worn over most personal prescription eyewear with a brow guard bar that fits snugly to the forehead for extra protection from flying particles. A universal bridge fits a wide variety of nose sizes comfortably and snugly, eliminating any pressure points. Side shields should not be removed. They provide lateral eye protection. Vertically vented side shields can be added for unrestricted airflow around face and eyes, reducing heat buildup and lens fogging, which will encourage your workers to use them.

If the safety glasses have a CSA Z94.3-M88 compliance, it means they have a safety-lens scratch-resistant coating that is permanently bonded to the lens surface in a continuous-dip coat process. These glasses are extremely scratch-resistant and very durable, with a fair to excellent optical quality. Though a little more expensive, they are long-lasting and resist a wide range of chemicals used in landscaping operations. The coatings have antistatic, UV protection, and antifog properties that are perfect for hot, humid outdoor conditions requiring impact and abrasion resistance, plus antifog to keep lens from steaming up. The better ones have full optical-quality lenses for distortion-free vision.

Extra eye protection also can be obtained by the use of goggles. Designed to fit tight to the worker's face and surround the eye area, goggles shield the eyes from a variety of hazards, such as impacts, splashes, and sparks. Goggles for impact protection are usually ventilated for comfortable wearing and proper airflow to minimize lens fogging. Splash goggles also offer impact protection but have indirect venting. Specialty goggles have special features for their intended uses, such as welding. Some have a low-profile design to provide a snug seal and fit when worn with respirators, hard hats, and personal glasses up to around 58 mm thick. Chemical-resistant goggles resist mild acids, caustics, aromatic hydrocarbons, and methylene chloride. They are designed with a glass-like coating that is permanently bonded to polycarbonate lenses and is not affected by solvents, bases, or acids (except hydrofluoric acid). Gas-proof goggles seal out vapors, fumes, and dust where airtight protection is needed.

Remember, code requires that you store safety glasses in clean and sanitary containers. You must also meet the maintenance requirements of ANSI Z87.1-1989, which states, "Protectors should be cleaned at appropriate intervals. Protectors must be maintained in a usable condition."

Face shields

Face shields offer workers secondary eye protection and are required wherever there's a severe danger of impact or chemical splash when opening insecticides, pesticides, or other hazardous chemicals. They also provide lightweight protection from sparks and debris. But they're still only *secondary* protection. According to ANSI, "Face shields are secondary protectors and must be used only with primary protectors." Primary protection comes from the safety eyewear workers wear underneath the face shield. When you or your workers are opening pesticides, never fail to have the added safety margin of face shields.

Polycarbonate face shields have an adjustable crown strap and ratchet adjustment knob on thermoplastic headgear, which permits easy sizing and firming up of the sweatband. After correct fitting, the face shield should not slip or slide out of position on the worker's head. A special brim should be attached that prevents fluids from splashing down inside the face shield window. The shield should extend below the chin for full face protection.

Chemical-resistant face shields are specially treated with chemically bonded clear silicone protective coatings that reduce shield wear. The coating on the outside creates an inert barrier against corrosive and harmful chemicals for longer service life in chemical splash situations. These face shields are designed for use with mild acids, caustics, aromatic hydrocarbons, and methylene chloride (with the exception of hydrofluoric acid).

Hard hats

Hard hats are required ANSI Z89.1-1986 head protection for you and your crew at the work site. Compliant hard hats have a durable injection-molded rigid shell with high dielectric strength made from lightweight high-density polyethylene. They must have an approved six-point nylon web suspension system inside that provides an airspace between the wearer's head and outer shell and absorbs impacts. Compliant hard hats have an adjustable sweatband strap and ratchet adjustment knob, which permits easy sizing and firming up of the sweatband. After correct fitting, the hard hat should not slip or slide out of position on the worker's head. You can now get hard hats with your favorite sports team helmet painted on them. And they meet specs.

For severe hazards, such as chainsaw tree-limb cutting, a double-walled hard hat is required by code. These hats have a polycarbonate-alloy outer shell with an expanded foam core, a dual polyethylene crown cushion, and an ABS plastic inner shell for dual-wall helmet protection. For landscaping work, hard hats should be purchased with accessory slots that allow the worker to add earmuffs or face shields as necessary. An optional elastic chin strap should be supplied that holds the hat securely in place in elevated work situations. Added safety measures like these keep your worker's comp costs down and give your workers a more confident working environment.

Hearing protection

Hearing protection for your workers is mandated by law. The cheapest form of hearing protection are soft foam earplugs that provide sanitary comfort and a close-fitting seal against harmful noises. These types of earplugs are soft polyurethane foam with a hygienic smooth surface that is easily washable with a mild detergent for continued reuse. Some have a triangular contoured shape that provides for a tighter fit in the ear canal. Their preshaped and tapered design exerts virtually no pressure on the ear canal, for exceptional fit and comfort. Because of the comfort of these new types of ear plugs, workers are encouraged to use them instead of the old style, which can cause pressure headaches with prolonged use. They're also handy if your spouse snores.

Polyurethane earplugs are made from new-technology, expand-to-fit material that allows the use of one size for most workers, cutting your inventory requirements and costs. It is a self-adjusting foam that forms a low-pressure seal against noise with excellent sound attenuation (blocking). Individually packed pairs are boxed in cardboard dispensers for easy access by workers. They must meet sound-attenuation specifications set by ANSI S3.19-1974 and be labeled NRR: 29dB through NRR: 33dB. This information should appear on the cardboard dispenser. Do not purchase any earplugs without these ratings appearing on the box.

High-impact plastic earmuffs provide added side-of-head protection and high-attenuating hearing protection when using high-decibel small engines, such as trimmers, blowers, and chainsaws. Deep earmuffs provide excellent sound attenuation in an outdoor work environment. These earmuffs should have large ear and head cushions to spread pressure over a wider area of the head or attach directly to the aforementioned accessory slots on hard hats. Dielectric earmuffs have better noise attenuation than standard earmuffs, even at low frequencies.

Footwear

Choosing the right protective footwear for construction work prevents costly foot and toe injuries. Always protect your feet by wearing steel-toed work boots and require that your workers wear the same around tractors and heavy machinery, in wet, muddy conditions, or in high-heat areas. Lightweight, versatile styles of construction boots make wearing work boots comfortable for a variety of construction applications, including landscaping. The ANSI Z41 Standard states voluntary performance requirements and testing methods. However, all quality work boots have steel toe caps, weatherproof leather uppers with oil-resistant soles, and puncture-resistant soles.

Overboots give the wearer a full spectrum of added protection from heavy-duty wear conditions such as mud or concrete, to single-use chemical-resistance contamination control. Overboots are made from a wide range of materials, such as PVC (polyvinyl chloride), latex, butyl, natural rubber, polyethylene, neoprene, and vinyl. They offer protection from chemicals, oils, fuels, solvents, and acids. Stretchable latex rubber overboots protect workers' boots from dirt, mud, water, and some chemicals, plus they help increase traction on slippery surfaces. The better-quality ones go through a secondary dipping process in which the soles are dipped in a latex-rubber mixture containing wood fiber for even greater slip resistance.

For general landscaping duties, the most durable overboots are injection-molded PVC overboots that are made in a two-stage injection-molding process. With this process, two different compounds are injected at the same time. They are specifically blended to offer improved cold-weather flexibility and cut resistance and are formulated for wet or muddy conditions in all general-construction applications. The result is a softer, more flexible upper combined with an abrasion-resistant outsole. These boots resist salts, alkalis, ozone, acids, blood, grease, tar, oil, and gasoline. Most have adjustable, nonconductive polyester straps with nonmetallic or plastic buckles and snap fasteners to keep moisture out. Puncture-resistant steel-shank midsoles are combined with steel toe caps for extra foot protection.

Overboots used in pesticide and hazardous-chemical applications must meet NFPA 1991 requirements. These boots must be tested by a third party. Boots must resist permeation for one hour or more against each chemical in the NFPA 1991 battery. The battery consists of 15 chemical liquids and two chemical gases. The boots must also pass a flammability resistance test. They are manufactured from high-molecular-weight PVC that is then injection-molded with a urethane blend into a one-piece boot with no seams. These types of overboots provide the most chemical resistance available. Table 1-1 shows the NFPA chemical resistance guide regarding the manufacturers' degradation test results for each boot material and chemical listed. Actual applications and conditions may vary from laboratory testing, and therefore, the information contained in Table 1-1 should be used as a guide only.

Clothing

General-use overalls are often your best bet in protective clothing for most landscaping operations. The next step down is a long-sleeve cotton shirt and tear-resistant trousers. Loose or baggy clothing on workers is an open invitation for injury while operating equipment and power tools. T-shirts may be acceptable within your company's guidelines; however, they don't present a professional image for your company (unless they're company shirts). If you are going to supply your crew with company shirts, I suggest polo-type shirts that have a collar on them. These are more business-like, make a much better impression on your customers, and are just as comfortable as crew-neck T-shirts. Remember, light colors reflect the heat better and make for a cooler, more wearable shirt for the landscape worker.

Table 1-1. NFPA Chemical Resistance Guide

Hazardous chemical	Polymere	Heavy-duty polymere	Polyblend	Standard
Acetic acid	G	G	G	G
Acetone	F	NR	NR	NR
Ammonium hydroxide	E	E	E	E
Benzene	F	NR	NR	NR
Ethyl alcohol	E	E	E	G
Formaldehyde	E	E	E	E
Gasoline	G	G	G	NR
Grease	E	E	E	G
Hydraulic oil	E	E	E	G
Hydrochloric acid	E	E	E	E
MEK	F	NR	NR	NR
Methyl acetate	F	NR	NR	F
Methylene chloride	F	NR	NR	NR
Naptha	G	G	G	NR
Nitric acid	F	F	G	G
Perchloroethylene	G	F	F	F
Sodium hydroxide	E	E	E	E
Sulfuric acid	E	E	E	E
Toluene	G	NR	NR	NR
Trichlorethylene	G	F	F	F

Key: E = excellent
         G = good
         F = fair
         NR = Not recommended

Rain gear is a necessity for all landscapers. Rain gear has different levels of quality according to the materials used to make it. Vinyl polyester rain gear is an extremely lightweight PVC material that offers a reasonable initial barrier to rainwater penetration. The problem is that you sweat like a pig under it because the fabric does not breathe. PVC-coated fabrics are a broad class of synthetic thermoplastic polymers that cover many liquid/chemical applications. The degree of waterproof protection varies depending on specific formulation and the thickness of the coating. Rubber-coated fabrics are very flexible with a smooth surface that keeps water from pooling in crease areas. For heavy-duty use, choose a heavy fabric that offers rugged abrasion resistance. These are the economical choice for general-purpose construction.

Neoprene-coated fabrics are the next step above natural-rubber rain suits. This synthetic rubber is one of the most widely used materials for all-around abrasion resistance. They are lightweight and flexible in cold or heat, and they do not tear easily. Polyurethane-coated fabrics are lightweight materials that shed liquid easily and are very flexible. The fabric's breathability depends on the thickness of the coating and material additives. They offer good tear resistance for general landscape work and are a durable, cost-effective form of general rain-gear protection. Nitrile-coated fabrics are especially well-suited for use with petroleum and fuels because of their excellent resistance to oils and grease. Their thin-gauge material offers excellent flexibility, yet it is tough enough to resist cuts and punctures. However, they are for *general-use applications* only when handling chemicals.

Vests and chaps

Early morning hours and dusk bring low light and reduced visibility situations on the job site, which increase your workers' risks tremendously. Fluorescent-orange traffic vests accented with reflective striping at front and back enhance visibility of these workers and provide increased safety when working around machinery or vehicles. Made from lightweight knitted polyester, they are soft enough to wear against the skin and tough enough to wear over work clothes. They range from nylon mesh to solid cotton engineer's vests and can also be personalized with your company name on the back for a professional look.

Chainsaw chaps are necessary protective clothing that provide maximum protection without extra weight. The best of these are made from multiple layers of Kevlar in the chaps, which are designed to jam a chainsaw blade and reduce the severity of leg injuries from chainsaw accidents. Two layers of woven Kevlar and two layers of Kevlar felt are enclosed in a polyurethane-coated nylon shell. The chaps are secured by a heavy nylon belt and quick-release buckles on 1-inch-wide nylon leg straps at the sides of the chaps. If they meet these rated standards, the label will say they are made in accordance with U.S. Forest Service Specification No. 6170-4D. This specification indicates the chaps are rated to 3300-fpm chain speeds. If they don't display this acceptance rating tag, they don't meet specs, so don't buy them.

Gloves

Gloves that are applicable for landscaping can be divided into two categories: work gloves and chemical-handling gloves. To provide all your workers with dependable abrasion protection and to protect their hands while handling sharp objects, general-purpose leather work gloves are the traditional choice. There are many styles and grades of leather work gloves that will meet your protection, durability, comfort, and budget requirements. The most durable grade of leather for work gloves is premium side-split leather. It offers the best glove for extra-sturdy hand protection. Side-split leather withstands abrasions and scrapes better than other grades because it contains the strongest and densest fibers. Next is select shoulder leather, which offers a consistent-quality work glove at a more economical price. Most work gloves come with a safety gauntlet cuff, which is a band of material permanently attached to the glove that protects the wearer's wrists.

A new-technology work glove has come onto the market that has superior cut resistance over leather, and the prices are now reasonable. These work gloves last twice as long as leather and offer superior cut and abrasion resistance without sacrificing manual dexterity or comfort. They are made from fabrics using DuPont's remarkable Kevlar. Kevlar gloves also protect hands against heat. They won't burn because the aramid fiber is inherently flame-resistant and only begins to char at about 800°F. They are lightweight, seamless, washable, and reversible. Kevlar aramid fibers outperform steel, offering your workers improved comfort and increased protection against common cuts and abrasions. Their knit design construction fits with superior comfort and allows the skin to breathe, which lessens hand fatigue. They are also an ambidextrous design, which saves on lost single-glove throwaways.

Chemical-handling glove selection is based on the chemicals used in your operations. Your MSDS should have glove-handling requirements under the permissible exposure limit (PEL). Different glove materials and manufacturing processes produce different gloves for different applications. Make sure you are using the proper glove for the chemicals you are handling. Laminated gloves resist most chlorinated and aromatic solvent chemicals. PVC plastic laminates are thick enough to protect hands against most chemicals and insecticides. Neoprene-coated gauntlets protect for 24-hour rated contact against acetone, benzene, carbon tetrachloride, chloroform, epoxy, MEK, styrene, toluene, trichloroethylene, and xylene. Fluoroelastomer gloves offer the highest degree of impermeability and chemical resistance. Water-soluble PVA gloves have a coating that protects against aromatics, ketones, and chlorinated solvents, such as xylene, MIBK, and trichloroethylene. However, PVA coating is water soluble, so do not use these gloves in water or water-based solutions.

Fall protection

Working at heights off the ground, especially tree-limbing work or on cherry pickers, exposes your workers to severe risks every moment. So OSHA requires harnesses, lanyards, lifelines, and waist belts for many conditions in elevated work areas. A full-body harness combined with a lanyard or lifeline is the best choice for fall protection. In the event of a fall, the harness evenly distributes the fall-arresting forces among the worker's shoulders, legs, and buttocks, reducing the chance of further internal injuries. Made from lightweight nylon webbing and forged steel hardware, they are designed without a tight waist belt so workers have a full range of motion while climbing and working. Whether you choose nylon or polyester harnesses and ropes depends on your job application. Both nylon and polyester are high-strength, flexible, and abrasion-resistant fibers. Nylon is lighter than polyester, more weather-resistant, and the best all-around choice for most landscaping applications. But when it comes to chemical resistance, polyester may be your best choice. It resists most mineral acids, chemicals, bleaching, and other oxidizing agents.

Shock-absorbing lanyards are the preferred safety connectors for harnesses over traditional lifelines. Specially treated lanyards have a built-in shock-absorbing system to greatly reduce fall-arresting forces like a bungee cord, lowering them to under 900 pounds. OSHA lanyard force comparison testing using a 130-pound test weight showed polyester webbing exerted 2410 pounds in fall arrest, $\frac{9}{16}$-inch spun nylon rope exerted 1730 pounds in fall arrest, and shock-absorbing lanyards exerted 900 pounds in fall arrest. (**Caution:** Lanyards must be taken out of service after being subject to fall arrest, per OSHA 29 CFR 1910.66 regulations. They cannot be reused even if they appear fine.)

Waist belts should be used for lateral positioning only. They are not recommended for fall protection because if a worker falls wearing a waist belt, all the fall-arresting forces are centered on the abdomen, greatly increasing the chance of damage to the internal organs. Even more serious is the fact that workers have actually slipped out of a waist belt while awaiting rescue, resulting in serious injury or death. As a further note, OSHA 29 CFR 1926.502 (d) states that, effective January 1, 1998, body belts are not acceptable as part of a personal fall-arrest system.

Respirators

Breathing-protection respirators are grouped into two divisions: air-purifying respirators (particulate masks, cartridge style respirators, gas masks, and powered air protection respirators) and supplied-air respirators (self-contained breathing apparatus [SCBA], airline systems, and emergency escape breathing apparatus [EEBA]). Choosing the right respirator for your chemical application needs is a three-step process:

1. *Identify the contaminant.* Always consult the material safety data sheet (MSDS) on file for each chemical used in your work processes. It gives you a good starting point for dealing with the hazards your workers face. The physical form of the chemical will help you determine the type of respiratory protection you'll need:

   - *Dusts* are tiny, suspended particles resulting from a mechanical process such as grinding. Depending on the material, an air-purifying respirator—a particulate mask or a cartridge-style facepiece with filters—may provide adequate protection.
   - A *mist* is an aerosol composed of liquid particles. To meet minimum protection requirements, be sure to choose an air-purifying respirator having a filter specifically designed for use with mists.
   - *Fumes* are even smaller particles formed by a condensing gas or vapor (as in welding). At minimum, use a filter specific to fume protection.
   - A *vapor* is the gaseous form of a liquid or solid material. Depending on the chemical, an air-purifying respirator with hazard-specific chemical cartridges may provide adequate protection.

2. *Determine the concentration level.* OSHA has established a permissible exposure limit (PEL) for many contaminants in your workplace. Any worker exposed to a concentration level higher than the PEL for that substance must take precautionary measures, including respiratory protection. Modern sensitive monitoring instruments can give you a precise reading of the concentration level, which can help you determine which type of respirator to use. For example, if the concentration level is above the IDLH (immediately dangerous to life or health) level, you have only two options: an SCBA or a pressure-demand airline system equipped with an escape bottle.

3. *Evaluate the conditions of exposure.* Any number of variables can affect your choice of protection. Always keep these factors in mind:

   - *The nature of the task.* How long will the worker be exposed to each hazard? Is the work strenuous, requiring a higher level of oxygen?
   - *The characteristics of the work area.* Is the area well ventilated? A confined space? Will air temperatures be hot or cold? Could mixings of hazards occur?
   - *The work process itself.* The way chemicals are combined, treated, or applied often results in new hazards. For example, when using an air-purifying respirator for a spraying operation, you'll probably need both a filter for the mists and a cartridge for the vapors.

Caution

Air-purifying and airline respirators are not designed to be used in conditions that are immediately dangerous to life or health (IDLH). Failure by the user to properly select the appropriate respirator for all the materials and concentrations to which the respirator wearer may be exposed may result in serious illness, disability, or death. Immediately leave the area and replace the respirator if:

- Breathing becomes difficult.
- Dizziness or other distress occurs.
- You sense irritation.
- You smell or taste contaminants.
- The respirator becomes damaged.

The respirator selected must properly fit the wearer. Carefully follow fitting directions, fit tests, and fit checks in the manufacturer's instructions accompanying each respirator to ensure proper fit and operation. Save these directions in your MSDS file. Tight-fitting respirators should not be used by individuals with beards or other facial hair that passes between the sealing flange of the respirator's facepiece and the wearer's face. Facial hair may cause leakage or interfere with the proper operation of the respirator exhalation valve, thereby exposing the wearer to the hazardous contaminants. If the worker is exposed to two or more contaminants for which different air-purifying elements are recommended (e.g., ammonia and benzene) and a combination element is not available, then a supplied-air respirator should be used.

Some toxic contaminants are readily absorbed through the skin. In these cases, appropriate gloves and protective clothing may be required to protect other areas of the body. Air-purifying respirators should not be used for sandblasting or for gas or vapor contaminants with poor warning properties. Any air-purifying respirator, when properly selected and fitted, will significantly reduce but not completely eliminate the breathing contaminants of the wearer. The wearer, when working in atmospheres containing substances that are reputed to cause cancer in amounts below their permissible exposure limit (PEL), will obtain better protection from a continuous-flow or positive-pressure air-supplied respirator. Always check your MSDS for substance PEL and other information before mixing and working with pesticides and chemicals. When in doubt, call the manufacturer or OSHA for any needed information. A phone call is cheaper than a funeral.

MSDS

OSHA law requires all businesses to maintain an ongoing safety and hazard communication program. An excerpt from Section 29 CFR 1910.1200, Hazard communication, reads:

> *The purpose of this section is to ensure that the hazards of all chemicals produced or imported are evaluated, and that information concerning their hazards is transmitted to both employers and employees. This transmittal of information is to be accomplished by means of comprehensive hazard communication programs, which are to include container labeling and other forms of warning, material safety data sheets (MSDSs), and employee training.*

Material safety data sheets may be kept in any form, including operating procedures, and may be designed to cover groups of hazardous chemicals in your working or mixing area where it may be more appropriate to address the hazards of a process rather than individual chemicals. However, the employer must ensure that in all cases the required information is provided for each hazardous chemical and is readily accessible during each work shift to employees when they are in their work areas. These MSDSs come directly from the material supplier and become your responsibility to maintain. Normally they are kept in the required right-to-know center in your mixing or storage area. Three-ring binders help organize, store, and transport MSDSs to the job site or anywhere MSDS information is required. A sturdy wall-mounted rack provides convenient storage and high-visibility access to binders containing important hazard information, giving workers instant reference when working with potentially dangerous substances, which is the requirement of the law.

Keeping your workers informed helps create a safer work environment, because trained workers know how to prevent and avoid hazardous situations and accidents. Material safety data sheets can help let workers know how to work safely with the chemicals they use, but having the right MSDS on file is only part of the story. OSHA also requires employees to be trained on the company's hazard communication (haz-com) program, including how to use MSDSs, labels, and signs. In addition to MSDS binders, centers, and posters, other training support is required for both supervisors and employees from you, the employer.

Signs compliance

Landscape contractors invariably have employees. This fact, added to the fact that landscaping involves amendments, pesticides, and other hazardous chemicals, makes you, the landscape contractor, liable for other related safety-compliance laws. As an employer, you are required to have warning, caution, and notice signs in compliance with OSHA law. Are your shop and job site signs in compliance? I have included the following information, an excerpt from OSHA 29 CFR 1910.145, Specifications for accident prevention signs and tags, so that you can make sure. As used in this section, the word *sign* refers to a surface prepared for the warning of or safety instructions for construction workers or members of the public who may be exposed to hazards. The following apply:

- All workers must be instructed that **Danger** signs indicate immediate danger and that special precautions are necessary. **Danger** indicates an imminently hazardous situation that, if not avoided, could result in death or serious injury. This signal word is to be limited to the most extreme situations.
- **Warning** signs indicate a potentially hazardous situation that, if not avoided, could result in death or serious injury. This signal word is to be limited to the warning of extreme situations in job operations. It is not for property damage accidents unless personal injury is also present.
- **Caution** signs must be used only to warn against potential hazards or to caution against unsafe practices. Employees must be instructed that caution signs indicate a possible hazard against which proper precautions should be taken. **Caution** indicates that a hazard may result in moderate or minor injury.
- **Notice** signs are used to state a company policy. The signal word **Notice** should not be associated directly with a hazard

or hazardous situation and must not be used in place of "Danger," "Warning," or "Caution." Notice and emergency signs are not for use with a physical hazard. These signs provide information only related to the safety of personnel or protection of property.

- **Emergency** signs are for fire extinguishers and fire escape egress, which fall under the domain of the fire codes and NFPA.
- **Safety instruction signs** must be used where there is a need for general instructions and suggestions relative to safety measures.
- **Sign design features**. All signs must have rounded or blunt corners and be free from sharp edges, burrs, splinters, or other sharp projections. The ends or heads of bolts or other fastening devices must be located in such a way that they do not constitute a hazard.

ANSI standards from ANSI Z535.1-1991 set further regulations concerning safety-color code and color tolerances, as well as product and symbol production standards, but these pretty much apply specifically to the product manufacturer, so I won't bore you with all that.

2

Maintaining plants

Here are some of the terms and definitions used in this chapter:

crown The portion of a plant at the junction of the root and stem or trunk

cuttings Detached vegetative plant parts that have the ability to develop roots and shoots, forming a new plant

dormant Not actively growing, but capable of resuming growth when environmental conditions become favorable

drip line An imaginary line drawn from the outside limb tips of a tree or shrub down to the ground

edging A border that helps to retain plants within an area and retard unwanted plants from spreading into the area

foliage Collectively, the leaves of a plant

hardening off Acclimating plants to environmental conditions

heaving Alternate freezing and thawing of the soil that can force small plant materials out of the ground

heeling in Temporary storage of plant materials in a shallow ditch or trench with moisture-conserving materials or soil covering the root system

mulch Any loose, dry material such as straw, leaves, peat, etc., used as a thin protective covering over the soil

peat pellets Compressed peat and soilless growing mix that expands when wet to form small pot-like containers used for seeds, cuttings, and seedlings

rhizomes Underground rootlike stems producing leafy shoots above and roots below

shingle-tow Shaved wood used to retain moisture around packaged plants

soil amendment Chemical or mineral element added to the soil to improve soil characteristics

starter solution A dilute fertilizer solution applied following transplanting to provide water and quickly available nutrients

stolons Stems growing horizontally on or below the soil surface, forming leaves and roots at the nodes

sunscald Damage resulting from drying and blistering of plant tissue

tree wrap Protective wrappings around the tree trunk that help to prevent sunscald, dried bark, and trunk borer damage

Classes of plants

Plants can be classified according to growth habits, landscape form and use, root forms, and special forms.

According to growth habits

Woody plants are plants that have a protective outer layer of bark and an inner layer of annual growth rings. They persist above ground from year to year in regions where they are hardy. *Deciduous* plants lose their foliage at the end of the growing season. *Evergreen* plants retain most of their foliage throughout the year.

Herbaceous plants have more or less soft or succulent tissue (not woody). *Perennials* are plants that continue to live year after year. Their tops may die in cold climates, but the roots and rhizomes persist. *Annuals* are plants that complete their life cycle in one growing season. *Biennials* are plants that complete their life cycle in two years. They produce leaves the first year and flowers, fruits, and seeds the second year, and then they die.

According to landscape form and use

Trees are woody, perennial plants that usually having a single main axis or stem (trunk) and usually exceed 10 feet in height at maturity. *Shade trees* are trees grown primarily for their broad-spreading form, which creates shade in the landscape. *Ornamental trees* are trees with outstanding form, flowers, or foliage grown primarily for decorative effect in the landscape. Ornamentals are usually smaller than shade trees. *Windbreaks* are columnar trees or low-branching trees grown primarily to shield certain areas from undesirable winds.

Shrubs are woody, perennial plants usually having multiple stems and are usually smaller than a tree. *Vines* are woody or herbaceous perennial plants whose stems require support from other plants or objects. *Ground covers* are low-growing, spreading plants used to cover areas, exclude undesirable plants, or prevent erosion. *Bedding plants* are primarily annuals that are preplanted and growing in small packets for transplanting in groups to cover a prescribed area (bed). They are used for their showy flowers or foliage effect in the landscape.

According to root forms

Balled and burlapped (B&B) plants are dug with most of their roots and soil left intact (for example, larger trees and shrubs). *Container-grown* plants are usually grown in 1- to 5-gallon containers and are transplanted with all roots intact. *Bare-root* plants are dormant plants that are field grown and dug leaving no soil on the roots (for example, deciduous trees, shrubs, and a few seedling evergreens). *Small packet* or *package* plants are grown in small containers usually less than 1 gallon in size (for example, bedding plants, ground covers, and vines).

Special forms

A *tree-spaded* tree is dug up by a tree spade with a large percentage of roots and soil intact and transplanted directly to the site. It allows the immediate landscape effect of larger trees. *Containerized* plants are bare-root plants placed in various-sized gallon containers. The roots are not as established as container-grown plants. *Limited-use containers* are papier-mâché pots, machine-made balls, and polyethylene bags commonly used for quick, mass sales of common plants by discount stores and large landscape stores (for example, field-grown trees, fruit trees, shrubs, rose bushes, perennials, seedlings, and summer bulbs).

Characteristics of various root forms

Balled and burlapped (B&B) plant materials have less disruption of the root systems, but they are a very expensive root-form method, the plants are heavy and bulky to ship, and they may require larger equipment for harvest, transporting, and planting. This form allows the harvest of larger trees and shrubs, which can be a desirable feature in a newly landscaped plan. The root coverings can be made of burlap, plastic mesh or webbing, or wire baskets.

Bare-root plant materials have a severely reduced root system, which makes it an inexpensive root-form method. They are lightweight, easy to transport, and may be sent by mail order. The roots are covered with moisture-retaining peat, plastic wrap, or shingle tow for shipping. Smaller deciduous trees or shrubs are harvested while dormant, and these plants have a limited storage life.

In container-grown plant materials, the plants have intact root systems and are grown in the container. This form is less expensive than B&B plant materials, but more expensive than bare-root. The growing media adds weight for handling and transport. Containers are commonly made of metal or heavy plastic, and the plants can be maintained or "held" for long periods, but they may become root-bound.

For small packaged plant materials, plants are seeded, rooted, and grown in containers with the roots intact. They are lightweight and easy to transport. Package forms may be peat or plastic pots, cell packs, bands, peat pellets, clay pots, or paper or poly bags. These types of plants may provide one-season interest (for example, annuals, chrysanthemums, or pansies).

Standard procedure for handling all plant materials is to inspect plant materials and check for broken, rubbed, or frozen limbs. For B&B plants, check root bindings to make sure they are secure but not constricting. Replace torn or deteriorated wrappings, rope, or twine, especially after long periods of storage. Maintain an evenly moist root ball. Use drip line or sprinklers on hard-to-wet burlap. Here, a word of caution: Too much water may cause burlap to deteriorate. Grasp the root ball or rope bindings, not the trunk or crown. Heel in or mulch. Maintain a high humidity level in storage coolers and keep mulching materials evenly moist. Use sprinklers, misters, or hand watering for plants that are heeled in.

For container-grown plants, replace damaged, unusable pots, washed-out growing media, and missing identification tags. Repot usable overgrown plants. Discard or treat and isolate diseased and insect-infested plants. As always, it's wise to know your supplier's policy concerning unusable plants received from the supplier before unloading. Correct any problems, such as damaged wrappings or pots. Group on weed mats or bare ground and mulch if necessary. Build or move to structures such as plastic greenhouses, lathe houses, and windbreaks for protection. Remember, plants are received in a dormant state and should not be stored for long periods. Container-grown plants dry out more rapidly than heeled-in B&B or bare-root plants. Use sprinklers, drip lines, or hand watering. Pick up pots with special can carriers, gloved hands, or in groups on a pallet, not by the trunk or crown.

For bare-root plants, remove packing materials and bindings. Prune damaged roots and discard diseased plants. Remove dead foliage and flowers. Prune leggy plants. Heel in or mulch. Place at proper temperature and humidity. Replace or add identification tags. Protect from adverse climatic conditions. Use sprinklers, misters, or hand watering for plants that are heeled in. When moving the plant to its transplant hole, grasp the trunk or limbs gently.

When you receive small packaged materials, discard diseased or insect-infested plants. Repot usable plants if needed. Group on weed mats, bare ground, or in greenhouses. Grouping plants close together helps maintain moisture. However, those around the outside edges dry more quickly and require supplemental watering. Remove dead foliage and flowers. Prune leggy plants. Repot usable plants if needed. Water as needed. Packaged plants wilt readily and dry out unevenly due to different soil mixes, pot sizes, and plant types. Use sprinklers and hand watering. Pick up plants properly. Group into trays or flats and lift in groups. Protect from dehydration and bruising in transit. Transport in closed trucks or cover with tarps on open truck beds. Bind or wrap flexible limbs. Wet foliage of recently watered plants promote disease when tightly covered or closed in an unventilated truck. Do not leave a plant load in the full sun without adjusting covering.

Techniques for planting and transplanting materials

Ideally, roots should be given the chance to develop before shoots and foliage begin growing. The best times for planting vary from region to region. All root systems should be placed deep enough to allow the crown to be even with the surrounding surface or at the previously grown depth. Certain conditions and planting soils may require special planting depths.

Plant spacing should allow plants to reach mature size without restricting their natural form. Some plants may be spaced closely to form thick hedges or solid ground cover. The hole should be large enough to accommodate the root system without causing unnatural bending, twisting, or wrapping of roots. Many opinions have been expressed about proper hole sizes, ranging from 6 inches wider and deeper than the root system to 50 percent wider and deeper.

Adding nutrients at planting time can be beneficial if slow-release fertilizers or low concentrations are applied and care is taken to keep the material from direct contact with roots or foliage. Plants should be watered before transplanting, during backfilling, and after final leveling around plant.

When cleaning up after planting, dispose of all discarded pots, wrappings, tags, sod, weeds, and excess soil. Remove wires of all tags remaining on plant materials. Rake fresh soil off sod and smooth the surface area. Form a neat basin or saucer from excess soil around trees and shrubs for water conservation. Redefine bed edges if necessary.

Plants should be staked only if absolutely necessary. The common methods of staking plant materials are the two-stake method, for small to medium trees, and the three-stake method, for large trees. One stake should be toward the prevailing wind for time of year planted. The standard procedures for staking are as follows: Remove staking materials as soon as roots become established. Wrap wires, place them through sections of landscape hose, or use other soft material strips or cotton ropes. Stakes driven close to plants should not touch stems or trunks. Check all wires and stakes after wet or windy weather conditions. Do not use eyebolts screwed into the trunk. These holes can provide entry points for insects and diseases. Soils must be treated according to their textures and particles, as shown in Figure 2-1.

Trimming and grooming practices

The practical reasons for pruning back plants are to remove dead, dying, diseased, or damaged plants parts, to manipulate the plant's

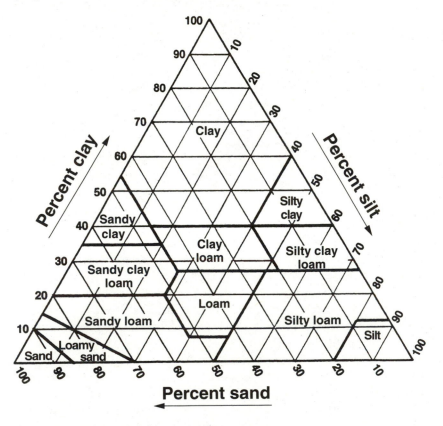

2-1 *Soil textures and their particles.*

growth, remove low limbs (for safety reasons), remove crossover limbs (limbs that rub against each other), or improve or maintain the general form or size. Remedial pruning prevents future damage to the plant, property, or persons nearby. Proper pruning also increases flower or fruit production. Grooming is important to all flowering plants because to keep blooms coming all season long, the landscaper interrupts nature's seed-producing process by removing old blossoms before the plant can begin seed formation. With its reproductive cycle never triggered, the plant remains in a flowering stage. Pruning procedures are a necessary part of landscaping maintenance because injuries to the trunks of trees are quite common. Left untreated, serious damage may occur, leading to the death of the tree by borer attack or by heart-rot organisms that weaken the trunk and destroy it from the inside out.

Pruning, if done right, invigorates or rejuvenates a plant, stimulating new growth. Particular attention must be paid to the pruning cut. Shape the pruning cut so that it is oblong. This technique keeps water from collecting on the pruned area and encourages rainwater to drain from the pruning cut, decreasing the chance of heart rot. Bevel the bark at the sides of the pruning cut so that when the bark starts to cover the pruning cut, it does not roll and curl over itself. The bark and underlying cambial layer only grow from side to side, gradually covering the exposed heartwood. Seal the pruning cut with an appropriate sealant to repel water and borers and to discourage animal pests from causing further damage by chewing on the bush or tree. Do not use tar, paint, or any material with a petroleum base as a sealant because it poisons the tree and eventually causes death. Never use any pruning-cut sealant that is not specifically intended for use on plant materials. Dispose of pruned debris immediately—don't leave branches lying around. They harbor insect pests, promote plant disease problems, and quickly become rodent hotels. Dispose of pruned branches, return tools and equipment to the job-site storage area, and clean and put them away properly under lock and key.

Trim plants to remove dead branch tips; however, do not top trees (see section on tree topping). Deciduous plants and large evergreens are groomed by removing longer branch tips and older growth. This technique allows the shorter, younger branches to shape the desired form. Allow shorter limbs to set the form. Cut back into shrub to a bend on the limb. Pine trees may be kept more dense by breaking out part of the candle before needles emerge in the spring. Breaking out part of the candle typically encourages new growth. The time to prune depends on the types of vegetation you wish to prune. Different seasons are best for different trees, shrubs, and ground covers. The following are general guidelines that may need to be adjusted for your region.

Deciduous trees, which lose their leaves during the fall, should be pruned during the winter. Many trees can also be pruned in July because of a head-induced dormancy. Known bleeders, such as maple, elm, mulberry, and birch, should be pruned in the winter. To test for "bleeding," cut off a small branch two or three hours before pruning and observe any sap that exudes from the cut. If there is no exudation, it is probably safe to prune.

Fruit trees and grapevines should be pruned in the dead of winter. Generally speaking, the more miserable the weather, the better.

Pine trees or evergreens should be pruned only if absolutely necessary. If the need exists, clip back the new candles as they are produced during the early spring.

Flowering shrubs such as lilac, forsythia, and flowering quince should be pruned in the spring. These shrubs flower on growth that is one year old. Therefore, they should be pruned after they have flowered to encourage more branching and subsequent flowering the following year. Flowering shrubs such as crape myrtle, glossy abelia, and roses should be pruned in the summer, before the current growing season, since flowers are produced on the current season's growth.

Ground covers such as vinca, honeysuckle, and monkey grass or Liriope should be pruned before the spring flush of growth occurs.

Bulbs should be allowed to retain their leaves until they naturally turn yellow because the leaves of bulbs are totally responsible for the production of food (carbohydrates) used for producing the next year's flowers.

Damaged plant parts, such as broken limbs caused by wind storms, should be pruned whenever they are noticed, regardless of the time of the year.

To shear hedges, cut soft new growth usually in early spring and then as needed to maintain neat compact growth. Remove suckers. Cut suckers under the soil surface or flush with the trunk. For example, Yaupon holly plants must be inspected and suckers removed monthly. Buds sprouting on cleared limbs can be rubbed off.

Typically, we remove old canes to promote new growth. You can maintain the plant's natural shape by thinning out older canes. This care is needed by winter jasmine, forsythia, and nandina. Slightly remove the top growth. Cut away above-ground growth to provide space for new growth in plants like Liriope and pampas grass. Remove dead, damaged, or diseased limbs and make pruning cuts 12 inches below any disease. Cut limbs to a bud or branching Y. Do not leave a stub. Remove any dead flowers and foliage. Faded flower heads should be removed to prevent seed heads from forming. Remember that dead foliage can promote disease or insect pests, so always collect and remove all trash and plant debris. Rake and smooth mulch and soil surfaces. Hoe out weeds and unwanted grass (hoeing weeds is easier if the soil is moist). Use shallow, short strokes to up-root unwanted plants and to avoid striking roots of adjacent plants.

Pruning

Proper pruning involves making the right type of cuts at the right time and in the right places so that the plant takes on a desired shaped and continues to be healthy. This careful trimming of the plant or tree, if also done to neighboring similar plants, creates symmetry in land-scape design and is generally pleasing to the human eye as it creates a uniform visual panorama. A proper pruning cut induces a certain type of sealing bark called *callus*. Callus is the healing bark a tree produces to heal its pruning cuts—nature's bandage, if you will. If the pruning cut is made right, the callus quickly seals off the pruning cut, reducing the chance for decay or pest infestation. Landscapers prune to achieve any of the following:

- To control or direct the plant's growth.
- To maintain plant health by removing dead or diseased branches.
- To increase quality or yield of flowers or fruit.
- To train young trees to ensure a uniform shape and strong trunk structure.

Every landscaper needs to know how to make good pruning cuts. There is a right way to make pruning cuts, and many wrong ways that provide avenues for disease to infect the plant. You want to avoid leaving stubs, and you also want to avoid undercutting the bud or branch. If you cut a branch beyond its uppermost growing part, you leave nothing in the stub itself to maintain growth. The stub, no longer a part of the plant's active metabolism, withers and dies. In time it will decay and drop off, leaving an open patch of dead tissue where it was attached. However, if a pruning cut is made just above a growing point, callus tissue begins to grow inward from the cut edges, sealing the pruning cut. The proper cut positions the lowest part of the cut directly opposite and slightly above the upper side of the bud or branch to which you are cutting back. There are four ba-sic different types of pruning:

1. Thinning
2. Heading back
3. Pinching out
4. Shearing

Thinning is the removal of a lateral branch at its point of origin or the shortening of a branch to a smaller lateral branch (at least 30 percent of the size of the branch being removed). Thinning serves to open a plant to sunlight and reduce its size (if desired) while accentuating its natural form. In most cases thinning cuts are preferred over heading cuts.

Heading back (also called cutting back) involves cutting a currently growing shoot to a bud or cutting an old branch back to a stub or a tiny twig. Pinching and shearing are forms of heading. With a few exceptions, including pruning fruit trees to establish main framework branches, shearing hedges to keep them compact, and pruning roses for flower production, heading is a less-desirable type of pruning. The reason is simple: Heading results in vigorous growth below the cut, usually from several to many buds, depending on the severity of the heading. While a plant that has been headed does become more compact, its natural shape is ruined and is difficult to repair. In addition, new growth is often weakly attached and prone to breaking. Beautiful trees are often ruined when they are headed back instead of thinned.

The first opportunity you have to control or direct plant growth is to remove (to *pinch* out) new growth before it elongates into stems. This technique is especially useful with young plants that you want to make bushier. For example, you can pinch all the terminal buds on every branch of a young fuchsia plant, forcing growth from buds that are at the leaf bases along the stems, creating perhaps two, three, or four new side branches instead of just one lengthening branch. When this happens, you get all-over growth. Conversely, if you want a plant to gain height, keep side growth pinched back so that the terminal bud on the main stem continues to elongate.

Shearing is the only form of pruning that could be called indiscriminate. It is more of a chainsaw massacre than pruning, really. Ignoring all advice about cutting just above growing points, you instead clip the surface of densely foliated plants. Shearing is the process that maintains the even surfaces of formal hedges and topiary work. Because the plants that normally are used for these purposes have buds and branches that are close together on their stems, every cut is close to a growing point.

When you cut with pruning shears, be sure that the cuts are sharp: Clean cuts callus over faster than cuts with ragged edges. Use shears that are strong enough for the job. If you can't get them to cut easily through a branch, the shears are too small, too dull, or both. Switch to a stronger pair of shears or use a pruning saw instead. With hook-and-blade pruning shears, remember to place the blade, not the hook, closer to the branch or stem that will remain on the plant.

If the position of the shears is reversed, you will leave a small stub. Pruning saws come in handy when you need to cut limbs that are too thick for shears or loppers or when a plant's growth won't allow your hand and the shears to get into position to make a good cut.

Larger limbs—from wrist-size upward—are heavy and need special care in removal. If you try to cut through one with a single cut, the branch is likely to fracture before you've finished the cut. The limb may fall, tearing wood and bark with it and leaving a large, ugly pruning cut. To cut a larger limb safely, make it a three-step operation. The final cut should be made very carefully. For years, the recommended approach was to cut the branch flush to the trunk. That has changed slightly. To avoid decay, make the final cut slightly outside the branch bark ridge (the compressed bark in the branch crotch) and branch collar (the natural circles or ridges where the branch meets the trunk). If no collar is visible, the angle of the cut should match the angle formed by the branch bark ridge and the axis of the trunk.

In pruning for shaping, the landscape design determines what shape the plant should take. Every plant has a natural shape; its growth tends to conform to a natural pattern, whether round, gumdrop-shaped, wide-spreading, vase-shaped, or arching. Observe what a plant's natural shape is, and then prune the plant in a manner that allows the natural form to continue to develop. Remove any excess growth that obscures the basic pattern or any errant growth that departs from the natural form. Use thinning cuts. When pruning to shape, make your cuts above a bud or side branch that points in the direction you'd like the new growth to take. If you have no preference, remember that generally it is better for a new branch to grow toward an open space than toward another branch. Also, it is generally better for growth to be directed toward the outside of the plant than toward its interior. Try to eliminate branches that cross and touch one another. Crossing branches may rub together, suffering injury, and are usually unattractive, especially in deciduous plants out of leaf.

Pruning for flower production involves flowering shrubs that bloom either from new growth or from old wood, depending on the plant species. Before you prune, determine which sort of growth bears flowers. In this way, you can avoid inadvertently cutting out stems that would give you a flower display. Most spring-flowering shrubs bloom from wood formed during the previous year. Wait until these plants have finished flowering before pruning them (or do some pruning by cutting flowers while they are in bud or bloom). Growth that the shrubs make after flowering provides blooms for the next year. Most summer-flowering shrubs bloom on growth from the spring of the same year. These are the shrubs you can prune during the winter dormant season without sacrificing the next crop of blooms. A few shrubs bloom twice or throughout the growing season (many roses, for example). Spring flowers grow from old wood; later blooms come both from recent growth and from wood of previous years. During the dormant season, remove weak and unproductive stems and, if necessary, lightly head back remaining growth. During the growing season, prune as necessary to shape while you remove spent blossoms.

Pruning conifers depends on the class. These evergreens fall into two broad classes: those with branches radiating out from the trunk in whorls and those that sprout branches in a random fashion. Spruce, fir, and most pines are examples of random-branching conifers. Pruning guidelines differ for the two groups. On whorl-branching types, buds appear at the tips of new growth, along the lengthening new growth, and at the bases of new growth. You can cut back the new growth "candles" about halfway to induce more branching, or you can cut them out entirely to force branching from buds at their bases. The point to remember is that you must make cuts above potential growth buds or back to existing branches. Cutting back into an old stem—even one that still bears foliage—won't force branching unless you're cutting back to latent buds. The random-branching conifers can be pruned selectively, headed back, even sheared; new growth will emerge from stems or branches below the cuts. But when you shorten a branch, don't cut into bare wood below green growth: most kinds (yew is an exception) won't develop new growth from bare wood.

Some conifers (chiefly the random-branching kinds, plus cedar and hemlock) can be kept at a controlled size or height, either as dense specimens or as hedges. When growth reaches within a foot or so of the size you desire, cut back all but about 1 inch of the new growth to produce enough small side branchlets to make full, dense foliage. Once this bushy growth forms at the ends of the branches, you can hold the plant to a small size year after year by shortening new growth that develops and cutting out any wild shoots.
Basic professional pruning safety rules:

- Wear a hard hat when pruning large limbs.
- Wear goggles as needed to protect the eyes.
- Wear ear protection when operating loud machinery such as a chainsaw.
- Use care and full attention when operating any machinery.
- Watch out for the cutting edge of all pruning saws.
- Make sure other workers are clear of the area before pruning.

Mulches

Requirements for a good mulch are that it holds moisture, is attractive, and controls weeds. A good mulch layer also controls erosion and prevents rapid temperature fluctuations. It should not compact easily, nor should it wash or blow away. Good mulch does not tie up nutrients, is not a fire hazard, and should not encourage disease development.

- *Peat* is not a mowing hazard; is attractive; is available in various grades; retains water well; can be fibrous or powdery; is hard to wet; deteriorates; scatters in the wind; and is expensive for large areas.
- *Bark* is not a mowing hazard; is attractive but turns gray with exposure; comes in various sizes; may be a fire hazard if very dry; washes away; and needs to be replaced every one to two years.
- *Manure bedding* is a variable expense. It is readily available; has a strong odor initially; contains weed seeds, straw, or wood shavings; must be decomposed before use; molds; and may pack down.
- *Pecan shells or almond hulls* are attractive; uniform in size; and extremely durable; but they have limited availability and are expensive.
- *Ground corn cobs* mold; have limited availability; turn gray; and control weeds.
- *Sawdust or wood shavings* decompose slowly and are not uniform. The material generally contains chips and splinters; packs down; may attract insects; and is low in plant nutrients.
- *Pine needles* are attractive and durable; have limited availability; and do not pack.
- *Peanut hulls or cotton-seed hulls* are durable; pack down; are attractive to rodents; mold; and retain too much water in a rainy season. They may carry verticillium wilt, which affects some plants.
- *Tree leaves and lawn clippings* are excellent humus; pack down; are readily available; may contain herbicides; scatters; washes; and decomposes rapidly.
- *Hay and straw* are inexpensive; readily available; control erosion; have limited life; must be replaced often; pack; are unattractive; are flammable; and tend to scatter.
- *Crushed stone, marble chips, brick chips, or river rock* are durable and attractive materials that present a mowing hazard and are heavy and nonflammable. Light colors tend to

discolor and these materials have limited use. Crushed stone adds calcium.

- *Shredded tires* are durable; they have limited availability and are unattractive and flammable.
- *Plastic* is inexpensive. Black plastic retards weed growth. It allows heat buildup; sheds water; deteriorates; and is slippery.
- *Fiber mats* allow limited weed control. Quack grass grows through mat and seeds germinate on mats. Mats are commonly used under other mulches; they allow water and air penetration; are expensive; and deteriorate if exposed to sunlight.

Organic or inorganic mulching materials must be replaced regularly due to natural decomposition, erosion, weed seed germination, and decline in appearance. Old mulching materials should be removed before adding new material to prevent layers building up or burying and killing plants. Plant materials must also be replaced when plants are dead or damaged, overgrown, or unattractive. Plants that are leggy or too open in the centers sometimes cannot be rejuvenated. Perennials, especially flowering plants like iris, Shasta daisy, and Liriope multiply and need to be divided. There are advantages and disadvantages to using mulches.

- Advantages
  ~Conserve moisture (lessen evaporation and runoff)
  ~Reduce temperature fluctuations
  ~Suppress weed growth
- Disadvantages
  ~May attract rodents and other pests
  ~Require periodic replacement due to deterioration and washing away
  ~May retain excess water during prolonged rainy periods

Disease problems

The first line of defense against plant diseases is prevention. Whenever possible, choose disease-resistant plants. Make sure that planting locations and conditions don't encourage disease-producing organisms that are troublesome in your region. Different kinds of organisms cause plant disease. Most leaf, stem, and flower diseases result from bacteria, fungi, or viruses. The most prevalent soil-borne diseases are caused by fungi. Sometimes disease results from plants interacting with unfavorable environmental factors such as air pollution, a deficiency or excess of nutrients or sunlight, or the wrong local microclimate for the plant.

Specific symptoms are associated with each disease and are found on both shoots and root growth. When looking at symptoms, concentrate on the outer, advancing edge of diseased area. Look for such things as color of blade, leaf tip, leaf margins, leaf lesions, streaks, mottling, leaf wilting or curling, and slimy substances on leaves. General thinning and browning of turf may be caused by numerous diseases. Circular patches of dead grass are symptomatic of one disease; circular rings of darker green or dead grass are symptomatic of another.

Disease problems may stem from soil compaction in the form of pedestrian shortcuts, chemical burns resulting from spilled fertilizer, dog urination, or mower gasoline. Thatch build-up harbors lawn disease and may stem from mowing with dull mower blades. Symptoms include gray color and shredded edges of turf, as well as distinct patches of dead grass. There are proven ways to prevent disease problems from starting, including

- Clean all equipment carefully before and after use.
- Buy healthy plants from a reliable source.
- Select resistant cultivars.
- Promote vigorous turf growth.
- Water infrequently and deeply.
- Control thatch, which can harbor disease.
- Apply chemicals to prevent infection or correct existing problem.

Disease problems frequently involve insect problems. Pesticides used to control them are such an environmental issue that pesticide laws have been passed in every state to implement federal laws and regulations that deal with pesticide application. Many jurisdictions require that they be applied only by a certified pesticide applicator, an individual who is certified to use or supervise the use of any pesticide that is classified for restricted use. In some states, this person cannot supervise others. Private applicators are certified after completion of training available at their county cooperative extension service offices and the completion of an application form. There is also usually a fee. Certification is good for a set number of years depending on the state (one, three, or five years) and may be renewed either by reexamination or by obtaining a set number of continuing education units in the category by attending various meetings and completing training during the time period.

Symptoms of insect problems can be found by examining root and shoot growth as well as surrounding soil for actively feeding insects. Damage may not be obvious until it is well advanced and appears similar to that caused by drought, heat, disease, nematodes, or nutrient deficiencies. Symptoms include irregular brown patches of dead grass, plants defoliated to the soil line, sod that separates from soil easily, and stunted or thin turf with individual plants turning brown and drying. Also look for soil mounding or tunneling that smothers or lifts turf, resulting in drying and plant death. The ways to prevent insect problems are pretty much the same as disease prevention:

- Clean all equipment carefully before and after use.
- Use approved chemical and mechanical preplanting controls.
- Select resistant cultivars.
- Promote vigorous turf growth.
- Apply approved chemicals to prevent or control insect infestations.

The symptoms of nematode problems show up as a general decline in plant vigor. Often a yellowing leaf color is followed eventually by stunted plant growth. In advanced stages, the plant wilts and roots have lesions, knots, or excessive root branching. The ways to prevent nematode problems are also the same list: Clean all equipment carefully before and after use, promote vigorous turf growth, apply chemicals and mechanical preplanting controls. Treat soil with chemical fumigants or heat.

What makes disease so devastating to turfgrass is that if you give turf diseases an inch, they'll take a whole yard. Or a golf fairway. Or anywhere else turfgrass grows. Just as there's no such thing as weed-free turf, there's no disease-free turf, either. When conditions are right, turf disease organisms spread and grow. Most turfgrasses are weak against disease invasion. Disease symptoms, especially those of patch diseases, may occur in the year of inoculation or wait one or two years to appear. When they do appear, they tend to reappear in the same location for one to three years or longer. Symptoms aren't telltale, either—field or lab tests may be needed. When disease strikes, they show one of three main symptoms:

- Overdevelopment of tissue, such as galls, swellings, leaf curls, and uncontrolled growth acceleration
- Underdevelopment of tissue, such as yellowing, dwarfing, thinning, lack of chlorophyll, and incomplete development of organs
- Death of tissue, such as blights, leaf spots, wilting, and cankers

Most turfgrass disease is caused by microscopic organisms called fungi. They're plants with no leaves, roots, stems, or chlorophyll, so they can't make their own food. That means they must feed on living plants or decaying matter to survive. Altogether, there are more than 100,000 different species of fungi, but only about 8000 of these cause plant disease. Fortunately, only a very small number of these are economically important to turfgrass. Fungal organisms take advantage of the right conditions to feed on turfgrass. These conditions include a susceptible host plant, which includes most varieties of turfgrass, and a favorable environment for fungi to develop, which includes the proper temperature and moisture levels. The temperature range may be wide or narrow, depending on the fungi. Even selected fungal strains of the same organism may vary in their response to temperature. But a definite maximum and minimum temperature can be established for fungal germination, growth, infection, and spore production. Most fungi need plenty of water on the leaves of turfgrass during their germination, growth, and infection stages. High humidity (over 90 percent) can also encourage active fungal growth. All of these factors must be present at the same time for disease to occur on turfgrass.

Many fungal organisms are always present in the soil and turfgrass, just waiting for the right moment to strike. When they do, they attack in four stages:

1. *Infection*, when fungal organisms penetrate the turfgrass host.
2. *Incubation*, when these organisms begin living off the host.
3. *Symptom development*, when the host plant begins to show visible signs of disease, such as lesions, wilting, or stunted growth.
4. *Inoculum production*, when the fungal organisms reproduce, spreading the disease to other turf hosts, ready to begin another cycle. Most fungi reproduce by spores in tremendous numbers. Like seeds, some can remain dormant for weeks, even months, before acting.

Ironically, many modern landscaping practices may even help fungal disease develop, especially on high-maintenance turfgrass. Practices such as close mowing, heavy fertilization, and intense irrigation actually encourage disease in turfgrass because they promote the conditions necessary for fungi to grow and thrive. It's no wonder that highly managed turf is more prone to fungal organisms than other turfgrass areas. Good control is difficult, but not impossible. It starts by creating an environment that's more favorable to turfgrass than to fungi.

Diagnosis may be difficult, but it's not impossible. It's easier when you know what fungi have been active on turfgrass recently.

Just use the information in this guide and conduct a field test. Remove 5 to 10 affected turfgrass plants. Place the plants in water to remove soil from roots. Place the washed plants in a container of water and spread the roots apart. Carefully examine the blades, roots, crowns, and stems with a hand lens. Infected roots may show a few dark strands of fungal mycelial growth. If you still can't identify the disease, just collect turf plugs of 1 to 4 inches in diameter from the outer edge of the damaged area. Send the sample, along with soil and healthy turfgrass plants, to your state or university extension plant pathologist for accurate identification.

Fire blight
Common host plants for fire blight are pears, pyracantha, quince, and others. On affected plants, leaves and new growth are black. New shoots show typical "shepherd's crook." The optimum seasons for fire blight are spring and summer.

Black spot
The common host plants for black spot are roses. Dark circular spots appear on the leaves of the plant. Black spot causes eventual defoliation of the plant. Seasons to watch for black spot are spring, summer, and fall.

Dutch elm disease
Common host plants for Dutch elm disease are American elm and certain other elms. It causes limbs to die, browning of the vascular system, and wilting and dying of smaller branches. Seasons are spring, summer, and fall.

Anthracnose
Common host plants for anthracnose are sycamore, sweet gum, oak, and redbud. Small triangular dead specks appear in the leaves. Leaves can curl. The leaves' interveinal spaces turn brown, and leaves drop. Seasons are spring and summer.

Wilts
The common host plant for wilts is honeysuckle. The plant suddenly wilts, collapses, and dies. Seasons are spring and summer.

Blight
Common host plants for blight are junipers and other similar plants. Branches turn brown. Affected branches usually are scattered throughout the plant. The seasons for blight are spring, summer, and fall.

Canker
Canker has many common host plants. You will notice swelling at ground level or at the base of stems or limbs. Canker affects plants in all seasons.

Nematode
Nematode also has many common host plants. Plants appear sickly, stunted, and yellow. Its seasons are spring, summer, and fall.

Powdery mildew
Lilac, crape myrtles, roses, and zinnias are common host plants for powdery mildew. The leaves and stems of affected plants have a white, powder-like appearance. Powdery mildew first appears as small gray or white circular patches on plant tissue, spreading rapidly to form powdery areas of fungus filaments and spores. Powdery mildew can infect leaves, buds, flowers, and stems, depending on the exact kind of mildew and the host plant. It attacks the young growth of some woody plants, such as roses and sycamores, and mature leaves of nonwoody plants, such as dahlias, chrysanthemums, peas, beans, and squash. Infected leaves may become crumpled and distorted. Seasons for powdery mildew are spring, summer, and fall.

Spotted spurge
Spotted spurge has many common host plants. Plants appear sickly and stunted. A demon in warm weather, the very aggressive summer annual spotted spurge grows from a shallow taproot in exposed areas such as sparse lawns, landscape walks, and flower beds. It spreads fast; in as little as a month, each plant can produce several thousand seeds in clusters of tiny pinkish seed capsules. Oblong ¼- to ⅜-inch leaves have reddish green undersides. Cut stems exude a milky juice. Plants turn red-orange and decline in the fall (especially noticeable in lawns) as temperatures drop. Seeds germinate as early as January in Palm Springs, and seedlings start active growth when temperatures climb in spring. Control is difficult. Hoe out isolated plants early, before they produce seed, or spray them with glyphosate. On lawns (except dichondra), use a preemergent broadleafed herbicide appropriately labeled to control spotted spurge. Watch for small plants in areas that have had problems in past years. A vigorous, well-fertilized lawn provides tough competition for spotted spurge. For cool-season lawn grasses, mowing the grass higher helps to discourage this weed.

Texas root rot

Texas root rot has many common host plants. Plants appear weak and break at trunk stem. Texas root rot is a damaging and widespread disease in the semiarid and arid Southwest at elevations below 3500 feet—from California's Imperial and Coachella valleys through Arizona and New Mexico and eastward. It is caused by a specific fungus (*Phymatotrichum omnivorum*) that destroys the outer portion of roots, thus cutting off the water supply to the upper parts of the plant. The first symptom of the disease is a sudden wilting of leaves in summer, with the wilted leaves remaining attached to the plant. When this occurs, at least half the root system has already been damaged. The fungus is favored by high temperatures and a highly alkaline soil low in organic matter. Fortunately, the fungus does not compete well with other soil-inhabiting organisms. Therefore, control measures focus on lessening alkalinity (by adding soil sulfur) and increasing the population of organisms that "crowd out" the fungus (by adding organic matter that decomposes rapidly). Contact your local nursery or county agricultural agent office for specific recommendations.

Verticillium wilt

Verticillium wilt has many common host plants. Plants appear sickly and stunted. Verticillium wilt is one of the most widespread and destructive plant diseases. The verticillium fungus invades and plugs the water-conducting tissues in the roots and stems of plants. A common symptom is wilting of one side of the plant. Leaves yellow, starting at their margins and progressing inward, and then turn brown and die. The dieback progresses upward or outward from the base of the plant or branch. Affected branches die. If you cut one of these branches, you may find that the sapwood (the outer layer of tissue just under the bark) is discolored—it frequently is streaked olive green, dark brown, or black. Development of the fungus is favored by cool, moist soil, but wilting of foliage may not show until days are sunny and warm and the plant is under water stress (the leaves transpire water faster than the diseased roots and stems can supply it). The fungus can survive in the soil for years in the absence of susceptible plants. Even rotation (the growing of nonsusceptible plants in the infested soil) does not rid the soil of verticillium fungus. Highly susceptible crops—such as tomatoes, potatoes, cotton, strawberries, and various melons—frequently leave the soil infested.

Mildly affected plants may recover from an attack. You can aid recovery by deep but infrequent irrigation. If a plant has been neglected, apply fertilizer to stimulate new root growth. However, shrubs and trees showing lush growth should not be fertilized after the disease appears. No measures will kill the fungus once it has invaded a plant. If you are planting shallow-rooted plants, you can control the fungus before you plant by having the soil fumigated. A commercial fumigation specialist uses chloropicrin (tear gas) or methyl bromide. But fumigation has not been successful with deep-rooted shrubs and trees. The most certain solution to verticillium wilt is to grow wilt-resistant plants. Choices include cedar, cotoneaster, euonymus, holly, oleander, pyracantha, rhododendrons, and bulbs such as amaryllis, narcissus, and tulip. For additional advice on plants that resist verticillium wilt, contact your local nursery or county agricultural agent office.

Purslane
Purslane is a mat-forming annual weed. It thrives in damp or dry conditions and warm weather. Look for succulent, fleshy green-to-red stems and dark green leaves, often tinged with red, and pale yellow flowers that open on sunny mornings. It spreads by seeds and stem fragments that root in damp soil. The weed is usually easy to dig out. Chemical controls include glyphosate and appropriately labeled pre-emergent herbicides.

Root rots and water molds
The diseases caused by the water-mold fungi are seldom mentioned as such. But they are indirectly referred to in directions that specify "infrequent but deep watering," "sharp drainage" or "well-drained soil," "good aeration," or "keep plant on the dry side." These phrases advise you how to avoid water molds. Free water (excess water that fills the air spaces in the soil) can suffocate plant roots. But water can pass through the root soil continuously without damaging roots if it carries air with it. The damage that occurs to roots from over-watering is, in almost all cases, not caused by water itself but by water-mold fungi that thrive when free water stands too long around roots, especially when the soil is warm. Weakened plants are much more susceptible. To offset problems caused by water-mold fungi, take steps to improve soil drainage (if necessary) for susceptible plants, and be sure not to overwater. The only symptom that almost always indicates a need for more water is wilting. Other signs, such as poor growth, dropping leaves, and yellowing, suggest other problems, including root rot. Two chemicals, metalaxyl and fosetylal, have proven effective against water molds, but they are costly and often hard to find.

Integrated pest management (IPM)

The notion of pest control (where control implies eradication) has been superseded by the concept of pest management. The management concept acknowledges that many perceived "problems" are natural components of the landscape, and the presence of pests doesn't necessarily spell trouble. In a diversified landscape, most insect pests are kept in check by natural forces such as predators and weather. If pests reach damaging levels, however, temporary intervention may be needed to restore a balance. Because of this natural system of checks and balances in a landscape, it makes sense to determine which form of intervention will return the situation to a normal balance with the least risk of destroying helpful and harmless organisms that maintain the equilibrium. Action choices range from doing nothing (giving nature a chance to correct the imbalance) or using restraints such as washing plants or repelling or physically destroying the damagers with biological controls and, as a last resort, chemical controls.

More and more landscapers are turning to physical restraints and biological controls as a first defense against landscape pests because they want natural landscapes that are safer for children, pets, and the environment. Yet almost all horticulturists acknowledge the need for at least occasional treatment with chemical controls. This approach—the preferred use of natural and mechanical controls plus chemicals as a discretionary second choice—is called integrated pest management (IPM). Increasingly, IPM is being used in parks, city landscapes, and public areas. IPM is a philosophy of pest control proven in years of practice, especially on golf courses. But I'd like to remind you of its goal—managing pests and the environment while balancing costs, benefits, public health, and environmental quality. To meet this goal, you need to do two things:

1. Gather technical information on each pest. See how it interacts with the environment. Study each one closely, and monitor its populations in your area to get the best results.
2. Take advantage of all pest control options. Choose a combination of the following control options to keep pest damage to minimum (and know when direct action such as pesticide application is necessary). Make a positive identification. Some common pests are shown in Figures 2-2 and 2-3.

Nature can help balance the populations of pests, but it doesn't always do it the way you want. Obviously, you can't change it, but

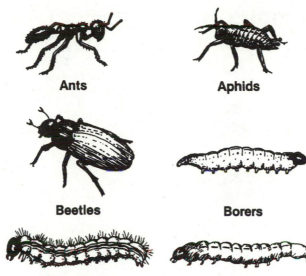

Ants　　**Aphids**

Beetles　　**Borers**

Caterpillars　　**Cutworms**

2-2 *Insect pests.*

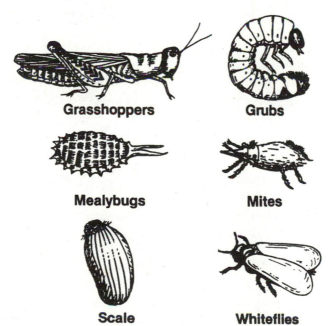

Grasshoppers　　**Grubs**

Mealybugs　　**Mites**

Scale　　**Whiteflies**

2-3 *Insect pests (continued).*

you can take advantage of it whenever you can. These forces include climate and adverse weather conditions, natural enemies of pests, soil type (heavy, poorly drained soils, for example, favor some pests), and the food and water supply pests need to live. Many pest-resistant turfgrass varieties are available to keep pest populations below harmful levels. It works two ways. You can either add chemicals to the host to keep pests from completing their life cycle or plant pest-resistant cultivars to add vigor to turfgrass for extra tolerance against pest aggression. Select the cultivar that adapts to your landscape environment and fits the level of use and management intensity you plan to give it. You can also reduce pest numbers by using naturally occurring enemies of the pest, such as certain insect predators or parasites. Most of these occur naturally, but you can release extra numbers to supplement your control. Control is very limited, but research on this method is continuing. Mechanical controls such as screens, barriers, electricity, and other devices can help prevent the spread of insects or reduce their infestation. They also alert you to heavy pest populations to help you time your pesticide applications for best results. Also use lights, heat, and fans to change the environment to help suppress some pest populations.

Healthy, vigorous turfgrass is the first step to effective pest control. It doesn't give weeds any room to grow and is a strong defense against diseases and insect aggression. Here are some important management practices that help turfgrass withstand pest competition:

Fertilize for proper nutrition. You can maintain healthy turf growth by fertilizing twice—once in the fall to help turf recover from summer stress and prepare for winter hardiness and early spring growth (taking advantage of cool weather for maximum turf development with less competition from weeds) and the second time in early spring just before the growth cycle. Water deeply and infrequently to foster an extensive root system and greener, thicker turf. Amounts vary greatly according to soil type, turf species, climate, and weather changes. When the soil is dry at 2 or 3 inches deep, irrigate enough to moisten the full rooting zone. In hot, humid weather, pathologists recommend frequent, light watering so there's no standing water to foster disease. Mow at recommended height. Never cut off more than 30 to 40 percent of the grass blades in any one cutting to help grasses develop more extensive roots and withstand environmental stresses better. Control thatch buildup. By soil aerating (coring) and verticutting (power raking), you can increase the rate of thatch decomposition and improve absorption of valuable air, water, and nutrients.

For intensively maintained areas such as golf greens, you may also want to top-dress (see Chapter 5). Cultivate properly. When soils become compacted from heavy traffic, the result is less air, water, and nutrients for turfgrasses, as well as increased vulnerability to environmental stresses. By timely cultivation with selective tillage or coring, you can reduce compaction, speed up drying of persistently wet soils, and improve turfgrass response to nutrients and many pesticides. Enrich the soil. Add peat moss, mulches, or other organic matter to improve drainage and encourage turfgrass growth.

These control methods don't always offer satisfactory pest control by themselves, so you'll need to include pesticides in your program. They offer the most effective way to prevent and treat weeds, diseases, and insects in turfgrass, but only when you know how to use them wisely. When it comes to responsible pest management, knowledge is your most powerful tool. The first rule with pesticides is to read the product label. Even though the print may be small and some of the terms unfamiliar, study it for directions, mixing instructions, precautions, and limitations so that each product performs as intended. Apply a little knowledge for the best control. Sometimes it's tempting to apply more pesticide to make up for a lack of other control measures, but to get the highest levels of control, it pays to use all control methods in an IPM program, including the proper use of pesticides.

Integrated pest management for weeds takes advantage of all control methods—cultural, mechanical, biological, and herbicidal. All should work together to control weeds and costs. Herbicides offer an effective way to control many types of weeds in most situations but only when they're used like they're supposed to be. You must choose the right herbicide for IPM. All herbicides control certain weeds. That makes your decision tough. How do you know which one is best for your landscaping job? Should you apply less herbicide more often? When should you apply? Review these factors before deciding:

- *Weed species.* Before you apply any herbicide, you should know exactly what weeds you have. Make sure they appear on the label of the herbicide you apply. Hard-to-control weeds may require split applications.
- *Stage of weed growth.* Young, actively growing weeds are more susceptible to postemergence herbicides than larger, more mature weeds.
- *Growing points of weeds.* Those that are sheathed or located below the soil can't be reached by many foliar herbicide sprays.

- *Plant tolerance.* Always check the label first and apply only those herbicides labeled for your specific turfgrass species.
- *Weed-free turf.* Preemergence herbicides can't control established weeds. Eliminate as many existing weeds as possible through the use of postemergence herbicides, hand-weeding, or tilling.
- *Thatch.* A thick layer of thatch has been shown to reduce the effectiveness of preemergence herbicides. Cultivation such as core aerating, verticutting, or top-dressing can eliminate thatch to increase herbicide contact with the soil.
- *Soil moisture.* The most effective weed control results when at least ½ inch of rain or irrigation follows your preemergence herbicide application, which allows the herbicide to mix adequately with the soil.
- *Soil temperature.* When you know the proper soil temperature for weeds to germinate, you know when to apply your preemergence herbicide.
- *Soil type and organic matter.* Studies have shown that different soil types affect the effectiveness of preemergence herbicides. In general, the higher the soil organic matter, the higher the herbicide rate you need to control weeds.

Here are a few helpful steps to follow to keep problem weeds from spoiling turfgrass:

- Encourage turf growth to reduce weed competition. Cultural practices help enhance the growth of healthy turfgrass, which helps crowd out unwanted weeds. These include fertilizing, dethatching, mowing, watering, aerating or verticutting, cultivating, and ensuring adequate drainage.
- Remove all established weeds before applying preemergent herbicide. Because preemergents do not control existing weeds, you should take them out by hand or with a postemergent herbicide. Also clean your landscape area of weed residues, prunings, and trash as much as you can to allow your preemergent herbicide to reach the soil and do its best job.
- Prevent weed growth with a preemergent herbicide. That way, the customer won't have to look at dead or dying weeds left over from a postemergent herbicide application or worry about filling the holes in turfgrass these weeds can cause. When you choose a long-lasting preemergent herbicide, you reduce the need for additional sprays later in the season.

- Spot-treat any weed escapes. Nothing can give you 100-percent IPM control, so you'll need to take out weed escapes by careful spot-treating with a postemergent herbicide. The best control from a postemergent comes when you time your treatments early—while weeds are actively growing. It's also important to keep perennial weeds such as dandelion, dollar weed, or white clover from getting established.

Nothing knocks weeds down like postemergent herbicides. They're very effective against only the weeds you see (except for those with soil residual activity). But this IPM practice has a few drawbacks. It allows unsightly weeds to litter turfgrass. It also leaves behind dead or dying weeds after application (which can leave holes in turf). Turf may sometimes be discolored for a short time, too. And you usually have to reapply several times throughout the season. With preemergent herbicides, you prevent weeds from spoiling turfgrass. Most of them have several weeks of residual activity to save herbicidal applications throughout the season (giving truth to the adage about an ounce of prevention). But they're not as effective as postemergents on tougher perennial weeds. Both practices serve a valuable purpose. The choice of using either or both (or a tank-mix of both) depends on your turf management program, a sample of which I have supplied you in Figure 2-4.

IPM requires the right fungicide. Before you apply any fungicide, you should know which diseases are affecting your turf and make sure they appear on your fungicide's label. It's difficult to predict where diseases will show up, but usually they appear in areas where they've occurred before. Fungicides work best when you use a recommended fertilizer program for your species of turfgrass and extra irrigation to prevent stress-induced turf dormancy. Always check the label first and apply only those fungicides labeled for your turfgrass species. Thatch can make fungicides less effective. By coring, verticutting, or top-dressing, you can increase fungicide contact with the soil for more effective control of pathogens. In general, weather conditions such as rainy, foggy weather and poor drying conditions favor foliar diseases, and wet soils favor most root-decay diseases. The most effective disease control results when you reduce the amount of time moisture is on the foliage or affects the roots to reduce the opportunity for disease infection. Diseases under "heavy pressure" (meaning very severe) require higher application rates. When you know the proper soil temperature that favors patch disease development, you know when to apply your fungicide for best results. It's very important to start a preventative disease program before the onset of disease for more consistent results. The faster you control

Cool-season grasses:

	JAN	FEB	MAR	APR	MAY	JUNE	JULY	AUG	SEPT	OCT	NOV	DEC
Weed control												
Insect and disease control					pests	vary						
Watering					as	needed						
Fertilization X-Quick O-Slow	X	X	X	X	X	X			X	X	X	X
			O	O	O				O	O		
pH adjustment												
Mowing					as	needed						
Aeration												
Thatch control												
Lawn installation												

Warm-season grasses:

	JAN	FEB	MAR	APR	MAY	JUNE	JULY	AUG	SEPT	OCT	NOV	DEC
Weed control												
Insect and disease control					pests	vary						
Watering					as	needed						
Fertilization X-Quick O-Slow	X	X	X	X	X	X			X	X	X	X
				O	O	O	O	O	O	O		
pH adjustment												
Mowing					as	needed						
Aeration												
Thatch control												
Lawn installation												

These are only samples. Tasks and when they are performed will vary for different locations and turf uses.

2-4 *Sample turf-management calendars.*

existing disease, the better your chances of keeping it from spreading. Curative programs usually require higher rates.

There is a way to get a stranglehold on fungi. By using the kinder, gentler approach of integrated pest management, you can control them with regards to the environment we all love. These suggested steps can help the landscaper prevent or treat turf diseases:

- Encourage turf growth to reduce disease risks. (Applying nitrogen, for example, can reduce the severity of anthracnose but may provoke brown patch.)
- Never let water linger. Try to reduce the amount of time moisture is on the plants. Timing varies by region and conditions. Also encourage good soil drainage.
- Use disease-resistant varieties of plants. By choosing a resistant cultivar, you can greatly reduce the need for multiple fungicide applications while keeping healthy, well-foliated turfgrass.
- Make a positive disease identification. Make sure you diagnose correctly, using field or laboratory tests if necessary, so you can choose the right control methods.
- Prevent diseases with fungicide control. Choose the fungicide that matches your turf disease problems and your management program. Apply when weather conditions favor disease development. Many long-lasting fungicides also reduce the need for additional sprays later in the season.
- Cure existing diseases with fungicide control. It takes quick work. When disease does break out, you must correctly identify it, choose the right fungicide, and apply it right away, usually at higher rates for effective control. Rotate two or more fungicides regularly if one fungicide isn't enough. Repeated use can cause some resistance problems, especially if you use a systemic fungicide with a specific site mode of action. That's why many turf managers rotate two or more fungicides in a regular program for optimal disease control. Make sure you rotate fungicides with different modes of action for effective resistance management.

Turf patch diseases are troublesome to deal with. A disease-control program that includes a foundation fungicide can help prevent and treat major patch diseases. As a preventive measure, make a single application in April and May. Follow label directions for rates. Applications in turfgrass should be thoroughly irrigated. For season-long control, make split applications in May, June, and July. Treatment is effective even in areas with a history of summer patch disease. Follow label directions for rates and spray intervals. Applications usually require thorough irrigation. One to two applications of a foundation fungicide in early spring can prevent disease all season long.

Turf pests and others

Turf pests include mites, ticks, spiders, sowbugs, centipedes, and millipedes. They're often called "insects" because of their similarities in size, shape, life cycle, and habits, but they're not really insects. They're insect relatives. Mites, for instance, have eight legs, not six, and their bodies have two main parts, not three. They also lack wings and antennae common to most insects. But since the same insecticide and cultural practices can control both insects and their relatives, both are regarded as "insects" here (Figure 2-5).

The more you know about how insects live, the better your chances of effective control. You should time your control methods to coincide with susceptible insect stages. For example, if you spray a tree for caterpillars after it has been defoliated, you're wasting your

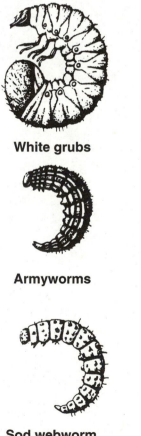

White grubs   **Billbug grubs**

Armyworms   **Mites**

Sod webworm   **Chinch bugs**

2-5 *Common turf insect pests.*

time and insecticide because the caterpillars are done feeding and are now pupating. You can also spot a pest invasion before it ruins turf-grass. Look for two different life cycles.

Complete metamorphosis includes very distinct stages: egg, larvae, pupae, and adult. The young (called larvae, caterpillars, maggots, or grubs) look entirely different than the adults (which have legs, wings, antennae, and reproductive organs). Beetles, butterflies, flies, mosquitoes, fleas, bees, and ants are common examples.

Incomplete metamorphosis includes a very gradual change from young to adult. The young (called nymphs) resemble the adult in form, eat the same food, and live in the same environment. Wings (when present) become fully developed only in the adult stage. Examples are grasshoppers, earwigs, cockroaches, and aphids.

Insects don't just eat the choicest foods from the picnic table. They'll even eat the table—and the turfgrass under it. The damages that result to turfgrass vary according to their principal mouthparts. Chewing insects are more common among turf insects. They directly consume plant tissue, leaving holes or notches in grass blades, tunnels in stems, and missing epidermis from leaves. They even completely sever plant parts or prune its roots. Webworms, cutworms, beetles, armyworms, grasshoppers, and weevils are common examples. Most do their damage as immature larvae and nymphs. By feeding on leaves, they rob plants of their ability to manufacture food, slowing or stunting their growth. And by injuring roots, these pests slow water and nutrient absorption, causing plants to wilt or even die.

Sucking insects use hollow, needlelike tubes to pierce plant tissue and withdraw sap the same way you'd use a straw. Common examples are chinch bugs, aphids, leafhoppers, and mites. Both adults and nymphs can damage turfgrass. When sucking out a plant's sap, they drain nutrients necessary for plant growth. Some even inject toxic saliva that inflicts more damage. The results are yellowing, wilting, stunting, or curling of leaves, followed by browning and death. What's worse, some of these insects also act as vectors, spreading diseases from one plant to another. A single aphid species, for example, can transmit more than 50 different plant viruses.

How can insects thrive in harsh conditions when so many other animals can't? One reason is their incredible ability to adapt to heat, cold, famine, and inhospitable environments. Another is their protective strategies. Some (like scales) use camouflage to escape detection. Still others live between the thin walls of a leaf. Insects also have their skeletons on the outside of their bodies to protect against injury and moisture loss. And unlike most animals, insects have wings to make it easier to search for food and escape from enemies. They also have

keen sensory perception to locate choice food. Perhaps the biggest
reason for insects' success is their reproductive powers. What else in
the animal kingdom can produce several generations in a single season? Or multiply in vast quantities to meet changes in their surroundings? Or even reproduce without mating, in some cases? Take beetles,
for example. There are more species of beetles alone than all other
animals combined. Current counts are at more than 1.5 million
species altogether, and that grows by 7000 to 10,000 every year as
scientists make new discoveries. (To put this number in perspective,
it would take more than 6000 pages to list them all here.) Fortunately,
less than 1 percent of these are harmful, and only a few hundred are
considered serious pests. Only insects that are common landscaping
problems are discussed in this guide.

Annual bluegrass weevil
The annual bluegrass weevil is a dark-colored pest about ¼ inch long
with a beak-like snout that, like all weevils, plays dead when you
pick it up. It preys primarily on annual bluegrass (*Poa annua*), causing damage ranging from scattered, small yellow-brown spots to
death of turf. The damage is most noticeable in late May or early June
when you can easily pull up damaged turf to see the hollow stems.

Ants
Ants are not considered to be serious landscaping pests, although
some types may damage young seedlings. However, they are closely
associated with honeydew produced by sucking insect pests and are
often the most visible clue that the pest is present. Ants often maintain aphid colonies, fighting off parasites and predators to feed on the
sticky honeydew that aphids produce. They are considered to be a
nuisance pest for the nest mounds they make, not because they feed
on turf. These nest mounds vary by species, but in the northern states
they're usually 2 to 3 inches tall, replaced rapidly, causing damage to
mowers as well as shading out turf to cause small dead spots. Some
ants culture aphids in their colonies by placing them on turf roots.
Others kill grass surrounding their nests. Getting rid of the ants often
permits natural aphid controls to reestablish themselves. To keep ants
out of plants, encircle trunks with bands of a sticky ant barrier,
put out diazinon or chlorpyrifos granules, or use poisonous ant baits.
Use chemical insecticides only as a last resort.

Aphids
Aphids are soft, oval, pinhead- to matchhead-size insects that cluster
together on young shoots, buds, and leaves. They come in various

colors, including green, pink, red, and black, with and without wings. Numerous creatures keep aphid populations in check. Often the best tactic is to do nothing and watch natural controls go to work. Lacewings, ladybird beetles, syrphid flies, predatory midges, parasitic wasps, even lizards and small birds are among the many natural aphid controls that may live in the landscape. If you spray with a toxic insecticide, you risk killing the insect predators along with the problem.

Fortunately, you can get rid of most aphids with a blast of water from the hose. For greater effectiveness, wash them off with an insecticidal soap. The soap kills aphids but won't linger to harm other insects later. The most troublesome aphids curl leaves around themselves or stay in protected places like the inside of young buds. The best control for these aphids is anticipation. If you had them last year, expect them again this year. Hose or wash them off when the aphid colony is still young and leaves are still open. A dormant oil spray is effective in killing overwintering eggs of many species of aphids on trees and shrubs. On herbaceous plants, clean up old plant debris before growth starts in spring. If an aphid infestation is severe, spray with an insecticidal soap, pyrethrum, rotenone, diazinon, malathion, or acephate (on nonedible plants only). Resort to chemical insecticide only as a last resort.

Black turfgrass ataenius

These pests are primarily a problem of golf courses. As grubs feed on the roots of turfgrass, they damage fairways, greens, and tees by causing plants to wilt despite abundant moisture. Under heat stress, plants eventually die in small, irregular patches that later join to form large dead turf areas. Affected turf rolls up easily to reveal countless numbers of mature larvae, pupae, and even adult pests.

Bluegrass billbugs

A severe threat to turfgrass, especially in summer, billbugs overwinter as adults, emerging in spring to lay eggs in holes they gouge out of grass blades. Larvae feed within stems and hollow them out, then feed on plant crowns and roots so that grass stems within the dead areas can be easily pulled out of the soil. The result is wilted turf and small, circular patches that become yellowish or brown.

Clover mites

These pests are similar in size and appearance to winter grain mites, but they have a slightly pink body with pale-colored legs. The damage they cause is also similar. They live and feed on the underside of grass blades, preferring clover and similar plants. Clover mites can kill turf next to building foundations and often enter buildings in winter in search of warmth. Up to 5000 mites a square foot are possible across an entire lawn.

Cutworms

A large variety of hairless larvae of night-flying moths make up the diverse group called cutworms. They feed at night and on overcast days, and most can cut off young plants at the ground—hence their name. These larvae are highly destructive pests. They are most active at night. During the day, they curl up into a ball in a trench they've dug about an inch below ground. Visible damage is uncommon on home lawns, but they can cause significant damage to golf greens. Adult moths don't damage turf. Three or four generations are possible each season. Susceptible seedlings should be protected from cutworms by putting a physical barrier around each seedling the day it sprouts or the day you plant it. As these pests are voracious and quick, I recommend the latter. One simple barrier is a cut-off milk carton sleeve: Sink it 1 inch below soil level, allow 2 inches above, and provide at least 1 inch of space between the sleeve and the plant. As an extra precaution, put petroleum jelly or a sticky ant barrier on the upper edge.

Some cutworms crawl up into plants and eat the buds, leaves, and fruit. One way to keep them out is to spread a sticky ant barrier around the base of each susceptible plant. If you have too many to easily employ barriers, try hand-picking cutworms at night. Or try trapping them by placing cardboard, plywood, wide boards, or heavy paper sacks in landscape paths. During daylight, lift the traps and destroy the worms that have taken refuge beneath. Resort to chemical insecticide only as a last resort.

Deer

Deer may be pleasant to watch, but they can ravage a landscape in no time by nipping off flower heads and eating tender young shoots. As wild plants dry out, deer spend more time looking for food in landscapes on the fringes of suburbia. They develop browsing patterns, returning regularly, most often in the evening. Fond of a wide array of flowering plants, especially roses, deer eat the foliage or fruit of nearly anything.

Fencing is the most certain protection, even though deer typically can jump vertically higher than their body height. On level ground, an 8-foot woven-wire fence usually keeps all but the most determined deer out. A horizontal "outrigger" extension on a fence makes it harder for a deer to jump it. On a slope, you may need to erect a

10- to 12-foot fence to protect against deer, because they are extremely clever and will go to higher ground to jump the fence. Because deer can jump high or wide—but not simultaneously—some landscapers have had success with a pair of parallel 5-foot fences, with a 5-foot "no-deer's-land" in between. The old traditional method of hanging small cloth bags filled with blood meal on plants works initially, but blood meal attracts dogs and smells horrible when wet. Never use chemicals or poisons on deer.

Earwigs

Earwigs are known to eat almost anything soft. They normally eat aphids and their larvae, which means that earwigs can be an important natural control of plant pests. Unfortunately, earwigs also feed on soft parts of plants, such as flower petals and corn silks. A large earwig population can significantly damage desirable plants. Earwigs hide during the day but are active at night. When dawn comes, they scurry back into tight, cozy places. You can trap earwigs by providing the type of tight-fitting, moist shelter in which they like to spend the day. At night, put moistened rolled-up newspapers, rolls of corrugated cardboard, or short sections of landscape hose on the ground. In the morning dispose of the accumulated insects. Use chemical insecticides only as a last resort.

Geranium budworm and corn earworm

The geranium budworm has appeared in damaging numbers in some mountain regions across the nation. It is closely related to the corn earworm. Both are larvae of stout-bodied, dull-colored, night-flying moths. The typical geranium budworm lives through the winter as a pupa in the soil. Then, in late April or May, a mature gray moth emerges and lays eggs on geranium buds—one egg per bud. From the egg hatches a very small worm, which enters and feeds on the geranium bud (or on a rosebud or petunia bud). As the worm grows, it consumes the bud and moves on to the rest of the plant, taking on the color of the plant tissue it eats. Once you see a hole in a bud, pick the bud, squash it, and discard it. This may destroy the young worm that has already damaged the potential blossom. For heavy infestations where worms have outgrown the protective covering of flower buds, spray with *Bacillus thuringiensis*, pyrethrins, carbaryl, or acephate. Repeat weekly as needed.

Grasshoppers

During their periodic outbreaks, grasshoppers own much of the Midwestern and western states, except in areas where coastal weather prevails. By preference, they lay their eggs in dry, undisturbed areas such as along roadsides and in empty lots, but they also lay in landscapes. Eggs begin hatching from March to early June, depending on temperature and climate. Newly hatched nymphs resemble adults but are smaller and lack wings. The nymphs feed voraciously, sometimes stripping entire areas bare. When they mature and develop wings, they fly out and find new feeding areas.

When you are cultivating in fall, winter, or early spring, watch for and destroy egg clusters, which contain up to 75 cream or yellow rice-shaped eggs. In spring and early summer, while grasshoppers are still young and wingless, they are most vulnerable to chemicals and baits. Use malathion, diazinon, acephate, carbyl, chlorpyrifos, or barn-and-carybly bait. Grasshoppers roost at night in hedges, tall weeds, and shrubs. Observe their evening behavior to locate roosting sites, then spray in these areas after dark. Your best early defense against large numbers of grasshoppers may be to protect desirable plants with floating row covers or netting. In summer, when grasshoppers are mature and less vulnerable to chemicals, hand-pick them early in the morning. The disease-producing organism *Nosema locustae* causes grasshoppers to produce fewer eggs. Over large areas (over a ranch for example), applying this commercially packaged material can help reduce grasshopper problems in later years.

Greenbug aphids

Greenbug aphids are tiny but very damaging pests that pierce grass blades and then drain them of sap and inject toxins, causing rust-colored patches under trees that turn brown and die. Left untreated, these pests can kill an entire lawn. Damage occurs primarily after mild winters and cool springs. Forty or more of these pests may be seen on a single grass blade at the same time. They are also common carriers of viral plant diseases.

Ground squirrels

Throughout the nation, ground squirrels are especially troublesome in landscapes that border fields or wild land. The California ground squirrel is the most common kind in California, western Oregon, and southwestern Washington. It lives in burrows, usually 2 to 4 feet underground, where it stores food, raises young, and hides from its chief predators: foxes, hawks, and owls. During the spring and summer, the ground squirrel scurries around most actively in mid-morning or late afternoon (except in very hot weather), nibbling through vegetable patches, digging up bulbs, gnawing roots and bark, and climbing trees after fruits and nuts. Methods of control include using a baited (with an almond, walnut, or a slice of orange tied to the trigger) box-type gopher trap placed outside the burrow. Baits should be placed in one or more bait stations near the squirrel burrows and must be available to the squirrel for at least a week to achieve maximum control. Metal guards around tree trunks can keep ground squirrels out of trees. Protect bulb beds with a cover of fine-mesh chicken wire. Before you try any type of trapping or baiting, check with your county agent or farm advisor because laws in some areas prohibit catching certain types of ground squirrels.

Grubs

Grubs are larvae of many kinds of beetles that are whitish or grayish in color with three pairs of legs that distinguish them from legless billbug grubs. As they feed on turfgrass roots, they cause dead brown patches that roll back easily like carpet. Their presence can lead to damage from birds, moles, raccoons, and skunks looking for grubs. They are difficult to control because they insulate themselves in thatch and soil.

Hairy cinch bugs

A tiny pest (only $\frac{1}{16}$ to $\frac{1}{4}$ inch long), cinch bugs can wipe out entire lawns by sucking the sap out of grass blades. When feeding, they inject a toxin that causes the blades to turn brown and die, resulting in large, distinct, circular patches in sunny areas of turfgrass. They prefer hot, dry weather. Both adults and nymphs cause turf damage. Most have distinctive black marks on their white wings (Figure 2-6).

Leaf rollers

The most common leaf rollers (a group of larval landscape pests) are the fruit-tree leaf roller and the oblique-banded leaf roller. Despite its name, the fruit-tree species feeds on oaks as well as fruit trees. In spring, summer, or fall adult moths can lay egg clusters that they cover with a waterproof cement. In some species, the eggs hatch early and overwinter in cracks in the bark of the host tree, whereas other species don't hatch until spring. For the first few weeks after hatching, while the green larvae are about the size of long rice grains, they eat day and night. Then, when they are about half grown, they begin to hide during the daytime by folding leaves together, and when disturbed, they thrash about violently. At night they crawl out and feed on the plant. At some point in maturity, the larvae pupate. From the pupa (a light brown or green segmented cylinder within the rolled-up leaf) emerges the adult moth. The oblique-banded leaf roller produces one or two generations a year; the fruit-tree leaf roller produces just one.

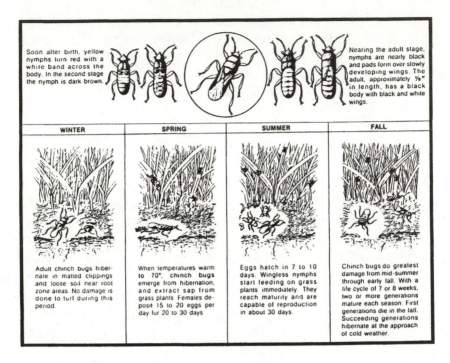

2-6 *Chinch bug life cycle.*

A number of parasitic insects usually keep populations of leaf rollers low. Light infestations are easy to take care of physically—just pick off and destroy rolled leaves or squash leaf rollers in place. Use sprays only when leaf rollers threaten serious damage. The favored control is *Bacillus thuringiensis*; the surest chemical sprays are diazinon, carbaryl, and acephate.

Mealybugs

Closely related to scale insects, mealybugs have an oval body with overlapping soft plates and a white, cottony covering. Unlike most scales, a mealybug can move around at a very slow crawl. These pests suck plant juices, causing growth stunting or death. Often a black, sooty mold grows on the honeydew they excrete. Mealybugs are prime landscape pests everywhere. For any minor infestation, daub mealybugs with a cotton swab dipped in rubbing alcohol. Hose plants with jets of water or insecticidal soap every 2 to 4 weeks to remove adult mealybugs, their eggs and young, and the black mold that deters beneficial insects. Ants have the same symbiotic relationship to mealybugs as to aphids and scale insects, so aphid control measures stated previously work for them as well (Figure 2-7).

Natural predators, such as ladybird beetles, can help control mealy-bugs, as can some commercially available predators such as Crypto-laemus beetles and lacewings. Cryptolaemus beetles are "sheep in wolves' clothing": They look like mealybugs but have chewing mouth parts and a ropey wax covering. When mealybug infestations are heavy, spray with malathion, diazinon, acephate, or horticultural oil.

Mites

To the naked eye, mites look like tiny specks of red, yellow, or green. In reality, they are tiny spider relatives (each has eight legs). Spider mites are especially troublesome in interior regions of the nation. The first (and sometimes only) sign of spider mite damage is yellow-stippled leaves. But there are many reasons for leaf yellow-ing. To confirm that mites are the problem, hold a piece of white paper beneath the stippled leaves and sharply rap the stem from which they are growing. If mites are present, the blow will knock some of them onto the paper where they will look like moving specks. Some mites also make fine webbing across leaves (espe-cially on the undersides) and around stems. Citrus bud mites dis-tort lemon fruit and foliage in coastal areas. Control measures are rarely necessary.

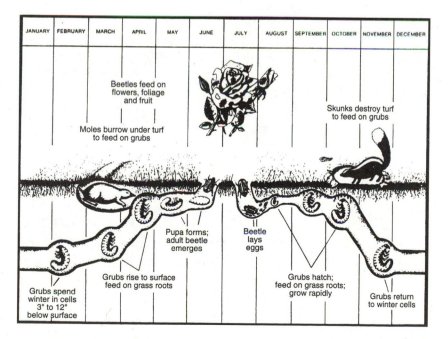

2-7 *Beetle/grub life cycle.*

If the plant is small, you might jet it thoroughly with water to wash off the mites. Insecticidal soap added to the water spray will increase the spray's effectiveness. Dust that settles on leaves encourages mites, so continual hosing helps control mite populations. Increased humidity also helps. Drought-stressed plants are more prone to mites. Many natural predators keep mites in check most of the time. Some of these predators (lacewing larvae and five different species of predatory mites) are bred and sold by biological control companies. If you can't wash the plant or if washing is not effective, try spraying. Summer horticulture oils are especially effective because all stages of mites, including eggs, are destroyed. Sulfur can also be effective, but don't use it in combination with oil sprays because it can be toxic to plants. If the infestation is severe, you can try dicofol outside California. (Dicofol is not registered or legal in California.)

Moles

Notorious pests in good soils through the nation, moles have short forelegs pointing outward; large, flattened hands; and claws for digging tunnels. Townsend's mole (common in the Pacific states west of the Sierra-Cascades chain of mountains) has velvety, blue-black fur and a nearly hairless tail and snout. Moles are primarily insectivorous, eating earthworms, bugs, and larvae, and only occasionally nibbling greens and roots. Irrigation and rain keep them near the soil surface where they do the most damage as they tunnel, heaving plants from the ground, severing tender plant roots and disfiguring lawns. A mole's main runways, which are used repeatedly, are usually 6 to 10 inches underground and are frequently punctuated with volcano-shaped mounds of excavated soil. Shallower burrows, created while feeding, are used for short periods and then abandoned.

Due to their feeding habits, moles are very difficult to control with poison baits. And moles, like gophers, are difficult to control with toxic gas. To be successful with this method, place gas "mole bombs" directly in the main runways and block all holes. Be persistent with follow-up treatments. Trapping is the most effective way to control moles. The spear- or harpoon-type trap is the easiest to set because you simply position the trap above the soil. A scissor-jaw trap must be carefully set into the main runway (probe with a sharp stick to find it) because a wily mole will spring, heave out, or walk around a faulty trap. Out here in the frontier West, we sit on the back porch after work with a couple of cold beers and a .22 rifle, and wait for them to stick their heads out. Of course, city authorities frown on this type of varmint control.

Oak moths

The pale-brown oak moth can damage mature oak trees. It can be a major problem in coastal regions. The tan, inch-wide moths lay eggs in live oak trees twice a year (three times if winters are unseasonably mild). The first generation of larvae hatch in November and overwinter on live oak leaves, growing and eating more as weather warms in spring. About an inch long, full-sized worms have bulbous brown heads and olive green bodies with distinct black and olive or yellow stripes. The moths emerge from their pupae in June and July, and their offspring larvae eat leaves again from late July to October. The worms aren't a problem every year; however, populations may become heavy enough to defoliate trees for two or three years in a row and then disappear for several years.

Pillbug and sowbug

These two familiar creatures have sectioned shells and seven pairs of legs. Pillbugs roll up into black balls about the size of a small pea; sowbugs are gray and cannot roll up as tightly. Their principal food is decaying vegetable matter.

Pocket gophers

Pocket gophers are serious pests in many areas of the nation, and in coastal regions, they rank among the top three landscape pests. Like little bulldozers, they dig out a network of tunnels (usually 6 to 18 inches below the surface) with strong, clawed forefeet. Tunnels near the surface are for gathering food; deeper ones are for sleeping, storing food, and raising young. Gophers eat roots, bulbs, and sometimes entire plants by pulling them down into their burrows. Well suited to burrow life, they have small eyes and ears that don't clog with dirt and the flexibility needed to turn around in tight spaces. The first sign of gopher trouble often is a fanshaped mound of fresh, finely pulverized earth in a lawn or flower bed; this soil is a by-product of burrowing operations, brought to the surface through short side runs opening off the main burrow. A plug of earth is used to close the hole.

Trapping is the most efficient method of gopher control. Avoid the temptation to place a single trap down a hole. Your chances of catching a gopher are much greater when you dig down to the main horizontal runway connecting with the surface hole and place two traps in the runway, one on either side of your excavation. Attach each trap to a stake on the surface with a chain or wire (to prevent a trapped gopher from dragging the trap farther into a burrow). The Macabee trap is the most effective. Box-type traps also work and are easier to set, but they require a larger hole to be dug for insertion.

When the traps are in place, plug the hole with a ball of carrot tops, fresh grass, or other tender greens; their scent attracts gophers. Next, place a board or soil over the greens and the hole to block all light.

Check traps frequently, and clear tunnels if the gopher has pushed soil into the traps. Be persistent: A clever gopher may avoid your first traps. Poison baits are very effective for the control of trap-wise gophers. Probe for the deep burrows with a rod or sharp stick, insert bait, and close the hole. These baits are hazardous to other living things, so be sure not to spill any on the ground. And although poisoning of dogs and cats from eating poisoned gophers is rare, it can happen. If your landscape is subject to ongoing invasion by gophers from neighboring fields or orchards, or if all your trapping efforts fail, you can protect roots of young plants by lining the sides and bottom of planting holes with light-gauge chicken wire. If they get through that, use heavy-gauge hog wire.

Root weevils
More than one dozen different kinds of root weevil are found in the western United States and throughout the Midwest. From the moment they emerge in spring through fall, flightless gray or black adults eat notches from leaf edges of many plants. They especially like azaleas and rhododendrons, roses, and viburnums. In late summer, the weevils lay eggs on the soil or in folds of leaves. Eggs hatch into legless larvae with pinkish or whitish bodies and tan heads; these burrow into the soil and eat roots, particularly of strawberry plants. Use acephate to control adults (which feed only at night) on nonedible plants. Parasitic nematodes are effective for controlling larvae.

Slugs and snails
The worst pests in all landscaping for fruits and vegetables are slugs and snails. Similar creatures (a slug is simply a snail without a shell), they feed on various plants by biting tissue with rasping mouths underneath their bodies. Both hide by day and feed at night, although they may be active during daytime hours on gray, damp days. Nobody ever gets rid of slugs or snails for good. They always return from neighbors' lots, on new plants, or even in new soil (often in container-grown plants) as eggs. The eggs look like clusters of ⅛-inch pearls; look for them under rocks, boards, and pots, and destroy those you find.

The most popular chemical controls are packaged baits containing metaldehyde or methiocarb in pellets, meal, or emulsion form. Metaldehyde is the most widely used, but its effectiveness is limited during periods of high humidity. Methiocarb, commonly used in slug bait, should not be used around fruit and vegetables. If you put out pellets, scatter them so there is space between them, rather than making piles. And be careful using baits where dogs live or visit, because the bait can poison dogs, too. Never apply it when dogs are present: It may look as though you're putting out dry dog food.

Hand-picking is an easy way to control snails: You simply grab them by their shells and dispose of them however you wish. (Slugs are harder to pick up because they have no shell to grab. Some landscapers kill them with a 5-percent ammonia solution in a hand sprayer.) The best hunting time for slugs and snails is after 10 P.M. You can also trap slugs and snails. One easy-to-set trap is a wide plank or piece of plywood elevated about an inch off the ground. Place it in an infested area. It offers a daytime hiding place for them to group in from which you can collect and dispatch the pests. Squash a slug or snail on the board's underside; this will attract other slugs and snails. Beer or a solution of sugar water and yeast appeals to slugs' fondness for fermented foods. Put the liquid in a saucer or other shallow container, and set it in the landscape so the rim is even with the soil. Slugs will crawl into the dish and drown. Refill the container daily with fresh liquid. You can prevent snails from damaging such plants as citrus by wrapping copper bands around the tree trunks. Snails and slugs will not cross this barrier.

Decollate snails feed on the brown landscape snail, but, although they do not usually molest mature landscape plants, they will feed on succulent leaves or berries near the ground, especially once the supply of brown landscape snails has been depleted. Their sale is legal only in certain regions of the country.

Sod webworms

Also called the lawn moth in the adult stage, the sod webworm is a serious pest that chews off blades of grass close to the ground, then drags them into silk-lined tunnels to eat them, resulting in small, saucer-shaped, brown patches on turf. The moth itself doesn't damage turf but drops eggs into grass that develop into hungry caterpillars. Sod webworms generally feed at night, preferring slopes and other hard-to-water areas (Figure 2-8).

Squash bugs

About ⅝ inch in length, squash bugs are a problem on many plants of the squash family, particularly in high desert and mountain areas. Damage is usually greatest on winter squash and pumpkin plants: The bugs can cause leaves to wilt completely and also damage the

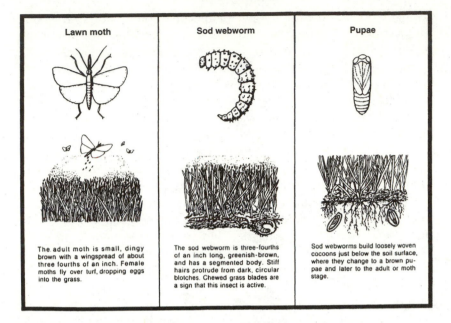

Lawn moth	Sod webworm	Pupae
The adult moth is small, dingy brown with a wingspread of about three fourths of an inch. Female moths fly over turf, dropping eggs into the grass.	The sod webworm is three-fourths of an inch long, greenish-brown, and has a segmented body. Stiff hairs protrude from dark, circular blotches. Chewed grass blades are a sign that this insect is active.	Sod webworms build loosely woven cocoons just below the soil surface, where they change to a brown pupae and later to the adult or moth stage.

2-8 *Sod webworm life cycle.*

fruit. Summer squash, melons, and cucumbers are seldom affected. In spring, adult bugs lay their eggs on squash leaves. If you find a mass of hard brown eggs crowded together on a leaf underside, destroy them. Squash bugs spend nights under flat objects, so put out boards in the evening; in early morning, turn over the boards and kill the bugs (they can emit a very unpleasant odor). Carbaryl is an effective chemical control, but getting it applied to all the leaves is a problem—particularly on older plants with plenty of foliage. For best results, start control when plants are small or as soon as you see eggs. Sabadilla may also work.

Thrips
Almost microscopic pests, thrips feed by rasping soft flower and leaf tissue and then drinking the plant juices. In heavy infestations, both flowers and leaves fail to open normally, appearing twisted or stuck together and discolored. Look closely and you'll see stippled puckerings in flower or leaf tissue and the small black fecal pellets that thrips deposit while feeding. Leaves may take on a silvery or tan cast, distinguished from spider-mite damage by the black, varnish-like fecal pellets on leaf undersides. The Cuban laurel thrips are darker and larger than the more widespread kinds (which are about half the size) and cause a noticeable curl in the leaves of their host plant, Indian laurel fig (*Ficus microcarpa nitida*).

Thrips can be a problem starting in May (as early as March in the desert) and breed rapidly, increasing in numbers as the season goes on. Thrips are notoriously fond of white and light-pink rose blossoms and of gladiolus leaves and flowers. The natural enemies of flower thrips are numerous, including ladybird beetles and larvae, green lacewing larvae, and predaceous thrips and mites. The Indian laurel fig variety "Green Gem" is apparently resistant to Cuban laurel thrips. For serious thrips infestations on ornamental plants, try malathion, diazinon, chlorpyrifos, or acephate. On edible plants, use malathion or insecticidal soap.

Varmints

Other animal pest problems are caused by burrowing animals. The symptom of animal underground pests is simply tunneling. Moles and gophers are the usual culprits. Other digging and burrowing animals include crayfish, armadillos, birds, dogs, skunks, ground squirrels, and mice. The ways to control animal pests involve trapping, poison baits, fumigation, eliminating the attractive food source such as grubs, gopher-proof wire installed below subgrade, and constructing or planting barriers such as fences or thorny shrubs. Use traps. Resort to chemical poisons only as a last resort.

Whiteflies

Aptly named, whiteflies are annoying winged insects (about $\frac{1}{8}$ inch long) that fly up from a plant when you brush or touch it. Turn over an infested plant's leaf and you see winged adults, stationary pupae, nymphs that suck plant juices and exude a sticky substance, and (with sharp eyes or a hand lens) tiny eggs and freshly hatched, mobile young. Whiteflies are on the list of the top 10 pests in every part of the West and other semiarid regions.

Nature keeps whitefly populations in check most of the time with tiny wasp species that are parasites of the nymphs and pupae and other predatory creatures that feed on them. When you spray with a chemical insecticide, you may also kill those parasites and predators, resulting in an increase of whiteflies. So before you decide to use a chemical control, consider these options: Eliminate highly susceptible plants from your landscape. Hose off infested plants, hitting both sides of all leaves to wash off adults and crawlers (newly hatched nymphs); repeat every few days. Insecticidal soap can be more effective than water, and it is less harmful than insecticides to natural enemies. Place yellow cards or stakes covered with sticky material among infested plants. The color attracts adult whiteflies; the sticky material captures and holds them. Buy and release in your landscape a commercially reared natural parasite: *Encarsia formosa* wasps. They are parasites of the greenhouse whitefly (common species) and will kill them in a greenhouse or outdoors.

On plants like squash, get rid of old, nonproductive yellow leaves in the center of the plant. These leaves carry many whitefly nymphs. On edible plants, use pyrethrins or malathion. On nonedible plants, you can use systemics, neem, chlorpyrifos, or summer oils. Increase spray effectiveness by spraying at night, while whiteflies are resting. Recent outbreaks of introduced species of whitefly, including the ash whitefly, are not effectively controlled with chemical sprays. Instead, massive releases of parasitic wasps by state agencies have been successful in bringing these annoying pests down to reasonable levels. In cool climates—including all of Colorado and areas to the north and northwest—whiteflies don't overwinter outdoors; all landscape infestations originate from indoor plants or are imported as transplants. Inspect greenhouse and indoor plants and eliminate any whiteflies you find. When you buy new plants for your landscape, particularly bedding plants that may have started their lives in a greenhouse, carefully examine the undersides of leaves for the nymphs.

Watering techniques

Improper watering results in too much excess water, leaches fertilizer, reduces plant growth, increases erosion, compacts soil, increases irrigation costs, increases plant diseases, decreases rooting depth, and decreases soil aeration. Not enough water reduces plant growth, promotes soil cracking, contributes to wind erosion of soil, and may completely kill plants, causing increased cost for plant replacement. A balance must be maintained.

Methods for correcting water problems include using water-conservation methods, selecting appropriate irrigation systems, use of appropriate mulches, installing drainage systems, and selecting proper plants. Waterlogged soils are caused by fine-textured, compacted soils, lack of surface and internal drainage, water accumulations in depressions, and excessive irrigation or rainfall. Waterlogged soils result in poor soil aeration, reduced number of roots and plant vigor, increased disease occurrence, and increased soil compaction. Terms and definitions involved in this section include

drainage tile Clay or plastic tube beneath the soil surface that carries away excess surface runoff water.

evaporation Water lost as vapor.

growing season Period between beginning growth in the spring and cessation of growth in the fall.

irrigation Application of supplemental water.

mulch Material applied to the soil surface around plants to reduce water loss, decrease soil temperature fluctuation, and discourage weed growth.

necrosis Death of tissue.

pH Measure of acidity or alkalinity on a scale with values running from 0 to 14, with 7 representing neutrality, less than 7 acidity, and greater than 7 alkalinity.

psi Pounds per square inch; a unit for measuring pressure.

relative humidity The amount of water vapor that air can hold compared to water-saturated air at the same temperature.

runoff Surface flow of water from an area.

slope Incline of the surface of a soil.

soil permeability Quality of soil that enables water to move through it.

soil texture The proportions of particle sizes in the soil. Sand is recognized as the largest particle size, silt as medium size, and clay is the smallest particle size.

soluble salts Dissolved minerals in water that affect water quality.

swale A shallow depression in a turf area.

water (H_2O): Up to 85 percent of a plant's fresh weight.

waterlogged Soil condition in which large and small pore spaces are filled with water.

Supplemental irrigation may be needed to offset uneven rainfall distribution, unseasonable high temperatures, or higher individual plant water requirements. Some plants desired in the landscape require more water than naturally falls as rain in their native environment. Therefore, irrigation must be used in caring for that plant. Irrigation affects plant performance by promoting deep rooting, in contrast to frequent shallow watering, which causes shallow rooting. Supplemental irrigation also helps maintain plants' health and growth. Cold damage on evergreens can be avoided by proper watering during fall and winter. Inadequate watering can kill a plant or severely stunt its growth. Factors affecting water requirements are

- *Plant species.* Some species simply require more water than others.
- *Stage of plant establishment.* Water is more critical for young and newly transplanted plants. Grass seed requires frequent watering for germination and establishment. Newly planted trees should be watered immediately after planting.
- *Soil texture.* Coarse-textured (sandy) soils require more frequent watering than fine-textured (clay) soils.

- *Temperature.* Warmer temperatures increase water use. Some water loss due to evaporation may be avoided by watering when temperature is lower.
- *Wind.* Greater wind velocities increase water demand. Some water loss due to evaporation may be avoided by watering when wind velocity is low.
- *Relative humidity.* Lower relative humidities increase water loss.
- *Mulch.* Mulches can be used to reduce water loss. When no mulch is used, soils lose more water to evaporation and require more water.
- *Plant competition.* Greater plant densities increase water use.
- *Growing season.* Demand is higher when plants are growing than when they are dormant.
- *Site orientation.* Southern slopes receive more wind and sun. Areas with large tree roots compete for water. Areas along street curbs, patios, walls, and driveways receive heat from the pavement. Different areas of the landscape may require varied watering schedules.

Irrigation water quality is obtained from water quality analyses. These analyses can be done through the water quality board at your county extension office. The factors that affect the irrigation water quality are

- Presence of suspended particles or silt (sand, soil, algae).
- Presence of chemicals (chlorine, water softeners, industrial waste).
- High soluble salts or high sodium concentrations (salts make it difficult for plants to extract the moisture from soil).
- High or low pH.

Proven water conservation methods are

- Remove weeds and undesirable plants to reduce competition.
- Avoid aerial applications in high winds.
- Water in early morning.
- Water the depth and frequency needed to maintain plant health.
- Use trickle (drip) irrigation systems where possible.
- Mulch around trees and in flower beds.
- Use drought-tolerant plants.
- Cultivate compacted soil areas to reduce runoff.
- Remove dense thatch in lawn to reduce runoff.
- Use the shut-off valve on hose end.
- Clear patios and sidewalks by sweeping with a broom or with a portable blower rather than by washing with a landscape hose.

Plant symptoms resulting from excess water application:

- Dark, spongy roots
- Light-colored (chlorotic) new growth
- Reduced shoot growth
- Leaf fall
- Sudden wilting during warm temperatures
- Plant poorly anchored in soil

Plant symptoms resulting from deficient water application:

- Few healthy, bright-colored roots
- Discolored foliage (greenish gray, purple tinge, light green)
- Marginal leaf necrosis
- Reduced shoot growth
- Leaf fall
- Wilting
- Reduced bloom size
- Reduced number of blooms
- Fruit and bud drop

Fertilizing

To ensure uniform disbursement of fertilizer, the person who calibrates the spreader must spread the fertilizer. Partially fill the spreader with fertilizer and mark the level on the side of the hopper. With the spreader set at a middle setting, operate it over an area of known dimension. For example, if the spreader has a 6-foot spreading swath and is operated for 50 feet, it will have covered 300 square feet. Some spreaders are equipped with catchers that can be emptied and weighed when calibrating. Place a piece of cloth on the inside of the hopper and pour in fertilizer until it has reached the marked level. Remove and weigh the amount of fertilizer that was added to refill the hopper to the marked level. Record this weight in ounces.

Uniform distribution is a problem, but it can be controlled by overlapping. To uniformly spread a fertilizer, apply half of the material in one direction, and the other half at right angles to the first. This means that when the rotary spreader is calibrated, it will be for half the recommended rate. Determine the amount of material (A) to be spread per 1000 square feet. Determine the total area (B) to be covered with fertilizer, i.e., 50 feet (length of test area) by 6 feet (width of spreader swath) = 300 square feet. Set up the proportion with (C) divided by 2 equals the amount of materials that should fall from the spreader:

(A) ounces/1000 square feet = (C) ounces/(B) square feet

where (C) = (A) × (B)/1000 square feet and

(C)/2 = amount of fertilizer that should be added to the hopper

The final answer should equal the weighed fertilizer. If the weighed value is less that the calculated value, set the spreader with a larger

Fertilization Record

Client: _____ Phone: _____ Address: _____

Dates of fertilization	Fertilizer analysis	Sq. ft. of lawn	Amount of fertilizer	Next application date

2-9 *Fertilization record.*

opening and repeat the procedure. Spread the fertilizer uniformly by applying *half* of the material in one direction, and the other *half* at right angles to the first.

After using the fertilizer spreader, remove all excess material from the spreader. Never store unused material in the hopper. Thoroughly wash the inside of the hopper as well as external surfaces. Dry the spreader to minimize rust formation, which can severely affect the uniformity of fertilizer application. Apply a thin coat of oil to exposed metal surfaces. Do not forget to oil the wheels. Check for worn or broken parts. Replace those parts prior to the next use. Store the spreader with the opening in the wide-open position.

Mixing a complete fertilizer into the soil before planting generally supplies enough nutrients to last at least half the growing season. In cold-winter zones, an application of fertilizer after bloom is under way tides most plants through their season. Where winters are warmer and the growing season is correspondingly longer, give plants another fertilizer application in late summer. Keep a record, as shown in Figure 2-9.

3

Starting plants

Planting techniques

Proper planting techniques depend on the type of plant (annual, perennial, shrub, tree, etc.) and how the plant is sold or propagated (as seed, bare-root, or in containers). Special techniques for various types of plants and planting approaches are explained in this chapter. To get plants off to a good start, you should also have an understanding of soils and soil amendments.

In nature, seeds are scattered randomly from seed-bearing plants. Scattering, or *broadcasting*, seeds is a common method for planting seeds of lawn grasses and wildflowers. To plant seeds of most common plants, though, the landscaper sows seeds more carefully in the open ground or in some sort of container.

You can buy seeds of most ornamental plants in three different forms. The traditional packaging is the seed packet with a picture of the flower, fruit, or plant on the outside, the loose seeds within. You also can buy packets or packages of pelletized seeds: Each seed is coated, like a small pill, to make handling and proper spacing easier. The third form is seed tapes, which are strips of biodegradable plastic in which seeds are embedded, properly spaced for growing to maturity. You just unroll the tape in a prepared furrow and cover it with soil. In all three cases, you find planting instructions on the package. One advantage of sowing seeds directly in the earth is that you usually avoid the need to transplant. The seeds germinate and grow into mature plants in one place. Their growing energy is not interrupted in transplant shock. You may need to thin seedlings to prevent overcrowding, filling in a few sparse spots with thinned plants. But most of the seedling plants need no handling once they break ground.

Sowing seeds

Landscapers commonly choose between two seed-sowing methods, broadcasting and row planting, depending on the results desired. Seeds planted in rows will probably need to be thinned later. Native wildflowers make a reasonably good show if simply scattered in time to catch fall rains and take where they are intended to grow. But they do even better if the ground is first cleared of weeds and grasses and prepared a bit by tilling and adding organic amendments. If you plan to broadcast seeds in drifts or patterned plantings or if you wish to sow a broad area with tough, easy-to-grow plants (such as sweet alyssum or California poppies), you can achieve a more even distribution by mixing the seed with several times its bulk of fine sand. After you have scattered the seeds or seed-and-sand mixture, rake lightly, then carefully sprinkle the area with water. Cover the area with a very thin mulch to prevent the soil from crusting and to hide the seeds from predators. (Be prepared, though, for some loss to birds and rodents.)

Most annuals can be sown in place, but they benefit from a bit more attention than simple broadcasting calls for. With a fork, spade, or rotary tiller, prepare the seedbed, working in soil amendments and a complete fertilizer (read the label and apply only the recommended amount). Smooth the prepared soil with a rake and moisten it well a few days before you intend to plant (if rains don't do the watering for you). Then follow the sowing and covering directions outlined for broadcasting. If you intend to grow annuals in patterned rows, prepare the soil as described previously. But you can omit the fertilizer and apply it, instead, at seeding time in furrows 1 inch deeper than the seeds and 2 inches on either side of the seed row (again, consult label recommendations for the proper amount of fertilizer per foot of row). Follow the seed-packet instructions for optimum planting depth and spacing of the rows, and plant them in a north-south direction so that both sides receive equal sunlight during the day.

When seedlings appear, thin out excess plants (if necessary) so that those remaining are spaced as directed on the seed packet. Bare seeds scattered in furrows almost always come up too thickly; pelletized seeds are easier to sow at the proper spacing, and seed tapes do the spacing for you. Thin out seedlings while they are still small. If you wait too long to thin them, the plants develop poorly, and it is more difficult to remove one without disturbing those around it. Work quickly but gently, replanting the surplus seedlings elsewhere as you go. Many plants get off to a better start when they are sown in containers and later transplanted into place in the landscape. Most nurseries stock seedling plants in flats or other containers, ready for planting. In choosing a container, almost anything that holds soil and has provision for drainage will do for a seed-starting container.

Plastic or wooden nursery flats accommodate the largest number of seeds; other choices are clay or plastic pots, peat pots, aluminum-foil pans (the sort sold for kitchen use), foam or plastic cups, cut-down milk cartons, or shallow wooden boxes that you can make yourself. Remember to punch holes for drainage in the bottom of any container that holds water. If you make your own wooden flats or boxes, leave about a $\frac{1}{4}$-inch space for drainage between the boards that form the container's bottom. If you use containers that have held plants before, give them a thorough cleaning to avoid the possibility of infection by damping-off fungi, which destroy seedlings. A vigorous scrubbing followed by a few days of drying in the sun usually does the job.

Unless you plan a large-scale seed-planting operation, you'll find it easiest to buy a prepared planting-soil mixture for starting seeds. Nurseries carry a variety of mediums called "potting soil." For sowing seeds in a container, gently firm the mixture into the container and level it off about $\frac{3}{4}$ to 1 inch from the top of the container. If the mixture is powdery dry, water it thoroughly and wait a day or two to plant. Very fine seeds can be broadcast over the surface and covered with sand. Larger seeds can either be planted in shallow furrows scratched into the surface or poked in individually. Always remember that seeds should be planted no deeper than recommended on packet labels; a good general rule is to cover seeds to a depth equal to twice their diameter.

Cover seeds with the proper amount of prepared mixture, press down gently but firmly, and then water. Direct watering of the soil surface can sometimes dislodge the seeds. Instead, place the container in a tub, sink, or bucket containing a few inches of water. The planting mix in the container will absorb enough water within a few hours. Thereafter, keep the soil moist but not soaking wet. For slow-sprouting seeds or for plants whose seedlings develop slowly, you can sow seeds in a pot and tie a clear plastic bag around the pot. Place the pot where it receives good light but not direct sunlight. Air can get through the plastic, but water vapor cannot get out; the seedlings will have enough moisture to complete germination without further watering. If you use this technique, be sure that your planting mixture is sterile and that the container has not been used for planting before.

Planting balled-and-burlapped or bare-root plants

Planting techniques for balled-and-burlapped plants are different. Certain plants have roots that won't survive bare-root transplanting.

Instead, they are dug with a ball of soil around their roots. The soil ball is wrapped in burlap (or another sturdy material), and the wrapping is tied with twine to keep the ball intact. These are called balled-and-burlapped (or B&B) plants. Available in this fashion are some deciduous shrubs and trees, evergreen shrubs such as rhododendrons and azaleas, and various conifers. Treat B&B plants carefully: Don't use the trunk as a handle, and don't drop them, because the root ball could shatter, exposing the roots. Cradle the root ball well by supporting the bottom with one or both hands. If it is too heavy for one person to carry, get a coworker to help you carry it in a sling of canvas or stout burlap. Many B&B plants are grown in clay or fairly heavy soil that holds together well when the plants are dug up and burlapped. If your job-site soil is medium to heavy in texture (heavier loam to clay), you can plant without amending the soil you return to the planting hole (called backfill soil). But when the B&B soil is more dense than the soil of your native landscape, there can be a problem in establishing the plant: its dense soil will not absorb water as quickly as the lighter native soil around it. In such situations, the soil ball around your B&B plant can become dry even when the landscape soil is kept moist. To avoid this problem, amend the backfill as needed.

For successful bare-root planting, the roots should be fresh and plump, not dry and withered. Even if roots appear fresh and plump, it's a good idea to soak the root system overnight in a bucket of water before you plant. Dig the planting hole broad and deep enough to accommodate roots easily without cramping, bending, or cutting them to fit. But cut back any broken roots to healthy tissue. In areas with shallow or problem soils, a wider hole speeds establishment. After the initial watering, water bare-root plantings conservatively. Dormant plants need less water than actively growing ones, and if you keep the soil too wet, new feeder roots may not form. Check the soil periodically for moisture (using a trowel, fingers, soil-sampling tube, or any pointed instrument) and water accordingly. If the root-zone soil is damp, the plant doesn't need water. When weather turns warm and growth becomes active, you need to water more frequently. Do not overwater: Check soil for moisture before watering. If hot, dry weather follows planting, shade the new plant at least until it begins to grow. And be patient—some bare-root plants are slow to leaf out. Many will not do so until a few warm days break their dormancy.

In planting, dig a hole twice as wide as the root ball. If the root ball is wrapped in burlap or another biodegradable fabric, you can leave it in place. But if a synthetic material encases the root ball, carefully remove it so that the roots can grow into the surrounding soil. Then fill the hole half full with backfill soil, firming it with your fingers or a stick. If your soil is light to medium (your B&B soil is heavier), mix one shovelful of organic amendment to each three shovelsful of backfill soil. Doing so improves the water retention of the backfill soil, creating a transition zone between the root ball and landscape soil. Use peat moss, ground bark, nitrogen-fortified sawdust, or similar organic amendments (but not animal manures). If you are setting out a B&B plant in a windy location, you should stake it. Drive the stake firmly into the soil beneath the planting hole on the side of the plant that faces the prevailing winds. During the first couple of years after planting, pay close attention to watering, especially if the root-ball soil is heavier than the native landscape soil. Keep the surrounding native soil moist (but never continuously soggy) so that the roots grow out of the root ball into the surrounding soil as fast as possible.

If a root ball becomes dry, it will shrink, harden, and fail to absorb water. Where there's a great difference between native landscape soil and root-ball soil, you can achieve better water penetration if you carefully punch holes in the root ball with a pointed instrument $\frac{1}{4}$- to $\frac{1}{2}$-inch wide, or use a root irrigator. After several years, when roots have grown out and become established in your landscape soil, the difference between soil types won't matter.

Planting container-grown plants

Plants grown in containers are popular for many reasons. Most broadleaf evergreen shrubs and trees are only offered growing in containers, and you can buy these plants in cans in all seasons. Available in a variety of sizes and prices, they are easy to transport and needn't be planted immediately. Even better, you can buy a container plant in bloom or fruit and see exactly what you are getting.

When shopping for container-grown plants, look for plants that have a generally healthy, vigorous appearance and good foliage. The root system should be unencumbered, i.e., not badly tangled or constricted by the plant's own roots. Two signs of a seriously rootbound plant are roots protruding above the soil level and husky roots growing through the container's drainage holes. When selecting young trees, feel for circling roots around the trunk in the top 2 inches of soil. Additional indicators of crowded roots are plants that are large for the size of their containers, leggy plants, and dead twigs or branches. If you find any of these signs, pass it by and look for another plant.

Removing plants from containers takes knowledge of the container. Nurseries sell plants in a variety of containers: metal cans (1- and 5-gallon are standard sizes), plastic or fiber pots, clay pots, and wooden boxes for large specimen shrubs and trees. With straight-sided metal cans, slit the cans down each side with tin snips. The best time to cut the cans is just before you plant, but you may prefer to have the cans cut at the nursery before taking the plants to the job. Handle the cut edges with care. If planting is delayed, keep the plants in a cool place (out of the hot sun) and water often enough to keep roots moist (water gently so that you don't wash out soil). With tapered metal cans and plastic containers, you can easily knock the plants out of their containers. Tap sharply on the bottom and sides to loosen the root ball so that the plant slides out easily. With fiber pots, it's often easier to tear the pots away from the root ball.

Pollination

Plant propagation also occurs through pollination. The transfer of pollen from stamens to pistil accomplishes pollination, which leads to seed formation and thus to a new generation of plants. Usually pollination happens by natural means (insects, birds, self-pollination, wind), although landscapers can transfer pollen from one flower to another to ensure fruit or to attempt a hybrid cross. An insect or animal that carries pollen from one part of a flower to another, or from one plant to another, is referred to as a pollinator. Some plants produce separate male flowers (with stamens only) and female flowers (with pistils only). These may appear on the same plant (in pecans and walnuts, for example) or on separate plants (as in hollies). In the latter case, you need a male plant nearby to produce fruits on the female plant. To get a crop from some fruit and nut trees, you need to plant two varieties—either because a variety will not set fruit using its own pollen or because its own pollen will not be ripe when its pistils are receptive. A plant used to provide pollen for another plant is often called a pollenizer.

In landscaping usage, propagation refers to the many ways of starting new plants. These methods range from planting seeds to the more complicated arts of budding and grafting. With the exception of seed sowing, all methods of starting new plants are known as vegetative propagation: The new plants that result will be identical to the parent plant. Vegetative propagation therefore maintains uniformity that ensures, for example, that each plant of the rose 'Queen Elizabeth' is like every other.

Transplanting

Successfully transplanting seedlings requires good timing. When the new seedlings have developed their second set of true leaves, it's time to transplant or thin them. If you don't need many plants, you can thin them in place. Give them enough elbow room (1½ to 2 inches between them) to grow larger before you plant them out in the landscape. But if you want to save most of the plants that have germinated, you need to transplant them to larger containers for increased growth before planting outside. Preferably, transplant them into individual pots or cups; then when you plant out in the landscape, they'll suffer a minimum of root disturbance.

For a first transplanting, fill a new container with moist planting mix. Loosen the soil around the seedling plants and carefully lift out a seedling. Or lift a clump of seedlings and gently ease individual plants apart from the tangled mass of roots. Handle a seedling by its leaves to avoid bruising or crushing its tender stem. Poke a hole in the new container's planting mix, place the seedling in the hole, and firm the soil around it. Water the transplant right away. Do this for each seedling plant until all are transplanted. Keep these plants out of direct sunlight for a few days until they have adjusted. For a final transplanting, again wait for the best time. A few weeks to a month after the initial transplant, the seedlings should be ready to plant in the landscape. During that month, you can help their development by watering once with a half-strength liquid fertilizer solution or by sprinkling lightly with a slow-acting fertilizer.

Planting techniques for annuals and perennials are different. Landscapers typically buy sprouted and growing annuals and perennials from a nursery supply. Some perennials are sold as bare-root transplants during their dormant seasons. Many of these plants, as well as some ground covers and hedge plants, are sold in plastic cell packs, individual plastic pots, peat pots, and flats. You'll get the best results from small plants in pots and flats if you prepare the soil well, as you would for sowing seeds. Be sure not to let these plants dry out while they're waiting to be planted. For all small plants, plant so that the tops of their root balls are even with the soil surface.

When you transplant from plastic cell packs, each plant will be in an individual cube of soil that is easy to remove. Push down with your thumb on the bottom of a soil cube, and remove the root ball with the other hand. If you see a mat of interwoven roots at the bottom of the root ball, tear it off—the plant will benefit from its removal. Otherwise, loosen the roots by pulling apart the bottom third of the root ball. Plants in individual pots can be dislodged by placing one hand over the top of the container, with the plant stem between index and middle fingers, and then turning the container upside down. The plant and its root ball should slip out of the container into your hand. If the plant is in a peat pot, plant it pot and all;

the roots will grow through the pot. But make sure that the peat pot is moist before you plant it. A dry peat pot takes up moisture slowly from the soil, so roots may be slow in breaking through it. This can stunt the plant's growth or cause roots within the peat pot to dry out completely. Several minutes before transplanting, set the peat pot in a shallow container of water. Also be sure to cover the top of a peat pot with soil, because exposed peat acts as a wick to draw moisture out of the soil. If covering the peat would bury the plant too deeply, break off the top of the pot to slightly below the plant's soil level.

For plants in flats, a trowel is a handy transplanting tool. Separate the plants in the flat by cutting straight down around each one. Many landscapers prefer to separate individual plants out of flats gently with their fingers; they lose some soil this way, but they keep more roots on the plant. If you work quickly, there will be little transplant shock.

Nurseries carry trees and shrubs at all times of the year. You can purchase trees and shrubs for immediate planting: bare-root in the dormant season, balled-and-burlapped generally in the cooler months, and planted in containers the year around.

The season dictates transplanting bare-root plants. In winter and early spring, you can buy bare-root plants at many retail nurseries and receive them from mail-order nurseries. A great many deciduous plants are available in bare-root form: fruit and shade trees, deciduous flowering shrubs, roses, grapes, and cane fruits. Why go out in the cold and wet of winter to buy and set out bare-root plants when you can wait until spring, summer, or fall and plant the same plants from containers? There are two valid reasons. First, you save money. Typically, a bare-root plant costs only 40 to 70 percent of the price of the same plant purchased in a container later in the year. Second, the manner in which a bare-root tree or shrub is planted makes it establish itself faster and often better than it would if set out later from a container. The advantage of bare-root planting is that when you set out the plant, you can refill the planting hole with the backfill soil that you dug from the hole, so the roots grow in only one kind of soil. In contrast, when you plant from a container or balled-and-burlapped, you put two soils, usually with different textures, in contact with each other. The two different kinds of soil can make it difficult to get uniform water penetration into the rooting area.

Propagation

Good soil, the foundation on which successful landscape propagation depends, requires some advance preparation. Whether propagating seeds or setting out small plants, first refer to the soil preparation advice in Chapter 2. Plants (mainly annuals) suitable for massing in beds for their colorful flowers or foliage are propagated together and called bedding plants. Propagation of plants involves the following terms and definitions:

asexual propagation The duplication of a whole plant by methods other than seeding; for example, stem-tip cutting and crown division.

crown The transition area from trunk or shoots to roots.

fumigate A chemical in a volatile gas form that kills nematodes, weeds, seeds, and other pests in a confined area.

lesion An area of dead tissue.

nematodes Microscopic roundworms that are found in plants, soil, and animals.

overseeding, winter Seeding a cool-season turfgrass over a warm season grass to maintain green turf while the warm-season lawn is dormant.

plug A piece of sod used to establish or repair an existing turf area.

reestablishment A method of lawn management that requires complete removal of existing turf, basic site preparation, and replanting with new seed or sod.

renovation Restoring turfgrass through overseeding or vegetative planting in an existing lawn without complete clearing and reworking of the soil.

rhizome A stem that grows horizontally partly or completely under the soil surface.

sexual propagation Reproduction of plants by seed.

sod The top few inches of soil and established turf.

sprig A piece of grass stolon or rhizome.

stolon An elongated stem or shoot that grows along the soil surface with leaves and roots developing at nodes.

thatch Buildup of old clippings, roots, and stems in growing turf.

weeds Plants growing where they are not wanted.

Identification of commonly used plants

Landscape plant materials terms and definitions:

accent plant Any plant, placed in contrast to its surroundings, that has distinctive form, foliage, texture, or color that calls attention to itself.

acclimatization The adjustment of a plant to a climatic zone or area to which the plant is not native.

botanical name Latin identification of plant materials divided into genus and species. The botanical name is used as the standard in the industry for precise plant selection.

broadleaf evergreen Plant material that has leaves that are broad (not needle-like) and that are retained year-round.

common name Plant name used by the general public. A plant may have several common names but only one botanical name.

compound leaf Leaf made up of several leaf-like blades attached to a central stem.

conifer A cone-bearing plant that is usually also evergreen and needle-bearing.

cultivar A cultivated variety of plant that, when reproduced, retains its distinguishing features.

deciduous Plants that lose their foliage (leaves) at the end of the growing season.

dormant Not actively growing, but capable of resuming growth when environmental conditions become favorable.

evergreen Plants that retain most of their foliage throughout the year.

foliage Leaves of the plant.

hardiness zone A geographical zone in which a plant is considered to be hardy; generally based on temperature.

hardy Capable of living over the winter without artificial protection.

hybrid A genetic cross between two species of plants.

lateral bud A bud extending from the side of the stem.

leaf margin The edge of the leaf.

lenticel One of the pores in the stems of woody plants by which air penetrates to the interior. The presence or location of the lenticel may aid in identification.

ornamental A plant grown for the beauty of its form, foliage, flowers, or fruit, rather than for food, fiber, or other uses.

petiole The stem of the leaf.

pruning Selective cutting of plant parts.

resistant Tolerant and capable of withstanding adverse conditions or pests.

specimen plant Any plant that is displayed to its best advantage either singly or in multiple plantings.

spp Abbreviation for the plural of species.

terminal bud Bud at the end of a stem.

The parts of a plant's Latin botanical name are its *genus* (the first part of a botanical name; always capitalized and italicized or underlined); species (the second part of a botanical name; not capitalized but also italicized or underlined); cultivar (cultivated + variety); and the named variety of the plant (the lister after the species name; capitalized and surrounded by single quotation marks). The meanings of common botanical names follow:

Albidus, albus White

Aureus Golden
Baccatus With berries
Bi Two (2)
Brachy Short; for example, brachycarpus (with short fruit) and brachyphyllus (with short leaves)
Chinensis From China
Compactus Compact, dense
Cyaneus Blue
Diffusus Spreading
Domesticus Domesticated or cultivated
Elatus Tall
Elagans Elegant or handsome
Fallax False or deceptive
Flavus Yellow
Florepleno With full or double flowers
Floribundus Free-flowering, blooming abundantly
Fragrans Fragrant
Gracilis Graceful, slender
Grandifolius With large leaves
Grandiflorus With large flowers
Japonica From Japan
Luteus Yellow
Macro Large; for example, macrocarpus (with large fruit)
Major Large, larger
Micro Small; for example, microphyllus (with small leaves)
Minor Small
Mono One
Nigra Dark, black
Paniculatus With flowers in compound racemes or panicles
Poly Many
Procumbens Flat or trailing
Pungens Piercing, sharp-pointed
Repens Creeping
Robustus Strong, robust
Roseus Rosy, pink
Rubens, rubra Red, ruddy
Sempervirens Evergreen
Speciosus Showy, good-looking
Stellatus Star-like
Tri Three (3)
Variegatus Variegated, usually of different colors
Virens, viridis Green
Vulgaris Vulgar, common, usual

The characteristics used in plant identification are flowers, fruits, leaves (including their shapes, tips, margins, types, and arrangements on the stems), stems, bark, and overall form. Flowers and fruits are good identifying characteristics because they are less subject to change by growing conditions for the plant. However, they are not always present on the plant. Common flower forms are single, head, unbel, spike, raceme, and loose cluster (panicle). Common leaf shapes are deltoid (triangular), elliptic (oval), linear, needle-shaped, oblong, obovate (inverted ovate), orbicular, and ovate (egg-shaped).

Common leaf tips are pointed, rounded, and notched. Common leaf margins are smooth (entire edge), wavy (undulate), serrated, dentate (double serrated), and crenate (lobed). Basic leaf types include the number of leaves in a grouping and how they are arranged on the petiole. They are simple (one leaf blade), compound leaf (several leaf-like blades attached to the petiole), pinnately compound (leaflets attached on either side of the main petiole like feathers), palmately compound (leaflets radiating from one point on a single petiole, like your palm), or trifoliate (three leaflets per petiole). Leaf arrangements on a stem are alternate (leaves attached to the stem at points along the stem in an alternating form), opposite (leaves attached to the stem directly across from each other), and whorled (leaves attached to the stem in a cluster around the stem). Lenticels can be used as a major identifying characteristic on stems by observing if they go around the stem, run up and down the stem, or are diamond-shaped on the stem. Some plants have many, some have only a few, and some have none at all.

Differences in bark are also used in identification. Often the differences are only very small but can be used as an identifying characteristic to some extent. Bark textures can be smooth or furrowed and can have a very distinctive pattern. Bark colors usually range from grays to browns. Unusual bark colors are very helpful in identification.

Lastly, basic overall forms of plants are used in identification. These forms include upright, rounded, oval, spreading, pyramid, and vase-shaped (inverted pyramid).

Common plant groups

Common name: Elm
Botanical name: *Ulmus spp*
Size: Large trees, 40 to 80 feet tall with 20- to 60-foot spread
Form: Vase-shaped
Exposure: Sun
Texture: Fine to medium

Leaves: Simple, alternate, usually lopsided with serrated margins
Color: Medium to dark green
Flowers: Not showy
Fruit: Small winged seed
Cultural notes: Many elms are susceptible to diseases and weak wood, but most will grow virtually anywhere. They are extremely tough and durable. The best example is lacebark elm, which is highly disease- and insect-resistant and tolerates parking lots, poor soil, restricted root systems, and soil compaction. Lacebark elm gets its name from the characteristic patches or orange bark that is exposed when the outer bark peels off. Other examples are American elm and Siberian elm.

Common name: Pine
Botanical name: *Pinus spp*
Size: Large trees except for dwarf varieties
Form: Usually pyramidal; can be loose or compact
Exposure: Sun
Texture: Needle-like
Leaves: Needles
Color: Light to deep green
Flowers: Not showy
Fruit: Cones
Cultural notes: Pines grow well in different soils, prefer a well-drained soil but usually tolerate other soils, except for very heavy clay. Examples are pinyon, slash, Austrian, Japanese black, Scotch, cluster, ponderosa, white, and loblolly pines.

Common name: Juniper
Botanical name: *Juniperus spp*
Size: Varies greatly
Form: Upright, spreading, or ground cover
Exposure: Sun
Texture: Fine
Leaves: Scale-like leaves
Color: Varies from blue-green to light or dark green
Flowers: Not showy
Fruit: Usually small, round, bluish or purple-blue berries
Cultural notes: Most varieties are easy to grow in any type of soil, except very wet. Examples are Chinese, parson's, Rocky Mountain junipers, or Eastern red cedar.

Common name: Holly
Botanical name: *Llex spp*
Size: Small to medium shrub
Form: Some are upright; most are rounded

Exposure: Sun to part shade
Texture: Coarse and thick
Leaves: Coarse, thick leaves with spines; broadleaf evergreen
Color: Varies from blue-green to deep green
Flowers: Not showy
Fruit: Most have red berries
Cultural notes: Hollies grow well in most landscapes, but they don't like poor drainage or hot, dry wind. Examples are burford, blue, Japanese, Chinese, yaupon, Foster's, 'Nellie R. Stevens,' and American hollies.

Common name: Maple
Botanical name: *Acer spp*
Size: Some are small; most medium to large trees
Form: Mostly rounded or oval
Exposure: Sun to part shade
Texture: Medium
Leaves: Simple, opposite, usually deeply lobed with a coarsely toothed margin
Color: Medium to dark green; good fall colors
Flowers: Not showy
Fruit: Flattened, winged seeds
Cultural notes: Most species grow well in a wide variety of soils if adequate water is given. Maples are attractive trees that are used often in landscapes. Examples are trident, hedge, amur, paperbark, Japanese, Norway, red river, and sugar maples and boxelder.

Common name: Red oak
Botanical name: *Quercus spp*
Size: Large trees; 60 to 100 feet tall with 30- to 60-foot spread
Form: Pyramidal to oval
Exposure: Sun
Texture: Medium
Leaves: Simple, bristle-tipped lobes or the tip of the leaf terminates in a single bristle
Color: Leaves are deep, dark green. Bark is generally dark gray to gray-black, is smooth when young, and hard and rigid when mature, but not flaky.
Flowers: Not showy
Fruit: Acorns take two seasons to mature and taste bitter.
Cultural notes: Pores in the wood are open and do not hold water. Red oaks grow well in urban areas with fair to good soil. They can be transplanted in late fall, winter, or early spring. Examples are Northern and Southern red, blackjack, sawtooth, water, pin, willow, and shumard oaks.

Common name: White oak
Botanical name: *Quertus spp*
Size: Large trees; 60 to 100 feet tall with 40- to 60-foot spread
Form: Rounded
Exposure: Sun
Texture: Medium to coarse depending on species
Leaves: Simple, rounded at the tips with no sharp bristles or points
Color: Leaves are deep green to slightly blue-green. Bark is light gray or brown and becomes scaly or flaky.
Flowers: Not showy
Fruit: Acorns mature in a single season and are generally sweet to the taste.
Cultural notes: The wood has pores that are plugged with a plastic-like material called tylose, which makes the wood valuable for making barrels that are capable of holding water or other liquids. White oak needs fair to good soil with a moderate supply of moisture. Examples are white, swamp white, bur, chinquapin, English, and post oaks.

Annuals

A plant that completes its life cycle in a year or less is called an annual. A seed germinates and the plant grows, blooms, sets seed, and dies all in one growing season. Examples are zinnias and marigolds. The phrase "grow as an annual" or "treat as an annual" means to sow seed or set out plants in spring after the last frost, enjoy the plants from spring through fall, and pull them out or let the frosts kill them at the end of the year. Some plants that mild-winter landscapers treat as annuals are planted in the fall, grow and bloom during winter and spring and then are killed by summer heat.

Think of annuals as the real workhorses of the landscape. Their lives are short, but that brief lifetime is extremely productive. Annuals can bloom literally for months, from the moment the plants are mature enough to bear flowers until they are cut down by frost. In areas of no frost or mild frost, certain annuals can brighten even a winter landscape with blossoms. Some landscapers prefer to sow their own annual seeds, or you can buy a wide selection of popular types and varieties already started at nurseries. They are sold in small individual containers in packs of four or six or in flats.

In mild-winter regions, there are two principal times of the year for planting annuals: early spring for those that bloom in late spring, summer, and fall (warm-season annuals); and late summer or fall, for the winter and early-spring bloomers (cool-season annuals). Both are periods of moderately cool temperatures. Landscapers in cold-winter regions can start plants only in the early spring. The summer-flowering annuals need to establish roots before really warm days come along to hasten growth and bloom. Winter-blooming annuals should be set out while days are still warm enough for good plant growth but nights are lengthening. Winter annuals set out while days are longer than nights may perish or rush to maturity as stunted, poorly established plants.

The secret to success with annual plantings is to keep the plants growing steadily. The keys to plant growth are watering, fertilizing, and grooming. Sprinkling is an effective way to water annuals, although the spray of water may topple tall or weak-stemmed plants. An economical and thorough way to water annuals grown in rows or in block beds is to irrigate in furrows between the rows. With a small bed of annuals, you may be able to hoe up a shallow dike around the bed and irrigate by flooding. Drip irrigation, using any of the various emitters available, offers a range of watering options. Mulching helps conserve water and reduce weeds.

Biennials

Plants called biennials complete their lifecycle in two years. Two familiar biennials are foxglove and Canterbury bells. Typically, you plant seeds in the spring or set out seedling plants in the summer or fall. The plants bloom the following spring, then set seed and die.

Perennials

A perennial is a nonwoody plant that lives for more than two years. The word is frequently used to refer to a plant whose top growth dies each winter and regrows the next spring, but some perennials keep their leaves all year. Perennials are as diverse an assortment of plants as you'll find under one collective heading, yet all have two traits in common: Unlike shrubs, they are not woody, and unlike annuals, they live from year to year. Typically, a perennial has one blooming season each year, from only one week to more than a month long. Some perennials store reserve food for the coming season in specialized underground tissues in their roots.

After blooming, the plant may put on new growth for the next year; it may die down and virtually disappear until the time is right, some months later, for growth to resume; or it may retain much the same appearance throughout the year. Many of the popular perennials are grown for the beauty of their flowers and any attractive foliage is merely a bonus. Conversely, a smaller group of perennials (artemisias, for example) are grown for their foliage alone, the flowers being inconsequential or even unattractive. Like annuals, perennials provide color masses, but unlike annuals, they bloom several years in a row without having to be dug up and replanted. Perennials are thus more permanent than annuals but less permanent than flowering shrubs. In fact, their semipermanence is a definite selling point. You can leave perennials in place for several years with little maintenance beyond annual cleanup, some fertilizing, and routine watering, but if you want to change the landscape, perennials are easy to dig up and replant, much more so than the average flowering shrub.

Many perennials are sold in nurseries or by mail order as bare-root plants during their dormant periods. The roots of these bare-root perennials should be kept moist until planting. Before planting dormant bare-root perennials, prepare the soil well and moisten. Be sure to set out each plant at its proper depth and spread the roots out well in the soil, gently firming soil around them. Then water thoroughly to establish good contact between roots and the soil. Feed perennials with a nitrogen fertilizer just prior to the normal growth cycle, in fall or late winter to early spring. Repeat after bloom. With perennials that are periodically dug up, divided, and replanted, you can renew phosphorus and potassium when you prepare the soil for replanting. But even the "permanent" perennials, such as peonies, respond to replenishment of these nutrients from time to time. The best way to apply them is to use a complete fertilizer high in phosphorus and potassium. Carefully dig it in, apply it in deep trenches, or use fertilizer stakes or tablets.

Routine watering during the growth and bloom periods satisfies most perennials. After a perennial has finished blooming, remove the old blossoms to prevent the plant's energy from going into seed production. Later in the season (usually in the fall), remove dead growth to minimize overwintering diseases and eliminate hiding and breeding places for insects, slugs, and snails. In cold-winter regions, many landscapers routinely mulch their perennials to protect them from alternate freezing and thawing. After the ground first freezes, apply a lightweight mulch that won't pack down into a sodden mass. Straw is one popular choice; evergreen boughs are good where available. Over time, many perennials grow into such a thick clump that performance declines because the plants are crowded. When this happens, dig up the clump during its dormant period and divide it.

Soil amendments

Soil amendments improve aeration and water penetration and thus improve the efficiency of organisms in making nitrogen available to the plants. The final product of the action by soil bacteria and other organisms on organic materials is humus. This soft, sticky material improves aeration and drainage. And in sandy soil, humus remains in pore spaces and helps hold water and nutrients. The types of amendments are varied. Soil amendments are divided into four basic classifications: organic, inorganic, chemical, and physical. Various inorganic soil amendments may be useful in special situations, but because they provide no nourishment for microorganisms in the soil, they are no substitute for organic amendments. Use inorganic materials only to supplement organic amendments when a specific need arises.

Organic

Because all organic materials are continuously being decomposed by soil organisms, even the best of soils benefit from periodic applications of organic amendments. Included among organic soil amendments are ground bark, peat moss, leaf mold, sawdust and wood shavings, manure, compost, and many other plant remains. When you add organic amendments to your soil, be generous and mix them deeply and uniformly. For the most marked improvement, add a volume equal to 25 to 50 percent of the total soil volume in the cultivated area. Mix in thoroughly, either by spading and respading or by rotary-tilling. The mixture adds air to the soil, and amendments help keep it there.

Organisms that break down organic materials need nitrogen to sustain their own lives. If they cannot get all the nitrogen they require from the organic material itself, they will draw on any available nitrogen in the soil, in effect "stealing" the nitrogen that is vital to plants' roots. The result can be a temporary nitrogen depletion and reduced plant growth. To use raw wood shavings, ground bark, straw, or manure containing much litter (such as straw or sawdust), you need to add nitrogen. After application, use 1 pound of ammonium sulfate for each 1-inch-deep layer of raw organic material spread over 100 square feet. A year later, apply half as much ammonium sulfate, and in the third and fourth years, use one-fourth as much. Liberal and prolonged use of organic matter can significantly lower soil pH (increase its acidity). Where soil already is neutral or acid, it can result, over a period of time, in an overly acid native soil. A simple soil test can reveal your landscape soil's pH.

The best soil amendments for general landscaping are wood or bark products or other relatively dry organic matter materials. They should not contain any noxious vegetation, pathogenic viruses, herbicides, or chemicals that could inhibit plant growth. All amendments should comply with the Federal Food and Agriculture Code.

Organic soil amendments are vital to the fertility of all soils. Organic matter is particularly needed in sand and clay. Landscapers therefore incorporate organic soil amendments into their soil to improve or maintain the soil's texture and thereby encourage healthy root growth. Organic soil amendments immediately improve aeration and drainage of clay soils by acting as wedges between particles and particle aggregates. In a sandy soil, organic amendments help hold water and dissolved nutrients in the pore spaces, so the soil stays moist and holds dissolved nutrients longer. As organic matter decomposes, it releases nutrients, which add to soil fertility. But the nitrogen released by decaying organic matter isn't immediately available to plants. First it must be converted by soil microorganisms (bacteria, fungi, molds) into ammonia, then into nitrites, and finally into nitrates, which can be absorbed by plant roots. The microorganisms that do this converting are living entities themselves and need a certain amount of warmth, air, water, and nitrogen to live and carry on their functions.

Physical

Physical amendments are a group of mineral amendments that includes perlite, pumice, and vermiculite. Perlite is a mineral expanded by nature's heating to form very lightweight, porous white granules useful in container soil mixes to enhance moisture and air retention. These materials improve the texture of clay soils and increase the capacity of sandy soils to hold water and dissolved nutrients. But their relatively high cost limits use to small-scale projects like amending soil in containers or in small planting beds. Perlite and pumice are both hard, sponge-like, materials that are inert (as sand is), but their porosity makes them water-absorbent. Soft-textured vermiculite (expanded mica) can absorb nutrients as well as water and contribute some potassium and magnesium, which are essential to plant growth. Vermiculite breaks down after several years; perlite and pumice last considerably longer.

Chemical

Chemical amendments are lime and gypsum, both sold as fine powder or granules to be scattered over the soil surface and dug or tilled in. Although lime is the traditional remedy for raising the pH of overly acid soils, both lime and gypsum may improve some clay soils by causing the tiny clay particles to group together into larger units, or "crumbs," which produces larger spaces between particle aggregates, with a corresponding improvement in aeration and drainage. Which material to use depends on the pH of your soil. Where soil is alkaline and high in sodium (the "black alkali" soils of the low-rainfall Southwest and West), gypsum (calcium sulfate) reacts with the sodium and clay particles to produce the larger soil crumbs. If your soil is acidic (generally in regions of plentiful rainfall), lime is the material that might be most useful. Lime adds calcium to soil; gypsum furnishes both calcium and sulfur. Either material may be used as a nutrient supplement in regions (such as parts of the Pacific Northwest) where these minerals sometimes are deficient. Before using either lime or gypsum, check with your county agricultural agent for advisability and guidelines.

For disease and pest control in soil amendments, remember that all chemical controls must be applied under the strict supervision of a licensed and qualified pest control applicator, per the manufacturer's recommended label application procedures and your county health ordinances. Healthy plants and lawns should be able to withstand minor disease and insect damage without controls. Routine applications of pesticides should not be permitted, as this practice destroys natural predator-prey relationships in the environment. In general, with proper fertilization and irrigation practices, the incidence of serious disease and insect problems can be reduced. Where unusually high infections or infestations occur, an accurate identification of the disease or insect should be made and the control product selected with care prior to application. Insecticidal soaps should be used whenever possible.

Calcium

Calcium is the largest consumed element of all soil amendments. It improves soil structure by aggregating the colloidal clay and humus particles of native soil, provides a better place for soil organisms, increases available potassium, and improves air and water penetration into the soil. Calcium also corrects soil acidity and sodium alkalinity (pH does not indicate calcium availability). Soils average 1 percent calcium but vary from 0.1 to 2.2 percent calcium. High levels of nitrogen made available to the plant reduces calcium availability. Calcium is immobile in the plant; it does not move from old leaves to new ones. Seeds contain too little calcium to supply the plant beyond seedling emergence, and high levels of potassium or heavy applications of potassium fertilizers reduce calcium availability. Grains and grasses contain 0.25 to 0.5 percent calcium. Cotton, soybeans, and alfalfa plants average 2.096 percent calcium. Ten tons of dry alfalfa forage could contain as much as 280 pounds of calcium. Cotton at three bales level needs 84 pounds of calcium. Thirty tons of sugar beets remove 36 pounds of calcium from the soil. Orange trees must be able to take up 210 pounds of calcium to produce 30 tons of fruit. Peaches need almost as much calcium as potassium.

Calcium is necessary for plant cell elongation, protein synthesis, normal cell division, uptake of water, uptake of plant nutrient from the root system, and translocation of carbohydrates. It regulates cell acidity and permeability, grain and seed production, terminal growth, and bud production. Environmental factors influence calcium stress disorders more than soil-available calcium. Stress usually affects fruiting parts on the growing point of plants.

Gypsum is a natural mineral that is mined or quarried. Chemically, it is calcium sulfate dihydrate. Gypsum's most familiar use is in drywall panels, notably Sheetrock-brand gypsum panels. Gypsum is also used in plaster of paris, portland cement, various interior finishes, and in landscaping turfgrass soil amendments. Gypsum makes its calcium available to plants far faster than limestone. Though similar in chemical composition, gypsum is 150 times more soluble than limestone. Gypsum won't upset soil pH balance because it is a neutral material, with a pH value near 7.0. Limestone and other lime products are alkaline materials that raise soil pH to levels detrimental to plants that love acidic soil. Gypsum won't change the chemical makeup of plant nutrients, whereas an increase in soil pH induced by adding limestone can change the chemistry of plant nutrients. Sometimes the affected nutrient becomes insoluble and is not available to plants. So, even with sufficient plant nutrients in the soil, an alkaline condition can be created that causes plants to starve for nutrients. You should also know that if you grow acidic-soil-loving plants or trees, such as rhododendrons, azaleas, roses, pin oak, evergreens, or flowering dogwood trees, and you have already established the correct soil pH, you can safely apply gypsum.

Gypsum can play a significant role as a clay soil conditioner. In this role, gypsum is used to flocculate (or aggregate) the clay particles. In the presence of sufficient organic material, the gypsum-initiated flocculation can pave the way for a more permanent aggregation of the soil. In the absence of organic matter, the flocculation continues only as long as sufficient calcium is present in the soil. Clay is present in most soils in widely varying proportions. The clay friction is the most reactive part of any soil, and clay's reactions are governed by its properties as a colloidal. A colloidal is defined as organic matter with very small particle size and a correspondingly large surface area. A second definition of a colloidal is a substance that consists of particles too small for resolution. With an ordinary light microscope and in suspension or solution, a colloidal fails to settle out. The colloidal clay friction of the soil (which, as stated previously, is the most reactive part of any soil) directly or indirectly affects the following soil properties:

- Plasticity
- Swelling
- Shrinkage
- Cohesion
- Flocculation and dispersion
- Plant exchange capacity and soil reaction

These properties are surface-related phenomena and are highly dependent on the amount and nature of the specific surface area presented by the soil colloids. Flocculation is a term applied to the coagulation of dispersed particles. Remember that flocculation is not granulation, because granulation (the formation of stable granules) is best attained in the presence of organic matter. Flocculation really only sets the stage. The presence of organic matter and other cementing agents is necessary before stable granules form. The main reason for the tendency of a clay colloid to flocculate in the presence of gypsum is that when gypsum is applied to a soil containing sodium ions, the calcium ions (after gypsum goes into solution) replace the sodium ions on the colloidal clay particles. The sodium ions released into the soil solution combine with the sulfate ions, and the sodium sulfate can then be leached out. Because sodium ions cause colloidal clay particles to disperse, their replacement by the calcium ions initiates a flocculation of the colloidal clay.

Herbicides

Herbicides are used to control and inhibit weed growth, but they must be selected with extreme care. Preplant, preemergent, contact, and translocated herbicides are available to the landscape contractor. All herbicides must be applied in strict accordance with the manufacturer's label application procedures.

The effectiveness and certain desirable attributes of glyphosate herbicide have made it one of the most widely used herbicides in the world today. Glyphosate-based herbicides are broad-spectrum herbicides with no soil residual activity. The family of glyphosate-based herbicides is made up of more than 90 different brands used in agricultural, industrial, and residential markets in more than 100 countries worldwide. Glyphosate was introduced as a herbicide in 1974 in several markets worldwide. The U.S. Environmental Protection Agency

(EPA) approved registration in 1976 for many agricultural uses and in 1982 approved another glyphosate-based product for aquatic uses. Glyphosate, used primarily in forestry and utility rights-of-way settings, was registered in 1986.

Glyphosate-based herbicides exhibit certain desirable soil characteristics. For example, they have no long-term residual activity. Tests have shown that they bind tightly to the soil and will not harm nearby vegetation. As a result, there is extremely low potential for contamination of groundwater when used according to label directions. Once in contact with the native soil, glyphosate is broken down by soil microorganisms. The process of glyphosate degradation doesn't harm the microorganisms either. The active ingredient in glyphosate (the common name for N-phosphonomethyl) is glycine. Glyphosate is usually formulated as a water-soluble salt to meet a variety of weed-control needs. Glyphosate inhibits an enzyme that is essential to formation of specific essential amino acids in the plant. When properly applied to the leaves of actively growing vegetation, glyphosate-based herbicides are absorbed into the above-ground parts of weeds such as green leaves or green stems. Once there, glyphosate moves or "translocates" throughout the plant. Obvious signs of treatment may not be visible for four days in annual weeds and up to seven days or more in perennials. Visible effects include gradual wilting, yellowing followed by complete browning, deterioration of plant tissue, and ultimate decomposition of the underground roots and rhizomes. Since glyphosate works only on plants that have emerged through the soil, it will not affect seeds that have not yet sprouted.

Hundreds of separate studies on glyphosate products have been reviewed by the EPA for health, safety, and environmental effects. In addition, state agencies have carefully reviewed these studies, examined the product's use for specific geographies, and are responsible for strict registration standards as applied to pesticides. Glyphosate herbicide has one of the most extensive worldwide health, safety, and environmental effects databases ever completed on a herbicide, and studies continue today as new requirements come into existence. Extensive testing by the EPA classified glyphosate in Category E (evidence of noncarcinogenicity for humans) based on a thorough review of results from extensive toxicological tests required by the agency. This very positive rating means that glyphosate has been placed in the most favorable category possible, one that has been given to only a limited number of pesticide active ingredients. (The categories are rated from A through E, with E being the most favorable.) Toxicological testing with laboratory animals serves as a model for evaluating the potential of a substance to cause adverse effects in humans. Toxicology studies measure the effects of direct and indirect exposure to myriad substances including herbicides and pharmaceuticals. In addition to these standard tests, numerous studies have also been conducted with glyphosate products on other nontarget species, such as birds, deer, mice, chipmunks, and various aquatic organisms.

For example, this diverse testing focused on specifics such as how glyphosate and other herbicides affect birds' ability to lay eggs, the ability of the eggs to survive, and the thickness of the egg shells. Other studies examined the impact of glyphosate on habitat change and bacteria in the soil. The results of acute (single-exposure) oral toxicology tests using rats are expressed as LD50 values, or the amount of the substance that produced death in 50 percent of the test animals. The EPA places herbicides into one of four categories, with I being the most toxic and IV the least toxic. Glyphosate is rated as an EPA Category IV compound in oral rat tests. Here are the approximate oral LD50 values for rats fed glyphosate and some other familiar substances help put these numbers into perspective. The smaller the LD50, the greater the toxicity. (Glyphosate is less toxic to rats than table salt following acute oral ingestion.) The mg/kg rating for LD50 values is in milligram test substance per kilogram of body weight. The acute skin LD50 is greater than 5000 mg/kg. In acute skin studies using laboratory animals, glyphosate was nonirritating.

A common-use spray solution of glyphosate was rated as "slightly irritating" in eye studies. The eye irritation observed following exposure to the spray solution was completely reversible. Recent summaries of accidental eye exposure to Roundup herbicide, for example, showed 97 percent exhibited no or slight irritation or were unrelated to exposure. The remaining 3 percent showed moderate but temporary effects (Cardinal Glennon Regional Poison Control Center, St. Louis). Glyphosate does not turn into vapor or gas, and inhalation is extremely unlikely when the product is used according to label directions. Since glyphosate has a low vapor pressure, it does not tend to vaporize. The likelihood of vapor inhalation and redistribution by air movement is thus very low.

Long-term (chronic) toxicological studies have been conducted to determine the effects of prolonged exposure to glyphosate. These studies were conducted on rats, mice, and other laboratory animals. High doses were administered on a daily basis for the average lifetime (two years) of rats and mice and for one year for dogs. Again, these results contributed to the extensive toxicological database reviewed by EPA. The results of long-term toxicity tests on glyphosate resulted in glyphosate being classified as Category E. Long-term feeding studies have also shown that glyphosate does not cause birth defects or reproductive problems in laboratory animals. Pregnant rabbits and rats given high-dose levels of glyphosate delivered normal offspring. In a study in which glyphosate was fed continuously over two generations, weight reductions were seen only at a very high dose level. Lower dose levels in this study and in a three-generation study did not affect the ability of rats to mate, conceive, carry, or deliver normal offspring. Nor were any significant adverse effects observed on the ability of those offspring to develop into normal adults. An extensive battery of mutagenicity and genotoxicity assays designed to evaluate three major objectives—gene mutations, chromosome aberrations, and DNA damage and repair—were also performed using glyphosate. The results of these studies show glyphosate does not interfere with the genetic make-up of cells.

The high water solubility of glyphosate suggests that it should not bioaccumulate, which has been confirmed by numerous studies. Work done with laboratory animals shows that glyphosate is poorly absorbed when ingested. Any absorbed glyphosate is rapidly eliminated, resulting in minimal tissue retention. Feeding studies with chickens, cows, and pigs have shown extremely low to no residues in meat and fat following repetitive exposure. Negligible residues have also been reported in wild animals, such as moles, chipmunks, hares, and moose, after feeding in treated areas. Similarly, a series of bioaccumulation studies was done to determine if glyphosate concentrated in the edible portions of fish and marine organisms. The results clearly indicated that glyphosate did not accumulate. Moreover, transfer of the organisms to glyphosate-free water resulted in virtually complete elimination of glyphosate. Therefore, the data obtained for numerous studies with mammals, birds, fish, and marine organisms firmly support the conclusion that glyphosate will not bioaccumulate in the food chain.

In addition to toxicology tests, a completely different set of tests are conducted to determine how a herbicide behaves in the environment. One series of tests is conducted to measure what happens to the herbicide itself when it enters the environment. Some studies measure the tendency of the chemical to bind to the soil and its likelihood of moving through the soil after rainfall. Other tests measure the ability of microorganisms in the soil to degrade the product. The results of these tests show that glyphosate-based herbicides exhibit favorable environmental-fate characteristics. In fact, these properties facilitate the routine use of glyphosate herbicides in the delicate work of wildlife-habitat restoration. Glyphosate degrades in the soil. The average half-life in soil is less than 45 days. The breakdown of glyphosate takes place primarily by normal soil microbial degradation. Studies have shown that glyphosate binds tightly to soil particles but that it does not accumulate in soil environment after repeated applications over several years or after repeated applications in one year.

Metabolism studies are conducted on crops to determine how a herbicide is metabolized or processed by plants. Residue studies then determine the amount of the parent herbicide or its metabolites that remain in the crop when the herbicide is applied under normal-use conditions. Dissipation and residue studies are carried out in a number of locations over a wide geographic range to ensure that the effects of various climates and soil types are examined. If residues are found, studies are then performed to determine if there is any concentration in a particular food fraction, such as in flour or vegetable oil. Based on the results of these residue studies, the EPA establishes tolerance levels, or maximum legal limits, for a herbicide on various edible crop commodities. These limits are set to ensure that human exposure does not exceed an acceptable level, referred to as the Acceptable Daily Intake, or ADI. This level is generally 100 times lower than the dose that produced no effects in any animal study. The tolerances set by the EPA are then enforced by the Food and Drug Administration (FDA), which is responsible for monitoring residue levels in domestic and imported crops.

Recent summaries of accidental human eye exposure directly related to glyphosate herbicide show 97 percent exhibited no or slight irritation. The remaining 3 percent showed moderate but temporary effects (Cardinal Glennon Regional Poison Control Center, St. Louis). Chronic toxicity studies have also been performed to determine the effects of prolonged exposure to glyphosate. Glyphosate herbicide does not persist in the environment. In soil, both glyphosate and its surfactant, an ethoxylated tallowamine (added to the glyphosate formulation to aid adherence and penetration of the active ingredient into the weed), are degraded by microorganisms naturally present in the soil, and the process of degradation doesn't harm the microorganisms. Microbial degradation of herbicide occurs under both aerobic (with air) and anaerobic (without air) conditions. The average half-life of glyphosate in soil is less than 45 days. Studies show that glyphosate does not accumulate in soil environment after repeated applications over several years or after repeated applications in one year. The average half-life of the surfactant in soil is typically less than seven days. In addition, glyphosate itself has a low vapor pressure and is considered nonvolatile, meaning vapor inhalation or off-site vapor movement is highly unlikely. Although glyphosate herbicide is not labeled for "aquatic use" in the United States, the stability of glyphosate and the surfactant in water has been studied. In water, glyphosate and the surfactant are degraded by naturally occurring microbes. The half-life of glyphosate in natural water is less than eight days.

Because glyphosate-based herbicides are widely used throughout the world, ecosystem studies have been conducted to assess what effect, if any, the use of glyphosate had on an ecosystem. The wildlife diversity and complex nature of the forest ecosystem presented an ideal setting to assess the ecological effects of glyphosate herbicide. Results from two landmark, independently conducted, and comprehensive ecosystem studies—the Canadian Carnation Creek Study and the Oregon State University study—showed glyphosate herbicide:

- Degrades in soil.
- Is essentially immobile in soil.
- Is not a threat to either groundwater or surface water.
- Does not cause adverse health or migrational changes in fish.
- Has no effect on aquatic or terrestrial invertebrates or waterfowl, when used according to label directions.

Of particular interest was the effect of glyphosate herbicide on fish and other aquatic organisms. The Oregon State University and Carnation Creek studies helped clarify what environmental effect glyphosate herbicide would have following accidental release in natural bodies of water. In the Oregon State University forestry ecosystem study, glyphosate herbicide was applied at the rate of 4 quarts per acre. Streams within the treatment areas were intentionally oversprayed. Glyphosate residue in the stream water peaked at approximately 0.27 parts per million (ppm) one hour after application and decreased rapidly to less than 0.1 ppm in five hours. Streamwater concentrations of glyphosate herbicide were calculated based on the measured glyphosate concentration level in the stream water. The calculated concentration levels of glyphosate herbicide were compared to LC50 values for sensitive, juvenile aquatic fish species and were less than the lowest glyphosate herbicide LC50 values reported for either rainbow trout or salmon fingerlings. This study shows that, at labeled rates, there is a large margin of safety in the unlikely event of a direct application of glyphosate herbicide to water.

Mixing and loading herbicides

It is strongly recommended that special care be taken in mixing and loading any herbicide product. Gloved hands should be placed on the container in such a way as to avoid any possible drip or splash. Correct procedures for mixing and loading are provided in the manufacturer's label instructions. If you will handle a total of 60 gallons or more of a product per day, you must use a mechanical transfer system for all mixing and loading operations. If a product is packaged in a 30-gallon drum, you must use a mechanical transfer system that terminates in a drip-free hard coupling that may be used only with a spray or mix tank that has been fitted with a compatible coupling. If you do not presently own or have access to a mechanical transfer system with this type of coupling, contact your dealer for information on how to obtain such a system or to modify your present system. When using a mechanical transfer system, do not remove or disconnect the pump or probe from the container until the container has been emptied and rinsed. The pump or probe system must be used to rinse the empty container and to transfer the product directly to the mixing or spray tank.

Fill the spray tank one-half to three-quarters full with clean water. Begin agitation and add the recommended amount of product. If tank mixing with wettable powder, soluble powder, flowable, or dry flowable products, add the powder or flowable product first. After the herbicide is thoroughly mixed with water, add the recommended amount of any additive, and add water to the spray tank to the desired level. Maintain sufficient agitation to ensure a uniform spray mixture during application. Use only tank mixtures with herbicides and insecticides registered for use on approved sites. Refer to the specific site section for rate recommendations and other restrictions. Always mix one product in water thoroughly before adding another product, or compatibility problems may occur. Never mix two products together without first mixing in water. If a spray mixture is allowed to set without agitation for short periods of time, be sure to agitate until uniformly mixed before application. Use of pesticides must be recorded as shown in Figure 3-1.

If tank mixing, a compatibility test is recommended to ensure satisfactory spray preparation. To test for compatibility, use a small container and mix a small amount (0.5 to 1 quart) of spray, combining all ingredients in the same ratio as the anticipated use. If any indications of physical incompatibility develop, do not use this mixture for spraying. Indications of incompatibility usually appear within 5 to 15 minutes after mixing. To ensure maximum crop

Pesticide Utilization Record

Certified Supervisor _____

Applicator _____

Date: _____ Time a.m. _____ p.m. _____

Location _____

Pesticide Name _____

Amount of Pesticide Concentrate Used _____

Total Solution Applied _____ gal(s) or lb(s)   Rate/acre _____

Target Pest(s) _____

Plant Material(s) Treated _____

Equipment Used _____

Wind Direction _____   Wind Velocity _____

Temperature _____   Sunny _____   Cloudy _____

Dew: None _____   Light _____   Heavy _____

Equipment Cleaning:
Rinsed _____   Washed _____   Neutralized _____

Notes: _____

_____

Supervisor's Signature_____

Applicator's Signature_____

W.O. #_____

3-1 *Pesticide utilization record.*

safety and weed control, follow all cautions and limitations on the label and the labels of products used in the tank mixture. When tank mixing with liquid fertilizer, always add the fertilizer to the spray tank first and agitate thoroughly before adding herbicide. Always predetermine the compatibility with liquid fertilizer by mixing small proportional quantities in advance. Agitation must be maintained during filling and application operations to ensure that the herbicide is evenly mixed with the fertilizer.

Fertilizers and spray additives can increase foliage leaf burn when applied with herbicides. Do not apply fertilizers or spray additives if leaf burn is a major concern due to environmental conditions or plant or variety sensitivity. Do not apply herbicides in combination with fertilizers or spray additives if restricted under the individual product-use directions.

In ground applications, use a standard herbicide boom sprayer that provides uniform and accurate application. The sprayer should be equipped with screens no finer than 50 mesh in the tips and in-line strainers. Select a spray volume and delivery system that ensures thorough and uniform spray coverage. For optimum spray distribution and thorough coverage, the use of flat-fan nozzles (maximum tip size 8008) with a minimum spray pressure of 30 psi at the nozzle tips are recommended. Other nozzle types that produce coarse spray droplets may not provide adequate coverage of the weeds to ensure optimum control. Raindrop nozzles are not recommended because weed control with herbicides may be reduced.

In general with herbicides, an average minimum spray volume of 10 gallons per acre (GPA) is recommended for optimum spray coverage. A minimum of 5 GPA with a minimum spray pressure of 50 psi may be used with higher speed or low-volume ground application if ground terrain, plant, and weed density allow effective spray distribution. When using higher-speed equipment, a maximum speed of 10 mph is suggested if field conditions cause excessive boom movement during application and subsequent poor spray coverage. Ground applications made when dry, dusty field conditions exist may provide reduced weed control in wheel track areas. Do not apply when winds are gusty or when other conditions favor poor spray coverage or off-target spray movement. When weed infestations are heavy, use of higher spray volumes and spray pressure are helpful in obtaining uniform weed coverage. If you are unsure of the infestation level or size of application necessary, consult your local county farm agent extension service.

Most cases of groundwater contamination involving phenoxy herbicides such as 2,4-D have been associated with mixing and loading and disposal sites. Caution should be exercised when handling 2,4-D pesticides at such sites to prevent contamination of groundwater supplies. Use of closed systems for mixing or transferring this pesticide reduces the probability of spills. Placement of the mixing/loading equipment on an impervious pad to contain spills helps prevent groundwater contamination. Do not apply 2,4-D directly to or permit to drift onto cotton, okra, grapes, tomatoes, fruit trees, vegetables, flowers, or other desirable crop or ornamental plants that are susceptible to 2,4-D herbicide. Do not apply near susceptible plants since very small quantities of the 2,4-D will cause severe injury during the growing or dormant periods. Crops contacted by 2,4-D herbicide sprays or spray drift may be killed or suffer significant stand loss with extensive quality and yield reduction. Do not apply when a temperature air inversion exists. Such a condition is characterized by little or no air movement and an increase in air temperature with an increase in height. In humid regions, a fog or mist may form. An inversion may be detected by producing a smoke column and checking for a layering effect. If you have questions pertaining to the existence of an inversion, consult with local weather services before making an application. Use coarse sprays to minimize drift. Do not apply with hollow cone-type insecticide or other nozzles that produce fine spray droplets. Drift from aerial or ground application may be reduced by five steps:

1. Apply as near to the target as possible to obtain coverage.
2. Increase the volume of spray mix per acre.
3. Decrease the pounds of pressure at the nozzle tips.
4. Use nozzles that produce a coarse spray pattern.
5. Do not apply when the wind is blowing toward susceptible crops or valuable plants.

Herbicide products are toxic to aquatic invertebrates. Drift or runoff may adversely affect aquatic invertebrates and nontarget plants. Do not apply directly to water except as specified on the label. Do not contaminate water when disposing of equipment washwater. Do not apply when weather conditions favor drift from treated areas. Do not use the same spray equipment for other purposes unless thoroughly cleaned. Do not contaminate water used for irrigation or domestic purposes (except as specifically recommended on the label) especially in areas where grapes, cotton, tomatoes, or other susceptible plants are grown. Do not treat irrigation ditches in areas where water is used to overhead-irrigate susceptible crops, especially grapes, tomatoes, tobacco, and cotton.

When you use a preemergent herbicide, you have to get the weed seeds one to two weeks before they germinate. Exactly when do they germinate? When they have the right combination of environmental conditions to germinate: abundant sunlight, water, soil nutrients, and the right temperature. For problem weeds, such as crabgrass and goosegrass, it's not air temperature, it's soil temperature. Here's a good rule of thumb: Crabgrass germinates when there are three consecutive days with these soil temperatures (at a 2-inch depth):

Goosegrass germinates at a higher soil temperature of 60 to 65°F. It's important to take the soil temperature at the right time. I recommend

Table 3-1.

Soil texture	Soil temperature (between 7 & 8 A.M.)
Loam	50–52°F
Heavy wet clay soil	53–57°F
Sandy soil	49–51°F

7 to 8 A.M. That's the daily low point of your soil temperature. It rises as the day progresses, usually 10 to 15°F by midafternoon on a sunny, moderately dry day in late April and May. Several factors can affect soil temperature:

- Soil in wet turfgrass usually warms up more slowly than dry soil.
- Turfgrass on south-facing slopes warms up faster than that facing north.
- Dark soil warms up faster than light soil. Thin grass areas warm up faster than thicker turf.
- Wet clay soils may require up to three or four times more heat than when they're dry.

It also pays to study your weather forecasts to see if soils stay at adequate soil temperatures for good crabgrass and goosegrass germination. Generally, a forecast for below-normal temperatures, with dry and sunny conditions, results in little or no change in the seasonal warming trend of the soil. But if cloudy, cold, wet weather is forecast, then soil temperatures will quickly decline. A forecast of warm, dry, sunny weather, on the other hand, results in a moderate rise. Crabgrass and goosegrass germination also depends on abundant sunlight near the soil surface. A tall, dense turf or a heavily shaded area delays or eliminates the potential for crabgrass germination and, hence, herbicide application. Moisture is vital also, not just for germination, but for survival. Crabgrass and goosegrass germinate later than you probably think. Be sure to consider all these factors when applying your preemergent herbicide. For example, dry, sandy areas should be treated in early spring. Poorly drained lawns could be delayed until mid to late spring. Use two or more of these environmental guidelines to predict when crabgrass germinates to help make the most of your preemergence herbicide application:

- Night temperature is consistently higher than 65°F.
- Daytime temperature is consistently between 55 and 75°F.
- Soil temperature is 55 to 60°F for seven to 10 consecutive days.
- Seedbed is moist.

Because weather conditions are an important factor, always refer to the product label before applying. You can effectively control crabgrass, goosegrass, and most other annual weeds on cool-season turf for up to 20 weeks with a single application of a preemergent herbicide. Granular preemergent herbicide products have several uses: Summer annual grassy weed control requires applying 75 to 150 pounds (1.5 to 3 pounds active ingredient) per acre in the spring for up to 20 weeks of control. For areas with heavy goosegrass pressure, apply the high rate (150 pounds). Split your application program. Apply a cumulative rate of 150 pounds (3 pounds active ingredient) per acre and time your applications about eight to 10 weeks apart. For annual control, apply 75 to 100 pounds (1.5 to 2 pounds active ingredient) per acre in late summer or early fall. Repeat in late winter or spring one to two weeks before weed seeds germinate. Some products available from leading formulators combine crabgrass and goosegrass control with a dry fertilizer of your choice in one convenient application for landscapers with fertilizer programs who want to do two jobs at once.

4

Hand tools

Hand tools used in landscaping are defined by their traditional usage. I have set up the first part of this chapter in list form for ease of reference to help you find what you're looking for quickly. Headings locate the terms, and definitions follow accordingly.

The following list identifies characteristics you should consider in choosing hand tools for particular jobs.

- Type of soil. (For example, heavy clay or rocky soil requires a sturdy tool.)
- Height and strength of the user. (A shorter worker needs a shorter handle.)
- Size of job. (Digging a trench requires stronger tools than digging a planting hole. Smaller tools may be easier to use, but the job takes longer.)
- Handle length. (If you are standing, you need a cultivator with a long handle, but if you are kneeling, you need a hand cultivator.)
- Right tool for the job (For example, when digging a ball-and-burlap planting hole, a spade would be better than a hoe or scoop shovel.)
- Degree of cant. (When scooping leaves and excess soil, a higher degree of cant helps avoid laying the shovel flush with the ground to lift material.)
- How often the tool will be used. (A shovel may be used to dig a planting hole rather than a spade if only one small hole is needed.)

Hand-tool construction

This list identifies various features of hand tools.

- Handle lengths
  ~Rakes—50 to 60 inches

121

~Shovels—40 to 48 inches
~Spades—30 to 40 inches
- Handle grips
  ~Straight handle
  ~"D" handle
  ~"T" handle
- Handle materials
  ~Metal
  ~Hardwood—ash, hickory
  ~Fiberglass
- Head attachment
  ~Forged socket and shank
  ~Tang-and-ferrule
  ~Eye
- Head weight—light or heavy (For example, heavy pick and mattock heads add to the striking force of the tool.)
- Head materials
  ~Forged steel
  ~Stamped sheet metal
  ~Heavy plastics
  ~Stainless steel
  ~Cast iron
  ~Aluminum alloy
  ~Plated steel
  ~Bamboo
- Reinforcement
  ~Socket—closed is stronger than open
  ~Straps—forged-steel straps that extend more than half the handle length
  ~Grip—"D" handle
  ~Tines—square tines add strength to forks

Characteristics of high-quality hand tools

- Metal heads are made of stainless or forged steel in one piece.
- Heads are attached tightly by closed socket.
- Handles are made of rolled steel, fiberglass, or smooth hardwood such as hickory or ash.
- Grains on wooden handles should run in the same direction as the force exerted on the tool.
- Reinforced tool handles and heads are meant for heavy use.

- Saw teeth are beveled, providing a good cutting edge.
- Wide tires on carts and wheelbarrows are best for use on turf.
- All moving parts work smoothly.
- Cutting edges have no nicks or burns.
- All screws and bolts are placed correctly and securely.

Hand-tool metallurgy

burr A rough edge left on metal

degree of cant Position of a shovel or spade blade in relation to the handle. The greater the degree of cant, the more leverage the tool has in lifting. A lesser degree of cant is best for digging straight down the sides of a hole.

forging Hammering and compressing steel, making it more dense, uniform, and therefore, stronger

rust Material resulting from a corrosive process promoted by the presence of moisture on metal

sharpening Beveling the cutting side of a blade to a keen edge

sprung A condition resulting from forcing pruning tools to cut through limbs by twisting the tool back and forth

Hoes

- General landscape hoe
    - ~Loosening and moving light soil
    - ~Breaking soil surface
    - ~Weeding
    - ~Cultivating plant beds
    - ~Slightly angled blade 5 to 7 inches wide
    - ~One to three sharp beveled edges
- Grading hoe (also called grub or eye hoe)
    - ~For tough jobs
    - ~Chopping weeds and small brushy shrubs
    - ~Loosening hard, compacted soil
    - ~Planting bed preparation
    - ~Head fits directly onto handle
    - ~Various blade sizes
- Scuffle hoe
    - ~Weeding by cutting off tops of plants
    - ~Light cultivating of loose, rock-free soil
    - ~Heads angled flat to the ground
    - ~One to three sharp edges

- Triangle hoe
  ~Light cultivating
  ~Breaking stubborn soil
  ~Weeding by uprooting the whole plant
  ~Reaching tight spots under shrubs
  ~Making rows
- Push hoe
  ~Weeding by moving back and forth, cutting both directions
  ~Edging
  ~Sharp front and back blade

Rakes

- Flathead rake (also called a gravel rake or asphalt rake)
  ~Planting beds and vegetable landscapes
  ~Smoothing surfaces
  ~Final cultivating of seed beds
  ~Breaking clods
  ~Raking rocks and twigs but not heavy soil
  ~13- to 16-inch-wide steel head
  ~Flat, straight tines (not for use on lawns—tines will damage turf)
- Bowhead rake
  ~Planting beds and vegetable landscapes
  ~Leveling soils
  ~Raking heavy soil
  ~Flexible, wide steel head (not for use on lawns—will damage turf)
- Leveling or grading rake
  ~Installing new lawns
  ~Breaking up and spreading soft soil
  ~Smoothing seed bed
  ~Straight 4-inch tines
  ~Very wide head, 25 to 30 inches
- Thatching rake
  ~Removing matted materials
  ~Pushing and pulling through turf
  ~Cutting blades or curved tines
  ~Some heads adjust to various angles
- Leaf or broom rake
  ~Sweeping or raking debris, leaves, and clippings without damaging turf
  ~Metal, polypropylene, or bamboo heads

Shovels

Shovels and trenching hand tools are supplemented by power trenchers, as shown in Figure 4-1.

- Round-nose shovel
  ~Lifting loose sand and soil
  ~Scooping
  ~Cleaning trenches and drains
  ~Digging ditches
  ~Preparing planting holes
- Square-nose shovel
  ~Lifting heavy materials
  ~Scooping soil, sand, gravel, concrete, rocks
  ~Flat face and high sides
- Scoop shovel
  ~Lifting lightweight materials (can pull heavy loads along ground instead of lifting)
  ~Scooping sawdust, mulch, snow, rocks, and debris
  ~Not for digging
  ~Wide face and high sides
  ~High degree of cant

Spades

- Landscape spade
  ~Digging straight-sided, flat-bottomed planting holes
  ~Cutting bed edges
  ~Removing sod layer
  ~Flat blade with no sides
  ~Socket or straps extend to bottom of handle for strength
  ~Small degree of cant
- Tree spade
  ~Digging deep, rounded planting holes
  ~Slicing heavy soils
  ~Digging trenches
  ~Wide steps
  ~Curved, long, narrow blade with square nose
  ~Steel straps reinforce half, three-quarters, or full length of handle
- Transplanting spade (trencher)
  ~Digging out plant materials to be moved
  ~Digging ditches and trenches
  ~Narrow curved blade with pointed or rounded nose

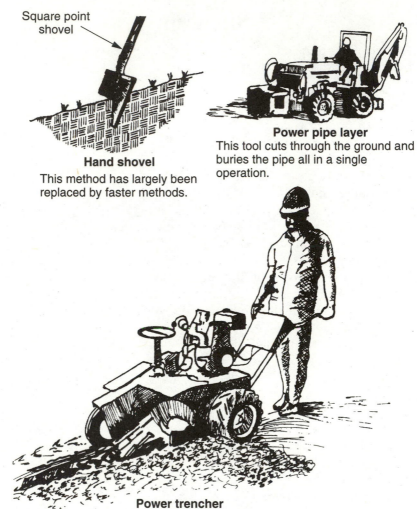

Square point
shovel

Hand shovel
This method has largely been
replaced by faster methods.

Power pipe layer
This tool cuts through the ground and
buries the pipe all in a single
operation.

Power trencher
This tool cuts a narrow ditch and places the excavated earth alongside the
trench.Sod should be removed before trenching

4-1 *Trenching tools.*

Forks

- Landscape fork
  ~Working planting beds
  ~Lifting soil
  ~Dividing perennial plant clumps
  ~Digging heavy soil
  ~Small head

~Diamond-shaped or square tines
~Short handle
- Manure forks
  ~Lifting or moving loose materials
  ~Mulching
  ~Not for digging
  ~Four or five long, tapered tines
  ~Long tapered or "D" grip handle
- Scoop fork
  ~Scooping compost
  ~Lifting debris from usable mulch
  ~Not for digging
  ~Multiple, curved tines
  ~Long socket
- Tine cultivator (sometimes called a potato fork)
  ~Coarse raking
  ~Raking debris from under shrubs
  ~Cultivating deeper than rake
  ~Breaking up clods
  ~Four or five round tines
  ~Tines bent at sharp angle

Hand pruners or shears

- Bypass (scissor-cut) blade pruners
  ~Cutting up to ¾-inch-diameter twigs
  ~Clipping very close to main limb
  ~Clipping flowers and stems, shrubs, and trees
  ~Preferred by professionals
- Anvil blade shears
  ~Cutting twigs to ¾ inch in diameter
  ~Cutting in open spaces
  ~Cannot cut very close to main limb
  ~Clipping flowers and stems, shrubs, and trees
  ~Can crush stems

Loppers

- Bypass (scissor-cut) lopper
  ~Cutting in narrow spaces
  ~Cutting up to 2-inch-diameter limbs
  ~Cutting shrubs and trees

- Anvil loppers
  ~Cutting up to 2-inch-diameter limbs
  ~Cutting in open areas or wide crotch
  ~Heavy cuttings
  ~Cutting shrubs and trees
  ~Can crush stems
- Pole pruner
  ~Cutting overhead branches from the ground
  ~Cutting branches $1\frac{1}{4}$ to $1\frac{3}{4}$ inches in diameter
  ~Commonly has hook and blade (scissor-cut) action operated
   by a rope or metal rod through a pulley or lever system
  ~Pole may be one-piece, sectional, or telescoping
  ~Pole may be wood, metal, or fiberglass (**Caution!** Wood and
   metal poles conduct electricity and should not be used near
   electrical lines. Fiberglass may be acceptable.)

Pruning saws

Depending on the saw, the cut is made on the push or pull motion,
sometimes both.

- Folding saw
  ~Cutting branches 1 to 3 inches in diameter on small shrubs
   and fruit trees
  ~Blade 6 to 8 inches long
- Curved blade saw
  ~Cutting limbs 3 inches in diameter and larger
  ~Sawing limbs at various angles
  ~Cutting green and dead wood
  ~Pruning trees and large shrubs
  ~Rigid handle
  ~Blade 12 to 30 inches long
- Bow saw
  ~Pruning trees and large shrubs
  ~Difficult to use in crowded branches
  ~Cutting limbs 10 to 25 inches in diameter
  ~Narrow tip
  ~Blade 15 inches or longer
- Double-edged saw
  ~Cutting both green and dry wood
  ~Fine-tooth edge for cutting small branches and dry wood
  ~Coarse-tooth edge for cutting green or sap wood
  ~Coarse, raker teeth pull sawdust out to prevent jamming

(**Caution!** Top edge may damage desirable branches while cutting with lower edge.)
- Pole saw
  ~Cutting limbs 3 inches and larger
  ~Cutting overhead limbs 4 to 6 feet away from user

Combination pole saw/pruners are also available.

Wheelbarrows and carts

- All-purpose wheelbarrow
  ~Hauling soil, rock, and debris
  ~Mixing amendments, concrete, and soil
  ~Light to heavy weight
- Sod and tile barrow
  ~Hauling sod, tiles, plants, etc.
  ~Hardwood body on metal frame
- Utility cart
  ~Moving large, bulky loads
  ~Available with various sizes and types of beds and wheels
- Nursery cart or "truck"
  ~Moving plants and materials
  ~Wide tires are recommended for use on turf areas

Spreaders

- Hand-held broadcast spreader
  ~Applying seed, fertilizer, granular pesticide, and ice melters
  ~Easy to use on rough surfaces
  ~Can be used to spread material over planted beds and shrubs
  ~Covers large areas quickly
  ~Hand crank distributes the material to be spread
  ~Made of various materials and sizes that hold 2 to 10 pounds
   of material
- Push broadcast spreader
  ~Applying seed, fertilizer, granular pesticides, ice melters, and
   soil amendments
  ~Primarily for use on smooth, level surfaces
  ~Various sizes hold 20 to 80 pounds of material (Broadcast
   spreaders distribute material in a full circle, applying less ma-
   terial at the edges than middle. Patterns should be overlapped
   for even coverage.)

- Drop spreader
  ~Applying granular fertilizers, ice melters, and pesticides
  ~Seeding new lawns
  ~Use on smooth, level surfaces
  ~Various models are designed to push by hand or pull by tractor
  ~Various sizes hold 30 to 80 pounds of material (Drop spreaders distribute material in an even band the width of the hopper through holes in the bottom. Overlap the wheel tracks for uniform application.)

Caution! Never leave materials in spreader hoppers because they are very corrosive. They absorb moisture and will cause rusting of the spreader.

Specialty hand tools

- Pick
  ~Breaking up hard, rocky soil
  ~Breaking up root-filled soil
  ~Trenching
- Mattock
  ~Loosening heavy, compacted soil
  ~Digging narrow ditches
  ~Cutting roots
  ~Chopping
- Pick-mattock
  ~Breaking up hard, root-filled soil
  ~Loosening soil
  ~Digging
  ~Chopping
- Post-hole (clamshell) digger
  ~Digging holes for fence, deck, and other support posts
  ~Digging holes in hard, rocky soil
  ~4-foot-long handles
- Hedge shears
  ~Shaping shrubs and hedges
  ~Cutting level or vertical sides of hedges
  ~Cutting young, tender growth up to ½ inch thick
  ~Limb notch is used to cut individual thick stems
  ~Serrated or plain blades
- Rotary edger
  ~Cutting lawn edges flush to the drive and walk edges

~Has 6-inch cutting blade that rotates with the rubber-tired wheel
- Turf edger
  ~Cutting soil and turf along walks
  ~Recutting overgrown edges
  ~Edge may be curved or straight
- Trowel
  ~Planting bedding plants, ground covers, bulbs
  ~Digging furrows in soft soil
  ~Weeding
  ~General landscape work
- Grass shears
  ~Trimming grass and foliage along drives, walks, bed edges, and posts
  ~Scissor cut
- Cultivator
  ~Loosening soil
  ~Mixing amendments
  ~Raking
  ~Weeding
  ~Breaking up clods
  ~May have long or short handle
- Pry bar
  ~Dislodging (prying) heavy rocks, roots, etc.
  ~Breaking up heavy clay soils or rocks
  ~Available in various lengths and diameters
- Soil probe
  ~Collecting soil samples for testing
  ~Checking depth of soil moisture
- Grass whip
  ~Cutting grass and succulent weeds
  ~Reducing high grass to a mowable height
- Swing blade, weed cutter
  ~Cutting heavy, fibrous weeds at ground level
  ~Has double-edge V-shaped cutting blade
- Grass hook
  ~Cutting high, heavy, fibrous weeds
  ~Has single edge, curved cutting blade
- Snow shovel
  ~Scooping snow or debris
  ~Blade made of lightweight materials such as aluminum or plastic

- Clean-up caddy
  ~Picking up small objects, trash, cans, and bottles without bending; some models have a metal spring in tip for gathering debris, others are designed like large tongs or pinchers.
- Can cutter
  ~Splitting plant material containers open
  ~Makes removal of root mass easier
- Roller
  ~Firming soil, mulch, seed beds, and sod
  ~Available as push or pull types
  ~Designed to be filled with sand or water for weight
- Ax
  ~Chopping woody plants
  ~Splitting wood
  ~Clearing brush
  ~Available with single or double edges (bits)
- Sledgehammer
  ~Driving stakes
  ~Installing edgings
  ~Heavy-duty hammering
- Lawn sweeper
  ~Picking up fallen leaves, twigs, and grass clippings
  ~Use on smooth, level ground

Sprayers

Most sprayers used today are the hydraulic type in which the spray pressure is built up by direct action of the pump on the spray mixture. Essentials of effective spraying include correct timing of application, proper chemicals and rates, and proper equipment used correctly. The basic types of sprayers are *large boom* (hydraulic or manual), *hand-held*, and *backpack*.

The parts of a sprayer:

- An *antisiphon device* is installed between the domestic water source and the sprayer to prevent chemicals from being siphoned back from the sprayer into the water source, thereby contaminating it.
- The *tank* holds the chemical solution to be sprayed.
- The *agitator* keeps the liquids in the tank properly mixed.
- The *pump* raises, moves, and compresses liquids from the tank to the hoses.

- *Hoses* convey liquid through the sprayer.
- *Strainers* catch solid debris while liquid passes through.
- *Valves* regulate the flow of liquid through the sprayer.
- *Nozzles* turn the liquid leaving the sprayer into droplets in a specific pattern and size.
- The *boom* contains nozzles a specified distance apart to cover a large area.
- Basic *nozzle spray patterns* are solid cone, hollow cone, or flat (fan).
- Basic parts of a nozzle are the *body, strainer, tip,* and *cap.*

To properly maintain a sprayer, the care and storage of the sprayer must include daily cleaning. Be sure to clean the sprayer according to federal regulations in an area where the pesticide residue rinsed out will not contaminate the environment. Rinse out the tank and run half a tankful of water through the nozzles to rinse the system. Repeat this step. Clean nozzle tips and screens by removing them and using either kerosene or a detergent solution and a soft brush. Replace the nozzles. Use about half a tankful of detergent and water solution to agitate in the tank about 30 minutes, then flush through the nozzles.

If an organic phosphorous insecticide such as 2,4-D (check the label) was used, these additional steps must be followed:

Add one pint of ammonia for each 25 gallons of water in a half tankful of water. Agitate for about 5 minutes and flush a small amount through the sprayer. Keep the rest of the solution in the sprayer overnight. In the morning flush out the ammonia solution through the sprayer. Hose out the tank with clean water one last time and run a half tankful through the sprayer. **Separate sprayers should always be used for herbicides and insecticides.** Storage of the sprayer for winter requires removing the nozzle tips, strainers, and screens, and coating the sprayer in light oil. Store the sprayer in a clean dry area. Keep the pump from freezing.

The purpose of calibration of sprayers is to determine the volume of liquid sprayed per acre under specific conditions, so that the proper amount of chemical can be applied. In preparing a sprayer for calibration, make sure the sprayer has been cleaned according to the proper procedure. Flush the unit with plenty of clean water. Check all the hoses and connections for leaks. Check to see if the sprayer unit is working properly, using water to test. Select the proper pressure for the conditions with the tractor unit (or truckster) running. Plan to calibrate the sprayer under conditions similar to those under which it will be used on your project site.

General procedures for maintaining hand tools

- Remove soil and vegetation from tools as they accumulate. Be sure to clean open sockets or hollows, especially in the back of tool blades.
- Remove rust from metal parts when it appears.
- Condition weathered wooden handles with linseed oil so they can be used longer.
- Sharpen cutting edges of tools as needed.
- Tighten screws, bolts, handles, and heads on tools as they become loose.
- Replace handles as needed.
- Always return tools and materials to their proper storage places and in their proper condition—clean and dry.

Procedures for properly storing tools for the winter

- Wash all tools to remove soil, vegetation, chemicals, and let air dry.
- Lubricate movable parts and apply penetrating oil to metal surfaces.
- Tighten loose screws, bolts, heads, and handles.
- Replace and repair broken or bent parts.
- Clean and apply linseed oil to wood handles.
- Sharpen dull cutting edges.
- Place tools in dry, clean area on proper racks or hangers.

Techniques for sharpening hand tools

- Decide if a tool should be sharpened.
- Remove as little metal as possible.
- Follow the existing bevel edge of the tool blade. (The smaller the angle, the sharper the edge. Very sharp edges will nick, bend, and dull easily.)

Selecting the proper sharpening tool

- Grinders allow sharpening but are not good for beveling fine edges. Use on mower blades and axes.
- Files remove metal quickly for medium-sharp edges. Use on spades and hoes but not on shears or knives. Files are available in several coarsenesses. Coarse files can remove a great deal of metal quickly. Smooth files are for small burrs.

- Whetstones remove metal for very sharp edges. Use on knives, shears, and very small edge surfaces.

Standard safety precautions

- Do not leave tools on the ground near a work site where they may become covered with debris and stepped on. While working on a project, lay tools down with the tines facing the ground. Tines facing up on rakes or cultivators can be very dangerous!
- Keep the work site neat. Clutter allows accidents to happen.
- Work at a steady pace rather than hurrying.
- Always tighten loose tool heads before use, and check periodically during use.
- Do not use metal or wood tools near electric lines.
- Do not use the wrong tool for the job. The most common violation of this rule is using a shovel or spade as a pry bar.
- Do not overload a wheelbarrow. Unstable and overloaded wheelbarrows are hard to push and can topple easily. Always set the wheelbarrow down when you feel the load beginning to fall. Also do not walk too close to wheelbarrows operated by others.
- Do not carry hand pruners in your pants pocket.
- Do not twist pruners or loppers while cutting because you can damage both the plant and the tool.
- Locate all utility (underground and above ground) lines and pipes before using tools that can cut or damage these lines.
- Wear work clothes suitable for the job. Clothing should protect you from the environment and job hazards and be appropriate for work situations.
- Securely cover an unfinished work site, and place caution signs if it must be left unattended.

A good, all-purpose set of hand tools includes all of the tools shown in Figures 4-2 through 4-12.

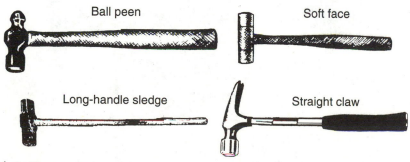

4-2 *Hammers.*

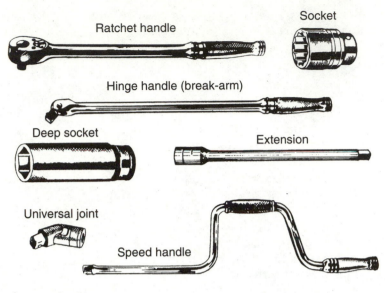

Socket

Ratchet handle

Hinge handle (break-arm)

Deep socket

Extension

Universal joint

Speed handle

4-3 *Socket sets.*

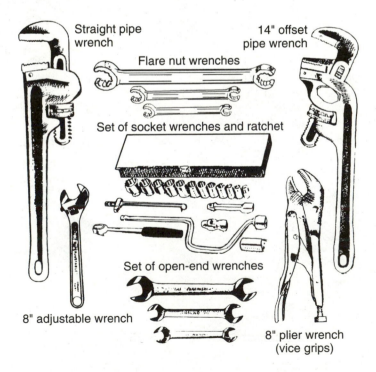

Straight pipe wrench

14" offset pipe wrench

Flare nut wrenches

Set of socket wrenches and ratchet

Set of open-end wrenches

8" adjustable wrench

8" plier wrench (vice grips)

4-4 *A variety of wrenches.*

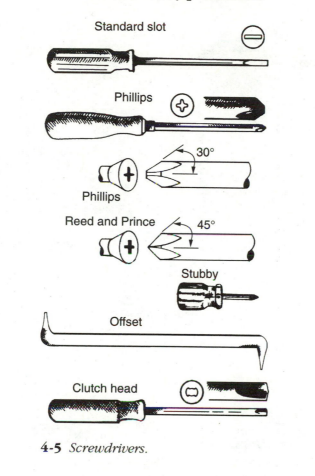

4-5 *Screwdrivers.*

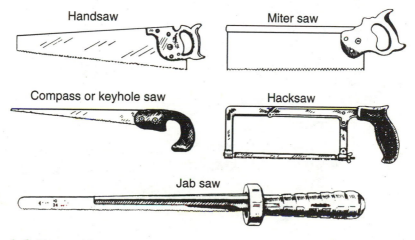

4-6 *Types of handsaws.*

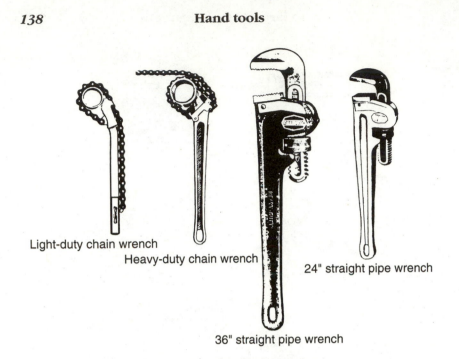

Light-duty chain wrench

Heavy-duty chain wrench

24" straight pipe wrench

36" straight pipe wrench

4-7 *Chain and pipe wrenches.*

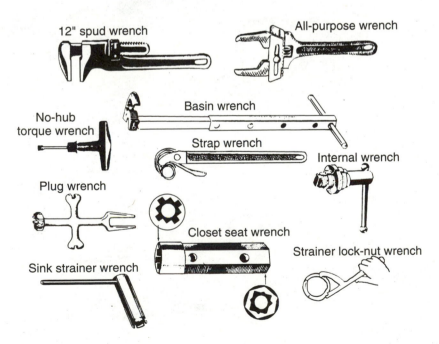

12" spud wrench

All-purpose wrench

No-hub torque wrench

Basin wrench

Strap wrench

Internal wrench

Plug wrench

Closet seat wrench

Strainer lock-nut wrench

Sink strainer wrench

4-8 *Specialty wrenches.*

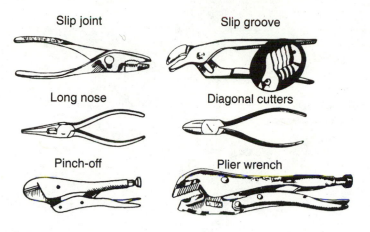

Slip joint

Slip groove

Long nose

Diagonal cutters

Pinch-off

Plier wrench

4-9 *Pliers.*

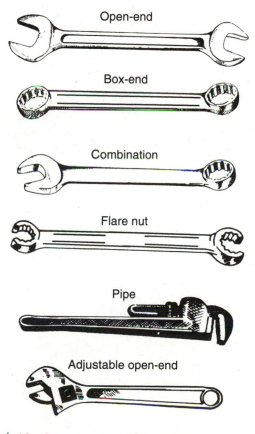

Open-end

Box-end

Combination

Flare nut

Pipe

Adjustable open-end

4-10 *Common wrenches.*

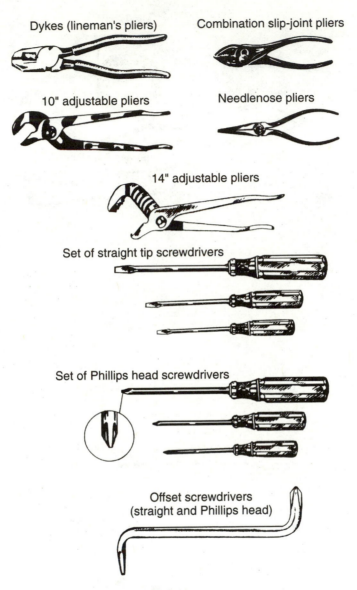

Dykes (lineman's pliers)

Combination slip-joint pliers

10" adjustable pliers

Needlenose pliers

14" adjustable pliers

Set of straight tip screwdrivers

Set of Phillips head screwdrivers

Offset screwdrivers
(straight and Phillips head)

4-11 *Screwdrivers and pliers.*

Steel tapes

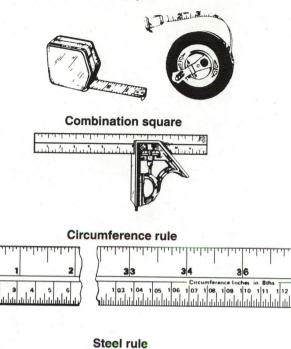

Combination square

Circumference rule

Steel rule

Folding rule

4-12 *Rules.*

5

Preparing and improving turfgrass

The different types of turfgrasses are classified by their optimum temperate zone growth environment:

Warm-season grasses have an optimum growth temperature of 80 to 95°F (26.7 to 35.5°C). These species are usually dormant below 60°F (15.6°C). Examples include Bermuda grass, St. Augustine grass, Bahia grass, zoysia, centipede grass, buffalo grass, and carpetgrass.

Cool-season grasses have an optimum growth temperature of 60 to 75°F (15.6 to 23.8°C). Examples include Kentucky bluegrass, rough bluegrass, chewing fescue, hard fescue, tall fescue, perennial ryegrass, Italian ryegrass, colonial bent grass, creeping bent grass, and velvet bent grass.

Methods of turf establishment

Turfgrasses can be established by a variety of methods.

- *Sexual propagation.* Seeding is done by spreading dry seed on a prepared soil surface. This technique is used with some Bermuda grass, buffalo grass, Kentucky bluegrass, tall fescue, and fine fescue.
- *Hydroseeding.* Hydroseeding is accomplished by applying a water, seed, and pulp-fiber mulch combination under pressure to a prepared soil surface. This method is frequently used on slopes, roadsides, and rocky areas.
- *Asexual propagation.* Turf areas established by asexual propagation should be established at least two months before

143

frost for good root development. This technique is used with Bermuda grass, centipede grass, and St. Augustine grass.

- *Sodding.* In sodding, strips of turfgrass with adhering soil are usually laid on the soil to form a solid, "instant" turf cover.
- *Plugging.* Plugs of turfgrass (2-inch pieces) with adhering soil are planted into the soil, spaced 6 to 18 inches apart. This method allows growth of a solid turf cover after one growing season. This technique is used with zoysia, Bermuda grass, and creeping bent grass.
- *Sprigging.* Turf material with leaves, stolons, and rhizomes are planted in rows or individual holes. Generally, 1 to 4 bushels of sprigs are used to plant 1000 square feet.
- *Stolonizing.* Stolons or rhizomes are broadcast or scattered uniformly over prepared soil, then top-dressed and pressed into contact with the soil. Generally, 5 to 10 bushels of material are used to cover 1000 square feet.

When establishing turf by seeding, the following factors apply. Seeding rate is based on pure live seed. Variable seeding rates are based on turfgrass species. Excess seeding rates produce weak seedlings and slow sod formation. Percent of germination refers to the seed that actually takes hold and germinates. For example, of 10 pounds of Bermuda grass seed spread, 8 pounds of seed sprout or germinate. The percent of germination in this example is 80 percent. Seed purity refers to the amount of good seed in a mix. Harvested seed may be mixed with crop or weed seeds and inert matter. Good-quality seed has a purity of 90 to 95 percent. Seed mixture refers to mixing different cultivars of the same species or mixing different species. These mixtures enhance establishment over a variety of conditions—for example, a site with full sun and full shade areas or a site with drought areas and wet areas. These mixtures should contain species or cultivars with similar color and texture. State and federal regulations control the minimum information on the seed label. It lists supplier, turf species or cultivar name, seed purity, germination percent, and test date.

Two techniques that may be used when establishing a turf are *top-dressing* and *mulching.* Top-dressing involves applying a thin layer of compatible soil or sand on a new or established turf area. It is used to fill depressions, help control thatch, retard drying of plant materials, and protect plants from temperature stress. Top-dressing can cause injury if the layers are too thick and exclude sunlight. Mulching involves applying a thin protective covering of natural or manufactured mulching materials over the soil. It is used to conserve moisture, protect against runoff and erosion, discourage weeds, and lessen temperature variations. Mulching can provide a favorable microclimate for seed germination and seedling establishment. Common mulching materials used when establishing grass include natural mulches such as straw, wood chips, peat, and compost. Manufactured mulches such as excelsior mat, jute net, burlap paper net, and pump fiber are used extensively for maintaining slopes.

Care and maintenance

After establishing the turf, irrigate new plantings daily, moistening the upper 2 inches of soil. As the turf becomes established, reduce irrigation frequency and increase irrigation depth to about 6 to 8 inches or as required by specific turf or regional climates. Water when the turf shows the first signs of wilt. Wilt is characterized by a blue-gray appearance and "footprinting," which is when grass does not return to an upright position quickly but shows the footprints when walked upon. Apply water at a rate the soil can quickly absorb to prevent runoff. Reapply fertilizer about three weeks after planting. Apply a recommended herbicide only when weed competition hinders turfgrass coverage and danger of damage to seedlings has passed. Mow turf as appropriate for the turf species, turf use, and season of the year.

Basic guidelines for mowing established turf involve first knowing the proper mowing heights. Correct height depends on the turf species, turf use, and season of the year. Mowing cool-season grasses higher during high temperatures protects the crown. Heights set too low seriously affect turf growth. The turf will have reduced root and shoot growth, less tolerance of environmental stress, and less wear resistance. How often the turf needs mowing depends on climatic conditions, growth rate of turf species, and purpose of turf area. When local temperature and rainfall conditions are ideal for the turf species, it grows faster and requires more frequent mowing. Removing more than one-third of the leaf area results in partial loss of the shoot or roots and eventually can destroy turf. Mowing too frequently reduces turf growth and increases maintenance costs. Different mowing patterns minimize turf wear and increase turf uniformity by alternating mowing directions or patterns each time you cut. Accepted mowing techniques for turfgrass are

- Mow across steep slopes, not up and down.
- Turn corners or directions slowly to prevent the mower's wheels from tearing the turf.
- Turn on a paved sidewalk or driveway when possible. However, do not turn on gravel surfaces.

- Make sure the mower's cutting blade is sharp before using it.
- Mow at a steady pace, slow enough to prevent clumpy, unevenly mowed turf.
- Check to make sure grass is dry enough to be mowed. Wet grass clogs equipment, spreads diseases, cuts unevenly, slows mower, and compacts soil.
- Overlap cutting passes by about 2 inches to prevent missed spots.

The advantages of clippings are that if turf is mowed frequently so that clippings are short, they disappear into the lawn. Short clippings decompose quickly, so they do not contribute to the thatch layer. Clippings are a source of plant nutrients, especially nitrogen. Moisture is also better retained. The disadvantages of clippings are that if turf is mowed infrequently so clippings are long, they clump and distort turf growth. Long clippings contribute to the thatch layer. Clippings may contribute to disease occurrence. In areas with low rainfall levels, clippings don't decompose.

Thatch is caused by rapid turf growth producing stems and roots faster than the vegetation can decompose. Its presence causes reduced microorganism, earthworm, and insect activity. When turf is allowed to grow too tall and then is cut severely (more than one-third of top growth), long clippings are left on turf and cause lawn disease. In planting of the more vigorous turfgrass cultivators, the damage caused by thatch buildup includes both increased disease and insect damage, unevenly mowed turf, shallow root development, and slow air and water movement through turf. Air and water movement is necessary to remove mildew. Telltale signs of thatch buildup are dry spots in the turf as growing shoots are shaded out.

Compaction is usually caused by heavy traffic over an area; it affects the upper 3 inches of soil. The methods of cultivating compacted soils involve such techniques as coring (which removes plugs of soil, leaving holes 3 to 4 inches deep); forking (hand-working a small area with a tined fork by pushing the fork into the soil 6 to 8 inches deep and then rocking or working the fork back and forth, loosening the soil, and repeating several times); slicing (vertically cutting slits 3 to 4 inches long and 3 to 4 inches deep); and spiking (which produces shallow holes $\frac{1}{2}$ inch long and $\frac{1}{2}$ to $\frac{3}{4}$ inch deep). Relieving compaction by loosening or puncturing the soil by mechanical means to increase water penetration and air permeability is called *aeration*. Aerating can be as simple as cultivating around newly planted seedling with a trowel or, in the case of turfgrass, can involve use of a gas-powered machine that removes small cores of soil from the turf. The response to aeration is generally improved turfgrass growth.

Before undertaking turfgrass fertilization, a soil test should be done to determine the nutrient level and pH of the area before lawn installation and as recommended in your area after establishment. Soil-amendment applications should be based on the soil test, existing turf condition, existing thatch, stress conditions, and presence of disease. Examples of these amendments are lime (adjust pH), sulfur (adjust pH), nitrogen (nutrient), phosphorus (nutrient), potassium (nutrient), and gypsum, all of which improve the soil conditions. Nitrogen is needed in the largest amounts by turfgrass. Nitrogen application is based on the appearance of the turf, use of the area, desired greenness, and whether or not clippings are removed.

Factors affecting fertilizer application include the strength of fertilizer material and whether it is dry or liquid. Nutrients can be specially mixed to serve a specific area. Pesticides can be mixed and applied with nutrients. Nutrients can be applied for foliar absorption. Turf should be irrigated after fertilizer application to avoid foliar burn. The equipment used to apply fertilizer are drop spreaders, rotary spreaders, and liquid applicators. Various sizes of spreaders, from push types to tractor-pulled models, are available for small to large jobs. Spreaders must be cleaned thoroughly after use. Mixes of different granular sizes of fertilizer are difficult to apply uniformly with rotary spreaders. Sprayers and irrigation systems are used for liquid fertilizer application. Liquid may be applied through existing irrigation lines, by injector systems, by hand sprayers, or by hose end sprayers. Liquid applicators must also be cleaned out completely after use.

Fertilizers and pesticides for turfgrasses are available in several forms, but only the liquid form can be used in sprayers. Spray drift is the portion of the spray material that moves outside of the target area. It can be either liquid or vapor (gas). Drifting chemicals could cause damage to susceptible, desirable species, or it could cause harmful contamination of air, water, soil, people, or animals. If the chemical leaves the target area, effectiveness within the target area is reduced. Several factors affect the amount of drift: droplet fall rate, droplet size, pressure, orifice size, humidity, wind speed, release height, air stability, and the size of the treated area. Liquid fertilizers supply plants with essential plant-food elements. Liquid pesticides kill or control pests, and insecticides are used to control insects. Herbicides control undesirable plants (weeds), and fungicides control fungus diseases.

Dry chemicals are commonly applied with drop or rotary spreaders. To establish a spreading pattern, spread half of a dry granular fertilizer in one direction and half in another, usually at a right angle to the first. Overlap the spreader wheel just inside the previous strip when using a drop spreader. Overlap the fertilizer pattern when using a rotary broadcast spreader.

Divide areas receiving liquid applications into units of two or four. Apply half or one-quarter of the liquid mix to each area. Turf should be fertilized as needed for the region, climatic conditions, turf conditions, and desired level of turf health. High-use areas such as athletic fields and golf fairways require more frequent and specialized fertilizer schedules.

Common causes of weed problems include thinned turfgrass resulting from soil compaction in high-traffic areas, mowing too low, nutrient deficiency, and drought or waterlogging. Weed seeds are spread by wind, contaminated (impure) top-dressing and mulches, water, equipment, traffic, birds, and animals. The best way to prevent weed problems by equipment contamination is by cleaning all equipment carefully before and after use. To promote vigorous turf growth, use chemical and mechanical preplanting control. Mow to reduce weed growth competition. Apply chemicals for selective weed control after turf establishment.

The terms and definitions used in turfgrass identification are

dicots Plants that germinate from the seed with two seedling leaves; these plants have characteristic veins that form a net-like pattern. Examples include clover, dandelion, and henbit.

drought Damaging climatic conditions brought about by heat and a lack of rainfall.

environmental stress Stress caused by naturally occurring factors such as drought, sunlight, or too much rainfall.

fungicide A material used in controlling fungi that attack plants and leaves.

herbicide A material used in controlling weeds on lawns or in other areas.

insecticide A material used to control insects on desirable plants.

local adaptation The ability of a plant to grow in a particular geographical region.

monocots Plants that germinate from the seed with a single seedling leaf; these plants have characteristic veins that run parallel to each other. All grasses are monocots.

nonselective herbicide A herbicide that kills every species of plant that it contacts.

postemergent herbicide A herbicide that kills after contacting leaves of the plant.

preemergent herbicide A herbicide that kills weeds as they germinate from the seed.

selective herbicide A herbicide that kills only certain species of plants.

surface-feeding insects Insects that do damage to plants by chewing or sucking on the part of the plant above the ground.

thatch A tight layer of dead and living stems, leaves, and roots that forms between the soil surface and green vegetation. Thatch development is normal; however, excessive amounts of thatch may be detrimental to the health of the lawn.

turf disease A naturally occurring disease of a lawn usually caused by a fungus. It is very dependent on environmental temperature and humidity and cultural practices (fertilization, watering, mowing, and thatch buildup).

turf pest Anything that damages turf, such as dogs, weeds, diseases, insects, humans, gophers, moles, even gasoline spilled on a lawn.

underground feeding insects Insects that do damage to plants by chewing the roots.

winter kill Damage caused by freezing temperatures or a combination of cold temperatures and lack of moisture.

Soil treatment

Before treating soil, you must determine the soil pH. The term *pH* is an abbreviation for potential hydrogen. It indicates the alkalinity or acidity of the soil. The pH scale ranges from 0 to 14, with 7 being neutral, below 7 acidic, and above 7 alkaline. A soil pH of 6.0 to 6.5 is desirable for most turfgrasses. However, many turfgrasses can tolerate a lower pH. When the pH goes above 7, minor elements (especially iron) can become deficient, which affects turf health. Soil tests give an analysis of the soil nutrients present as well as the soil's pH. Soil amendments may be used to change the soil pH or condition. Sulfur is used to lower the soil pH, and lime is used to raise the soil pH. Gypsum (calcium sulfate, a naturally occurring mineral) is used to condition heavy clay soils by making the clay particles lump together, creating needed air spaces in the soil. In the term *actual nitrogen, actual* refers to the amount of the specified nutrient (by weight) contained in a fertilizer. For example, we sometimes recommend applying a certain amount of actual nitrogen.

Major nutrients

Major turfgrass nutrients include nitrogen (N), which is the first nutrient represented in a fertilizer analysis. Nitrogen is responsible for growth of above-ground plant parts and for the development of chlorophyll, which is used as a food source in the development of plants and is the cause of the green color of turf. Turfgrasses use large quantities of nitrogen, which should be regularly replaced for a healthy turf. Phosphorus (P) is the second major nutrient represented in a fertilizer analysis. It is used by the plant for root growth and seed and fruit production and is fairly stable in the soil. Potassium (K) (potash) is the third and last major nutrient represented in a fertilizer analysis. It is used mostly by the plant for disease resistance. It also is fairly stable in the soil.

Minor nutrients

Minor turfgrass nutrients are nutrients that are needed by the plant in very small quantities but that are of major importance nevertheless. Most minor nutrients are available in sufficient quantities in the soil, although a soil analysis may detect deficiencies that need to be supplemented with calcium, sulfur, zinc, copper, magnesium, manganese, boron, molybdenum, or iron. When there is insufficient or unavailable iron in the soil, the turfgrass cannot produce enough chlorophyll, which causes a yellowing of the grass blades. This condition is known as iron chlorosis. Supplemental iron must be applied at regular intervals to correct this condition.

Cool-season grasses

Cool-season grasses withstand winter cold, but most types languish in hot, dry summers. They are best adapted to the Northeast and regions where a marine environment tempers summer heat. They also do well in mountainous regions where there is usually abundant summer rainfall. These grasses are started from seeds sold either in blends of several different grasses or as individual types. Lawns of a single grass type are the most uniform in appearance, most clearly expressing the characteristic you desire (fine texture or toughness, for example). The chief disadvantage of homogeneous lawns is that they may be wiped out by a pest infestation, a disease to which the grass is susceptible, or extreme weather (drought or unusually high temperatures, for example). A blend of several kinds of grasses is safer. Those that survive to maturity will be the one, two, or three that do best in the given soil conditions, climate, and maintenance practices. When buying seed, consider both the kind of lawn you want and the cost to cover your turfgrass area. Don't be fooled by the price per pound. Choice, fine-leafed blends contain many more seeds per pound than do coarse, fast-growing blends. Therefore, seeds of fine-textured grasses cover a greater area per pound.

When planting cool-season grass, it is preferable to get a broader survival rate by mixing different types of regionally acclimated grasses. This mixing serves many purposes, such as aiding in germination of more vigorous types, giving more-uniform coverage, and allowing for cover during different seasons due to the ability of some types to perform better during different times of the year. Grass seed in mixture can contain different varieties of bluegrass, rye, and fescue. Fine fescues are medium green in color; tillers spread the short creeping rhizomes. Tall fescues are medium to dark green in color and have coarse blades. Turf is often open and doesn't form a closely knit lawn. Tall fescue is often used where a low-maintenance lawn is desired. It is used in cooler regions of the United States and in shady areas in the warmer regions of the country. Fine fescue is used extensively in seed blends designed for sun and shade situations. This grass germinates rapidly and establishes quickly.

Seeding for cool-season grass is done by weight. Seeding rates for fine fescue are 3 to 4 pounds per 1000 square feet. Tall fescue seeding rates are 5 to 7 pounds per 1000 square feet. Cutting heights are $2\frac{1}{4}$ to 3 inches for tall fescue. Determine the frequency of mowing by the growth rate of grasses, not by a schedule. Remove no more than one-third of the leaf surface per cutting. During high-temperature stress periods, add 1 inch to the mowing heights. Use deep, infrequent watering. Water to a depth of 6 to 8 inches. Water again whenever fescue shows slight wilting or discoloration in the morning. Fescue typically wilts during hot afternoons. Fertilization rates are determined by the growing season and tend to vary from area to area; however, typical fescue fertilization requires that 1 to 2 pounds of actual nitrogen be applied in the spring and 2 to 3 pounds of nitrogen in the fall. Unless using a slow-release fertilizer, apply only 1 pound of nitrogen per 1000 square feet per application.

Ryegrasses have a medium to coarse texture and a light- to dark-green color. Leaves are heavily veined on the upper surface and glossy on the underside. Ryegrasses are used in full-sun environments in cooler regions of the United States and for shade grass in warmer region of the country. For ryegrass, use a seeding rate of 6 to 8 pounds per 1000 square feet. Optimum cutting height is $1\frac{1}{2}$ to $2\frac{1}{2}$ inches. Mow often enough so that no more than one-third of the leaf surface is removed per mowing. Water to a depth of 6 to 8 inches whenever signs of wilting or turf discoloration occur in the morning. Ryegrass fertilization requires 1 to 2 pounds actual nitrogen per 1000 square feet. In the spring, use 3 to 4 pounds actual nitrogen per 1000 square feet per application if using a water-released fertilizer. Again, fertilization rates are determined by the growing season and tend to vary from area to area.

Kentucky bluegrass is dark green in color with medium-textured blades. Its rhizomes are spread by tillers. It has the ability to form an attractive tight turf. Bluegrass is used in full sun in cooler regions of the United States and requires sun in the warmer regions. Propagation method involves seeding rates of $1\frac{1}{2}$ pounds per 1000 square feet. Optimum cutting height is $1\frac{1}{2}$ to $2\frac{1}{2}$ inches. No more than one-third of the grass blade should be removed per mowing. In watering procedures, Kentucky bluegrass withstands periods of drought by becoming dormant. Once irrigation begins, it must be continued throughout the period of drought. Water infrequently to a depth of 6 inches. For fertilization, use 1 to 2 pounds of nitrogen per 1000 square feet in the spring and 3 to 4 pounds of actual nitrogen per 1000 square feet in the fall. Thatch removal is important with bluegrass. In early spring or fall, remove as much thatch as possible.

Bent grasses are light to dark blue-green in color, fine-textured, and spread by an extensive stolon growth. This stolon growth, in combination with stems and roots, intertwines to form a thatch layer. Bent grasses are used in applications such as golf-course putting greens. Bent grass propagation is done most commonly by seeding, but bent grass can be sprigged. Seeding rates are $\frac{1}{2}$ to 1 pound per 1000 square feet. Cutting height is $\frac{1}{4}$ inch. In watering determinations, plugs should be taken from the greens and checked for moisture. The turf may have to be watered lightly several times a day to "cool" the greens. Fertilizer requirements for bent grass is a very exacting science and is determined by monthly soil tests. Whenever fertilizer is applied, it must be thoroughly watered immediately to avoid burning of the grass. Dethatching is usually accomplished by aerating the greens. This process usually enables the thatch layer to decompose naturally.

Warm-season grasses

Thriving in hot summer weather, warm-season grasses can form an attractive turf on at least 20 percent less water than cool-season grasses. Unlike the cool-season types, warm-season grasses grow vigorously during hot weather and go dormant in cool or cold winters. But even in their brown or straw-colored winter phase, they maintain a thick carpet of turf that keeps topsoil locked in place. The better warm-season grasses are grown from stolons, sprigs, plugs, or sod. Common Bermuda, hybrid Bermuda, and *Zoysia japonica* may be available in seed form, but seeding results are generally unsatisfactory and therefore the seeds are not widely offered. The hybrid Bermudas and St. Augustine grass cover quickly from runners, but most zoysias are relatively slow growers. Faster-growing zoysias are now becoming available as sod. All can crowd out broad-leafed weeds. Hybrid Bermudas require frequent, close mowing and thatch removal.

Bermuda grass is generally a fine-textured grass that is medium to dark green in color. Because of the extensive growth of stolons and rhizomes, Bermuda forms a very dense, thick turf. It requires a full-sun environment. Bermuda propagation can be done with sprigs, plugs, or sod. Seed is used occasionally but produces only common Bermuda. Seeding should not be attempted in areas that have hard freezes. The planting rates for variety-type Bermuda are 5 to 10 bushels of sprigs per 1000 square feet. Solid sod or plugs cut from sod can be used as desired. Seed should be planted at the rate of 2 to 3 pounds per 1000 square feet. Bermuda grass should be watered approximately 1 inch per week during March, April, May, and June; 2 inches per week if very warm and dry in July, August, and September; 1 inch per week in October and November; and 1 inch per month in December, January, and February. Cutting height is $\frac{3}{4}$ to $1\frac{3}{4}$ inches, never removing more than one-third of the leaf surface. In fertilization, use a good 3:1:1 ratio-balanced fertilizer containing iron, zinc, and sulfur. Apply 2 pounds actual nitrogen per 1000 square feet every six weeks starting when greening stolons are first observed in the spring. Stop fertilizing in the fall. Soil testing is important so that the fertility levels can be brought to recommended levels.

Dethatching common Bermuda grass is done every five years; U-3, every two or three years; tiff-type grass, on a yearly basis. In some regions of the country where Bermuda is the most common turf, overseeding the dormant sod with annual ryegrass is practiced. Care must be taken because you can never fully eradicate annual ryegrass, which will coexist with Bermuda for years and is considered unsightly by many. Overseeding does give the project a green lawn during the winter months when Bermuda grass is dormant.

Bermuda grass is a fast-growing perennial that provides a well-established lawn. However, it is also the second-most difficult landscape weed to control in the western United States at the lower elevations. Native to warm areas of the Old World, Bermuda grass spreads underground by rhizomes and above ground by seeds and stolons. If not carefully confined, its rhizomes and stolons invade shrubbery and flower beds and can be very difficult to eradicate once they are established. If stray clumps do turn up in flower beds, pull or dig them up before they form sod. Be sure to remove all of the underground stem—otherwise it can start new shoots. Or spray with fluazifop-butyl or sethoxydim, which can be applied over some ornamentals (check the label). Where patches are too big to be dug out of a lawn, apply glyphosate in summer or fall as Bermuda grass slows its growth. Avoid desirable plants nearby. Repeat applications may be necessary.

Zoysia is fine to medium in texture, dark green, and spreads by means of rhizomes and stolons. It is used in full sun to partial shade, hot to very cold climates, and is extremely wear-resistant. Propagation is done by plugs or solid sodding. Best results can be obtained by using solid sod due to the extremely slow spreading rate of zoysia. Cutting height is $\frac{3}{4}$ to $1\frac{1}{2}$ inches. In watering zoysia, remember that it is not drought-hardy, so soil moisture must be maintained at all times. Overwatering tends to drown out the turf. Frequent applications of fertilizer are needed to maintain vigorous growth.

St. Augustine is coarse in texture and is spread by above-ground stolons. Growth is so vigorous that thatch buildup causes major problems. St. Augustine is very sensitive to freeze damage and winter-kills if exposed to freezing and thawing weather for a period of two weeks. It is shade-tolerant and adaptable to most soils. St. Augustine propagation seed is rarely produced by St. Augustine, so sprigs or sod are the method used in installing a lawn. Cutting height is $1\frac{1}{2}$ to 3 inches. Frequent applications of fertilizer are needed to maintain good color and growth. Dethatching is necessary to prevent diseases such as brown patch. Insects such as chinch bugs and sod webworms thrive because of thatch buildup, so a good thatch-removal program is vital.

Centipede grass is medium to coarse in texture and is bluish-green in color. It is spread by stolons, which form good, dense, low turf. Its use is well-adapted to poor-acid soils, and it tolerates partial shade. However, centipede grass has poor traffic tolerance, poor salt tolerance, is sensitive to many herbicides, and usually goes dormant early in the fall and turns brown. Propagation of centipede grass is done by seed, sod, or stolonizing. Seeding rates are $\frac{1}{4}$ to $\frac{1}{2}$ pound per 1000 square feet. Centipede grass has poor drought resistance. Cutting height is 1 to 2 inches and should be done with a rotary-type mower. Centipede grass should not be overfertilized (no more than 2.4 pounds of actual nitrogen per 1000 square feet per year) and should be dethatched often to prevent turf decline.

Erosion control

Sediment and erosion control provides control of water runoff and short- and long-term protection from erosion as a result of construction operations. Erosion control includes the protection of a landscape's native vegetation, installation of sedimentation controls, control of slope construction, the stabilization of slope surfaces, control of runoff, protection of watercourses, disposal of excavated materials, and planting of exposed soils. Mulches most commonly used in erosion control include straw, wood fiber, wood chips or bark, and fabric or mats. Choice of mulch coverage should be based on the following factors or as specified in the contract:

- Effectiveness of materials
- Size of area
- Steepness of slope
- Soil depth and surface hardness
- Wind conditions
- Availability of materials
- Access to roadway and slope orientation (uphill or downhill)
- Fire hazard
- Weed growth
- Maintenance considerations

Choice of seed for ground cover should be based on the following factors or as specified in the contract:

- Rapid germination and growth
- Fibrous root mat
- Availability
- Fire hazard considerations
- Fertilizer requirements

All seeds should be labeled in accordance with the California Food and Agriculture Code. A density of 160 viable seeds per square foot for broadcast-type seeding is recommended in California. The rate of seed application may be adjusted according to erosion hazard or as specified. All fertilizers must conform to the requirements of the Food and Agriculture Code and should be used in accordance with manufacturer's recommended application rates. Native vegetation should be retained, protected, and supplemented wherever possible. When vegetation must be removed, the method should be one that minimizes erosive effects. Exposure of soil to erosion by removing vegetation should be limited to the area required for immediate construction operations. The native vegetative ground cover should not be removed more than 15 days prior to grading, unless otherwise approved by the engineer representing the permit-issuing authority.

Geosynthetic applications for erosion control, reclamation, regeneration, bioengineering, and soil mediation are just a few of the new technologies that are meeting the challenges of today's environmentally sensitive builders and landscapers. The need for both interim erosion control during construction and long-term biological stabilization of property site slopes, building pads, and contours is an ongoing challenge for today's builder, especially where unstable or demanding stress situations occur. Permanent erosion control is best achieved with permanent vegetation. Technology has never equaled nature's way, and nature's way is to heal erosion through the establishment of living organic matter, much in the way wounds of other organisms are healed through biological processes. Geotextile fabrics provide protection from erosion and stimulate natural healing through soil stabilization leading to rapid growth of vegetation. Geotextile fabrics come in a wide range of products from simple straw covered by hemp (jute) netting to high-tech polypropylene thermally spunbound nonwoven liners. These products serve a variety of soil-stabilization needs from drainage protection to maintaining flow and percolation to driveway and roadway stabilization.

Not all potential erosion is the same. Soil type, length of slope, moisture availability, fertility, and degree of slope are only a few of the variables to consider when planning erosion-prevention measures. Geotextile fabrics provide a variety of blanket types for different situations. A commitment to the earth's environment through the use of innovative materials and excellent technology applications has earned the American builder a world-class reputation for leadership in property-site development. Geotextile fabrics deliver fast, simple, and economical solutions to bioengineering—engineering demands where 100-percent biodegradable materials are required for turf reinforcement, erosion prevention, revegetation, and reclamation. To achieve natural regeneration or reclamation under erosion conditions, vegetation requires a natural environment that is stable under storm conditions for five years or more. Geotextile fabrics provide a lathwork of sturdy, natural fibers that are aesthetically and environmentally pleasing while meeting the high strength requirements of plant reclamation. They break up runoff from heavy rains and dissipate the energy of flowing water while providing lateral strength for construction integrity as vegetation becomes established.

Erosion-protection structures using geotextile fabric hold soil in place and dissipate hydraulic forces that cause erosion. Detailed guidelines are available from manufacturers for product selection and specifications based on application, site conditions, traffic conditions, aggregate used, and installation method. Installation of a geotextile fabric under heavy stone, rip-rap, gabions, or precast blocks is fast and easy. These fabrics have proven themselves to be time- and money-saving alternatives to traditional methods using graded aggregate or sand filters. Geotextile fabrics are made of 100-percent organic material woven into a high-strength matrix. As an organic material, geotextile fabric biodegrades into a natural humus, contributing to vegetation and avoiding the need for post-installation removal. When compared to unprotected areas, geotextile fabrics can reduce erosion and on-site soil loss by 99 percent. That's right, 99 percent! I build in the western coastal mountains that are subject to Pacific Ocean storm fronts, and we don't walk away from a job without this kind of erosion-control technology in place. This use of geotextile fabrics is standard procedure for erosion control in severe storm regions.

In areas on the property where slope stabilization is needed, long-term erosion control and soil stabilization are provided by geotextile fabrics in locations where rain runoff causes a continuous loss of the toe support of an embankment. They can also serve as an effective liner for severe-slope bank protection in unstable soil situations with high-velocity flooding during storm periods. The appearance of organic geotextile fabrics is particularly pleasing in recreation areas where long-term rehabilitation measures are required. On severe driveway slopes aggravated by loamy soil that produces pulp-like conditions when wet, geotextile fabrics have the density to hold back soil when it reaches over-optimum moisture content. They also function as effective liners to accommodate runoff of drains and culverts into a natural-environment storm-water overflow drainage system.

Designing geotextile-reinforced earth-retention systems requires an understanding by the builder of the physical properties of both soil and geotextiles. Tensile strength, elastic modulus, soil-fabric friction, and durability of the geotextile fabric must be known and understood at least as well as the soil parameters being used in design. Each design-influenced geotextile function must be considered and matched to the corresponding material's physical property. This "functional" approach to design is the basis for many recent developments in the field of geotextile-reinforcement technology.

Erosion-control liners are installed in the direction of water flow. Overlapping should be a minimum of 10 inches at the fabric ends and a minimum of 5 inches on the sides. Top and bottom ends of the liner are secured by anchor staples at least 6 inches deep, preventing undercutting of the liner. Staples should be a minimum of 11-gauge, 6-by-1-inch, and driven in a pattern of three per square yard of liner at intervals of 1 foot along sides and overlapping sections. If an anchor trench is used to secure liner edges, use check slots with liner buried at least 6 inches every 45 feet in ditches. Standard erosion-liner installation procedures are

1. Grade and smooth the slope.
2. Apply fertilizer and seed prior to installing fabric or liner.
3. Anchor fabric at top of the slope.
4. Unroll the fabric in the direction of water flow.
5. Place the fabric loosely and in full contact with the soil.
6. Overlap the fabric approximately 2 inches and staple.
7. Install the fabric so edge overlaps are shingled away from the prevailing wind direction.
8. Overlap the fabric ends 6 inches, placing the upper blanket over the lower blanket, and staple securely.
9. Cut excess fabric with scissors and anchor at the end of slope.

Erosion-control liners maintain their tensile strength almost unchanged in alternating dry, wet, and frozen conditions. The reinforcing strength and durability of erosion-control liners persist even when submerged. In highly volatile situations, they hold soil particles in place beneath the liner while the bottom is stabilizing. High-altitude environments generally require multiple seasons to produce an effective stand of vegetation to safeguard against erosion. Varying slope gradients and slope lengths of up to 400 feet require careful selection of a multiple-season erosion-control blanket. To satisfy environmental-erosion considerations, geotextile fabrics and preassembled silt fences control silt from water runoff at the site. Most states require that sediment-control plans, including silt fences, be submitted before construction on a site can begin. Quick and easy to install, geotextile-fabric silt fences are fabricated in a variety of ways to meet your state requirements.

Jute netting is another form of organic geotextile fabric that creates a microclimate within a flexible matrix of organic material, ideal for seed germination. Blended organic mulch is sandwiched between high-strength oriented netting and quilted with extra-strong thread. Being biodegradable, jute netting operates with an organic mulch that biodegrades slowly as vegetation grows. Prior to installation, a sprinkler system can be installed underground to ensure healthy germination of a seed bed. The jute netting provides high tensile strength to withstand the shear effect of wind and water over long slopes and ensures the mulch stays in place even in the heaviest of storms. Both the netting and thread photodegrade through exposure to ultraviolet rays in sunlight.

High-strength turf reinforcement requires a thick matrix of entangled fibers suitable for holding soil. Voids between fibers are infilled with soil to create a perfect seedbed for healthy and vigorous root development. The entrapped soil and geotextile fabric serve initially as an incubator for germinating seeds and eventually as a flexible matrix for root entanglement, which locks in the soil as vegetation matures. The product endures for years as it biodegrades, securely anchoring roots and preventing root compaction. For specialized soil reinforcement, geotextile fabrics meet a demanding range of site requirements for site development. High-strength geotextiles of polypropylene or polyester composition are designed to provide versatility, variety of purpose, and durable performance under severe conditions. High-tenacity woven polyester geotextiles are available for long-term reinforcement in critical performance structures. High tensile strength and modulus contribute to soil-structure reinforcement in cut-and-fills. Additionally, low strain under load minimizes the potential for horizontal slippage or creep deformation. These geotextile fabrics have the following advantages:

- Easy installation
- EPA approved
- Permitivity for drainage
- Cost-effectiveness
- Durability
- Conformity
- Resistance to rot and chemicals
- No concrete forming
- Maintenance of reinforcing integrity
- Distribution of soil-cover stresses

Geotextile fabrics used in drainage and septic systems provide a protective layer to prevent native soil intrusion into the drainrock field, which results in clogging of subsurface drains. In septic systems, geotextiles are a permeable separator, allowing liquids to percolate into the ground through the drainage field but restricting fine particles from passage. As an alternative to graded aggregate or sand filters, geotextiles are cost-effective and easy to work with and install. Lightweight or medium-weight nonwoven geosynthetic fabrics are proven to be excellent filters, allowing subsurface water to enter the drainage core while retaining the adjacent soil from entering and possibly clogging the system. When properly installed, nonwoven geotextiles are very effective in silty and clayey soil environments.

In facilities-maintenance asphalt overlay, geotextile fabrics called *petromats* have excellent grab, tensile strength, and tear resistance, stabilizing the subbase for greater seal and longevity of surfacing. Proven stabilization applications include paved and unpaved roads, driveways, walkways, and parking areas. Geotextiles are both durable and easy to handle for fast, efficient installation. Both woven and nonwoven geotextile fabrics are available, which allows the builder to select the most cost-effective product for a particular jobsite application and soil conditions. The surface performance of driveways, roadways, parking areas, and other traffic-bearing surfaces depends on the strength and stability of the subsurface foundation.

Asphalt mirrors the subbase job under it. The installer can't fake it here. It's like painting — if the preparation work isn't done right, the surface coat shows the bad spots underneath. Any soft spots in the pavement subexcavation result in low compaction areas in the road baserock. These settle in time, causing cracks and chuckholes in the asphalt surfacing. To prolong surface life and stabilize the subsurface foundation, geotextile petromats provide a rugged layer between aggregate base rock and subgrade. Case studies have shown improved resistance to deformation under repeated load, which means increased service life for asphalt or concrete surfaces and resistance to rutting on unpaved roads. In any application, roadway performance is improved. In addition to maintenance savings, geotextiles save costs by reducing roadbase aggregate depth and preserving the aggregate.

One final note of caution in selecting geotextiles. As a builder, I always assumed that permeability was a prime factor to use in evaluating geotextiles. When I was researching this book, I came upon case studies proving that this assumption was in error. Control studies have shown that permeability should not be used to evaluate the expected performance of a geotextile fabric. Permeability equals permitivity times the thickness of the fabric. Fabrics have varying thicknesses, and thickness can change under different load conditions. ASTM Committee D-35 on Geotextiles and IFAI recognize permitivity as the appropriate property value for determination of hydrodynamic cross-plane flow.

Turf management

Turf management is the process of following all maintenance practices to grow and maintain a quality turf. A breakdown of the individual tasks involved in turf management includes

- *Weed control.* The control or eradication of weeds from turf, whether by chemical (herbicides) or mechanical (such as hand weeding) methods.

- *Insect and disease control.* The control of turf insects and diseases with chemicals (insecticides and fungicides).
- *Watering.* The management of turf soil moisture by the use of irrigation.
- *Fertilization.* The management of turf's nutritional needs by the use of organic and inorganic fertilizers.
- *pH adjustment.* The process of applying either sulfur (to lower pH) or limestone (to raise pH) to alter the acidity or alkalinity to make a more desirable soil in which to grow turf.
- *Mowing.* The act of mechanically cutting the turf to its proper height.
- *Aeration.* The process of puncturing compacted soil to allow oxygen, nutrients, and water to reach the root system of turfgrass plants.
- *Thatch control.* The process by which turf is stirred and vacuumed to remove the buildup of grass clippings (thatch).
- *Renovation or lawn installation.* The process of improving a poor, weak lawn or establishing a new lawn.

Budget considerations in turfgrass management must also encompass the following:

- Labor costs (such as for mowing, edging, fertilizer, weed and insect control, watering, and aerification; labor is usually the largest cost).
- Equipment costs (such as for new machines, depreciations, repair parts and labor, tires, fuels, and lubricants).
- Chemical costs (such as for fertilizers and pesticides).
- Utility costs (such as for water and electricity use).

The five types of turf-management (maintenance) calendars for builders are residential (a schedule of tasks to be performed in the maintenance of a homeowner's lawn), commercial (a schedule for a business that serves both homeowners and commercial buildings in the maintenance of turf), institutional (for maintenance of an institution such as a school or church), golf course (for maintenance of a golf course, including fairways, tees, and greens), and athletic fields (for maintenance of baseball or football fields). These factors should be considered when developing any turf-management calendar:

- Type of grass.
- Expected use of area (athletic field, playground, lawn, etc.).
- Climatic factors (temperatures, humidity, rainfall, wind).
- Soil type.

- Budget considerations.
- Equipment needs.
- Soil analysis. (If the soil analysis shows chemical deficiencies, you must plan to correct this condition on the management calendar. The purpose of a soil test is to determine fertility and pH of the soil so that any necessary corrections can be performed.)

As stated earlier and repeated here for ease of reference are the nutrients essential to turfgrasses growth, broken down into two categories:

Major nutrients

- Nitrogen (N), necessary for growth and color (green) of the plant.
- Phosphorus (P), necessary for root development and cell growth and development of the plant
- Potassium (K), necessary for cell division and disease resistance.

Minor nutrients

- Iron (Fe), necessary for the synthesis of chlorophyll, which gives plants their green color.
- Manganese (Mn), essential to the synthesis of chlorophyll.
- Calcium (Ca), needed for root and stem growth.

There are several other minor nutrients, but they are usually present in sufficient quantities in native soil for turf growth.

The two categories of nitrogen sources are *quickly available* and *slow-release*. Quickly available indicates these materials are water-soluble, and the nitrogen is immediately available through liquid osmosis to the turfgrass. Fertilization results in a flush of growth and a rapid depletion of nitrogen, making it necessary to make several lighter applications to obtain uniform amounts of nitrogen in the soil. Urea, ammonium nitrate, ammonium sulfate, and diammonium phosphate are nitrogen sources that are less expensive per pound than actual nitrogen. Slow-release indicates that nitrogen is released as natural organic fertilizers decompose into inorganic ions or as synthetic organics chemically react with water to release nitrogen. Examples of slow-release nitrogen sources are activated sewage sludge, manures, animal tankage, isobutylidene diurea (IBDU), and coated nitrogen materials.

How we determine actual quantities of nutrients in fertilizer is based on fertilizer analysis, which designates the percentage by weight of nitrogen, phosphorus, and potassium in the product. For example, 10-20-10 contains 10 percent nitrogen, 20 percent phosphorus, and 10 percent potassium. The application calculations are the weight of the bag times the percent of the nutrient in the bag equals the weight (in pounds) of nutrient per bag. For example,

50 pounds × 10 percent nitrogen = 5 pounds of nitrogen per bag

50 pounds × 20 percent phosphorus = 10 pounds of phosphorus per bag

50 pounds × 10 percent potassium = 5 pounds of potassium per bag

Fertilizer ratios refer to the relationship between the percentages of nitrogen, phosphorus, and potassium. The determining ratios are arrived at by dividing each number by the smallest whole number in the grade or by the largest whole number divisible into all three numbers of the grade. For example, for 10-20-10, divide each number by 10 to get a ratio of 1:2:1. For 6-9-12, divide by 3 to get 2:3:4. By reducing to the lowest common denominator, we reduce the ratios until they cannot be reduced any more. Although 2-4-2 is reduced by 5 from 10-20-10, it is not correct until reduced to 1-2-1.

6

Irrigation systems

Modern landscaping technology can now convert a single sprinkler into a complete microwatering system or retrofit existing electro-mechanical controllers to the world of solid-state efficiency. Irrigation systems are designed around factors of coverage. You break the coverage down into its components and then add those components together. The following are the primary factors affecting the design and irrigation installation for facilities maintenance. These factors must be considered when determining what type of system delivers how much water and how often it should be applied:

- *Permeability of soil.* If the soil is not very permeable, water should be applied in smaller quantities with more frequent applications to avoid runoff. If soil is more permeable, water can be applied less often and in greater amounts.
- *Heat reflection and soil temperature.* In an area where soil temperature and heat reflection are greater, evaporation of water from the soil is greater, and the total amount of water needed is greater.
- *Wind.* If wind is more prevalent in a given area, more water must be applied to compensate for wind drift and extra evaporation.
- *Microclimates.* The effect landscaping has on the overall climate must be taken into consideration when determining water needs. For example, a berm may alter the situation by causing the east and south sides of the berm to get more sunlight, thus requiring more water due to evaporation.
- *Macroclimate.* Warmer areas require more water, as do areas with low humidities.
- *Surrounding vegetation.* Plants nearby slow down evaporative losses.
- *Surrounding buildings.* Buildings nearby raise the temperature and increase water needs.

- *Precipitation.* The amount of rainfall that occurs naturally in an area affects how much water is needed from the irrigation system.
- *Use.* The use of the area should be known so the irrigation turns on and off at the appropriate times. For example, residential and commercial areas are watered in the early morning before people are using the areas.

The fundamentals of good irrigation design begin with designing the irrigation system so that the area is watered completely and uniformly. Use full-circle lawn heads for most efficient coverage of turf. Use part-circle heads along property boundaries, building walls and windows, drives, and other nonturf areas to keep from wasting water and to avoid inconvenience from wet walkways. In general, plan to irrigate ornamentals separately from turf since their water requirements and growing environments are different. Ornamentals usually have deeper roots that require longer cycles for adequate water penetration. Ornamentals also are usually mulched, which increases the holding rates of water. Excessive watering of ornamentals can cause as many problems as deficient watering. Plan to use shrub sprays, bubblers, or drip irrigation on ornamentals. Do not exceed the manufacturer's recommendations for head spacings. Underspacing heads (too close) is not an efficient use of water. Overspacing heads (too far apart) results in dry spots. The terms and definitions used in irrigation systems follow:

absorption rate The rate at which the soil absorbs water.

application rate The rate at which water is applied to the turf by the sprinklers.

backflow Water that drains back or is sucked back from irrigation lines. Backflow preventers or antisiphon devices are commonly used on lines to prevent backflow water, which could contain insecticides, fertilizers, or bacteria, from contaminating the domestic water supply.

block of heads A section (or manifold) of sprinklers controlled by one valve.

circuit Section of sprinkler heads operating at one time and supplied with water and pressure by one valve.

class of pipe Pipe is grouped according to the working pressure at which it can be used. For example, Class 160 pipe can be used where pressures do not exceed 160 psi.

cycle One complete run of a controller through all programmed stations.

distribution curve Curve showing the rate of water application by a sprinkler at various points along the radius.

domestic (potable) water Water meant for human consumption; must be protected from any contamination.

elevation gain Pressure gained as water is used downhill from its source. This pressure is figured at the rate of 0.433 pounds per square inch for each foot of elevation.

elevation loss Pressure lost as water is used uphill from its source.

flow The movement of water through pipe.

flow restrictions Physical restrictions in the line of water flow; can be planned, such as valves or pressure regulators, or unplanned, such as corrosion buildup in the pipe.

friction loss Loss incurred when water is moving through an enclosure. Friction loss reflects smoothness of pipe, length of pipe, orifice sizes in components, mechanical restrictions, and volume of water being moved.

gallons per minute (gpm) Measure of the standard flow of water in irrigation design.

head-to-head spacing Spacing of sprinklers so that the radius of the sprinklers match their spacing.

heat reflection The reflection or throwing back of heat from objects in the landscape, such as concrete and buildings, which tends to increase the soil temperature.

infiltration rate The rate at which soil can absorb water, expressed in inches per hour. This rate is important because if the precipitation rate exceeds the infiltration rate, runoff and erosion occur.

lateral A pipeline of a smaller size than the main, branching off from the main.

main A large pipe sized to carry the feed water to the irrigation system. Usually sprinklers are not connected directly to the main.

microclimate The environmental conditions of a small place or region that is affected by very minute changes.

multicycling Programs of many short watering cycles rather than one long cycle.

overlap The amount one sprinkler's spray overlaps another one when installed in a pattern.

overspaced Sprinkler heads that are designed or installed farther apart than they should be.

permeability of soil The ability of soil to let water pass through it.

pounds per square inch (psi) The measure of the standard pressure of water in irrigation design.

precipitation rate The rate at which water is applied to the soil by the sprinkler system as expressed in inches per hour. For example, a system might apply water 1 inch deep over the lawn or shrub area in one hour.

precipitation rate The rate of rainfall.

pressure The force of water.

program The watering schedule set up by the turf manager, which regulates which areas receive water for how long and how often.

rating of pipe A rating given to pipe to indicate the wall thickness or pressure under which the pipe can operate.

runoff Water that is not absorbed by the turf to which it is applied. Runoff occurs when there is a severe slope or when water is applied at too great a rate or for too long a time.

schedule of pipe Classification of pipe based on the wall thickness.

section A group of heads or valves that operate on one station or at one time.

spacing The distance between sprinkler heads.

static pressure The pressure of water when it is not moving.

surge An energy wave in pipelines caused by sudden opening or closing of valves.

swale A gradient or inclined surface area that slopes downward on one side only.

underspaced Sprinkler heads that are spaced closer than they need to be.

uniform slope A gradient or inclined surface area that slopes at a uniform angle and degree.

velocity The speed at which water travels.

Soil moisture-sensing equipment provides an automatic override of the preprogrammed irrigation regimes, based on a continuous monitoring of soil moisture in relation to plant need. Manual instrumentation that does not override the automatic controls can be used to establish optimum programming or scheduling of the irrigation system. Two basic categories of moisture-sensing equipment are in general use. *Tensiometers* are hollow, water-filled tubes with a ceramic sensing tip at one end and a hermetically sealed vacuum gauge at the other. The tube is sealed by means of a cap-and-stopper assembly. Tensiometers measure soil suction (matrix potential) on a direct basis. *Electrical-resistance devices* use electrodes encased in a porous material (gypsum) to measure electrical resistance in the soil as an index to soil water. Data is calibrated for salinity, soil type, and temperature and then converted into either soil suction or water content, in a format similar to Figure 6-1.

Irrigation systems are divided into four categories: *surface, subsurface, aerial,* and *trickle* systems. In surface systems, water is conveyed directly over the area by flood irrigation, water hoses, etc. Its advantages are small power-usage requirement, less water evaporation, and the establishment of root-soil contact in new plantings. Its disadvan-

CODE	
PT = Pin Type NO = Normally open NCV = Normally closed vented or Normally closed	E = Electric A = All systems

Symptom	Problem	Action
Valves come on and system waters when it's not supposed to.	**PT or NO** Control tubing between valve and controller is severed.	**PT** Shut off valves by plugging tubing on the valve side. Repair with tubing coupler and two retainers. **NO** Repair the tubing or use a manual valve to shut off the water supply.
Valve will not come on.	**NCV** Control tubing between valve and controller is severed.	Tubing must be repaired using a tubing coupler and retainers.
	E A control wire between valve and controller is severed.	Wire must be repaired or spliced and waterproofed.
No valves will open. System does not water.	**A** Incorrect controller programming.	Make sure pin is inserted in hour wheel. Make sure day wheel pins are *removed* on watering day with 11 station controllers. Make sure stations are set for running time. Make sure hour wheel is at proper time. (If not, electric power has been interrupted, is now off, or controller is malfunctioning.) Make sure slide switch is set on "Automatic" on 11 station controller. Check main shut-off valves and other manual valves to make sure they are open. Turn each station on manually. If valves operate, recheck previous points since a controller problem is indicated. Check for blown fuse.
	E Blown fuse. Common line cut or broken.	Check 24-volt fuse. Check for low voltage on valve solenoid. A minimum of 19 volts is necessary for valve opening. With less, a clicking sound can be heard at the valve without it opening. Line must be repaired.
	NCV Cut or blocked supply tube at controller.	Check line by removing it from its controller connection. If strong flow of water is not present, tube is probably cut or blocked and must be repaired.
One or selected valves won't open. No water in one coverage area.	**A** Incorrect controller programming. Controller malfunction. Main valve is closed.	Check controller settings. Operate valves manually at the controller. If valves work, controller problem is indicated. Check manual gate valve and/or flow control valves.

6-1 *Irrigation controllers and maintenance.*

tages are uneven surface-water distribution, compacting of soil, high manual-labor requirement for constant monitoring and moving equipment, and the possible requirement of special land preparation (such as drains). In subsurface systems, water is released underground to move upward to plant roots. Subsurface irrigation requires permeable soil with a lower impervious layer to block downward water movement. Its advantages are minimal evaporative losses from soil, promotion of deep rooting, and use as a drain system during excessive rainfall. Its disadvantages are that land must be level or evenly sloped, water movement is uneven, visual inspection of the distribution system is very limited, and excessive rainfall can upset the application balance.

Aerial sprinkler systems release water into the air under pressure. Slower rates reduce compaction, erosion, and runoff. Its advantages are that both small and large systems are available, both portable and permanent systems are available, it is adaptable to uneven terrain, and various delivery rates are available. Its disadvantages include high evaporative losses, high cost of equipment, high power requirement, and uneven water distribution under windy conditions.

Trickle (drip) systems use frequent, slow water application directly to the soil near individual plants through small pipes, tubes, or emitters. Its advantages are that it conserves water because there is less evaporation and the water is directed to individual plants, not the soil in between. The systems have a small power requirement, and they aid weed control by watering the specific plants, not the area between, so surrounding weeds do not receive water. They can be automated and adapted to variable terrain and plant materials such as steep slopes, narrow planted areas in high-traffic areas, container plantings, etc. Trickle systems allow the combination of different plant needs on the same system, like large trees and individual flowers in beds. The disadvantages are that maintenance costs are high, the system requires a clean water source or a filtering system, and distribution pipes may be attacked by pests such as rabbits, deer, and ants.

Pipe and fittings

Unless otherwise specified in the contract, all rigid plastic pipe should be polyvinyl chloride (PVC), display a listed schedule (pressure rating), and conform to all requirements of the National Sanitation Foundation (NSF) product standards for PVC 1120, PVC 1220 (Type 1), or PVC 2120 (Type 2). All constant-pressure (main-line) pipes must be solvent-welded. All solvent-weld joint piping subject to constant pressure within the system should be Class 315. Schedule 40 PVC should be used for pipe sizes not exceeding 2 inches. Pipe that is 2½ inches and larger in diameter should be Class 200 ring- or gasket-joint pipe with proper thrust blocking at all Ts and 90-degree elbows. Lateral pipe (piping downstream of the operating valves not subject to constant pressure) should be a minimum of Class 200. All fittings for rigid PVC pipe should be either solvent-weld, ring- or gasket-joint, gasketed-compression, or IPS-threaded type. Rigid plastic pipe should not be threaded. Heavy wall nipples, schedule 80 with molded threads, are allowed by code. Backflow preventers must also be installed in piping, but they are so important they have their own section later in this chapter.

Solvent-welded fittings should be socket-type PVC schedule 40. Ring- or gasket-joint fittings should be of a type compatible with the pipe used and recommended for such application by the manufacturer. Compression fittings should be of a size and type compatible with PVC pipe, recommended by the manufacturer for such use, and pressure-rated to meet or exceed the pressure requirements of the system. All fittings for threaded valve assemblies should be threaded PVC schedule 80. All nipples used for riser, swing joint, valve, or other threaded assemblies should be a minimum of schedule 80 PVC with molded threads. Plain-end pipe should not be threaded because of the notch-sensitive nature of PVC pipe.

Compression fittings slide over the tubing and grip the outside. Various designs allow pressures up to 90 psi. Barbed inserts slip inside tubing to grip from the inside. For larger inner diameter (I.D.) tubing (1 inch and above), it should be used only with low pressures. Higher pressures may create stress cracks (longitudinal cracks along the barbed area) in poor-quality tubing exposed to sunlight. Barbed inserts with locking rings can be used at higher pressures than a barbed insert alone. These sometimes tend to leak when fastened in place and exposed to wide changes in temperature. Special compression fittings are required to hold polypropylene tubing in place or to clamp over barbed insert fittings.

In using flexible plastic material, all flexible plastic pipe should be virgin polyethylene (PE) PE 2306, PE 3306, or PE 3406 Class 125 or greater, as required to meet or exceed the pressure requirements of the system. Fittings should be insert- or compression-type designed for use with PE pipe, recommended for that use by the manufacturer, and pressure-rated to meet the system requirements. For galvanized steel piping, all steel pipe should be standard schedule 40 galvanized steel pipe. Fittings should be standard, malleable, galvanized-iron, screwed pattern fittings. Threaded nipples should be standard schedule 40 galvanized steel unless otherwise specified. For cast-iron piping, all pipe should be flanged or mechanically jointed (MJ) type, a minimum of Class 150. Fittings should be standard flange or MJ-type compatible with the pipe and incorporating all required sealing gaskets. For copper piping, all pipe should be Type L copper. Fittings should be standard solder-type wrought copper or cast bronze, 150 psi.

The different types of plastic pipe, along with their respective applications, diameters, grade, and type are shown in Figure 6-2, and an example of a piping system is shown in Figure 6-3.

Valves

Quick-coupling (or snap) valves are similar to hose bibs but are installed flush to grade with the built-in valve. They require a special

Type	Grade	Diameter range	Typical application
ABS	DWV	1¼" – 6"	Drainage, waste, and venting in residential construction
	Service	1¼" – 6"	Noncode applications
PVC	DWV	1¼" – 6"	Drainage, waste, and venting in residential construction
	Thin wall	1½" – 4"	Drainage, waste, and venting not enclosed within walls (not allowed by some codes)
	Pressure pipe	1½" – 6"	Selection based on pressure of fluid that is to flow through pipe
CPVC		½" – ¾"	Hot water lines
PE	High density	¼" – 12"	Gas piping
	Medium density	¼" – 48"	Irrigation, sewer mains
SR		½" – 12"	Storm drains, septic tank, and leach fields

6-2 *Types of plastic pipe.*

key to couple with and open the valve. These valves are typically used with a sprinkler attached to a key or coupler or as a hose outlet. Manual valves stop and start flow and control pressure on sprinkler equipment downstream of the valve's location. Main shutoff (gate) valves are used to control individual sections of irrigation systems for the purpose of repairs or modification. A gate valve's main requirement is that of low-flow losses. Due to low cycling (opening and closing), maintainability is not as important as it is in sprinkler control valves. Figure 6-4 shows a cross-section of a gate valve.

Spring-loaded check valves are installed for the purpose of allowing fluid flow in one direction while preventing flow in the opposite direction. Pressure-reducing and pressure-sustaining valves are installed to automatically maintain flow and pressure conditions downstream of their locations. Remote-control valves are any device that can be opened and closed from a remote source to control the flow of irrigation water. Valves in this class are controlled remotely by an electrical or hydraulic signal and used to operate a series of sprinklers much the way a manually operated sprinkler valve functions. They are typically made of brass, cast iron, or plastic. Their controlling signal comes via a wire or hydraulic tube from a controller located at some convenient place on or off the site. These assemblies are housed in valve boxes, which are reinforced plastic or concrete boxes specifically manufactured to house valves and prevent the valves from becoming buried in the surrounding soil. Valve boxes are available in various sizes to house single or multiple valves.

Glove valves serve a similar purpose. They work on a rising screw stem principle rather than a spring-loaded principle, as shown in Figure 6-5.

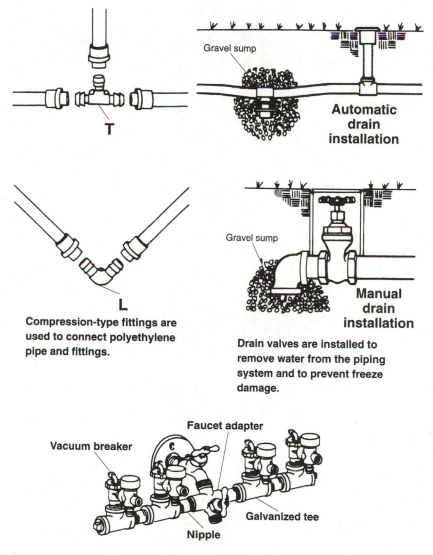

6-3 *Piping system.*

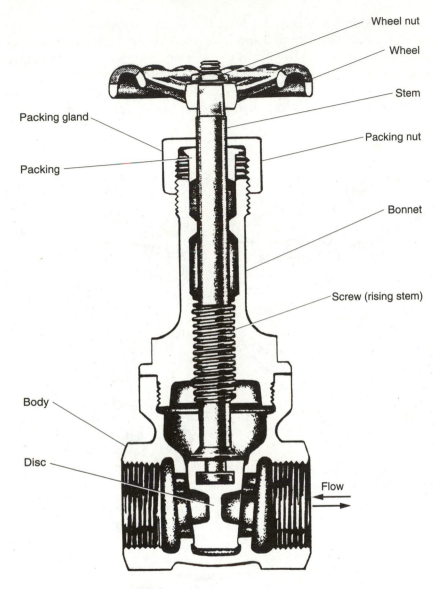

6-4 *Parts of a gate valve.*

Drip irrigation

Manual or remote control valves used in drip-irrigation applications must be designed to operate at minimal flow rates for cost-effectiveness. In addition, because pressure is at a minimum (no flushing action occurs), almost all drip-irrigation systems require filtration. Mesh or micron filters are recommended by most manufacturers. For mesh filtration, ratings are based on the number of openings per lineal inch (a

40-mesh screen passes particles up to 0.012 inch; a 100-mesh screen passes particles up to 0.005 inch; and a 150-mesh screen passes particles up to 0.0037 inch). For micron filtration, the ratings are based on one millionth of a meter (2.54 microns = 0.001 inch, 127 microns = 0.005 inch, or 100-mesh screen).

Tubing used can vary. The various plastics are described here:

- *Polyethylene* is a relatively inexpensive and extremely flexible tubing that lends itself most readily to drip use. Quality of resins, amount of ultraviolet light inhibitor (normally carbon black) added, and extrusion technique can cause prices to vary greatly. Most reputable manufacturers guarantee polyethylene tubing for five or more years.

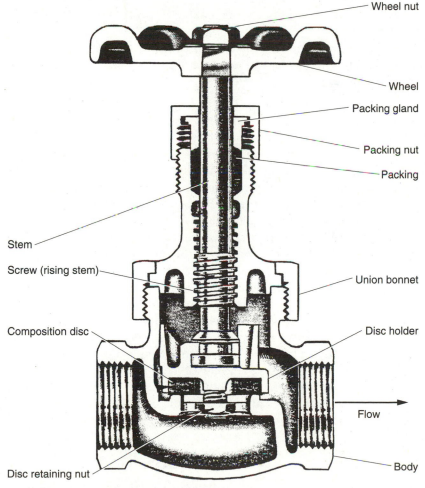

6-5 *Parts of a globe valve.*

- *Polypropylene* is less flexible and normally more expensive than polyethylene, but it is more resistant to high pressure and direct sunlight. It has more density than polyethylene and bends to retain its coil shape.
- *Polyvinyl chlorine* (flexible PVC) is heavier and more expensive than other drip tubing. Quality varies with resin quality and ultraviolet inhibitor. It is not as resilient as other tubing and is difficult to work with by comparison. However, it is less susceptible to mechanical damage and is used frequently when rodent damage is a problem.

All tubing must meet the following requirements:

- I.D. (inside diameter) and O.D. (outside diameter) must be published on the pipe.
- Minimum carbon black percentage in polyethylene must be 1 to $2\frac{1}{2}$.
- Tubing must be of a material to prevent algae growth inside.
- Tubing must withstand temperature extremes up to 140°C and water temperature to −40°C.

Emission devices for drip-irrigation systems include compensating emitters that give a fairly uniform flow through a predetermined pressure range. These are used with low- to medium-pressure systems when changes in elevation create a differential throughout the system. Noncompensating emitters do not compensate for pressure changes in the line. Mist sprayers are small mist nozzles usually made of plastic to provide airborne moisture for humidity-loving plants. They are also used for specialty planting.

Soakers are perforated or porous tubing designed to dispense water fairly evenly along the length of the tubing. In single-chamber soakers, water flows along the tubing and is dispensed out holes along the chamber wall. Multichamber soakers allow water to flow along the main channel and dispense through a lower-pressure chamber or chambers. Spacing of outlets is commonly 8 to 24 inches. Several variations are available, including emitters installed inside the tubing and holes drilled at a shallow angle into the tube, injected by laser. Spacing of outlets is commonly 12 to 24 inches. Porous tubing is an extruded material that allows the entire tube to weep. Low-volume sprinklers are miniature sprinklers in full- and part-circle patterns, used in ground-cover areas where emitters or soakers are impractical.

Controllers

Automatic irrigation controllers are any automatic timing device used to open and close remote control valves on a predetermined schedule for irrigation-system programming. These controllers include hydraulic devices, electric devices operated by mechanical control knobs, electric devices operated by an electronic touch pad (which includes memory with multiple functions), electric devices combined with a radio signal, solar-powered, and hybrid controllers combining electronic timing and controls with mechanical input. Control circuits are made up of any electrical circuit that controls the operation of remote landscape irrigation equipment by supplying signals or power to a solenoid, thermal motor, clock motor, or equivalent actuating or control device. Each circuit is any combination of conductors used to transmit hydraulic or electrical energy. Controller output circuits must be inherently power-limited remote-control circuits for signaling or actuating remote equipment used to control the operation of all or any portion of any type of landscape irrigation system. Figure 6-6 shows a typical residential controller, and Figure 6-7 shows a typical commercial controller.

Conductors on the load (output) side of the inherently limited power supply should be no smaller than #14 wire if single conductor or #18 wire if multiple conductor for physical strength, and should be

Individual station programming with extended run time and repeat cycles
Maximizes flexibility for diverse irrigation requirements

Easiest possible programming
Ends customer frustration and callbacks

Large, easy-reading display
One glance reveals entire station program and next watering day

Exceptional power surge and brownout protection
Reliable operation in harshest conditions

Global seasonal adjust 10-150%
One touch reprograms all run times

Silicone rubber keypad
Withstands at least one million presses per button

Durable, attractive locking cabinet for indoor and outdoor versions
Weather resistant and tamper-proof

Rain sensor circuit with detection and override capability
Automatically cuts off during rain if rain gauge installed; manual irrigation allowed, without disconnecting rain gauge

Large, easy-access wiring compartment with terminal strip
Makes installation fast and easy

6-6 *Typical residential automatic irrigation controller.*

Stand-alone intelligence automatically schedules and controls year-round irrigation based on local historic ET rates

Sophisticated water management

Large backlit display plus hard copy data printout

Single-knob programming and simple menu prompts

Automatic flow management

Shares sensor data and pump control when networked with other ETCs™

Two-wire communication between ETCs™

Flash ROM technology

Optional HALT:
Hunter Applied Lightning Technology

Maximizes watering efficiency without guesswork or reprogramming hassles

Customizes watering per plant ·type, soil and slope at each station

Everything you need to know, night or day

Programming was never easier

Matches gpm to available water supply

No central PC needed

You can update global data from any ETC™ location

Easy software upgrades in the field

Best-ever surge and lightning protection

6-7 *Typical commercial automatic irrigation controller.*

UF cable, rated at 300 volts, per UL Standard No. 493. Polyethylene-insulated golf-course and lawn-sprinkler systems wire for any direct burial should be rated at not less than 300 volts, per UL Miscellaneous Wires specifications, suitable for direct burial in the earth, with a covering that is moisture-, fungus-, and sunlight-resistant and has a jacket (insulation) thickness of not less than 30 mils. Bell wire is not acceptable. The inherently limited power source for a landscape irrigation-control circuit should be either a transformer approved for the purpose or a primary battery. The inherently limited power sources that follow require no overcurrent protection. Landscape irrigation-control circuits should be supplied by an inherently limited power source capable of supplying not more than:

- Circuit voltage (Vmax)   30 volts
- Volt amperes (VA)   100 VA
- Current (I)   100/Vmax
- Current limitation (Imax)   5 amps

Hydraulic controller tubing is any tubing capable of transmitting hydraulic pressure for the purpose of operating the hydraulic remote-control valves. All tubing should be flexible PVC, polyethylene, or copper, with a minimum pressure rating of 200 psi in standard nominal sizes such as ¼-inch O.D. (outside diameter), with a selection of sizing to be in accordance with the recommendations of the manufacturer of the control equipment as related to the type of equipment and the length of tubing. Hydraulic control tubing fittings should be standard solvent-weld, barb, or compression type, as recommended for the tubing used to maintain the 200-psi pressure rating of the control system. Strainers of the proper type should be installed at the control-system pressure connection, controller, and valves if so recommended by the manufacturer.

In all irrigation-controller installations, we start by wiring a controller and the valves. The typical tools and materials needed are a utility knife and wire strippers, screwdriver, long-nose pliers, electrician's tape, standard pliers, the valves, and the controller (timer). The wire for common ground is normally white. The procedure is to place the valve down and intercept the two wires coming from it. Straighten the wires and bring them toward the controller. Repeat these steps for all valves being used. Take one wire from each valve and twist these together. Prepare a "pigtail" (a short piece of wire about 1 inch long) and twist it together with the already twisted valve wires. Wrap the connection with tape. Connect the pigtail to the common terminal on the controller (timer). Take the other wire from each valve and connect one wire per terminal to the other terminals in sequence. Plug in the controller timer. Test the system by electronically opening and shutting each valve in sequence.

Use a flow gauge and the fittings necessary to connect to the water source. Turn the water on. Read the gallons per minute (gpm) on the flow-gauge dial to note the gallons per minute that flow out of the water source at maximum pressure. Some of the steps may have to have additional instructions from the manufacturer of the components to accommodate different designs of systems. Turn off the water supply. Cut into the service line. Remove a section of pipe large enough to put in a compression tee. Slip the tee over each end of the cut pipe and tighten the compression nuts. Install a short section of pipe coming out of the tee to serve as a stub-out. Attach a shut-off valve and then a backflow preventer to this section of pipe. Use stakes and string to locate where the pipe goes and dig a trench for the main line. Use stakes to mark the locations of the valves per the design. Protect valves by sheltering them in valve boxes. Attach the pipe main line to the service line by running pipe from valve to valve. Connect control valves to the main line using manifold tees.

Flush the main line by turning on the water and letting it run until water runs clear. Always remember to let the solvent on the pipes dry first. If the solvent hasn't had sufficient time to cure before you charge the system, leaks will occur. Flush the valves in the same way. Open the valves by using the manual-bleed finger screws. Install the automatic system controller according to the manufacturer's specific instructions. Install the circuits one at a time using the same procedures. Mark the location of the sprinkler heads with stakes. Dig the trenches for the pipe connecting the sprinkler heads to the valve. Lay the connecting pipe. At each stake where a sprinkler head belongs, put a tee or elbow in the line and attach a riser.

Install automatic drain valves at low points in each circuit. Attach the automatic drain valve to a reducer tee. Attach the reducer tee to a short section of pipe sloped downward at a 45-degree angle. Cover the short section of pipe with a bed of packed gravel to allow for proper drainage. Flush the system by sealing all the risers except the end riser with pipe plugs and turning on the water and flushing until the water runs clear. Install sprinkler heads to risers. Remove pipe plugs. Attach sprinkler heads to risers. Check the height of the heads. Cut the risers if necessary to adjust the head height. Turn on the water and open the control valve to check the proper operation of the system. Backfill trenches and clean up the area.

Hoses

When choosing hoses, check all of the following factors to determine the investment quality of the hose. The main parts of rubber-hose tubing are the outer skin, the inner layers or plies, and the core or center. The types of hose construction materials and their durability ratings are plastic (poor), vinyl (good), nylon (better), and rubber (best). Combinations of these materials have variable ratings. The smaller hoses ($\frac{3}{8}$ to $\frac{1}{2}$ inch) are primarily for homeowner use. Larger hoses are used commercially. Hose-tubing diameters and their general uses are

- $\frac{3}{8}$ inch—watering container plants.
- $\frac{1}{2}$ inch—watering container plants.
- $\frac{5}{8}$ inch—watering lawns and landscapes.
- $\frac{3}{4}$ inch—watering large yards, greenhouses, and nurseries.
- 1 inch—general construction work, watering large yards, greenhouses, and nurseries.

The smaller the diameter, the less water delivered. Length of hose also affects delivery rates. Diameters and their respective delivery rates are

- $\frac{1}{2}$ inch at 50 psi delivers $1\frac{1}{3}$ gallons per 10 seconds.
- $\frac{5}{8}$ inch at 50 psi delivers $2\frac{2}{3}$ gallons per 10 seconds.
- $\frac{3}{4}$ inch at 50 psi delivers $3\frac{1}{2}$ gallons per 10 seconds.
- 1 inch at 50 psi delivers 5 gallons per 10 seconds.

In choosing hose couplings and repair devices, use these factors: Solid brass (most durable), round brass (durable), galvanized steel (durable), plastic (least durable). Hose life can be extended by correct hose maintenance, which includes never letting the hose kink, always releasing water pressure before storing, removing from the faucet connector, and always hanging the hose on a wide support such as a hose hanger or reel. Shield hose from sunlight whenever possible and don't step on or drive over couplings or hoses. Always completely drain water from hoses after use, because the hose will be lighter to carry and water will not be retained to freeze inside the hose. Any water freezing in the hose can cause severe damage, such as cracking and splitting. Always clean couplings and fittings before joining. Connect the ends of a hose together when moving to keep dirt out of the hose. Types and characteristics of hose-end watering devices are

- Twist-control nozzle:
  ~Adjustable from fine mist to hard stream.
  ~Made of brass or plastic.
  ~Insulated nozzles are available.
- Pistol grip nozzle:
  ~Hand pressure on trigger controls water volume and spray pattern.
  ~Made of brass-plated zinc or plastic.
  ~Has a trigger lock.
  ~Accepts additional attachments.
- Sweeper or cleaning nozzle:
  ~Directs larger volumes of water in powerful streams.
  ~Made of brass or plastic.
  ~Not adjustable.
- Fan-spray head:
  ~Has wide spray with gentle delivery.
  ~Made of plastic or brass head set in plastic.
  ~Has an optional swivel-mounted spike.
- Water breaker or bubbler:
  ~Delivers high volume of water without erosion.
  ~Made of metal or plastic.

- Misting head:
  ~Produces a fine, fog-like spray.
  ~Adjustable from fine to coarse spray.
  ~Made of brass with removable jets.
- Wand (extension):
  ~Made of aluminum with vinyl or rubber hand grip.
  ~Has threaded tip.
  ~Shut-off valves are available.
- Shut-off valve:
  ~Made of plastic, zinc, or brass.
  ~Accepts attachments.
- Soaker hose:
  ~Seeps, trickles, or sprinkles.
  ~Made of canvas, plastic, or recycled rubber.

These and other sprinkler spacing factors are shown in Figure 6-8.

General maintenance procedures for hose-end attachments are to unclog jets and nozzle holes, shield plastic attachments from the sun when not in use, rinse often to remove soil and debris from the entire attachment, straighten or replace misshapen, cracked, or faulty attachments, and lubricate moving parts often.

Sprinkler systems

The product-delivery unit of any sprinkler system is the sprinkler head. Sprinkler heads are designed by many factors:

- *Arc of coverage* is the degree of coverage from one side of the throw of a sprinkler to the other side. A half head has a 180-degree area of coverage.
- The *cap* is the top of a sprinkler, usually a pop-up type.
- The *case* is the exterior shell or body of a pop-up sprinkler.
- A *cut-off riser* is a nipple with several areas of threaded sections that can be cut off to reduce the height of the riser. These are normally avoided in professional usage.
- A *flex riser* is made of flexible material so that it can be bent without breaking. It is usually used for mounting shrub or small lawn sprinklers to avoid damage to the lateral piping.
- *Flushing action* is the method used to flush debris from around the nozzle assembly of pop-up sprinklers as they are either rising to operate or retracting after operation. The term refers to water that bypasses the sprinkler riser seals before they seat.

Sprinklers are spaced after consideration of these factors:
- A. wind
- B. diameter/pressure
- C. sprinkler uniformity

The following chart depicts the general rule of thumb with varying conditions. No consideration is made for sprinkler uniformity.Three percentages of diameters are shown by a triangular spacing pattern, a rectangular spacing pattern, or a single row of sprinklers for the different climate areas:

Arid Southwest	Spacing type (% of diameter)		
Wind speed	Triangular	Rectangular	Single row
1-3 mph	55%	55% x 50%	45%
4-6 mph	50%	50% x 45%	40%
7-11mph	45%	50% x 40%	35%

Central & Eastern Sunbelt	Spacing type (% of diameter)		
Wind speed	Triangular	Rectangular	Single row
1-3 mph	60%	60% x 55%	50%
4-6 mph	55%	55% x 45%	40%
7-11mph	50%	50% x 45%	40%

All other moderate areas	Spacing type (% of diameter)		
Wind speed	Triangular	Rectangular	Single row
1-3 mph	70%	65% x 55%	50%
4-6 mph	60%	60% x 50%	50%
7-11mph	55%	55% x 50%	45%

NOTE: See product specifications for spacing recommendations.

Spacing of bubblers or emitters for turf areas

Type	Location	Quantity
Potted plants	At base of plant	1 emitter or bubbler
Shrubs (to 3'canopy)	At base of plant	1 emitter or bubbler
Shrubs & trees (3-5'canopy)	25% of the distance from the plant center to the canopy perimeter and equally spaced around the plant.	2 emitters or bubblers
Trees (5-10'canopy)		3 emitters or 2 bubblers
Trees (10-20'canopy)		4 emitters or 3 bubblers
Trees (over 20'canopy)		6 emitters or 4 bubblers

Soil percolation rates	
Soil type	Percolation rate, in/hr
Coarse-texture sand	.50" to 1.00"
Coarse-fine sandy loam	.35" to .75"
Very fine sandy loam	.25" to .40"
Clay loam	.20" to .30"
Silt-sandy clay	.05" to .20"

Precipitation rate (PR)

$$\text{Precipitation rate} = \frac{\text{Sprinkler gallons per minute} \times 96.3}{\text{Area within the sprinkler spacings}}$$

$$\text{Precipitation rate} = \frac{\text{Sprinkler gallons per minute} \times 96.3}{\text{Spacing} \times (.8 \times \text{dia.}) \text{ sprinkler}}$$

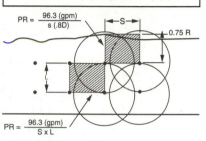

$$PR = \frac{96.3 \, (gpm)}{s \, (.8D)}$$

$$PR = \frac{96.3 \, (gpm)}{S \times L}$$

The formulas then take shape:

Application rate (AR)

Max. application rate =

$$\frac{\text{High GPM} \times 96.3 \times (CU) \times \text{relative humidity factor}}{\text{Area within sprinkler spacing} \times \text{grade variation}}$$

Min. application rate =

$$\frac{\text{High GPM} \times 96.3 \times (CU) \times \text{relative humidity factor}}{\text{Area within sprinkler spacing} \times \text{grade variation}}$$

Once the application rate is computed, calculate the station run times by using the following simple formula:

Station run time/day =

$$\frac{\text{Total water requirement/week (ET)}}{\text{Days/week of operation}} \div \text{Application rate}$$

Example:

$$\text{Station run time/day} = \frac{\text{Assume 2"/week (ET)}}{\text{7 days/week}}$$

= .286"/day ÷ assume .50"/hr.

= .57/hrs x 60 min./hr = 34 min.

$$\frac{\text{4 hours}}{\text{7 days/week}}$$ = .57/hrs = 34 minutes

6-8 *Spacing of sprinklers for turf areas.*

- *Positive retraction* is the feature of a pop-up sprinkler used to return it to the nonoperating retracted position, usually by means of a spring.
- *Radius* is the nominal distance water is thrown by a sprinkler.
- A *bubbler* is a sprinkler used for small planters or individual plants. A bubbler is mounted above grade on a riser and distributes water in either a stream pattern or a small fountain pattern.

- *Fixed spray* is a sprinkler in which the water delivery is continually being applied to the entire area of coverage.
- *Flush head* describes a sprinkler that is made for use in turf, without a pop-up feature. It is normally avoided in professional usage.
- A *hi (or high) pop* is a sprinkler that has a pop-up feature exceeding 2 inches. It is for use in taller turf installations or in ground cover and shrub areas.
- A *pop-up* is a sprinkler that is usually used in turf areas; it rises above the grass when operating and retracts when not operating.
- A *rotary sprinkler* is a cam-driven, gear-driven, impact- or impulse-driven sprinkler in which the water stream is rotated over the area of coverage to attain greater distance with a relatively low volume of water.
- A *shrub head* is a sprinkler used in shrubbery or ground cover areas; it does not have a pop-up feature.
- A *stream spray* is a sprinkler in which water is channeled into streams in the sprinkler, but the streams are stationary and do not rotate over the area of coverage.

These design features are illustrated in Figure 6-9.

Risers are the stems in a pop-up sprinkler to which the nozzle is affixed. If referred to in conjunction with the mechanics of installing a sprinkler, it is the nipple on which the sprinkler head is mounted. Risers can be either schedule 80 PVC, Marlex, poly, or galvanized steel. Swing joints and flex risers provide protection to lateral pipes in areas where sprinkler heads are subject to impact. In swing joints, the joint between the lateral pipe and the riser on which a sprinkler is mounted is articulated to move without breaking. Single-, double-, and triple-swing joints are fabricated from PVC, Marlex, galvanized steel, or a combination of fittings. Flex risers are manufactured, flexible PVC hose with fixed, threaded fittings on each end. Bulk flexible PVC should be IPS (iron pipe size) hose cut to desired length and solvent-welded to PVC fittings. IPS hose should not be used on the pressure side of a valve.

Sprinkler systems are designed around the sprinklers used for coverage in any given radius. For sprinklers covering a radius of 0 to 16 feet, use pop-up sprinkler bodies and incorporate an interchangeable variety of head nozzles. Low-pressure seals should be part of the heads that seat-flush only on retraction. Newer seal features prevent flushing on pop-up heads, which effectively enables more heads to be placed on the same zone, with low-pressure sealing at 15 psi.

Board across trench   Sprinkler head supported
by L hooks

Sprinkler heads can be supported with a board
across the ditch during backfilling. This assures
proper alignment of the sprinkler head with
ground level.

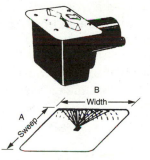

Wave type

Wave sprinkler head distributes water over
rectangular area.
Sweep × width = total area coverage

Rotary type

This rotary head can be permanently
mounted above ground level

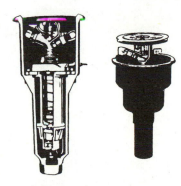

Spray types

Pop-up spray valves are generally installed in
systems for residential lawn areas

Pop-up rotary

Pop-up rotary type heads will cover large areas
of lawn. Cutaway shows spring attachment
which retracts nozzle after water is shut off

6-9 *Sprinkler heads.*

Retraction flushing of the head clears debris for a reliable pop-down system. Using new, finer-mesh filter screens prevents clogging of lower-gallonage nozzles.

Sprinklers covering a radius of 15 to 30 feet are stream rotors, easily recognized by their graceful "fingers of water." Ratcheting risers provide for an easy arc adjustment with about five levels of trajectory. Improved adjustments on new-tech stream rotors allow up to 25-percent reduction in radius and complete shut-off. Side inlet models are available on both 6-inch and 12-inch sprinkler bodies for easier installation. These sprinklers find their best use in medium to large lawn and shrub areas. Sprinklers that need to cover a radius of 30 to 52 feet should be precision-engineered, gear-driven sprinklers for medium to large residential applications. The spray nozzles need true matched precipitation rates. Matched precipitation rates ensure that all nozzles (every radius and pattern) apply water at the same rate, which eliminates fogging, conserves water, and provides precise flow rates.

Commercial sprinklers with a radius of 45 to 78 feet are designed with an adjustable arc and complete selection of color-coded nozzles for convenience in design, installation, and maintenance. A family component extends the range and control of the field satellite. Family components are designed for stand-alone or integrated control of high-density contiguous locations. These completely modular controllers are ideal for family applications requiring local and remote stations and sensors. The following table shows sprinkler coverages at pressure ratings:

Radius (feet)	Rate (gpm)	Operating pressure (psi)
0–16	0.05–4.58	20–75
28–43	1.01–10.81	35–75
35–50	1.2–6.7	25–75
25–52	0.8–9.75	25–75
47–67	6–25	40–150
45–78	4.8–30.1	40–100
Stream rotor:		
15–30	0.57–7.51	35–75 psi

Antidrain valves are used in sprinkler systems where elevation differences would cause a drainage of the sprinkler line through the lower sprinkler on the valve. These valves are also referred to as check valves. Some are adjustable. These valves hold back a given head of water to eliminate low-head drainage problems. Booster pumps can also be used to increase existing pressure to a higher pressure at a given flow. Booster pumps are typically centrifugal pumps driven by electric motors at 230/460 volts.

On the other end of the spectrum, drip-irrigation systems are achieved by subsurface pressure-compensating dripper lines that are designed for curved, angular, or narrow areas, high wind and perimeter areas, and locations subject to high foot traffic. These systems are ideal for confined planters, pots, or tree wells. Some modern innovative controller devices convert standard sprays and bubblers into complete microwatering systems.

Contamination-resistant plastic valves are electric in-line plastic valves that are flexible and easy to install, providing trouble-free performance in low-debris water applications. The 1- to 2-inch rugged valves feature a removable, fine-mesh, stainless-steel filter screen for easy cleaning in very dirty water. Also available are $1\frac{1}{2}$- and 2-inch pressure-regulating models, $1\frac{1}{2}$- and 2-inch normally open hydraulic, and $1\frac{1}{2}$-inch pin-type hydraulic models. These valves are all extremely versatile and rugged commercial valves designed to provide a wide array of options for a variety of water conditions. Brass valves come in 1- to 3-inch electric and normally open hydraulic models. The better commercial valves feature a three-way actuator designed for reliable, clog-free efficiency under dirty-water conditions. Pressure-regulating brass valves 1 to 3 inches in diameter are tough, long-lasting valves that regulate the water pressure to sprinklers, ensuring optimum sprinkler performance.

Sprinkler-head spacing patterns are geometric shapes for best coverage. In triangular spacing, all heads are placed an equal distance from each other in an equilateral triangle pattern. The distance between heads is usually 70 percent of the total wetted diameter for spray heads and 60 percent of the total wetted diameter for rotary heads. For example, for a sprinkler with a 10-foot radius (20-foot diameter), the distance between spray heads should be 70 percent of 20 feet, which is 14 feet. The distance between rotary heads should be 60 percent of 20 feet, which is 12 feet. The spacing between rows is less than the spacing between sprinklers. Multiply 0.87 times the recommended spacing to determine the altitude of the equilateral triangle, which is the distance between rows. For example, 14 feet × 0.87 = 12 feet altitude. An example of coverage design is shown in Figure 6-10.

Triangular spacing is commonly used because it provides a minimum of unnecessary overlap and uses a minimum number of heads for complete coverage. In square spacing, coverage is provided by all heads being placed an equal distance from each other. The distance between heads is usually 50 percent of the total wetted diameter for stream-type jet sprays; 55 percent of the total wetted diameter for rotary heads; and 60 percent of the total wetted diameter for spray heads. For example, for a sprinkler with a 10-foot

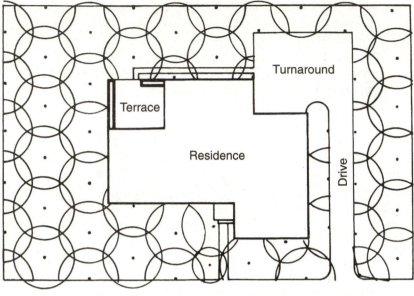

Street

6-10 *Sprinkler coverage design.*

radius (20-foot diameter), the spacing between rows is equal to the spacing between sprinklers. Square spacing is used less because it requires more heads for complete coverage; however, it is well-suited for small square or rectangular areas. In many residential landscapes, there are small or odd-shaped areas that do not adapt to any pattern. In these cases, "fill-in" heads are used for complete and uniform coverage.

The types of sprinklers and their characteristics are

- Fixed-spray sprinkler:
  ~Has no moving parts.
  ~Is commonly used in hard-to-reach areas.
  ~Standard heads have various patterns of holes.
  ~Adjustable heads contain several spray patterns.
- Oscillating sprinkler:
  ~Contains a row of nozzles in the single tube arm.
  ~Produces a long, rectangular pattern.
  ~Arm is adjustable from full to stationary movement.
- Revolving (rotary) sprinkler:
  ~Has two or more spinning arms.
  ~Head is mounted on wheels or skids.
  ~Changeable nozzle tips and arms are available.
  ~Produces a circular pattern from 5 to 50 feet in diameter or a locked narrow strip.

- Impulse sprinkler:
  ~Rotates as water strikes a counterbalance and spring-activated arm.
  ~Adjustable from spray to stream.
  ~Produces full- or partial-circle pattern up to 100 feet in diameter.
  ~Has exchangeable nozzle sizes.
- Traveling sprinkler:
  ~Drags hose as it moves.
  ~Hose-reel type rolls up hose as it moves.
  ~Requires hose pattern.
  ~Powered by water pressure.
  ~Affected by hose weight and length.
  ~Accepts various revolving and impulse sprinkler heads.

The basic parts of a sprinkler system are

- Sprinklers (sprinkler heads), which direct water through holes or nozzles called emitters to specific areas.
- Piping, which includes various types of pipes and fittings used to carry water from the source to the sprinkler heads.
- Control system, which consists of automatic valves and a controller that operates the sprinkler system according to preset programs.
- Miscellaneous equipment, which includes valves, regulators, pumps, and other devices used in a sprinkler system to regulate and control the flow of water.

Sprinkler distribution patterns are set in either a full circle (360 degrees) or partial circle (various arcs). Sprinkler heads distribute water in two ways:

- In a *fixed spray*, fixed nozzles distribute water throughout an entire area at one time. This type is used for relatively small areas of coverage (residential and small commercial).
- In a *rotary system*, rotating nozzles distribute water back and forth between set area limits. This type is used for large, open turf areas.

The types of sprinkler heads are

- *Fixed sprays*, which are stationary or fixed lawn sprays. This type sprays out water over the lawn area and is installed flush with the surface of the soil.
- *Pop-up lawn sprays*, which distribute the water the same way as the stationary lawn spray except that the water pressure pushes the nozzles up 1 to 12 inches above the grade. When the water is shut off, they drop back down to grade.

- *Stationary shrub sprays*, which are small heads installed above ground level on top of risers high enough for the spray to clear the top of foliage if watering is to be over the plants or on lower risers if water is to be distributed over the surface of the soil.
- *Bubble, flood, or spider heads*, which are small heads mounted just above the ground in flower or shrubbery beds where a spray of water would not be acceptable. These types of heads are used to gently flood the area.
- *Stream jets*, which are used for slow application of water. They are pop-up lawn heads or shrubbery heads that use nozzles that emit water in small, fine streams.
- *Rotary stream or rotary impact heads*, which are mounted above ground on risers or on couplers that fit into quick-coupling valves, are used in large lawn or landscape areas, have one or more nozzles, and emit water in streams.
- *Rotary pop-up heads*, which emit water through one or more nozzles. Their covers are flush with the grade and are raised or lowered by the rise or fall of the water pressure.

The types of modern landscaping pipes and fittings used for sprinkler systems are polyvinyl chloride (PVC) or polyethylene (PE or poly). Poly has relatively thick walls, is flexible, and is commonly used in colder regions because water freezing inside poly pipe will not burst the pipe. It is available in different schedules, up to 80 and 100 psi ratings. Common sizes for residential systems are ¾ and 1 inch. Poly pipe is installed by trenching or by pulling with a pipe puller. Pieces of poly pipe are connected with insert fittings that are placed on the inside of two pipe ends. A clamp is then used to secure the fitting. Insert fittings are available in various sizes of tees, elbows (ells), adapters, reducers, crosses, and couplings.

Polyvinyl chloride (PVC) is semirigid, has good tensile strength, and provides greater working pressure (160 psi and 315 psi) than poly pipe (80 psi and 100 psi). It also has better flow characteristics than poly pipe, which has flow restrictions caused by the internal fittings. PVC pipes are joined by solvent-weld processes, threaded fittings, or bell and spigot connections. The surfaces of solvent-weld joints must be properly primed, and the solvent cement must be uniformly applied. Liquid or paste sealants suitable for PVC pipe or Teflon tapes are used for leakproof threaded fittings. The fittings should be one to one and a half turn past "finger-tight." Do not over-tighten, because you will displace the primer/glue catalyst and create gaps, which in turn will become leaks under pressure. You will need the tools and fittings shown in Figures 6-11 and 6-12.

Knife

PVC cement   **PVC cleaner**

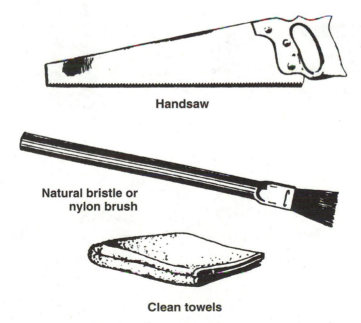

Handsaw

**Natural bristle or
nylon brush**

Clean towels

6-11 *Tools for making PVC joints.*

Tee

Tapped tee

90° female adapter

90° elbow

Male steel adapter

Male adapter

Coupling

Clamp

6-12 *Flexible plastic pipe (PE) insert fittings.*

Bell and spigot connections use gaskets or O-rings to prevent leaks between pipe pieces. These connections are commonly used on pipe 3 inches in diameter and larger, especially for longer runs. This type of connection allows for expansion and contraction, which would pull apart other joints. If water is allowed to freeze in PVC pipe, the expanding water (ice) will crack or burst the pipe. Therefore, all lines must be drained in the winter. PVC pipe is available in classes 160, 200, and 315 or schedules 40 or 80, types 1 and 2, and in various pipe sizes (½ to 6 inches). PVC is installed by trenching. PVC fittings are available in various sizes of tees, elbows (ells), adapters, reducers, crosses, and couplings. Examples are shown in Figures 6-13 through 6-16.

The methods of operating sprinkler systems are either *manual* (conventional valves control the water flow, which must be turned on and off by hand) or *automatic* (remote control valves are connected to a controller that turns the valves on and off automatically according to a preset schedule). Wire is used to link the electric remote-control valves with the controller, and polyethylene or PVC tubing links hydraulic remote-control valves and the controller. The related miscellaneous equipment used in a sprinkler system includes

- *Gate valves*, which shut off water in main lines and regulate the flow of water.
- *Angle valves*, which seal off the flow of water by a floating neoprene or rubber disc that closes against a brass seat.
- *Check valves*, which are installed in piping systems to limit water flow in one direction and prevent backflow.
- *Hose bibs*, which regulate the flow of water to hoses.
- *Quick-coupling valves*, which are attached to main lines or lateral lines under constant pressure and have a hinged lid. To get water, a coupler must be inserted and given a partial turn, which opens the valve. A sprinkler head or hose can be attached to the coupler.
- *Remote-control valves*, which are electrical or hydraulic circuit valves operated by a controller.
- *Manual drain valves*, which are used to drain the water out of pipes and sprinkler heads in freezing climates.
- *Automatic drain valves*, which are spring-and-ball combinations that close when the water is turned on and the pressure builds up to about 3 psi.
- *Pressure-regulating and relief valves*, which are used to control water pressure in the lines.

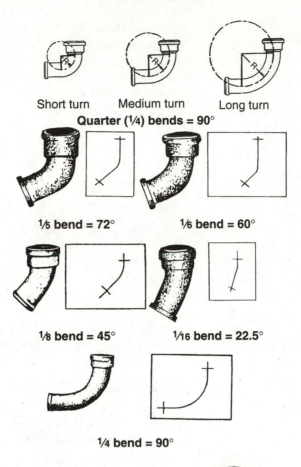

Short turn	Medium turn	Long turn

Quarter (¼) bends = 90°

⅕ bend = 72°	**⅙ bend = 60°**

⅛ bend = 45°	**¹⁄₁₆ bend = 22.5°**

¼ bend = 90°

Male street elbow
(copper)

Drop ear elbow
(copper to FIP)

Female adapter elbow
(copper)

6-13 *Basic plumbing bends.*

Sanitary tee

**Sanitary tee
with left side inlet**

**Sanitary tee
with two side inlets**

Horizontal twin tee
(Frog eye tee)

Fixture tee
Hub x Hub x FPT

Vent tee
(Straight tee)

Wye

Double wye

**Combination wye
and 1/8 bend**

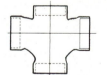

Double sanitary tee

**Double
sanitary tee
with side inlet**

**Double
combination wye
and 1/8 bend**

Cleanout tee
(Test tee)

Two-way cleanout

Upright wye

6-14 *PVC-DWV (drain, waste, vent) fittings.*

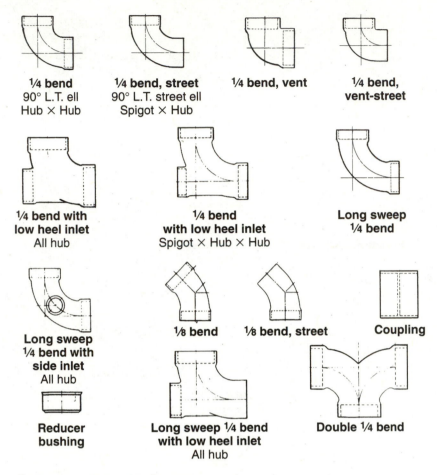

6-15 *More PVC-DWV fittings.*

- *Valve boxes*, which are used to protect valves and make it easier to get to valves in case service work is needed.
- *Controllers*, which are timing devices that can be set at a certain time to open and close the electric or hydraulic remote-control valves.
- *Electric wiring*, which is plastic coated, copper, direct-burial wire that transmits signals from the controller to the electric remote-control valves. For electrical-code requirements in your area, contact the local electrical inspector's office or your sprinkler-equipment dealer.
- *Hydraulic tubing*, which is PVC or polyethylene tubing that transmits signals from the controller to the hydraulic remote-control valves.

- *Antisiphon devices*, which are installed on sprinkler systems that use domestic (potable) water to prevent contaminates from being siphoned back into the water supply.
- *Risers*, which are connections between sprinkler heads and lateral piping. Risers should be of flexible material to withstand the shock of people walking on them or being struck by wheels of mowing equipment.
- *Pumps*, which are used as a prime pressure source in a system or as in-line pressure boosters.
- *Booster pumps*, which boost the water pressure in the system. A booster pump is used where water pressure is low or in a very large system.
- *System supply pump*, which supplies the system with sufficient water supply and pressure.

Hub adapter
Adapts C.I. to
ABS/PVC DWV

No hub adapter
Adapts C.I. no hub to
ABS/PVC DWV

Closet flange

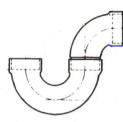

P trap

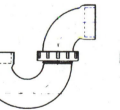

P trap with union

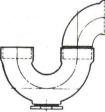

P trap with cleanout
(solvent vent)

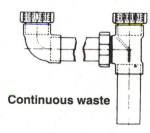

Continuous waste

Trap adapter

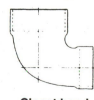

Closet bend

6-16 *PVC-DWV fittings (continued).*

Common hotspots in troubleshooting the sprinkler system are solved by observing the sprinkler problems. If there are random dry spots, check for plugged nozzles and screens, blocked nozzles, and correct arcs. Uniform dry spots mean you need to check the sprinklers for correct operating pressures and flow controls on master, antisiphon, and automatic valves. Also check for equipment breakage. Saturated spots and reduced operating pressure on the system means broken pipes or fittings. Saturated areas around the sprinkler heads usually indicate broken risers. Emergency troubleshooting repairs for water pipes are shown in Figure 6-17. Water hammer arrestors to prevent future breakage are shown in Figure 6-18.

Control-system malfunctions must be diagnosed in reverse. If the system won't operate, check controller and control lines. The lines may be cut or the controller may be malfunctioning or incorrectly

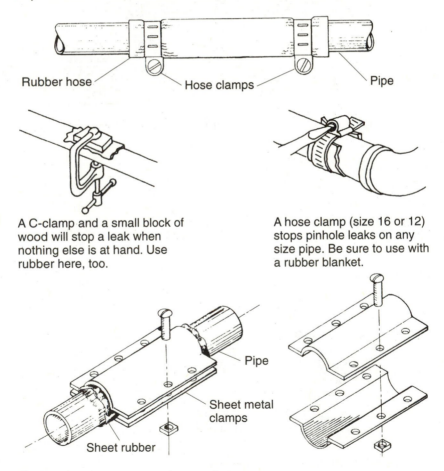

Rubber hose   Hose clamps   Pipe

A C-clamp and a small block of wood will stop a leak when nothing else is at hand. Use rubber here, too.

A hose clamp (size 16 or 12) stops pinhole leaks on any size pipe. Be sure to use with a rubber blanket.

Pipe

Sheet metal clamps

Sheet rubber

6-17 *Emergency water pipe repairs.*

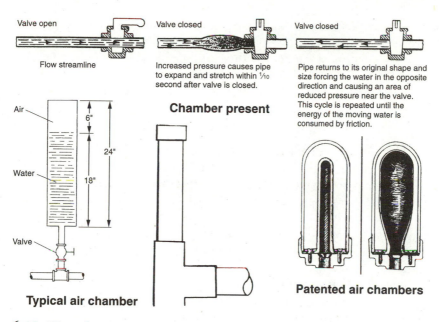

Valve open

Flow streamline

Air

6"

24"

Water

18"

Valve

Typical air chamber

Valve closed

Increased pressure causes pipe to expand and stretch within ¹⁄₁₀ second after valve is closed.

Chamber present

Valve closed

Pipe returns to its original shape and size forcing the water in the opposite direction and causing an area of reduced pressure near the valve. This cycle is repeated until the energy of the moving water is consumed by friction.

Patented air chambers

6-18 *Water hammer arrestors.*

programmed. If only part of a system won't operate, first check for sprinkler blockage, then check control lines, valves, and station selector circuit of the controller. Valves may be faulty, or the controller may be malfunctioning or incorrectly programmed.

If your region requires winterizing the irrigation system, you need to install drain valves. In freezing areas, automatic drain valves should be installed at low points in each circuit. These drain valves attach to reducer tees and empty through short sections of pipe into a bed of packed gravel to allow for proper drainage. Slope the drain pipe downward at a 45-degree angle. When the sprinkler system shuts off, the automatic drain valves open and release water so that no water is standing in the pipes at any time.

Backflow preventers

Backflow-prevention devices prevent the reverse flow of contaminated water from the irrigation system back into the domestic water supply. Backflow can occur through any cross-connection between an irrigation system and a potable water system. A cross-connection is any actual or potential connection in a water system where a potential contaminating material can come in contact with the potable water supply. Backflow through a cross-connection in an irrigation system can occur in one of two ways:

- Backflow due to "back-siphonage" occurs when the supply pressure is interrupted and a negative pressure or siphon occurs, most commonly due to a greater demand elsewhere in the system.
- Backflow due to "back-pressure" occurs when the downstream pressure exceeds the supply pressure due to pumping or pressure caused by elevation.

Elementary hydraulics and applied mechanics give us the reduced-pressure principle backflow preventer, which protects against backflow by maintaining reduced pressure downstream of the safe drinking (potable) water supply. By using a backflow preventer, water in a low-pressure zone cannot flow to a higher-pressure zone. Backflow preventers are designed to provide protection of the safe drinking water supply in accordance with national plumbing codes and water-utility authority requirements. They can be used in a variety of installations for backflow-prevention assemblies, including high-hazard cross-connections in plumbing and irrigation systems or for containment at the service entrance. When the supply-line pressure drops to a vacuum (pressure less than atmospheric), it is impossible to maintain a reduced-pressure zone. Backflow and back-siphonage protection then can only be achieved by allowing air to enter and break the vacuum. With the vacuum under control, the siphonage effect ceases and the potentially dangerous polluted or contaminated water is then drained out of the relief valve before it reaches the potable water supply. Vacuum relief is most important should the spring-loaded checks become fouled during a reversal of flow, which can displace debris.

Back-siphonage through a reduced-pressure principle assembly or device requires some method of preventing the vacuum from forming. Allowing air to enter, which breaks the vacuum (which caused the siphon), is necessary for the water to safely discharge. In hydrodynamic engineering, this is known as the *air-in/water-out concept*. The device's preventer valve has two channels: one for air-in to relieve the vacuum and one for water-out for protection of safe water. When the relief valve opens, one channel admits air to the top of the reduced-pressure zone and the other channel then drains to the atmosphere. Because contamination of potable water is a serious problem, most local codes require that backflow-preventer assemblies be installed by a licensed contractor who is recognized by the authority having jurisdiction and then be inspected for compliance with local safety codes. Certified testing and maintenance are required to ensure proper function and maximum effectiveness of assemblies. These services must begin at installation and be provided at intervals not to exceed one year and as system requirements warrant. Check your local code for other requirements.

Backflow prevention can be accomplished with an air gap, but this method is generally not practical in an irrigation system, since it requires a physical break in the supply piping and repumping for the irrigation-system pressure. Four types of backflow prevention devices can be used, depending on the application and local building code requirements:

- Atmospheric vacuum breaker.
- Pressure vacuum-breaker assembly.
- Double-check valve assembly.
- Reduced-pressure backflow preventer.

See Figure 6-19.

Atmospheric vacuum breakers protect against back-siphonage by means of an air inlet, which is closed by a poppet when pressure is on the device. As pressure is relieved, the poppet moves off the inlet, allowing incoming air to break a siphon. They must not be subjected to continuous pressure more than 12 hours of every 24 hours or to possible back-pressure due to pumping or elevation. This requirement also applies to a separate antisiphon device or a combination of an automatic or manual valve and an atmospheric vacuum breaker in one unit.

Pressure vacuum-breaker assemblies protect against back-siphonage by means of a check valve (as shown in Fig. 6-4) and an air inlet, which is closed when pressure is on the device. The poppet that closes the air inlet is spring-loaded to ensure that it opens even after being closed (pressurized) for long periods of time. These devices can be subjected to continuous pressure but cannot be subjected to possible back-pressure due to pumping or elevation. A typical application would be protection for an entire irrigation system, installed after the connection to the main (or meter) and before the manual or automatic sprinkler valves. Special consideration should be taken to ensure that these assemblies are not installed where toxic fluids or fertilizers may backflow.

Double-check valve assemblies protect against back-siphonage and back-pressure by means of two check valves in series, which prevent any backflow through the device. These assemblies can be subject to continuous pressure and to possible back-pressure due to pumping or elevation. They cannot be installed where the potential backflowing material is hazardous, as is the case with fertilizers or other chemicals. In their typical applications, they serve as protection

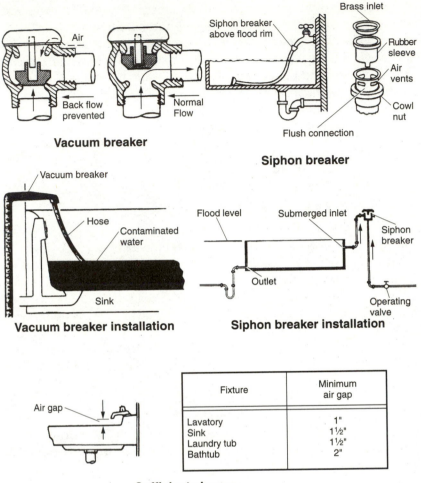

Vacuum breaker

Air

Back flow prevented

Normal Flow

Siphon breaker above flood rim

Brass inlet

Rubber sleeve

Air vents

Cowl nut

Flush connection

Siphon breaker

Vacuum breaker

Hose

Contaminated water

Sink

Vacuum breaker installation

Flood level

Submerged inlet

Siphon breaker

Outlet

Operating valve

Siphon breaker installation

Air gap

Fixture	Minimum air gap
Lavatory	1"
Sink	1½"
Laundry tub	1½"
Bathtub	2"

Sufficient air gap

6-19 *Methods of preventing water contamination (refer to local codes).*

for an entire irrigation system when chemical or fertilizer injection is not used, installed after the connection to the main (or meter) and before the manual or automatic irrigation valves. This device is considered a "low-hazard" device. Acceptance of double-check valve assemblies on irrigation systems is very controversial. Consult local building-code requirements before selecting this type of device. Different sizes are shown in Figure 6-20.

Reduced-pressure backflow preventers protect against back-siphonage and back-pressure by means of two check valves and a relief valve, which discharges the water from the "zone" between the check valves when a backflow occurs. The first check valve reduces the pressure, allowing the relief valve to "sense" a backflow condition due to a decrease in the inlet pressure (siphon) or an increase (back-pressure) in the reverse direction against the downstream side of the device. These devices can be subjected to continuous pressure and to possible pressure due to pumping or elevation. Reduced-pressure backflow preventers provide protection for an entire irrigation system, including systems where back-pressure due to pumping or

Model size	Dimensions (in.)						Weight (lbs.)	
	A	B	C	D	E	F	W/BV	L/BV
¼	9.44	5.62	2.00	3.50	2.75	1.50	6.50	6.00
⅜	9.44	5.62	2.00	3.50	2.75	1.50	6.50	6.00
½	9.88	5.62	2.00	3.50	2.75	1.50	6.50	6.00

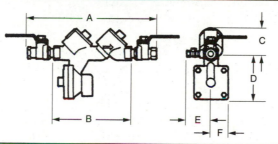

Model Size	Dimensions (in.)							Weight (lbs.)	
	A Ball valves	B Double ball valves	B Less ball valves	C	D	E	F	Less ball valves	With Ball valves
¾	11.88	14.00	7.75	3.75	5.00	2.75	2.00	9.25	10.25
1	13.00	14.25	7.75	3.75	5.00	2.75	2.00	9.25	11.75
1¼	17.00	N/A	11.13	5.00	6.63	3.38	2.13	17.50	21.46
1½	17.50	20.00	11.13	5.00	6.63	3.38	2.13	17.87	23.11
2	18.63	21.25	11.13	5.00	6.63	3.38	2.13	26.24	30.20

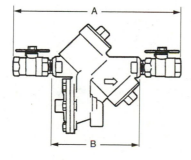
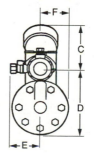

6-20 *Sizes of double-check valve assemblies.*

elevation could occur and where chemical or fertilizer injection occurs. They are installed after the connection to the main (or meter) and before the manual or automatic sprinkler valves. This device is considered as "high-hazard" protection and generally may be installed where the potential backflowing material may be hazardous.

One or more cross-connections may exist in any domestic water-supply system (Figure 6-21). Cross-connections usually are created without the knowledge of local plumbing and health inspectors. Usually the individuals responsible for creating them are not aware of it. Also, service contractors, plumbers, exterminators, or others using the facility's domestic water supply may fail to take precautions against backflow. Backflow hazards originating in domestic water-supply systems (facility systems) are beyond the jurisdiction of the water purveyor (municipal utility) to control. Dual check-valve backflow preventers provide protection for the public water supply (water purveyor systems) against backflow hazards originating in the facility (owner) system. Also, the owner water-supply system needs suitable backflow preventers at all cross-connections to protect drinking water against backflow hazards for the benefit of facility employees.

Dual check-valve backflow preventers are designed to be installed downstream of the facility's water meter. It is recommended that all water outlets, including sill cocks, toilet ball cocks, etc., be downstream and that all the facility's supply system must be in compliance with federal, state, and local codes. A properly installed and

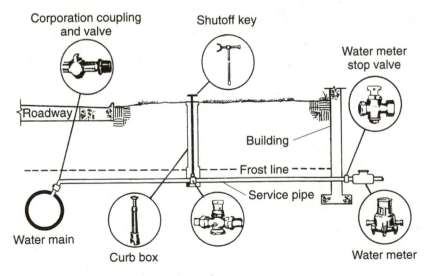

6-21 *Components of a residential water system.*

inspected domestic water-supply system is the first defense for quality drinking water. Installation of a dual check-valve backflow preventer has come to be relied on as a second line of defense. Any one or more of the following conditions not protected with a proper backflow preventer offer potential facility backflow hazards:

- Hose-attached spray bottles
- Hose-attached lawn sprinkler attachments
- Whirlpool adapters
- Water closet bowl deodorizers
- Backup water system wells
- Photo developing darkrooms
- Cooling tower and process water
- Commercial laundry machines
- Swimming pools
- Chemical plating tanks
- Heat exchangers
- Degreasers
- Misapplication of exterminator's equipment

Use ¾- to 2-inch reduced-pressure zone backflow preventers for backflow protection in cross-connection control and containment at the service entrance. Devices with high-capacity relief incorporate the "air-in/water-out" principle and substantially improve the relief valve's discharge performance. The emergency condition of combined back-siphonage and back-pressure with both checks fouled can defeat the effectiveness of a standard low-capacity backflow preventer. The installation of a drain line is recommended. When installing a drain line, an air gap is necessary. For vertical installations, a vent elbow is also necessary as the direction of flow may be up or down for ¾ to 2 inches. In applications for larger facilities, I recommend a double-check detector-assembly backflow preventer. These devices incorporate a meter that allows the water-utility authority to detect leaks with emphasis on the cost of unaccountable water (minimizing the losses that can occur due to water damage or sprinkler-system failure) and provide a detection point for unauthorized use. (Figure 6-22 shows available test equipment.)

Pressure vacuum breakers are similar to backflow preventers; however, vacuum breakers are not designed, tested, or approved to protect against back-pressure backflow or water-hammer shock. Pressure vacuum breakers are designed to prevent back-siphonage of contaminated water into the potable supply source and are ideally suited for industrial-process water systems and continuous-pressure piping-system applications where the water enters the equipment at

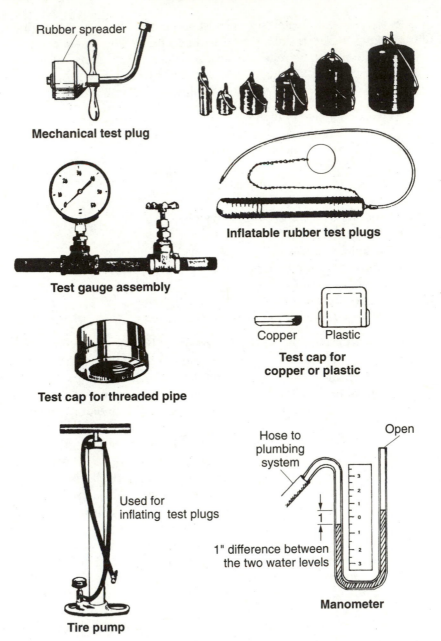

Rubber spreader

Mechanical test plug

Inflatable rubber test plugs

Test gauge assembly

Copper   Plastic

**Test cap for
copper or plastic**

Test cap for threaded pipe

Used for
inflating test plugs

Hose to
plumbing
system

Open

1" difference between
the two water levels

Manometer

Tire pump

6-22 *Test equipment.*

or below its flood rim. The disc- float and check-valve assemblies in pressure vacuum breakers are suitable for temperatures up to 140°F. When the supply-line pressure drops to 1 psi or below, the spring-loaded disc float opens the atmospheric vent, and the spring-loaded check valve closes the inlet, preventing the creation of a vacuum in the discharge line and preventing back-siphonage. As water flows through the valve, it pushes the check valve open and lifts the disc float, which closes the atmospheric vent, thus preventing leakage. The disc float is free-floating without close-fitting guides, which ensures freedom from sticking.

Pressure vacuum breakers must be installed with good plumbing practice. Pressure vacuum breakers are designed for installation in a continuous-pressure potable-water supply system 12 inches above the overflow level of the container being supplied. The valve must be installed with the supply connected to the bottom and in a vertical position, where it is available for periodic inspection, servicing, or testing. Remember, it is a continuous-pressure device. When there is less than $1\frac{1}{2}$ psi water pressure on the vent disc, some spillage of water may occur. Therefore, do not locate these valves in concealed areas or where spillage of water will cause damage.

Atmospheric vacuum breakers operate when the water-supply valve upstream of the vacuum breaker is open and a negative pressure is created in the supply line. The disc float drops, opening the atmospheric vent and at the same time closing the orifice opening, effectively preventing the creation of a vacuum in the discharge line downstream of the vacuum breaker and positively preventing back-siphonage. As water flows through an atmospheric vacuum breaker, it lifts the disc float and closes the atmospheric vent against water leakage. The domestic supply side of a well system is further protected by on-demand chlorination, as shown in Figure 6-23.

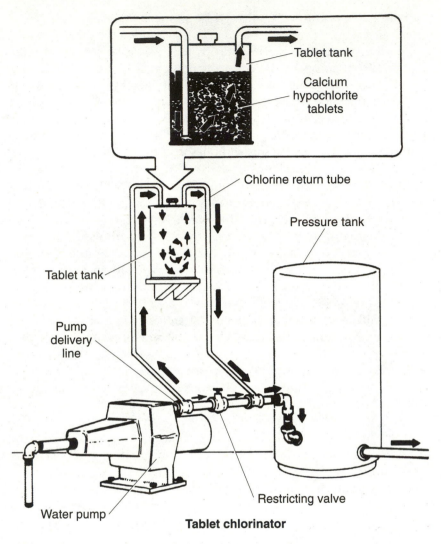

Tablet tank

Calcium hypochlorite tablets

Chlorine return tube

Pressure tank

Tablet tank

Pump delivery line

Restricting valve

Water pump

Tablet chlorinator

6-23 *Chlorine tablet method of disinfecting water.*

7

Landscape construction

Landscape construction can best be described as building structures that enhance the usefulness or beauty of a landscaped area (Figure 7-1). Common landscape construction projects include retaining walls (used to transform slopes into usable areas and to protect steep banks from erosion), paved walkways and drives (used for concentrated foot or vehicle traffic), patios (paved areas built at ground level adjoining dwellings that are used for outdoor entertaining or dining), and decks built to convert sloping, rocky, or undesirable terrain into usable space. Also included are contained planting areas, which allow plants to be placed in locations where they would otherwise be difficult or impossible to maintain, such as planters, flower boxes, raised planting beds, and planting beds with permanent edgings.

Fences, gates, and screens that are used to enclose an area, restrict movement, conceal unwanted views, or allow for privacy are profitable landscaping construction projects for the builder, as are patio covers and gazebos, which are overhead structures used to protect people from the sun or weather or to provide privacy. Additional site-enrichment items that fall under landscaping construction are natural or artificial features in the landscape that are not functioning as walls, ceilings, or floors in the landscaped area, such as permanent outdoor furniture (benches and tables), outdoor lighting, hot tubs, saunas, music systems, swimming pools, fountains, and birdbaths. Landscape construction terms, definitions, and conditions include the following:

aggregates Inert materials, such as sand, gravel, or stones, that are mixed with cement to form concrete.

batter The amount of lean-back on the front of a dry wall.

berm A raised, elongated mound or small hill of soil used to imitate natural features in the landscape or to conceal undesirable views or features.

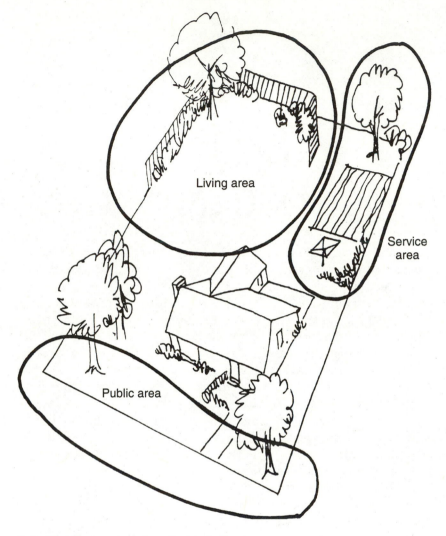

Living area

Service area

Public area

7-1 *Main areas in a landscaped plan.*

cement Substance used as a binder to hold other substances together.
chalk rocks Small rocks used when building a dry wall to keep large rocks level and solid.
concrete A hard, strong construction material made by mixing cement, aggregates, and water in a ratio that causes the cement to set, binding the entire mass.
course A single level, horizontal layer of material, such as bricks in a wall.
cut and fill Grading operations that change the contours of the earth's surface.

deadmen Metal, wood, or concrete members connected to a wall (or other structure) used to anchor and secure the wall.

dry wall A wall built without mortar.

galvanized Iron or steel coated with zinc to prevent corrosion.

masonry Construction projects made with bricks, stones, or blocks and mortar.

mortar A mixture of cement, lime, or gypsum plaster with masonry sand and water used between bricks, stones, or blocks to hold them together.

plywood A structural material consisting of sheets of wood glued or cemented together with the grains of alternating layers arranged at right angles.

screed A leveling device (such as a board) drawn over freshly poured concrete.

The supplementary building skills useful in landscape construction are carpentry (for all wood construction, such as building decks, outdoor furniture, planters, or even concrete forms), plumbing (for working with water and gas piping, as in irrigation systems, heated or unheated swimming pools, or water fountains), electrical wiring (for working with electricity, such as exterior lighting on walkways, yards, pools, or dramatic tree or shrub lighting), masonry (for working with bricks and stones in walks, patios, walls, and planting bed edgings), concrete work (working with concrete for drives, patios, walks, and planting bed edgings), surveying (for determining the sizes, shapes, and positions of features on a piece of land, as when locating a swimming pool or determining the slope of land), and earth moving or grading (for cutting and fill-ins of existing grade to meet a proposed grade, such as when trying to improve drainage flow or unusable areas).

The most common materials used in landscape construction are wood, concrete, brick, concrete block, stone (generally larger than 3 inches in diameter), gravel (generally 2 millimeters to 3 inches in diameter), soil, and asphalt. The types of woods commonly used in landscaping are cypress, red cedar, and redwood, which are naturally resistant to decay, and pressure-treated (PT) lumber, which are other woods that are chemically treated to resist decay before being used outdoors. These woods include cypress, red cedar, redwood, Douglas fir, spruce, Eastern white pine, and Southern yellow pine. They might be sold as solid lumber (boards) or manufactured sheets or boards such as plywood.

Concrete should always be poured freshly mixed from the delivery truck for the best compactive strength, but in small applications, hand mixing in a wheelbarrow is still appropriate. The standard concrete and mortar mix ratio is two parts sand, four parts aggregate (gravel), and one part cement. Add water to create the desired consistency (slump). Concrete can also be made from "ready-mix" bags from the local hardware store, which contain all these ingredients; only water is needed to activate the mix. To calculate concrete quantities, first determine the dimensions of concrete to be poured (length and width in feet). Then determine the depth of concrete slab to be poured. Convert to feet. Multiply length times width times depth to determine the cubic feet of concrete needed. Divide cubic feet needed by 27 cubic feet (1 square yard) to determine the number of cubic yards needed (which is how concrete is ordered). For example, if a patio is 15 by 20 feet and is 4 inches ($\frac{1}{3}$ foot) deep, the calculations would be:

$15 \times 20 \times 0.33 = 99$ cubic feet

99 cubic feet $\div$ 27 = 2.67 cubic yards

We always round up in construction, so you would order 3 cubic yards of concrete.

Bricks give a formal effect in landscape construction. They are held together in straight courses with mortar. They are most commonly used to tie in with other brick elements in the landscape, such as the house or sidewalks. Weep holes should be placed every 4 feet along the base of solid walls to allow water building up behind the wall to escape. Concrete block (CMU) gives a less formal effect in the landscape construction. These blocks are also held together in courses with mortar. In brick and block projects using mortar, the mix ratio is six parts masonry sand, one part hydrated lime, and one part cement. Add water to the desired consistency. (Mortar should be plastic-like, not stiff or sloppy.) Common brick patterns are running bond, herringbone, and basketweave. There are many other patterns used by professional masons. Many are more elaborate and some are just variations of these common patterns, such as the half basketweave. Dry stacked stone gives a natural effect to the landscape construction. These types of walls are nonstructural and must have 2 inches of batter per foot in height of wall to prevent collapse. Chalk rocks are used to level and solidify the wall.

Materials used for paved areas, such as sidewalks, drives, and patios, include solid paving concrete (concrete may have smooth, rough, or exposed-aggregate finishes), asphalt, wood planks, bricks, and stone pavers or flagstones. Brick and stone pavers should be laid in sand or in mortar. Stones may be irregularly shaped or cut into squares or rectangles and laid like bricks in patterns. Other materials include loose paving, gravel or stone, bark or wood chips, sawdust, and sand. Permanent edgings called ledgers or headers should be installed to contain the loose paving. The most common types of ledger edgings are decay-resistant wood (natural or treated), plastic (heavy black), metal (corrosion-resistant), and masonry (brick, concrete, stone). Ledger edgings help to retain the material within (plants or pavings), prevent grass from intruding, and give a neater appearance. A water-permeable, weed-preventing fabric should also be used under the paving to control weeds.

Considerations when designing contained planting areas in the landscape begin with size. Size should be determined by use. For annual plantings or flowers grown for only one season, the area could be basically any size suitable to the landscape plan. For permanent plantings or plant materials grown for more than one season (shrubs or ornamentals), the area should be large enough to accommodate the root system plus contain an adequate depth and width of soil to afford insulation to the root system to prevent winter injury to the plant material. Design and composition of the planter should be complementary to the style and composition of the building. For example, brick planters and edgings are generally not appropriate in front of stone houses. A railroad-tie planting bed is not suited for a formal-style building. Planting areas may be inground or freestanding. Adequate drainage should be provided, whether or not there is a permanent bottom in the box or planter.

In designing berms, care must be taken to make the berm look natural. This effect can be accomplished by imitating the flow of the surrounding terrain (contour). The berm can be surfaced with grass, shrubs, trees, ground cover, or a combination of these. The maximum slope if grass is used as the surface should not exceed a 1:3 gradient or 33-percent slope for mowing considerations. The berm should not drop or rise over 1 foot for every 3 feet in width. Consideration should be given to how the berm will alter the drainage of the area; a berm should never be allowed to act as a dam that restricts surface water drainage. If properly constructed, berms can be very beautiful, but they can be expensive. Consideration of how the berm alters the microclimate of the area can provide for a wider selection of plant material and should not be ignored or plants may be misplaced and grown poorly. For example, on berms 4 to 5 feet high, grass will become green a week or two earlier on the sunny slopes (south and west) than on the north and east slopes.

Lumber

Wood in landscape construction provides both functional and esthetic elements in the landscape design, including the construction of fences, decks, landscape stairs, benches, arbors, retaining walls, planter boxes, and header boards. Lumber stored at the job site should be protected from sun, rain, or other adverse weather conditions. The lumber should be stacked flat and kept off the ground at least 6 inches. Care should be taken when storing redwood on or near concrete paving; staining can occur if the wood becomes wet. Dimensional stability, strength, durability, and special beauty make redwood one of the most widely used and suitable materials for outdoor wood construction. Redwood is available in a variety of grades, grain patterns, seasonings, and textures. All redwood grades should comply with the grading accepted by the California Redwood Association. Different redwood lumber grade names may be used; however, the following grades are universally recognized.

- Architectural grades:
  ~Clear all heart (all heartwood with the graded face free of knots)
  ~Clear (includes sapwood in varying amounts and may have one or two small, tight knots on the graded face)
  ~B grade (contains limited knots and sapwood)
- Landscape grades:
  ~Construction heart (all heartwood with knots)
  ~Construction common (includes sapwood and knots)
  ~Merchantable heart (heartwood with larger knots)
  ~Merchantable (contains streaks of sapwood, larger knots, and some holes)
- Other grades:
  ~Select heart (all heartwood with knots slightly smaller than construction heart)
  ~Select (contains sapwood with knots slightly smaller than construction common)

Redwood lumber is available in either vertical or flat grain patterns. Landscape grades come in mixed grains. Vertical grain should be used where a smoother surface is desirable. Most redwood is available either unseasoned ("green") or air-dried. Architectural grades of redwood can be ordered "certified kiln dried" for applications requiring minimal shrinkage. As for texture, redwood is available in surfaced (smooth), rough-surfaced (rough), or resawn (slightly rough), which provides a special rough-textured, decorative face. The finish of surfaced lumber emphasizes the grain and color of the wood. Surfaced redwood is recommended for deck, bench, and other surfaces that will be touched or painted. Rough-surfaced redwood is appropriate for many uses in landscape construction and has excellent retention of penetrating natural oils and sealers and stain finishes. Resawn redwood is used when the special effects of this lumber treatment are desirable. All redwood used in ground contact or within 12 inches of the ground must be all-heart redwood.

Lumber that has been pressure-treated with wood preservatives that inhibit insect and fungi damage is most widely used anywhere wooden construction makes contact with the ground. Various types of treatment are used to preserve lumber for construction use, including above-ground, ground contact, freshwater, or saltwater application. Pressure-treated lumber is used by code wherever wood is to be placed in or within 12 inches of the ground or in water, in contact with masonry, or when exposed to wet or damp environments. All pressure-treated lumber should bear the American Wood Preservers Bureau *AWPB* stamp. All wood treated for ground contact will be marked *For Ground Contact* and will bear a designation such as "LP-22," which means it was treated with a waterborne preservative for ground contact or freshwater submersion. For above-ground use, an "LP-2" designation indicates the wood was treated for above-ground use only. Letters other than "LP" indicate that the wood was treated with other chemicals. Single digits are used for above-ground use treatments; double digits are used for ground contact or freshwater-use treatments.

All other lumber used for permanent landscape construction should be Douglas fir or western red cedar of an appropriate grade for the specific usage as recommended by the Western Wood Products Association or comparable grading bureau. All lumber should be clean, of standard sizes as required, and free of splits, shakes, wane, or other defects. No substitutions are acceptable for all-heart redwood or pressure-treated lumber when used in ground contact or within 12 inches of the ground. All exposed nails, screws, hinges, latches, or other fasteners should be galvanized or noncorrosive metal, sized as required. Noncorrosive connectors should be used for beams, joists, rafters, and posts, sized as required. All lumber used in wood construction should be protected from the elements to prevent the wood from excessive cupping, checking, and splitting. Wood-finish products include water repellents, water- or oil-based stains and paints, and specific wood preservatives. The choice of wood-finish products depends on the degree of durability and the appearance desired. All wood finishes should be chosen based on manufacturer's recommendations for the specific application.

Fences

Wooden fences that are not treated with an acceptable wood preservative will start to decay either at the joints or at any place where moisture is held. Therefore, the life of fences built with treated lumber will be greatly increased, thus lowering the average annual cost. Wood preservatives may either be applied in the field by a worker, or you can purchase commercially treated lumber. Commercially treated lumber is usually either pressure-treated or soaked. Pressure treatment gives the best protection, around 20 to 30 years for board fences. Sometimes costs or availability prohibit the use of commercially treated lumber. When this happens, you will have to apply the preservatives on site.

To apply preservative to lumber, first select the preservative. Use creosote, penta, or copper napthenate in heavy fuel oils on fences that are not going to be painted. Use penta or copper napthenate in light oils (mineral spirits is best, kerosene is fairly satisfactory) on fences that are to be painted. These preservatives should protect the fence for 5 to 15 years. Boards should be thoroughly air-seasoned. Green lumber will not absorb enough preservative to provide long-term termite protection. Cut the lumber to the desired lengths before treating the boards with the preservative, and coat all cut ends at least twice. Treat the lumber by soaking it in a vat filled with the preservative or by flooding on the preservative with a brush. When treating lumber by dipping it in a vat, soak the boards one hour for each inch of thickness. When treating lumber by applying the preservative with a brush, apply the preservative in thick coats. If treated wood is trimmed, bored, or otherwise cut, untreated wood may be exposed. You should brush-treat the exposed area with a preservative to avoid decay. Paint by itself will not prevent decay. However, when paint is applied over treated lumber, it helps the lumber retain the preservative.

To stake out the fence line, follow this procedure: Drive a stake at each end of the proposed fence line and stretch builder's stringline between the stakes. If your fence is to have a slight curve, outline the curve with additional stakes. If your fence is to be angular, drive additional stakes at the corners. Measure off the post spacings. The spacing between the first two posts should be about 7 feet, 10 inches from post center to post center. That allows 8-foot boards to extend across the face of the end post to the center of the second post. Using 8-foot centers for the rest of the spacing, drive stakes or make a mark in the ground next to the string. If the post spacing does not come out even, shorten the post spacings from 6 to 12 inches at one end until provision is made for the last panel to be almost full length.

To install the posts, dig each hole approximately $2\frac{1}{2}$ feet deep for each 7-foot post. Fences are generally about 50 to 60 inches high. A $2\frac{1}{2}$-foot hole allows for a 54-inch fence. Adjust the depth of the hole to obtain the desired height of the post plus 1 inch. Place the post in the ground aligned to the stringline so that the flat surface faces the side where the boards will be nailed. Set the post by tamping dirt firmly around the post, checking occasionally to make sure the post is plumb. Set a line post on each major rise or depression along the fence line and extend stringline along the top of each post. Set the remaining posts so that the top edge of the post touches the stringline.

Many different designs can be followed in nailing the fascia boards to the plates. The most popular design, the straight panel, is discussed here. Running horizontal 2-by-4-inch plate boards are nailed to the posts, end to end. The materials listed reflect the amounts needed to construct two panels of either a diamond-panel or straight-paneled fence.

- Straight panel: four pieces, $1'' \times 6'' \times 16'$. If top fascia (finishing) board is used, add one more board.
- Diamond panel: three pieces, $1'' \times 6'' \times 16'$; four pieces, $1'' \times 4'' \times 10'$ for cross member
- 2 pieces, $1'' \times 4'' \times 3'5''$ vertical fascia boards
- $\frac{1}{2}$ pound 10-penny galvanized common nails

Lay out the boards along the fence line. Place the correct number of boards for each panel. (A panel of board fence is the distance between two posts.) Place a 16-foot board at the top of the first two spans for rough measurement, and mark it for sawing. The board should be even with the outer edge of the end post and extend to the center of the third post. With other line posts, measurements are taken from center to center. Saw the ends of the board and apply wood preservative generously to the freshly cut end surfaces. Nail the board to all three posts with at least two nails in each post. (Three nails are better.) Stagger nails to avoid splitting the wood. Measure the second board from the first post to the center of the second post. The second and fourth boards for a straight-panel design are only 8 feet long (one panel) at the starting point. The first and third boards are 16 feet long (two panels) at the starting point. The second board for a diamond-pattern design is only 8 feet long (one panel) at the starting point. The first and third are 16 feet long (two panels) at the starting point.

Space and nail the fascia boards. For a straight-panel fence, space the second board 10 inches from the first board. Install fascia boards with a 2-foot level to ensure plumb members. Fascia boards are used to build the overall appearance of the fence; however, a running horizontal-top fascia board can also protect and strengthen the top plate of the fence. Saw the top of the posts even with the top of boards. Bevel the top of the post slightly so it slopes toward the side where boards are attached, or, better yet, chamfer 1 inch at 45 degrees off the top of each post, on each face. Apply preservative to the top of the post. Place the top fascia board (16-foot) on top of the posts and mark for saw lines. Plan to stagger fascia board joints so that both do not come on the same post. Square and saw the ends of the boards. Nail the boards in position. The boards should overlap both the top fence board and the end of the vertical fascia board.

In fence construction, all joints should be accurately made and securely nailed. Nails should not be driven close to ends of lumber where splitting may occur. Any boards or timbers split by fasteners during construction should be replaced. Splices in beams, rails, or similar units should not be allowed except on top of a supporting member. All posts embedded below grade must be all-heart redwood or pressure-treated lumber rated for ground contact. All wood surfaces should be sealed with an appropriate wood finish product, applied per the manufacturer's specific recommendations, to adequately protect the lumber from splitting or checking. Fence rails should be all-heart redwood. Boards should be a nominal minimum thickness of 1 inch. The actual dimension should be not less than $\frac{3}{4}$ inch. Boards can be surfaced or rough.

Care should be taken when laying out a fence on or near a property line. If a fence is constructed on the property line, it becomes a "community" fence and belongs to both property owners. Any licensed builder who builds without being aware of the exact property hubs is playing litigation Russian roulette. The height of fences and screens can vary according to application, location, and local building code restrictions. The most commonly constructed property-line fence is 6 feet in height. The size of the posts in length and dimension varies depending on the height of the fence. The typical 6-foot fence should be constructed using 8-foot-long, 4-by-4-inch posts. Posts should be spaced no further than 8 feet on center. The post hole size will vary, depending on the height and dimensions of the post. Post holes for the typical 6-foot fence should be a minimum of 12 inches diameter by 24 inches deep. All posts should be installed true to horizontal and vertical alignment. Posts should be set in five-sack wet concrete mix with $\frac{3}{4}$-inch aggregate or six-sack wet concrete mix with $\frac{3}{8}$-inch aggregate. The concrete should encircle the post the full depth of the hole to above grade to allow water to drain away from the post. The bottom of the post should not be encased in concrete. Metal flashing should be installed between posts and buildings or other structures as termite protection.

Fence rails should be evenly spaced on the posts, either level or parallel to the ground, and securely fastened with appropriate fasteners. The engineering rule of thumb is never to span more than 8 feet. The bottom rail should be a minimum of 6 inches above finish grade. The fence boards should be positioned on the rails with edges plumb and tops level and secured with appropriate fasteners. Wood gates should be structurally sound, functional for the intended use, and constructed to match or be compatible with the adjacent fence or structure.

Gate posts must be all-heart redwood or pressure-treated lumber rated for ground contact. The dimensions of posts can vary, depending on the design of the gate. Posts must have the strength to support the weight of the gate and resist stress when the gate is opened and closed. Posts should be set vertical and parallel in the same manner as fence posts. Gate frames should be constructed with butt joints, using 2-by-4-inch all-heart redwood minimum. The corner joints should be reinforced with wood gussets or metal braces. To eliminate sag when the gate is hung, a diagonal wood brace should be installed between the top inside corner on the latch side and the bottom inside corner on the hinge side. A tension cable may be used as an alternative and should be attached to opposite corners of the gate frame. The gate frame should be securely attached to the gate posts with 4-inch hinges. A minimum of three hinges should be used to properly support a 5- to 6-foot-high gate. A substantial latch should be installed with appropriate fasteners to securely hold the gate closed. Most gate latches are not designed to act as a gate stop. To prevent the destruction of the latch, appropriate gate stops should be installed.

Deck construction

In choosing the grade of lumber for decks, remember that various species of wood can be used in deck construction. The understructure of a deck is typically constructed from redwood or PTDF (pressure-treated Douglas fir). All lumber, including pier posts, beams, and joists, within 12 inches of the ground must be all-heart redwood or pressure-treated lumber rated for ground contact. Redwood is the most commonly used wood for deck boards, stairs, and fascia trim. Exposed surfaces should be surfaced lumber of chosen grade.

A building permit is required in most areas for decks constructed more than 30 inches above the ground. A licensed structural engineer may be required to design the structural portion of the deck. Support piers should be laid out to provide proper and adequate support for the deck structure, with correct spacing and alignment for the deck design. Pier spacing should be a maximum of 4 feet for 4-by-4-inch beams and 6 feet for 4-by-6-inch beams on edge. Deck design, soil type, and local codes determine the necessary type of pier construction. Pier holes should be a minimum of 12 inches in diameter by 12 inches deep and filled with wet concrete mix. If pier blocks are to be used, a standard concrete pier block should be set on the wet concrete true to line and level. The top of the pier block should be a minimum of 6 inches above grade to allow for proper clearance between wood and soil.

The soil excavated from the pier holes should be removed from the area or spread out evenly so as to not interfere with proper and adequate drainage under the deck. The area must be graded to allow water to drain away from the deck area or into a designed drainage system. All-heart redwood, adequately sized to support the deck structure, should be used for pier posts.

To support decks constructed close to ground level, 4-by-4-inch posts are normally used. Pier posts should be securely attached to the pier blocks or concrete footing with appropriate connectors.

To minimize swaying and lateral movement, cross bracing should be used where pier posts are 4 feet or higher. Material that is 2 by 4 inches or 2 by 6 inches is generally used, nailed to the lower portion of one post and the upper portion of an adjacent post. The bracing pattern varies, depending on the design of the deck and local building code requirements.

Two types of beam construction can be used: double beam, with 2-inch-thick boards nailed to each side of the pier posts, or single beam, with a 4-inch-thick board nailed to the top of the pier post. The size and spacing of beams should be determined prior to construction of the piers and pier post installation. The distance between beams is determined by joist size and spacing.

Joists are used to support the deck flooring. The size of the joists depends on the spacing of the support beams. The spacing of joists is determined by the structural strength of the deck boards. To avoid spring in the deck boards, 2-inch-thick redwood should be supported at a maximum distance of 30 inches, and 1-inch-thick boards should be supported at a maximum distance of every 12 inches. A 2-by-6-inch Douglas fir board placed on edge can span 6 feet without spring or deflection. Joists can be placed on top of or hung between beams depending on the design of the deck

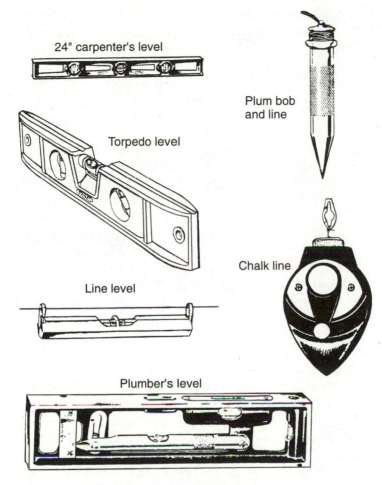

24" carpenter's level

Plum bob
and line

Torpedo level

Line level

Chalk line

Plumber's level

7-2 *Levels, plumb bob, and chalk line.*

structure and should be securely attached to the beams with appropriate connectors. Installation requires the tools shown in Figure 7-2.

Deck joists should be supported laterally with blocking at regular intervals. A board nailed between the joists on the top of the beam is one acceptable method of blocking. A ledger board is used to support the ends of the joists in place of a beam when a deck is attached to a building and the joists can run perpendicular to a wall. The ledger board should be set at an elevation low enough below doors so that water cannot run into the structure when the deck flooring is in place. Boards 2 inches thick by the width of the beams are usually used for ledgers. Flashing should be installed between the ledger board and the structure or a formed piece of flashing placed on top of the ledger board to provide moisture protection. Ledger boards should be bolted to a joist or beam behind the wall surface at the same elevation as the beams, using ⅜-inch lag bolts every 2 feet. Bolts should penetrate the support approximately two-thirds of its depth.

Deck boards should be installed with joints over support beams or joists. Boards should be laid with a maximum ⅛-inch space between adjacent boards. Wet lumber should be spaced closer, or tight, to allow for shrinkage. Boards should be securely nailed with two 16-penny galvanized common nails at each joint or end and at each supporting member. A trim board or fascia should be installed on the exposed edges of the deck to conceal beam and joist ends. The position of the trim or fascia should be determined by the design and layout of the beams and joists. The trim board can be nailed under the deck boards, allowing for a slight cantilever (1 inch) of the deck boards or can be nailed to the deck boards flush with the finish surface. Blocking should be installed to prevent warping or twisting of the trim boards. Flashing should be installed for termite protection at all points of contact to the structure, including beams, joists, ledger boards, deck boards, handrails or guardrails, and wooden planters attached to a structure.

When required, stairs and handrails should be constructed to be compatible with the deck design and constructed in compliance with local building code requirements. Depending on the elevation of the deck, guardrails may or may not be required. Section 1711 of the Uniform Building Code requires guardrails be installed on all decks that are more than 30 inches above grade. Guardrails should be 42 inches minimum height for nonresidential properties and 36 inches minimum height for residential properties. Guardrails should be constructed with intermediate rails or vertical elements spaced so a 6-inch sphere cannot pass through the opening. Guardrails should be compatible with the deck design and constructed in compliance with local building code requirements. Regarding deck stairs, all-heart redwood and pressure-treated lumber rated for ground contact are the only acceptable lumbers to be used in the construction of wood stairs that are constructed on or near the ground. Stairs should be supported at the lower end on a concrete slab or curb or, if free-standing, on concrete pier blocks. The upper end of stairs should be attached to another structure or supported on pier blocks. The maximum spacing between supports is 6 feet.

Stringers should be 2-by-12-inch lumber and should be securely nailed or bolted to the pier posts. Stairs up to 36 inches in width can be supported with one pair of stringers. Stairs exceeding 36 inches in width require additional stringers, evenly spaced. The riser-to-tread ratio is based on the height of risers, which should be not less than 4 inches nor greater than 7 inches and should not vary more than $\frac{3}{8}$ inch in any given run of stairs. The width of treads should be not less than 11 inches and should not vary more than $\frac{3}{8}$ inch in any given run of stairs. In the Uniform Building Code, a private residential exception allows for 8-inch maximum riser height and 9-inch minimum tread width. For easy ascent, a 6-inch riser is recommended. Normal riser-tread ratios can be arrived at by using the following formula: Two times the riser plus tread equals 26 inches, plus or minus. Open or closed risers may be used in the construction of stairs. Tread boards should be all-heart redwood, 2 inches thick by desired width, securely fastened to the stringers with galvanized nails.

On residential property, stairways having four or more risers are required to have a handrail. Handrails should be constructed similar to guardrails with the following exceptions. Handrails should be not less than 30 inches or more than 34 inches above the nosing of the stair tread. Handrails should be installed the full length of the stairs and should extend at least 6 inches beyond the top and bottom risers. The handgrip portion of the handrail should be 2 inches in width, should have a smooth surface, and when mounted on a wall should be a minimum of $1\frac{1}{4}$ inches from the wall.

For any deck to be properly built to exact elevations to match a building, you must also use a transit or builder's level, which brings us to the next section.

Using a builder's level

To set up and adjust a builder's level, we start with the mounting tripod. Set the leg shoes of the two nearest tripod legs in the ground about 3 feet apart. Swing the third leg out away from you to form a triangle, placing the legs on the ground so that the head plate is nearly level to the horizon. If the ground is not level, you may have to change the position of the tripod to keep the head plate level. In this case, always place two tripod legs on the downhill or uneven side. Hand-tighten the leg thumb nuts; do not overtighten. Recheck the tripod's head plate to assure that it is level with the horizon. Remove the level from its carrying case by lifting the level bar. Never grasp the telescope barrel while removing the instrument from the carrying case. Attach the level to the tripod. Keep a firm grip on the instrument until it is securely in position on tripod. Remove the dust cap from the lens and place the cap in the carrying case. Between uses, keep the dust cap in place to protect the lens from dust or scratches. Attach the sunshade to the instrument if it is not a permanent attachment.

Align the telescope barrel directly over one pair of leveling screws. The leveling screws are used just as their name indicates: to level the instrument. Firm up but do not overtighten the leveling screws, because doing so will warp the head plate. Rotate the leveling screws by moving your thumbs in opposite directions until the bubble is centered in the level vial. Turn the instrument clockwise 90 degrees to align the barrel over the other pair of leveling screws. Rotate those leveling screws by moving your thumbs in opposite directions until the bubble is centered in the level vial. Turn the instrument clockwise 90 degrees to bring it parallel with the first pair of leveling screws, and then center the bubble again. Turn the instrument clockwise 90 degrees to bring it parallel with the second pair of leveling screws, and center the bubble again. This process may have to be repeated several times for the bubble to stay in the center regardless of the direction the telescope is pointing. If the bubble does not stay in center, the instrument is out of level and must be readjusted until right. Avoid touching the tripod after the instrument is level. If the instrument creeps off level or is bumped during use, stop and reset the tripod, relevel the instrument, and start again from the last known good benchmark.

To shoot elevations, turn the eyepiece focusing ring until the cross hairs appear clear and sharp. The target may not be in focus, but you should be able to focus the cross hairs using the eyepiece focusing ring. Then rotate the objective focusing screw to bring the target into sharp focus. When both the cross hairs and the target are in sharp focus, you should be able to read the rod accurately. Read the number closest to the intersection and note it on a layout sheet in its relative position. Mathematical differences between different sightings (shots) are the height elevations relative to the instrument. When finished with noting all shots, replace the instrument's lens dust cap, remove the instrument from the tripod, and replace the level in its carrying case. Store the tripod and the builder's level (in its case) in your vehicle, not on the job site where it can get ruined due to someone's carelessness. A builder's level and related site layout tools are shown in Figure 7-3.

Benches

Benches can be constructed as part of a wood deck, in a concrete or masonry patio, or free-standing in the landscape. Each application requires different methods of post support. Posts should be all-heart redwood. The bench seat should be a minimum of construction heart redwood or equivalent grade of lumber. All trim should be the same grade as the bench seat. Posts should be of suf-

Hand level

Builder's level

Rod

Plumb bob

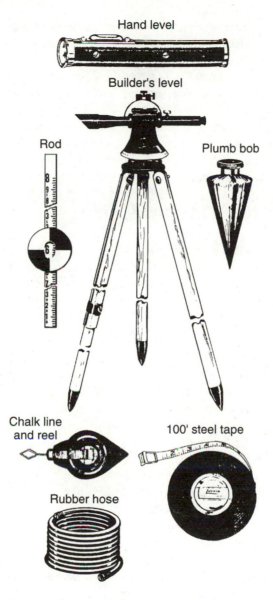

Chalk line
and reel

100' steel tape

Rubber hose

7-3 *Site layout and measuring tools.*

ficient size to support the bench and properly spaced to prevent any sag of the bench seat. On a deck, the bench posts should extend through the deck flooring to the bottom of the deck support structure. The posts should be attached securely to the beams, joists, and blocking as needed.

On a masonry patio, the bench posts should be set in 12-inch-diameter-by-24-inch-deep holes filled with concrete. To avoid the possibility of decay, wood posts can be set on heavy-duty metal post anchors embedded in the concrete pier hole, or galvanized metal pipe or tubing posts can be used. For a free-standing bench, posts should be set in 12-inch-diameter-by-36-inch-deep concrete-filled holes. Two bench-seat supports of sufficient size to support the bench should be bolted to the posts. The bench seat can be prefabricated or built in place. The seat should be constructed of 2-inch-thick material of an appropriate grade and surface finish. The understructure of the bench should be concealed with appropriate trim or fascia, using material to match the bench.

Planter boxes

Planter boxes should be constructed with the same methods used for low retaining walls and benches. All planter boxes should be provided with adequate drainage. Use only rated construction heart redwood or pressure-treated lumber rated for ground contact, sized as required.

Arbors

Free-standing or attached, arbors can provide both decorative and functional elements in the landscape. The design of an arbor and local building code requirements determine the type and dimensions of lumber used. Since arbors are considered a structure, most building departments require a permit for construction. In choosing the wood, remember lumber in contact with the ground should be all-heart redwood or pressure-treated lumber rated for ground contact. Structural-grade redwood, Douglas fir, or other approved species may be used for beams, rafters, and top boards. Lumber may be surfaced, rough, or a combination of both.

Arbors should be carefully laid out to properly locate the support posts. Free-standing arbors should have shear support in two directions. Attached arbors should be firmly anchored to a ledger board bolted to a stable structure. Ledger boards should be installed in the same manner as deck ledgers. All posts should be truly vertical and equally spaced. Sizing and spacing of the posts vary, depending on the design, size, and spacing of the beams. Post size should be a minimum of 4 by 4 inches, spaced not more than 8 feet apart. Depending on the design, arbor posts may be set in concrete or installed on top of a concrete slab or foundation pad with appropriate metal post anchors and adequate shear support (the recommended method) or attached to the support structure of a wood deck. Post holes for posts set in the ground should be a minimum of 12 inches in diameter and a minimum of 48 inches deep for an 8-foot-high arbor. Concrete should not enclose the bottom of the post.

The dimensions of arbor beams vary, depending on the design, type of construction, spacing of support posts, and the weight of the lumber to be supported. In a single-beam structure, a single beam (usually 4 by 6 inches to 4 by 12 inches) is set on top of the posts and securely anchored to the posts, using appropriate connectors. In a dual-beam structure, two beams (usually 2 by 6 inches to 2 by 12 inches) are used, one attached on each side of the posts and securely bolted together through the posts. Double beams should be blocked at the midpoint of each span. The dimensions of arbor rafters vary, depending on the spacing of the beams and the size of the top boards, if any. Rafters should be spaced 4 feet on center when using 2-by-4-inch lumber on edge and 6 feet on center when using 2-by-6-inch lumber on edge. Rafters may be installed with closer spacing, depending on the design, particularly when top boards are not used. Rafters should be nailed to each beam, and any necessary joining should be made only over a beam. Various depths of shade can be created when top boards are installed on an arbor. The lumber commonly used is 2 by 2 inches. The spacing of the top boards depends on the density of shade desired. Depending on the exposure, a 2-inch spacing between boards provides moderate shade. All top boards should be securely nailed to each rafter.

In using headers to form walkways, all stakes should be 1-by-2-inch construction heart redwood, 12 to 18 inches long. In layout, all headers should be laid true to line and grade. For straight headers, headers should be 2-by-4-inch lumber, laid on edge. Material can be surfaced or rough finish. Stakes should be spaced 4 feet on center maximum, with two at each joint, and securely nailed to the header with galvanized nails. For headers with a slight curve, two 1-by-4-inch boards should be tightly laminated, with joints staggered a minimum of 48 inches apart. Stakes should be spaced 3 feet on center maximum and at each joint and securely nailed to the header with galvanized nails. For headers with a strong curve, four or more $\frac{3}{8}$-by-4-inch boards should be tightly laminated, with joints staggered a minimum of 48 inches apart. Laminations should be nailed a minimum of 12 inches on center. Stakes should be spaced a minimum of 3 feet on center and at each joint and securely nailed to the header with galvanized nails.

For repair work in maintaining facilities, you need concrete demolition tools and pipe rethreading tools, such as those shown in Figures 7-4 through 7-6.

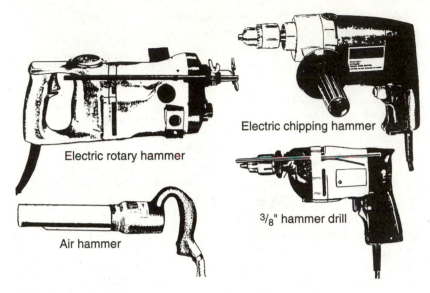

Electric rotary hammer

Electric chipping hammer

Air hammer

$3/8$" hammer drill

7-4 *Concrete tools.*

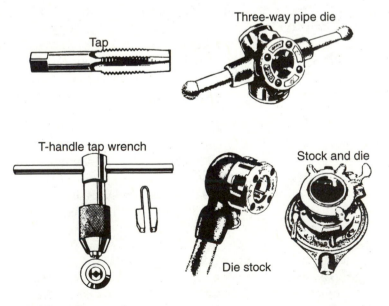

Tap

Three-way pipe die

T-handle tap wrench

Stock and die

Die stock

7-5 *Threading tools.*

Flaring tool and block

Bending spring

Swage punch

Lever-type bender

Geared ratchet-type bender

Tube reamer
and cutter

Reamer blade

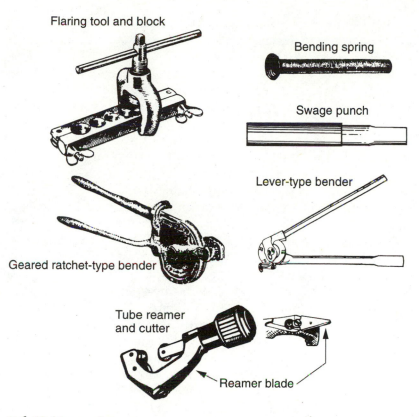

7-6 *Tubing tools.*

Retaining walls

In lot development for homes on uneven contoured land, retaining
walls are a common part of site work. Materials used for retaining walls
may be wood or concrete. Local codes may restrict the height of a retaining wall without an engineer's drawing. Railroad ties are often used
to give an informal, rustic effect to the landscape. The ties should be
straight, not excessively split, and not too heavily coated with creosote.
Layers are tied together (above and below) with large spikes. Deadmen
are used to stabilize the wall and prevent collapse. Drainfields are installed behind the wall to relieve hydrostatic pressure of wet soil. Landscape timbers or treated posts also give an informal effect to the
landscape, but they are less rustic than railroad ties. They can be used
like railroad ties, except that they are lighter and weaker than railroad
ties but cleaner to use.

All lumber used to construct retaining walls should be all-heart
redwood or pressure-treated lumber rated for ground contact.

Lumber can be surfaced or have a rough finish. Dimensions of posts and boards used in the construction of wood retaining walls vary, depending on the soil type and surcharge on the wall. Wood retaining walls exceeding 36 inches in height should be designed by a licensed structural engineer. Wood retaining walls exceeding 48 inches in height *must* be designed by a licensed structural engineer. Post holes should be a minimum of 12 inches in diameter and a minimum of 42 inches deep for a 36-inch-high wall. Walls up to a height of 36 inches usually require a minimum of 4-by-4-inch posts set in concrete, spaced a maximum of 4 feet on center. Concrete should not encase the post at the bottom of the hole.

A minimum of 2-inch-thick lumber should be used for walls up to 36 inches in height. Boards should be installed on the earth side of the posts and nailed with galvanized nails. If boards are placed on the front side of the posts, each board should be secured to the posts with two galvanized bolts and appropriate washers. Wall caps are usually constructed of the same species of wood as the wall. To avoid cupping of the cap boards, two or three $\frac{1}{4}$-inch-deep cuts should be made the length of the underside of the cap. All walls should be relieved of hydrostatic pressure. This relief should be accomplished by one of the following methods. Weep holes a minimum of 1 inch in diameter can be drilled at the bottom of wall boards every 4 feet. One cubic foot of $\frac{3}{4}$-inch drain rock should be placed behind each hole. Perforated drain pipe, encased in drain rock and filter fabric, should be placed at the bottom of the backside of the wall to create a drainfield. Retaining-wall boards can be attached to the posts with plus or minus $\frac{1}{2}$-inch spacings between the boards and the wall backfilled with drain rock. This can be done in conjunction with the installation of the perforated drainpipe.

Figure 7-7 shows an engineered retaining wall made from CMU concrete blocks. This wall will serve a 4- to 6-foot retention of light- to medium-density soil. The drainfield must be installed to avoid overload pressure of liquefied soil during rainy periods, which can cause wall failure. Before pouring, install all #4 horizontal and #4 vertical rebar as shown. Grout all cells with minimum 2000-psi concrete. Hold back rebar a minimum of 3 inches from any cell edge.

Embedment soil must have a *low plasticity index*. That's fancy engineering jargon for no expansive soils, such as clay, under the wall. Check local codes. If a permit is needed, these are the engineering specs you need to provide for the wall:

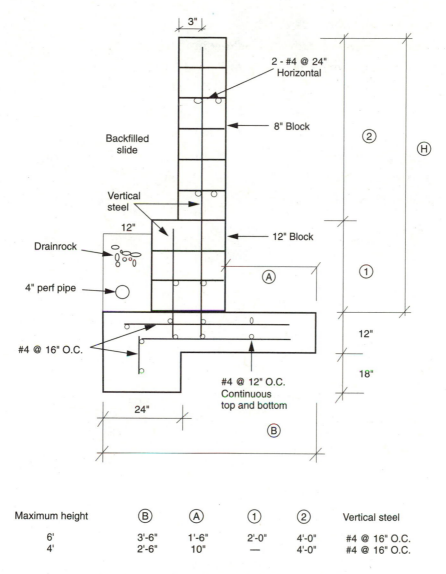

Maximum height	Ⓑ	Ⓐ	①	②	Vertical steel
6'	3'-6"	1'-6"	2'-0"	4'-0"	#4 @ 16" O.C.
4'	2'-6"	10"	—	4'-0"	#4 @ 16" O.C.

Material specs: Concrete block, Grade N - grouted solid.
Concrete: Fc = 2500 psi. Rebar: Grade 40 - All lap splices minimum 24".

7-7 *Retaining wall details.*

Design 6-foot-high retaining wall: EFW = 45 PCF

$H = 45 \quad (6)/2 = 810 \text{ lb}$

$M_C \text{ Stem} = 45 \quad (6)/6 = 1620 \text{ ft-lb}$

M_A = 810 [6/3 + 1] = 2430 ft-lb

Check overturning	Arm (ft)	Moment (ft-lb)
W_1 = 100 (1.33)(4) = 532	2.83	1506
W_2 = 100 (1)(2) = 200	3.00	600
W_3 = 92 (4) = 368	1.83	673
W_4 = 140 (2) = 280	2.00	560
W_5 = 150 (1)(3.5) = 525	1.75	919
W_6 = 150 (1)(1) = 532	3.00	450
2055		4708

S.F. = $\dfrac{4708}{2430}$ = 1.94 > 1.5 OK per code

Check sliding

Friction = .35 (2055) = 719

Key = 300 $(2)^3$/2 = 600

1319 lb

S.F. = $\dfrac{1319}{810}$ = 1.63 > 1.5 OK per code

Check soil pressure

X = $\dfrac{4708}{2055}$ = 2.29 ft

A = $\dfrac{2430}{2055}$ = 1.18

B = 2.29 - 1.18 = 1.11 ft outside middle third

P soil = $\dfrac{2055 (2)}{3 (1.11)}$ = 1234 Psf < 1500 OK per code

    These are the specs for a standard CMU block wall with solid grouted cells, code-spec rebar sizing and placement, and keyway footing. They are all over the nation, in your city, and in your neighborhood. I've built a hundred of them by now. However, if your local building department makes you recalculate these specs, don't blame me. The state gave me a license.

8

Drainage

Drainage refers to the movement of water over the ground and through the soil in a plant's root area. When water moves too quickly on the surface, erosion of topsoil results. However, when this movement occurs in the plant's root area, the drainage does not collect to the point of saturation, which causes root rot, and the soil is referred to as "well drained." For plants to grow, water must pass through the soil and not be retained for a long duration. Plant roots need oxygen as well as water, and soil that remains saturated deprives roots of necessary oxygen. Fast drainage (water disappears from a planting hole in 10 minutes or less) is typical of sandy soils; slow drainage (water still remains in planting hole after several hours) is found in clay soils and where hardpan exists. Water movement is subject to natural hydraulic principles, as shown in Figure 8-1.

Surface drainage

Methods for controlling surface drainage alter the contour of the ground to divert water away from depressions. Changing the contour is done by creating drainage channels that use gravity to channel water to natural outlets before it reaches the depressions. We can also create drainage channels that provide a path through which water can flow out of the depressions. On a flat terrain or where water can't flow to a natural outlet, channel water to an area above or below ground where it can be pumped away. Modify soil components to encourage vertical percolation (drainage) through the soil. (This process may involve removing the natural topsoil to a depth of 1 to 2 feet and replacing it with a mixture of sand, soil, and peat to provide a growth medium for turf, resist compaction, and permit rapid natural vertical percolation of the water. This system must be coupled with a subsurface drainage system to be effective.)

233

Static water presssure - defined

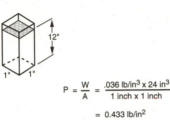

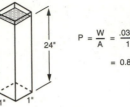

$$P = \frac{W}{A} = \frac{.036 \text{ lb/in}^3 \times 24 \text{ in}^3}{1 \text{ inch} \times 1 \text{ inch}}$$

$$= 0.866 \text{ psi}$$

$$P = \frac{W}{A} = \frac{.036 \text{ lb/in}^3 \times 24 \text{ in}^3}{1 \text{ inch} \times 1 \text{ inch}}$$

$$= 0.433 \text{ lb/in}^2$$

$$= 0.433 \text{ psi}$$

where:

W = weight of water in column
A = area at bottom of column supporting water

Elevation is the major influence on static water pressure. Thus, one foot of elevation change is equated to 0.43 psi pressure change, or one psi is equated to 2.31 feet of elevation change.

Static water pressure calculations

Water source

100 psi

50' 100'

Control valve
121.6 psi (static)

Example 1: In the illustration above, the water source is above the control valve. The static water pressure is calculated as:

100 psi + (50' x .443 psi per foot)
= (100 + 21.6) = 121.6 = 121.6 psi static

100' 50'

Control valve
78.4 psi (static)

Water source

100 psi

Example 2: In the illustration above, the water source is above the control valve. The static water pressure is calculated as:

100 psi + (50' x .443 psi per foot)
= (100 + 21.6) = 78.4 psi static

Working water pressure calculations
Example 1
Water source: 60 psi

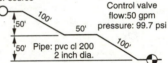

Water source

100'
50'
50'

Control valve
flow:50 gpm
pressure: 99.7 psi

50' Pipe: pvc cl 200
2 inch dia.
100'

Working water pressure = 60 psi (source) +
(100' x .433 psi/ft.) − (250' x 1.44 psi/100')
= (60 + 43.3 − 3.6) = 99.7 psi (working)

Example 2
Water source: 60 psi

Working water pressure = 60 psi (source) +
(100' x .433 psi/ft.) − (250' x 1.44 psi/100')
= (60 + 43.3 − 3.6) = 13.1 psi (working)

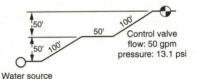

50'
50' 100'
50'
100'

Control valve
flow: 50 gpm
pressure: 13.1 psi

Water source

8-1 *Hydraulic principles and applications.*

Subsurface drainage

The factors affecting types of subsurface drainage systems are arrangement of the drains, slope, and terrain. The types of subsurface drainage systems are

- *Random drain*, which is used to drain several locations in an otherwise well-drained area.
- *Gridiron system*, which is used to drain areas with a uniform slope.

- *Herringbone system*, which is used to drain swale areas.
- *Interceptor drain*, which is used to drain areas wet by hillside seepage.

These systems are shown in Figure 8-2.

The parts of a subsurface drain are the inlet, drain pipe, and the outlet. The inlet must be constructed of durable material such as brick, stone, PVC plastic, concrete, sewer tile, or metal pipe, and water must enter freely. Protective grating must be placed over the inlet to allow water in but keep large objects out. The inlet must be at a higher elevation than the outlet. Drain pipe can be made from concrete tile, clay tile, PVC pipe, or corrugated plastic tubing. Water must flow out freely, and the outlet must be maintained frequently to check for broken or crushed pipe, deterioration due to freezing or thawing, displacement of tiles, or erosion of soil from the outlet. Soil textures and their related water intake and holding rates follow:

Table 8-1.

Soil texture	Water intake rate	Holding rate
Sandy soils:		
Coarse	High	Low
Loamy soils:		
Medium	Medium	High to medium
Clay soils:		
Fine	Low	High

Curtain drains and catch basins

Surface drainage systems use the contouring of the ground to direct the flow of water as sheet drainage or into swales. Provisions should be made for the best available routing of surface water to ensure that buildings or other site improvements are not endangered by runoff. Drainage swales should not carry runoff across walks in a quantity that makes the walks unfit for use. Walks should never be used as drainage swales. Drainage swales should receive a protective lining as required and whenever the concentration of runoff could cause erosion. Swales in lawn areas should be graded at a minimum of 2-percent slope for surface runoff drainage.

Subsurface drainage systems include the use of gravel-filled trenches, which may or may not contain perforated pipe, to intercept, collect, and direct subsurface water flow. French drains should be dug with a bottom slope of 1 percent minimum and should be limited to not

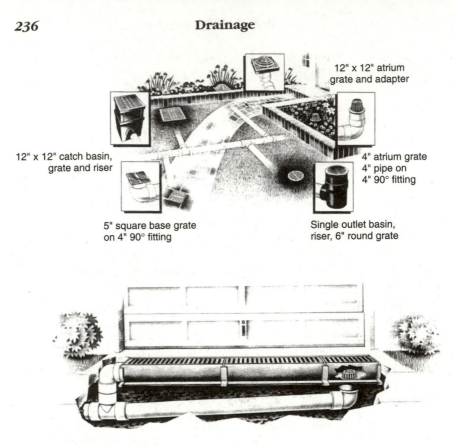

12" x 12" atrium
grate and adapter

12" x 12" catch basin,
grate and riser

4" atrium grate
4" pipe on
4" 90° fitting

5" square base grate
on 4" 90° fitting

Single outlet basin,
riser, 6" round grate

8-2 *Types of drainage systems.*

more than 50 feet in length. Drain rock should be large and irregular to provide adequate space for water flow.

A curtain drain is a trench filled with drain rock designed to intercept and divert the site's ambient groundwater with surface discharge via piping to another location. Curtain drains contain center-conductive pipes; French drains do not. Curtain drains are typically used to dewater areas upslope of a leachfield or a foundation and lower the water table. Cut a trench around the area to be dewatered and then backfill with clean, washed drain rock. Install clean, graded, washed drain rock around and under the pipe as well, to provide support and maintain a consistent invert (flow) line. Rock that is ¾ inch in diameter or bigger is recommended to provide large, irregular surface gaps within the rock field, providing good water flow. Install a 4-inch center-conductive perforated PVC pipe at the bottom of the drain field to provide flowline passage of water discharge. Envelop the drain rock with an approved soil filter fabric. Rock is also typically placed at the outfall to provide energy dissipation and lessen soil erosion during times of stormy weather. Cover the trench, filled with drain rock and a center-conductive pipeline, with nontreated building paper to provide a contamination barrier between the backfill soil and the drainfield. Backfill and grade a foot of native soil over the curtain drain.

Join pipe above ground or in place, in accordance with the manufacturer's recommendations for the specific type of pipe used. Do not move pipe and fittings after joining until properly cured or cooled and in accordance with the pipe manufacturer's tables for time delay between joining and use. Lay pipe with a minimum 1-percent slope, unless otherwise indicated on the approved plans. Lay perforated pipe with the perforations down. Types of inlet and outlet styles are shown in Figure 8-3.

Catch basins are used to act as collection points for surface runoff water. Adjust the final grade adjacent to drainage structures to provide positive slopes into catch basins without any standing water. The trick here is to make sure the sediment area in the bottom of the catch basin is cleaned annually, *before* the rains hit.

On completion of the site's drainage system, flush all pipes and drainage structures to make sure there is no buildup of dirt or debris. Check for a positive flow of water at the discharge point. A typical installation of a drainage system is for use behind a retaining wall to relieve hydrostatic pressure and prevent wall failure.

Septic systems

If your project involves underground piping around, repairs to, or landscaping to a septic system, you need to know the workings of the system. An individual sewage disposal system is not hooked up to a street main but rather provides for the disposal of sewage in a manner that does not create a public health hazard and does not degrade surface or local groundwater quality. Your landscape irrigation or piping may interfere with the system, so you must be aware of how a septic system works in the native landscape environment.

All sewage disposal systems, both existing and new, and all parts thereof must be maintained in a safe and sanitary condition at all times. The owner, lessee, occupant, user, or his or her designated agent is responsible for the maintenance of such systems. Where permitted, an individual sewage disposal system must be provided for each building designed for human habitation. The only exception is that a group of detached buildings designed for habitation, occupying land in one ownership and having a yard or court in common, may be serviced by a single individual sewage disposal system. Typically, septic systems are prohibited within 100 feet of potable wells.

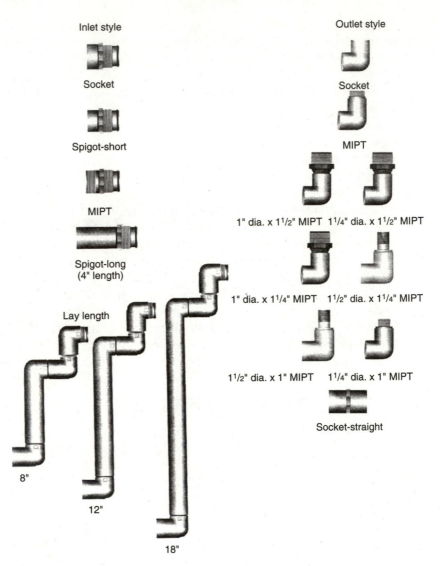

Inlet style

Socket

Spigot-short

MIPT

Spigot-long
(4" length)

Lay length

8"

12"

18"

Outlet style

Socket

Socket

MIPT

1" dia. x 1¹/₂" MIPT   1¹/₄" dia. x 1¹/₂" MIPT

1" dia. x 1¹/₄" MIPT   1¹/₂" dia. x 1¹/₄" MIPT

1¹/₂" dia. x 1" MIPT   1¹/₄" dia. x 1" MIPT

Socket-straight

8-3 *Inlet and outlet pipe joints.*

The building lot site is considered to be the parcel or parcels upon which an individual sewage disposal system is installed or is proposed to be installed, the size of which is total horizontal area included within the property lines of the site, excluding any rights-of-way for vehicular access. The installation, major repair, alteration, enlargement, improvement, or relocation of an individual sewage disposal system means a septic tank and drainfield or other approved means of sanitary disposal of sewage, including an alternative system or haul-away system. This may include any of the following types of systems:

- *Conventional system.* An individual sewage disposal system that uses a septic tank (with or without a sump or pump) and leaching trenches or pits.
- *Standard system.* A conventional system that is constructed in accordance with all sections of local code ordinances.
- *Nonconforming sewage disposal system.* A conventional sewage disposal system design that provides for insufficient leaching area as described in local code ordinances, that is in soils that percolate in the range 60 to 120 MPI or that requires seasonal haul-away of effluent. Use of a nonconforming system requires the use of water-conservation devices.
- *Alternative system.* An individual sewage disposal system that is not a standard system or a haul-away system.
- *Haul-away system.* An existing individual sewage disposal system for which the local health officer has ordered that the outlet of the septic tank or other sewage-holding container be permanently or seasonally sealed and the accumulated sewage pumped out and hauled away to an approved disposal site.

The septic tank size usually required for residences of from one to four bedrooms is 1500 gallons. An additional 250 gallons per bedroom is typically required for each bedroom in excess of four. Septic tanks have at least two compartments separated by a baffle or equivalent arrangement. The inlet compartment has a capacity of not less than two-thirds the total volume and is the big chamber that goes toward the house, as shown in Figure 8-4. The basic tank and system design is shown in Figures 8-5 and 8-6.

Access to each compartment is provided by a manhole approximately 20 inches in minimum dimensions with a close-fitting manhole cover equipped with a durable handle to facilitate removal. Septic tanks should be installed so that manhole covers are within 12 inches of the ground surface. If the top of a septic tank is deeper than 12 inches from the ground surface, the tank must be modified to extend the manholes and covers to within 12 inches of the surface. Material used to extend the manhole covers should be of the same material as the septic tank. A cleanout to finished grade must be provided between the house and the septic tank. Monitor risers that extend from each manhole cover to the surface of the ground so as to facilitate inspection and maintenance of the septic tank are currently required just about everywhere. These risers need to be of larger size than the manhole cover and constructed of durable material. Heart-grade redwood, PTDF (Pressure-Treated Douglas Fir), or an equivalent material is usually acceptable.

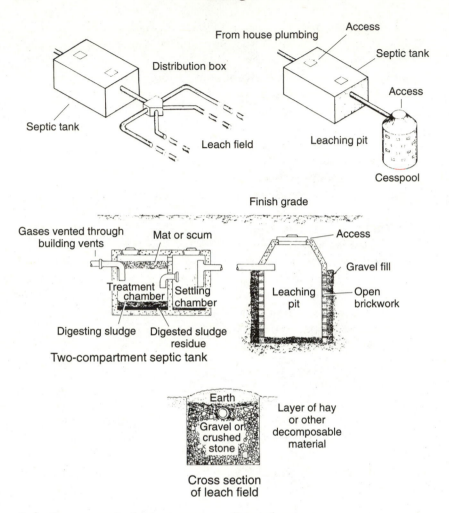

8-4 *Components of private sewage-disposal systems.*

Septic tanks are made of reinforced concrete, standard-weight reinforced concrete blocks, or approved noncorrodible synthetic materials. Metal septic tanks are no longer permitted in most states. Interior surfaces of concrete tanks must be coated with a bituminous or similar compound to minimize corrosion. Reinforced concrete and reinforced concrete block septic tanks are constructed with #3 ($\frac{3}{8}$-inch) steel reinforcing bars placed 16 inches on center vertically and 20 inches on center horizontally with all cells grouted. Concrete septic tank covers must also be reinforced.

Effluent flows from the septic tank via a *tightline* (so called because it is nonperforated) to leaching fields filled with drain rock. These may be either drilled holes or trenches. Soil suitability for leach

fields is determined by a combination of percolation test results, ex-
ploratory excavation soil logs, and soil structural and textural characteristics. Laboratory analyses of soil texture may be required by the
local health department. Percolation rate alone does not determine
soil suitability. Soil texture determines soil suitability where percolation test results are unclear or nonrepresentative. Soils with a clay
content of greater than 40 percent by weight are typically unsuitable
for conventional sewage-leaching devices. Leaching trenches are
18 inches to 36 inches in width, contain a perforated sewage conductor pipe, and are filled with permeable drainrock. The trench
depth required is dependent on soil conditions, and the trench length
required is dependent on sewage loading. Leach field trenches must
be placed in natural earth and in an unobstructed, not-to-be-
constructed-upon area.

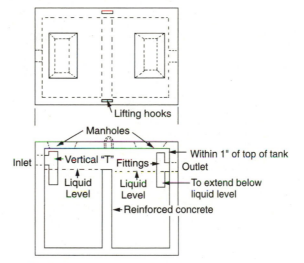

Typical precast concrete tank
3000 lbs. minimum strength concrete

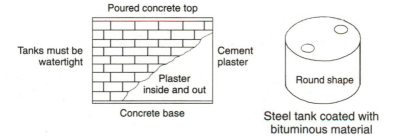

8-5 *Septic tank construction methods and materials.*

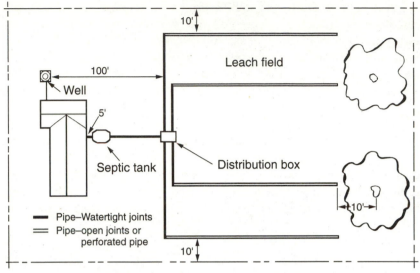

Typical layout for a private waste disposal system

8-6 *Basic design of a septic system.*

Leaching Area Requirements
(in average square feet).

Perc rate (minutes per inch)	1-5	6-30	31-60
One bedroom	500	600	900
Two bedrooms	625	750	1125
Three bedrooms	750	900	1350
Four bedrooms	875	1050	1575
Additional bedrooms	125 ea.	150 ea.	225 ea.

The effective leaching of a leach field is the total of the area of the bottom area and the sidewall area beneath the leach pipe. The minimum separation between the bottom of a leaching device and seasonally high groundwater for a minimum of 90 percent of the year is typically 5 feet where the leaching device is between 50 and 100 feet from a water body, 3 feet where the device is between 100 and 150 feet from a water body, and 1 foot where the device is more than 150 feet from a waterbody. Setback to a stream averages at least 50 feet, and setback to a seasonal drainage way averages 25 feet. If soils are at least 7 feet deep and conditions are otherwise suitable to prevent lateral surfacing of effluent, installation on steeper slopes, above 30 percent up to 50 percent, may be allowed if the distribution pipe is installed at least 2 feet below the surface (vertical depth) and a minimum separation of 5 feet is maintained between the leaching system and bedrock or other impermeable layer. Figure 8-7 shows how these factors affect contamination of water supplies.

Soil percolation tests are normally required prior to approval of a permit for a disposal system to serve new development. Percolation tests are performed by a registered civil engineer, a registered environmental health specialist, a licensed septic tank contractor who has a contract to install the individual sewage disposal system, a general engineering contractor, a registered geologist, or a soils scientist. Such tests are usually witnessed by the local health department inspector, who determines the number and location of percolation test borings. Percolation test procedures are established by policy of the local health department through the building permit process. For the soils where the leach trench is proposed, the minimum acceptable percolation rate is 60 minutes per inch (1 inch per hour). The maximum acceptable percolation rate is one minute per inch (60 inches per hour). For soils beneath the leaching device, the minimum acceptable percolation rate is 60 minutes per inch in the first 3 feet below the trench and 120 minutes per inch ($\frac{1}{2}$ inch per hour) from 3 to 10 feet below the trench.

When required by the local health officer (based on geomorphical and historical information), observation for seasonal high-water

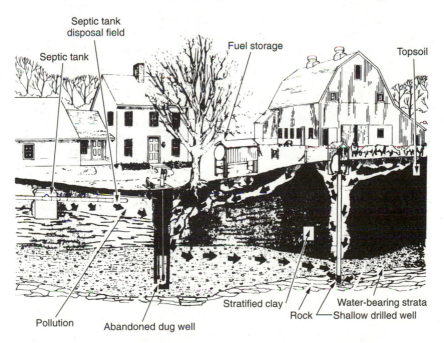

8-7 *Contamination of water supplies.*

tables may be required during the rainy season to check the cumulative rainfall. If the health officer expects the soils to have a percolation rate slower than 60 minutes per inch (1 inch per hour) or have a shrink-swell potential (due to high clay content, generally over 30-percent clay), the health officer may require perc tests during the time period for winter water-table observation. Any dispute over shrink-swell potential may be resolved by a soil texture (hydrometer method) and bulk density analysis. One or more soil excavations may have to be performed for each individual sewage disposal system to demonstrate the suitability of soil conditions. When effluent leaching trenches are to be used, the excavation should be made by a backhoe whenever possible and should extend to at least 10 feet below the bottom of the proposed trench leaching device.

Usually a required area equal to the amount of area necessary to install the leaching system must be kept available for future expansion and repair of the leaching system. No construction of buildings, sheds, permanent swimming pools, driveways, parking areas, or other permanent structures are permitted over the expansion area. For new development on previously undeveloped parcels, with soils that percolate in the range of 31 to 60 minutes per inch, the expansion system is installed at the time the primary system is installed. This second system is interconnected with the first by means of an approved flow-diversion device. The sewage disposal systems also must be located so as to be accessible for maintenance and repairs. Septic tanks must be located so as to allow vacuum pumping.

A minimum of 10 feet of permeable soil beneath the leach field is typically required by code. An average acceptable percolation rate for soils beneath the leach field is 60 minutes per inch in the first 3 feet below the trench and 120 minutes per inch ($\frac{1}{2}$ inch per hour) from 3 to 10 feet below the trench. Effluent leaching systems are not usually installed in or on slopes greater than 30 percent. Slope restrictions apply to the areas used for sewage leaching, including the area reserved for expansion of the leaching system. Slopes less than 30 percent are not acceptable when they have been created by grading or other modifications of slopes. Installations are restricted in areas subject to high water tables, whether seasonal or permanent. The bottoms of leaching areas must be separated from groundwater in accordance with the local environmental health code. Leach trench sidewalls should be left with rough surfaces to promote absorption. Drain rock used in leaching systems must be washed and reasonably free of sand, very fine silt, and clay. After backfilling with 1 foot minimum of native soil, leach fields should have a slightly sloped finished grade to promote surface runoff. Except in emergencies, leaching-system installation in clayey soils should only be done when soil moisture content is low, to avoid smeared infiltrative surfaces. Following this guideline is important to protect natural springs, as shown in Figure 8-8.

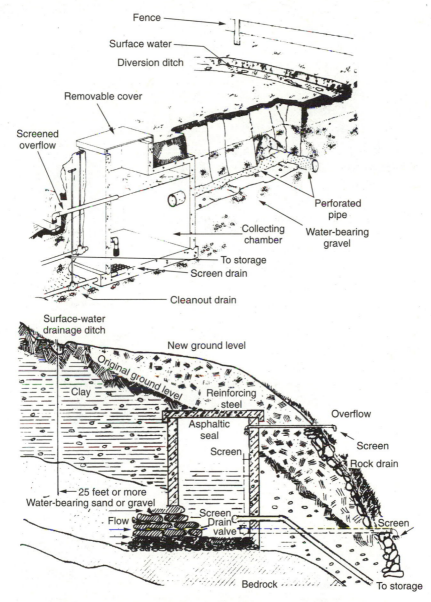

8-8 *A design for collecting water from a spring that provides protection against surface pollution and provides a means for entering and cleaning the collection chamber (top) and protection of a spring from surface contamination (bottom).*

Standard Construction Details
for Leaching Areas.

Width of trench	18 to 36 inches
Standard trench depth	Maximum of 14 feet ($2\frac{1}{2}$ feet effective depth)
Slope of drain line	1 inch per 4 feet minimum
Rock under pipe	Determined by local code
Rock over pipe	2 to 6 inches
Size of rock	$\frac{1}{2}$ to $2\frac{1}{2}$ inches
Spacing of trenches, edge to edge	Twice the effective depth

**Setbacks from leaching and curtain drains
(minimum distance in feet)**

Septic tank	3
Property line	5
Foundation structure bearing weight, building overhang	5
Water line	10
Stream, well, spring, water course	100
Steep slope over 67 percent	25
Embankment	4 × bank height
Pavement or driveway	5
Edge of road easement or right of way	10
Swimming pool	10

Leaching areas cannot be located in low-lying areas receiving storm water drainage or within 100-year flood-plain zones. Each individual sewage disposal system must typically be separated from streams, creeks, wells, springs, and watercourses by a minimum horizontal distance of 100 feet. Seepage pits must be separated from community wells by a minimum of 150 feet. The distance from streams and creeks is measured from the mean rainy season flowline. A watercourse is defined as a stream fed from permanent or natural sources, including rivers, creeks, runs, and rivulets, usually flowing in a particular direction (though it need not flow continuously) in a definite channel having a bed or banks, and usually discharging into some other stream or body of water. Leaching systems are also not permitted in areas containing fill. The building sewer line, or tightline, from the house is made of cast iron, ABS schedule 40 plastic, or other approved material. It has to have approved watertight fittings and be at least the same diameter as the building drain. Ells and bends of 90 degrees must be long turn sweeps (obviously), and cleanouts must be provided in accordance with the local code.

9

Operating equipment

Tractors

Earth-moving and landscaping tractors are classified by their usage and power rating:

- A *riding lawn mower* has a 5- to 25-horsepower engine mounted with a mower attachment. This equipment is primarily designed for mowing.
- A *lawn (small) tractor* has a 7- to 18-horsepower engine with a large variety of attachments. This equipment can be used for many jobs depending on the attachments used.
- A *lawn and landscape (large) tractor* has 18 to 80 horsepower or more with a large variety of attachments. This equipment is designed for the larger jobs.
- A *loader* is an earth- or materials-mover with more than 80 horsepower.
- A *backhoe* is an earth-mover with more than 80 horsepower.

Most of the following attachments are for use with a tractor, although many smaller mowers also have a few attachments that can be used. They are listed in order of size and capacity of machinery, rather than alphabetically.

- A *belly (deck) mower* is mounted to the bottom of the tractor or mower.
- A *grooming mower* rests on its own wheels for mowing height and can be attached to the front or rear.
- A *brush hog* is used for rough mowing of brush and pastures.

- A *box blade* is used for leveling and contouring surfaces.
- A *scraper blade* is used primarily for smoothing.
- A *post-hole auger* digs holes for setting fence posts or plants.
- A *sweeper* acts as a vacuum to collect leaves and grass clippings from lawn areas.
- A *sprayer* is used for spraying herbicides and insecticides.
- A *lawn aerator* is used to punch holes in lawn areas to encourage air filtration into the soil for healthier turf.
- A *truckster* is used for transporting materials, equipment, and personnel; hauling debris; and pulling various attachments such as spreaders and sprayers.
- A *front blade* pushes materials to a desired location.
- A *skid steer loader (Bobcat)* is used for moving loads and other jobs with the different attachments available, such as backhoe, bucket, forklift, and blade.
- A *power take-off (PTO)* is a supplementary mechanism enabling the engine power to be used to operate an attachment. The types of power take-off (PTO) drives that are used on tractors are hydraulic and hydrostatic. Both of these use liquids under pressure to transmit power from the engine to operate attachments.
- A *three-point hitch* is a mechanism on the back of a tractor with two hydraulic arms that connect to an implement and lift or lower it. It also has a top link used as a final connection between the implement and tractor PTO.
- A *tree spade* is used for transplanting large trees.
- A *stump chipper* or *stump grinder* is used for removing stumps.
- A *trencher* is used for digging narrow trenches for utility lines, edging, and sprinklers.
- A *backhoe* is used for digging trenches and large holes, scooping up dirt, and smoothing the ground after digging.
- An *excavator* is used for digging trenches and large holes. It has tracks that are well-suited for muddy, sandy, or rocky terrains without leaving deep ruts.
- A *hydromulcher* or *hydroseeder* is used for applying grass seed, pulp mulch, and fertilizer.

The basic types of tires used on tractors and landscaping equipment are

- *Pneumatic*: Air is added until recommended tire pressure level is reached.

- *Bar type*: Used primarily on tractors, it has a very deep tread for extra traction.
- *Ribbed*: This type aids in steering and turning and is used on many front tractor wheels.
- *Road*: Road tires are used for driving on paved surfaces at higher speeds.
- *Turf*: Turf tires are used primarily for driving on grass without leaving large ruts.
- *Greens*: Used for driving on golf course greens, this type leaves no track.
- *Solid*: No air is used. This type of tire is commonly used as attachment wheels and individual light power equipment wheels.

Operating any tractor equipment in proper control means the operator knows how to make the machine perform exactly as he or she wants it to, regardless of any external conditions. In some situations, it may even involve forcing the machine to do what the operator wants, within the limits of safety. When an equipment operator masters total control of his or her machine, common job site hazards and obstacles no longer prevent him or her from performing the work efficiently. Anything less may result in injuries or property damage or both. One common element that should be present in operating equipment is smoothness. It is impossible to place too much emphasis on this basic concept. Smoothly operating the tractor should be the constant goal of every operator. Smooth operation of equipment contributes to a longer machine life and enhances efficiency.

Control comes into play during the two basic areas of machine operation, namely, maneuvering the machine and hydraulic control. Again, the emphasis must be placed on control. Anyone can get on a machine and drive it around a job site, but it takes a skilled operator to exercise total control over it. Several variable factors affect the tractor's handling, such as weight distribution and how it can change during operation. A working knowledge of these factors and how to manipulate them is essential to operating-equipment control. The operator must develop a constant awareness of his or her machine's total operating weight (machine plus load) and how it is distributed.

With a larger tractor like a backhoe or a loader, the best way to maneuver the machine around a job site is to learn how to control its independent braking system. Each rear wheel is equipped with its own separate brake, with each brake controlled by a separate pedal. With the independent operation of the brakes, the tractor can be maneuvered in and out of surprisingly tight working situations. For example, when only one brake is engaged, that wheel locks while the other continues to drive, making the machine turn in a circle around the locked wheel. In many situations, the machine can actually be controlled better with the brakes than with the front wheels, which are actually designed to do the steering.

On slopes, learning to control the brakes reduces the instability usually caused by weight transfer. As the operator attempts to move the tractor up a sloped area, the front wheels tend to leave the ground, and control is soon lost as the machine veers off in the wrong direction. The effect of applying the brake forces the machine to travel in the desired direction, with or without the aid of the front tires to assist in the steering. This control of the brakes is most useful on tractors equipped with automatic, torque-converter transmissions because the brakes can be applied on one wheel while applying any amount of power to the other wheel at the same time. On standard-transmission models, the throttle is sometimes located near the brake, and it becomes impossible to use both, which the operator sometimes must do to control the machine the way he or she wants. Obviously, this use causes the brakes to wear more than they normally would. However, the extra wear is a small trade-off for the increased control and safety gained by mastering this technique of operating equipment.

There is also some loss of traction in most tractors when traveling in reverse, again due to the tendency of the weight to be shifted up and off the rear wheels. Backhoes are the exception because the hoe attachment serves as an effective counterweight. Placing so much weight on the rear wheels can tend to make the machine too light in the front, particularly when operating on slopes. In this case, the front loader bucket should be fully filled, stabilizing the weight distribution. When transporting material with the backhoe, which reduces weight on the front wheels, the brakes can be used for steering, or the operator can stabilize the front end by loading the loader bucket with heavy material, which returns steering control to the front.

A tractor's hydraulic system controls the movements of all attachments, as well as the side-mounted stabilizers and the loader bucket in the front. Its heart is a pump and fluid reservoir located in the tractor. The basic hydraulic power comes from fluid that is pumped through the system at a flow ranging from 15 to 35 gallons per minute, creating a high-pressure hydraulic ram and cylinder power system. The operator controls the flow with multiple valves located in a central valvebank at the control seat of the tractor. On a backhoe, these valves control the four basic hoe motions (the crowd, the boom, the bucket, and the swing), as well as the two side stabilizers. The control for the front loader bucket is located near the steering wheel.

Depending on how they are manipulated, these valves send hydraulic fluid through the system to the function or functions the operator wants to actuate. As resistance is built up in the hydraulic cylinders, the force necessary to move the various parts of the machine is created. This force may reach several tons in common backhoe operation, particularly when the boom, stick, and bucket are manipulated simultaneously. Since all power is controlled through these valves, the operator must become proficient in opening and closing them. This action determines how much force or speed is used to perform whatever task the operator faces. Each control is separate from the other, yet all are interrelated because they draw their power from the same pump. Therefore, if two or more valves are opened simultaneously, the oil flows to the one with the least resistance. If all four main backhoe controls were actuated at once, the flow each would receive would be about one-fourth as much as each function would receive if it were operated alone. So, much of what it takes to control the backhoe depends on the correct diverting of hydraulic fluid from point to point. Loaders and other types of heavy equipment use their drive wheels to control and direct their force, but on the backhoe this force is controlled strictly through the hydraulic system.

The way to master smooth operation is through a technique called *feathering*. Feathering is simply the opening and closing of the valves in combination in such a way that the flowing style from valve to valve mentioned earlier is created. The beginning operator, using one function at a time, will find the machine rough, jerky, and frustrating. High productivity is impossible to achieve at first. However, once the equipment operator learns how to combine the hydraulic functions in a smooth way, productivity rises.

A final note on tractor hydraulics is that systems are becoming more sophisticated all the time. Recent developments include electrohydraulic controls and limiting devices, which enhance precise operation. Also, an array of highly engineered valve stacks further smooth operation on tractor valve banks. Other examples of common valves found in tractors include flow-control valves and proportional-priority flow-divider valves, relief valves, and pressure-reducing valves. All of these contribute to increased operator control, ease of operation, and protection against hydraulic system damage. In addition, some backhoe models now feature two-lever systems instead of four-lever systems, combining two functions in each lever or joystick. The advantages of the two-lever system include less operator fatigue and increased control when using all four functions at once, which is much more difficult on four-lever models. The four-lever system, on the other hand, gives the operator slightly greater backhoe control, especially when propelling or maneuvering the machine with the backhoe itself.

Equipment safety

Always read the operator's manual before operating any tractor or equipment for the proper operation of that particular model of equipment. If you don't know how to use it, don't fire it up. Never bypass a manufacturer's safety device or guard on a machine or disconnect the back-up alarm. Don't wear loose, frayed, or bulky clothing, because it may become caught in revolving parts. Wear heavy shoes with steel toes. Wear a good respirator in very dusty conditions. Wear safety glasses or goggles when needed for eye protection. Wear hearing protection when using loud equipment.

Keep alert at all times while operating equipment to prevent injury or death to yourself and others. Check the tractor platform, steps, and pedals for mud or grease to prevent slipping. Stay alert and do not wear radio headphones when operating equipment. Be sure all guards and shields are in place before starting the engine. Check water, engine oil, and hydraulic oil levels before firing the engine. Always stay clear of any tractor's pinch points or articulation points. Many people have been crushed and killed or maimed by inattention to that last sentence.

Always use seatbelts as required, especially on tractors and equipment equipped with a roll bar. Make sure the seatbelt is in good condition and adjusted properly for your hips.

Let out the clutch slowly to avoid lurching forward. While operating with the tractor in motion, watch for hidden objects on the ground. Never drive into tall weeds that obstruct your view. Big holes may await. Watch for overhead hazards such as power lines and tree limbs. Remember to watch for those who may not be looking for you. Slow down when operating on slopes, and keep articulated parts pointed uphill. Back up hills if possible; it is safer than driving up hills. And keep the bucket low at all times. If your brakes go out while operating, that blade or bucket is your only emergency brake.

When going down hills, stay in gear to create a retarding compression brake on the engine in tandem with your mechanical brakes. Signal and slow down when turning. Always look carefully behind you when backing; keep your head (and attention) in the direction you're moving. Back-up alarms are OSHA-required equipment; it is illegal to disconnect or otherwise defeat them. Never horse around when operating machinery or let anyone so much as touch a lever unless that person is checked out on that tractor. Never give rides to other workers on a tractor, not even just to the other side of the job site. If your insurance company sees you driving around the job with your laborers riding on the fenders, you can kiss your low rates good-bye. Always lower all power implements when parking tractors.

Underground utilities

In open areas with no underground utilities present, the tractor operator is not required to maintain precise tractor control, because there is nothing within the backhoe's reach that can be damaged. The machine can be operated at maximum speed and efficiency. Open-field digging is an excellent opportunity for the tractor operator to practice and concentrate on developing a perfectly flowing, smooth digging cycle. The beginner can work on mastering the art of feathering the controls, enhancing smoothness. The best thing about this kind of practice is that it can be done on the job, as long as it is safe. Because there are no obstacles or restrictions, the tractor operator becomes accustomed to the tractor. This is not the case, however, when digging around tight work spaces and underground utilities.

When digging in developed areas, one hazard that almost always figures in the planning and execution of the job is the presence of underground utility lines. These lines include sewer pipes, gas lines, phone lines, fiber-optic lines, electrical cables, and so forth. Being able to locate and avoid breaking utility lines is a very important skill for the landscape tractor operator to develop; otherwise, even the simplest two-hour job can become a costly, drawn-out repair project. Also, in most areas, contractors who are judged to be responsible for utility breaks are charged for escaped gas or water. Breaking a fiber-optic phone cable can become an extremely expensive proposition (up to $1000 per second for any downtime), although important lines such as these are usually marked with warning signs and encased in concrete.

The more difficult tractor jobs include obstacles and restrictions that demand a high degree of control to prevent damage to the area or structures in the area. These restrictions can include houses and buildings; trees or bushes; new concrete, asphalt, or masonry surfaces; trenches or other excavations; existing footings; building materials piled on the site; cars and trucks; and stakes, hubs, or other surveyor's markings. The other set of obstacles exist underground. Pipeline transportation systems for gas, water, sewage, electricity, fiber optics, telephone wires, and cable television can pose problems, as can oil, steam, and cold and hot water lines. On some job sites, everything from water to hazardous gases and chemicals can be piped underground.

Some jobs may include only a few of these restrictions, while others are so complicated that safe, damage-free tractor operation can be next to impossible. However, it is the tractor operator's job to control the machine in such a manner that damage is prevented. It is also the operator's responsibility to know when job-site conditions are so restrictive that damage could be unavoidable. In these cases, the tractor operator must inform those in charge of the job, or, as a last resort, he or she should know when a job shouldn't even be attempted. Unlike the open area "blow and go" digging where the tractor operator can work at full speed without worrying about restrictions, digging around underground utilities means working in extremely tight situations, where one quick or thoughtless move could cause damage or other accidents. Digging around underground utilities creates a situation where every move must be planned and executed carefully, with the utmost precision.

The tractor operator will, after a time, develop a "feel" for underground pipes. He or she will often be able to tell a lot about an underground object simply from the way the bucket makes contact with it. The experienced tractor operator will know if he or she is hitting a rock, a chunk of concrete, or a pipe. If it is a pipe, the really good tractor operator will be able to tell what type of pipe it is, as well as the direction in which it has been laid. When looking over the job site, always inquire about possible locations, depths, and types of utilities that may be present. It may often be impossible to get exact location information. Even if they are marked, the markers may not be in the right locations, so there can be many surprises as the job progresses. The tractor operator should learn to take notice of the telltale signs of underground utilities. Learn to spot such things as the location of gas meters, water boxes, sewer cleanouts, stub outs, above-ground conduits, electrical vaults and pull boxes, and electrical signs or lights with an underground feed. Long, narrow depressions could be the sign of an old trench; in paved areas, trench or pothole patches could indicate underground lines as well. Also, don't ignore those other signs—the ones that read "BURIED UNDERGROUND CABLE." An old saying reminds us that "Nothing escapes the master's eye," and it is especially applicable to backhoe operations when digging around underground utilities. An observant tractor operator learns to spot these and other signs and avoid trouble with underground utilities most of the time.

There are generally four sets of conditions, or stages of alertness, that may exist on any job site with regard to digging around underground utilities. Knowing how to respond and proceed under any of these stages is vital to handling utilities successfully. Stage 1 exists when the tractor operator is working in an area where no utilities are expected to be encountered, including open areas, fields, rural sites such as farmlands, or new construction areas. When this is the case, the tractor operator can usually proceed ahead at full digging speed. He or she can work as quickly as his or her skills and safety allow, but he or she is also able to stop instantly if the bucket makes contact with anything unusual. At that point, the tractor operator should use an investigative procedure to determine the nature of the object.

Stage 2 is where information about utilities is limited or otherwise incomplete, and the tractor operator simply cannot tell if any are present. The area will probably have some utilities, but there are no obvious signs of them. These areas might include most urban locations and many open areas such as parking lots, large lawns, and so on, situated in or near any sizable human population. At any rate, Stage 2 is observed when it is believed no utilities are present. Here, the tractor operator can proceed at nearly full speed, but he or she must be much more careful than in Stage 1. Any bucket contact is usually checked out by hand, unless the tractor operator is certain about what he or she has hit.

Stage 3 exists when it is likely there are utilities in the area, including any time the tractor is operating within the boundaries of "city property," i.e., the street, the sidewalk, or even further in some cases. Signs warning workers about utility locations may be present. In this situation, the tractor operator must exercise great care. He or she should throttle the machine down and proceed very slowly. In this instance, the tractor operator's skills come into play as great care must be used at all times to avoid breaking a line. Here the cardinal rule is never to dig on public property or within the boundaries of any public easement without obtaining utility location information first.

Stage 4 is when the tractor operator knows utilities are in the area, whether marked or not. In this case, it is important to understand that officials of utility companies often make mistakes about the exact location of their lines; they usually try to determine a line's location and its depth, but they may be wrong on both counts. If the pipe has been located accurately, however, there is practically no excuse for breaking it. And, of course, there is no excuse for carelessly breaking a pipe that has already been exposed. The contractor pays damages in either case. Obviously, extreme care must be used in Stage-4 situations. The machine should be throttled down to about one-half, and the operator should proceed slowly and very carefully. Anything the bucket hits should be investigated by hand.

When the tractor operator is certain there are pipes in the area, and the machine is throttled down, he or she should proceed with great caution, taking only a few inches with each pass. When the bucket teeth come in contact with something, raise the bucket over the obstruction, come forward and continue digging carefully. At that point, another worker should go into the trench to identify the obstruction.

Engine-driven pumps

Engine-driven pumps are often used in landscaping construction to move excess surface water or dewater excavated holes. Self-priming pumps transfer a wide variety of liquids compatible with pump component materials. These range from 1½-inch clean-water pumps to 3-inch debris trash pumps that suck up mud and clods the size of baseballs. These are extremely portable pumps for high-capacity dewatering. Traditional pumps are made from cast iron with a removable cap for priming the pump and inlet line. Water must be poured in until it stops flowing down the inlet hose and backs up to the top of the chamber before the pump is primed.

Modern pumps have thermoplastic centrifugal pumps that self-prime up to 20 feet with the intake hose filled. They're made from thermoplastic components that are lightweight and give excellent corrosion resistance for long pump life. A standard 5-horsepower recoil-start gasoline engine delivers about 4000 rpm at upper governed operating range and pumps water smoothly from about 40°F to 160°F. The good ones have an automatic low-oil shutdown and clog-resistant impeller pumps that cut down on repair maintenance. A sediment basket installed at the point of intake cuts down on debris sucked into the pump, resulting in better head-pressure water flow and increased pump life.

The difference between a centrifugal pump and a piston pump is shown in the cross-sections in Figure 9-1. Figure 9-2 shows two types of jet pumps.

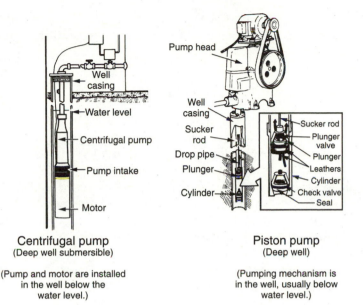

Centrifugal pump
(Deep well submersible)

(Pump and motor are installed
in the well below the
water level.)

Piston pump
(Deep well)

(Pumping mechanism is
in the well, usually below
water level.)

9-1 *Cross-sections of a centrifugal pump and a piston pump.*

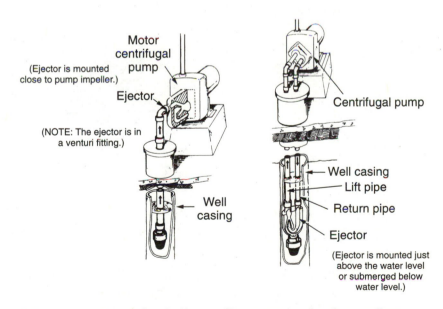

(Ejector is mounted
close to pump impeller.)

(NOTE: The ejector is in
a venturi fitting.)

(Ejector is mounted just
above the water level
or submerged below
water level.)

9-2 *Cross-sections of a shallow-well jet pump and a deep-well jet pump.*

Figures 9-3 through 9-5 show the operation of several different types of pumps. Types of pump controls are shown in Figures 9-6 and 9-7.

Chainsaws

Chainsaws are high-powered wood-cutting tools that consist of a special toothed chain and a gasoline engine (or electric motor) for driving it. The saw chain is flexible and is supported by a device called a guide bar. The saw chain revolves on this guide bar. The cutters on the chain sever the wood grain. Chainsaws are used by landscapers for a variety of tasks. Being portable, they are very useful in trimming branches, bucking (or sectioning) heavy wood, felling dead trees, or making through cuts in timbers or posts. Chainsaws may be used for both crosscutting or ripping with the tree grain. With proper operator training, they are safe and easy to control. Without proper training, they can be deadly.

A one-man chain saw is operated and controlled by grasping the handle bar with one hand and the grip with the other. The fingers of the hand on the grip are used to operate the throttle (or switch) and to pump the chain oiler lever. The handle bars are wrap-around types on most chain saws, allowing the guide bar to be positioned either vertically or horizontally. The better ones have an anti-kickback clutch

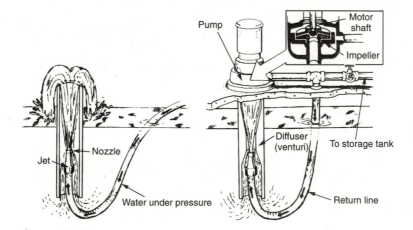

Water is supplied to jet nozzle under pressure. Water surrounding the jet stream is lifted and carried up the pipe as a result of jet action.

Jet used with a centrifugal pump

9-3 *Operation of a jet pump.*

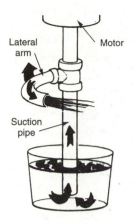

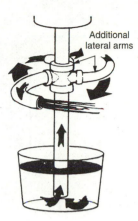

L-shaped pipe rotated rapidly pumps water out of a bucket.

More water can be pumped with addition of lateral arms.

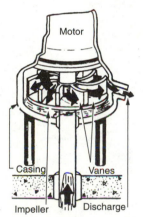

Manufactured pump with impeller replacing lateral arms.

9-4 *Operation of a centrifugal pump.*

brake that, when engaged, immediately stops the chain movement in an emergency.

Boring and notching cuts may be made by cutting with that portion of the chain at the end of the guide bar. For these reasons, the saws are excellent tools for notching timbers and topping posts. Chainsaws are very adaptable for cutting and framing decks or other landscape construction wood structures. There are three principal types of chainsaws, and there are also hydraulic and pneumatic chainsaws (the chain is driven by a compressed air or oil motor). There are also different chains for different jobs. We'll take them one by one. The two most common are discussed in the following text.

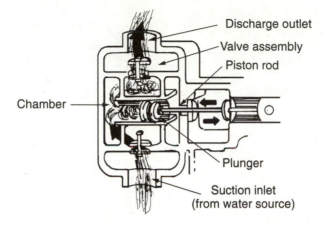

Single-acting piston

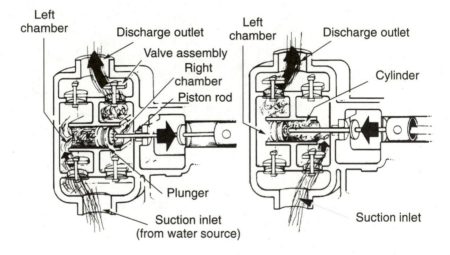

Movement of plunger to the right   Movement of plunger to the left

Double-acting piston

9-5 *Operation of a piston pump.*

Electric chainsaws

Electric chainsaws are used for light work where power is available and when cutting speed is not important. Electric chainsaws have limited power, due to the relatively heavy weight of the motors beyond ½ horsepower. Electric chainsaws use short (14- or 20-inch) guide bars. The saw chains used on these saws produce a relatively narrow kerf.

Direct-drive saws

Direct-drive saws have lightweight gasoline engines. A part of the lightweight feature results from not using reduction gears to reduce the chain speed. The saw chain is driven by a sprocket that revolves at the same speed as the engine's crankshaft. These saws, having their own power source, can be used in locations where electric power is not available. Modern direct-drive chainsaws are quite powerful. The

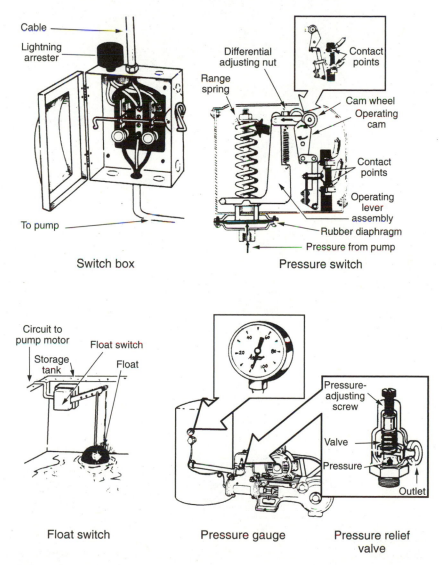

Switch box

Pressure switch

Float switch

Pressure gauge

Pressure relief valve

9-6 *Various pump controls.*

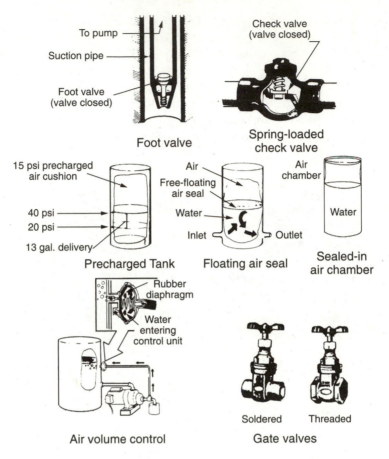

9-7 *More pump controls.*

range of guide-bar lengths extends from 14 to 42 inches. The saw chains are capable of creating the wider kerf that is needed to pass these longer guide bars through the cut. The chain speed is very fast, and cutting is accomplished with a minimum of time and energy.

Types of saw chains

There are three principal types (or styles) of saw chains. Each one has its own construction, operation, and maintenance features. Chainsaws, as used by carpenters, can be equipped with any one of the three types:

Chipper saw chain

Chipper saw chains are the most popular and widely used type, because they are very easy to sharpen and maintain the chain in a joined condition, which means it is not necessary to remove the chain from the machine. This type of saw chain has excellent cutting efficiency. It tends to produce a rough-sided cut edge unless its cutters are given a special shape. The loop of a chipper chain has a number of offsetting sequences. The right- and lefthand cutters alternate, except where the loop is fastened together with a master link.

Chisel saw chain

Chisel saw chains are somewhat more difficult to file and to join. However, they do operate much more smoothly than the chipper type. Their cutting efficiency is exceptionally good. The sides of the cut are relatively smooth. A loop of chisel-type saw chain is made up in the same manner as the chipper type. On chipper and chisel types of saw chains, the "bite" of the cutting edges is controlled by a device called a depth gauge. The height of the depth gauge is set, by filing, relative to the cutting edge. In softwood, the depth gauge setting is greater than that used for cutting hardwood. The depth gauge also acts to limit the self-feeding action of the cutters as they pass through the wood. To a degree, it also acts to limit the kerf produced by the chain.

Crosscut saw chain

Crosscut saw chains are made in a variety of patterns. A common pattern has rounded tops on the slitters and rakers. The tooth pattern is similar to that of a hand saw. The right- and lefthand slitters slice down through the cross-grain. The rakers, which follow the slitters, then chisel out the severed chip. Because a great number of slitters and rakes are always in contact with the wood, the cutting action is very smooth. The chain and guide bar are guided by the sides of the cut to produce a straight-line kerf. This pattern is sharpened by a grinding attachment that fits on the chain saw. The power of the chainsaw engine is used for the grinding. Other patterns of crosscut saw chain require time-consuming hand filing. This type has the highest cutting efficiency and is more abrasive-resistant than other types. They produce a narrow kerf. The power-sharpening feature is particularly useful when cutting posts or timbers that are dirty.

Standard safety rules for preparing chainsaws

Use the handle, not the guide bar, for transporting the saw. Lift the tool properly to avoid straining your back. Carry the saw with the guide bar pointed behind you. Be careful of your footing as you move. Do not "feel" the cutting edge of a saw chain. When checking the tension or oiling the chain, use gloves. Avoid infected cuts with these precautions. Never attempt to fuel a saw that has a hot engine. If you spill fuel mixture on the saw, wipe it off before starting up. Never start a gasoline saw in the same location that you refuel it. Never smoke while refueling. Never transport a saw while the engine is running. Stand in a position that gives you firm, solid footing. Stand on the control side of the saw. Do not attempt to steady a branch (or post) with your foot. Keep your hands, body, and clothing out of contact with the chain—even when it is not moving. Use the handle bar, grip, and spikes to retain full control of the saw at all times. Wear goggles or safety glasses. Avoid breathing the exhaust gases from gasoline saws. Remember, mufflers are hot and will burn skin, so avoid having any body contact with the muffler. Keep the saw chain in good cutting condition at all times. Always use a third-wire ground with electric saws.

The engines of gasoline chainsaws are equipped with "all position" carburetors and fuel systems. Thus, the saw may be held in the most convenient position for making the cut, even upside down. The cut is started by jamming the spikes (or dogs) into the wood, adjacent to where the cut is to be made. This action stabilizes the saw, allowing the guide bar to be properly aligned for the cut. When the cut is to be made along a branch or limb, check the guide bar position with the chain stopped (engine idling). Just before the cut is to be started, rev up the engine. Have the chain revolving at one-half to three-quarters of full speed. Then raise up on the grip until the chain is engaged for the full width of the cut. Keep the engine speed up so that the engine does not stall or the cutters "hang up" in the wood. Balance the saw engine (or motor) so that the cut runs straight and true. When the chain and guide bar are settled down in the cut, discontinue the use of the spikes. Allow the chain to self-feed down into the wood.

When cutting horizontally, control the cut with the spikes and apply enough pressure to keep the chain in contact with the uncut wood. Maintain a chain speed that allows you to retain *control* of the cut at all times. When a precise cutting line must be obtained, make a few end cuts further out to lessen branch weight prior to attempting the finish pass. When starting an underbuck cut, start on the lower side of the limb. Keep the chain up to full speed and apply pressure to the bar very carefully. When undercutting, you are using your arms and back as levers to keep the chain cutting wood. Work carefully to avoid losing control of the saw. Top cuts are easy to make with a chainsaw and they can be accurately controlled with the dogs.

Operating precautions for chainsaws

Pump the chain oiler lever frequently while cutting to keep the chain lubricated. Do not run the chain at full speed unless you are starting a cut (or are actually cutting). Check the tensioning of the saw chain frequently. Make tensioning adjustments with the engine stopped and when both the bar and chain are cooled down.

Chainsaws are precision working equipment. When not in use, they should be properly stored. Leave the cutting edges of the chain in good condition, ready for use. Slit a section of garden hose lengthwise for use as a chain guard. Store the saw so that it will not be tipped over, causing the fuel or chain oil to spill. Store the saw so that it will not be damaged by falling objects.

To perform a simple tune-up, start with a check of the air filter. Loosen the screws holding the air filter cover in place, and then remove the cover. Gently brush or blow all loose dirt and sawdust from the area around the air filter, and then lift the filter out. The opening beneath the filter is the carburetor's air intake. The intake area should be free of dirt and sawdust. If you find dirt or dust, it means the filter was not seated properly or was obstructed. Hold the filter up to a bright light. An opaque filter is plugged with dirt and should be replaced with a new one. If the filter is only partially obstructed, it can be cleaned. Wire-mesh and foam filters can be washed in soap and water or soaked in a nonoily solvent. Other types of filters can be gently brushed or blown clean. When the filter is clean, reinstall it.

Next check the spark plug. Chainsaw spark plugs cost about $1, so it's not worth struggling with an ancient plug to try to make it work; simply replace it. However, if a plug has been run for only a few hours, save your buck: A little simple maintenance is all that's necessary to keep it firing properly. Remove the plug and examine its business end, the end that screws into the saw. The curved piece of metal on the end of the plug and the upright metal post in the plug's center are the electrodes, where the plug's sparking occurs. Remove any foreign matter on and around the electrodes by wire-brushing or scraping with a soft tool (such as a piece of wood or plastic). Never use sand-blasting equipment meant to clean automobile spark plugs, because the tiny sand particles that may remain after sand-blasting are murder on a chainsaw engine. When the plug has been brushed or scraped clean, file the center electrode so that it is square and sharp-edged, and file the side electrode so it is bare, shiny metal. When the electrodes are filed, bend the outer electrode so its inner surface is 0.025 inch (0.64 mm) away from the center electrode. Use a feeler gauge to ensure that the gap is correct. Then reinstall the plug.

Remove the muffler assembly. Loosen the bolts holding the muffler assembly to the saw, and carefully lift the muffler away from the saw, making sure that no nuts, washers, spacers, or particles of debris fall into the saw body. Disassemble the muffler. A clogged muffler robs your engine of power, so take the muffler apart and use a scraping tool to remove accumulated carbon or dirt deposits in the muffler's internal passages. On a clean surface, lay out the parts of the disassembled muffler in a logical order so you'll be able to put them back together again in the correct sequence. The hole you uncovered when you removed the muffler is the exhaust port in the saw's combustion chamber. If the exhaust port is obstructed with carbon, use a soft tool, such as a wooden or plastic scraper, to remove the deposits. Then assemble and reinstall the muffler.

Check the starter-rope assembly housing. Chainsaw engines are cooled by means of a continuous stream of air drawn through the starter-rope assembly housing, so the air intakes in and beneath the housing must be clean and unobstructed. Clean the area, and check the starter assembly itself: If the starter rope is frayed, it should be replaced at this time. Buy an exact replacement from a chainsaw dealer, and follow the instructions supplied with the new starter rope. Remount the starter-rope assembly on the saw. Remove the sprocket cover. The saw's sprocket area is a Chinese puzzle of assemblies within assemblies, but it's not as complex as it seems. If you look at one assembly at a time, it all makes sense. Take the sprocket itself, the gearlike device that delivers power to the chain, for example. Obviously, it must be in good shape for the saw to run properly. Lift the chain away from the sprocket and examine the sprocket's teeth for wear. If the teeth are badly worn or chipped, replace the sprocket with a new one. (It unscrews.) If your saw is equipped with a chain brake, move the chain-brake lever with your hand to be sure the mechanism engages properly. The saw's clutch is usually located beneath the sprocket. Think back to the last time you used the saw: If the chain engaged or disengaged at the wrong time—that is, if it never stopped moving even when the saw was just idling, or if it didn't start moving until the saw was screaming—then the clutch may be to blame. Remove the sprocket and clean the curved pads of the clutch with a nonoily solvent. Most late-model saws have electronic ignitions, but if you own an older saw, the points (the electrical contacts that open and close to tell the spark plug when to fire) are usually located beneath the clutch. You can clean and file these points much the way you recondition spark plug electrodes. The points need to be regapped so they're the proper distance apart when open; your owner's manual gives the correct gap distance.

When you're through with the sprocket-area subassemblies, install a new chain or make sure that the existing chain is seated properly. Fit the chain around the sprocket so that the chain's cutters face outward and the chain's clawlike drive links engage the teeth of the sprocket. Working from the sprocket toward the tip or nose of the bar, insert the tangs of the drive links into the bar's groove. When the chain is fully seated on the bar, slide the bar forward (away from the sprocket) as far as it will go to take up the slack in the chain. Loosely reattach the sprocket cover by screwing the cover's mounting nuts finger-tight. Adjust the chain tension. Lift the nose of the bar as far as it will go without actually lifting the saw itself. (There may be quite a bit of free play.) Holding the bar in place, tighten the chain-adjusting screw until the chain is reasonably taut. Then, still holding the bar in place, fully tighten the sprocket housing nuts. Snap the chain to make sure there are no kinks: Pull the chain away from the top of the bar and let go. A properly tensioned chain will lift away from the bar only about $\frac{1}{4}$ inch. If your chain is too tight or too loose, slightly loosen the sprocket housing and reset the tension by turning the chain-adjusting screw, and then retighten the sprocket housing nuts. Make a final tension check by snapping the chain again, and then, wearing heavy gloves, slide the chain along the bar. The chain should move freely without binding.

Unless your chain is brand-new, it should be sharpened prior to each use. In fact, professional loggers will tell you that even new chains ought to be sharpened; in logging competitions, professional wood cutters may work for as much as 40 hours on a brand-new chain to achieve the fastest-possible cutting speeds. Of course, for everyday use, chain sharpening need only take a few minutes. Complete instructions come with the sharpening tools themselves, but shop carefully because different brands and types of chains need different-sized files, file guides, and file gauges. Use only the type recommended by your saw's manufacturer, and file to the correct angles recommended for your specific type of chain. If you've sharpened any chain more than five times yourself, it's a good idea to take it to a professional chain sharpener. For only a few dollars, he or she can remove any small errors that have crept into your work. Go over the entire saw, and tighten all nuts and screws (except the chain-adjusting and carburetor-setting screws). Make sure nothing is loose or out of place. Grip and twist the rubber handle covers to make sure they are not cracked or slipping. If they show signs of coming loose, have them replaced. Refill the saw with fresh gas and oil.

Chainsaws in storage should have their tanks completely dry. Fuel, if left in a saw for long periods, will gel and may gum up the carburetor and fuel lines. Most chainsaw manufacturers recommend leaded, regular-grade gasoline for their saws, although unleaded regular or unleaded premium gas can be used in a pinch. Four-cycle ("automotive") oil is not recommended for use either in mixing with a chainsaw's gasoline supply or for use in oiling the bar and chain. To lubricate a chainsaw's engine, use SAE-40 or SAE-30 two-cycle motor oil. SAE-40 two-cycle motor oil should be mixed in the saw's gasoline supply at a ratio of 1 part oil to 32 parts gasoline; that is, a pint of oil per 2 gallons of gasoline. SAE-30 two-cycle motor oil is mixed in a ratio of 1 part oil to 16 parts gasoline, or a pint of oil per gallon of gas. Oil and gas should be mixed in a separate container, never in the saw's own gas tank. When the oil and gas are thoroughly mixed, carefully fill your saw's tank. Then fill the saw's separate oil tank with a high-quality bar and chain oil. Make sure the gas and oil tank caps are replaced securely, and wipe off any spills.

Test-run your saw outdoors, at least 25 feet from the spot where you fueled your saw. Place the saw on solid ground and pin the saw to the ground by placing one of your feet on the rear handle and one of your hands on the front handle. With your free hand, flip the ignition switch on, and place the choke lever in full-choke position. Set the throttle lever in the start position. Pull the starter-rope grip out a short way until you feel the starter engage. Then pull the cord briskly to give a fast-cranking spin to the engine. Do not pull the starter rope all the way out. Holding onto the grip, let the cord rewind smoothly.

Normally, an engine that has not been run for some time takes at least three to five pulls just to be primed with fuel and several additional pulls to begin to run. When the engine finally begins to cough (fire erratically), move the choke lever to the half-choke position, and continue cranking until the engine runs. Reset the throttle to idle, and let the engine idle at half-choke until it warms up. If the saw won't run, adjust the carburetor setting as indicated in your owner's manual. There are usually two separate screws to adjust, one regulating idle speed and one regulating the richness of the fuel/air mixture. The adjustments are usually quite simple. When the saw is running properly, shut it off and place a sheet of plain, white paper on the ground. Restart the saw, and hold the nose of the bar 3 to 4 inches away from the paper. Rev the engine. A fine oil spray should appear on the paper. If not, there is a problem with the bar and chain oiler. Try pressing the manual oiler button several times, and rev the saw again. If the oil spray does not appear, the problem is serious: Consult the owner's manual or take the saw to a dealer for service.

10

Maintaining small-engine equipment

Oil

Small engines may require expensive repairs much sooner than they should. Often this problem occurs because of oil that is improperly added to the crankcase. Using the recommended amount of oil and adding it to the crankcase properly prolongs the life of an engine. Always follow the manufacturer's recommendations and the type of oil specified by the manufacturer. The dipstick or plug shows whether the oil is level with the full mark. It is important to check the oil level every time before firing up the engine because most small engines are not equipped with a warning indicator to show when oil pressure is low. There must be no oil leaks around the parts that have been removed and replaced when the engine is placed back into operation.

Small engines hold relatively small quantities of oil; however, all engines, regardless of their size or function, should be properly lubricated at all times. Many small-engine failures occur because they were operated without enough oil or with the wrong kind of oil. Damage caused by these oversights may be both costly and time-consuming to the owner of the small engine. Low oil levels can cause small engines to overheat, which in turn causes excessive wear. Overheating also causes oil to oxidize (or thicken), resulting in varnish deposits, stuck rings, and stuck valves. The function of oil as a lubricant is to

- Reduce friction and prevent wear.
- Reduce heat caused by friction between moving parts.
- Clean engine parts.
- Prevent engine corrosion.
- Help seal piston rings to prevent blow-by.
- Help increase the engine's power output by reducing friction.

Oil tends to break down and oxidize quickly because a small air-cooled engine operates at a higher temperature than a water-cooled engine. Oil also tends to become dirty faster in a small engine because of the lack of an oil filter. A small engine is often exposed to more dirt than a larger engine because it is usually operated near the ground. Small engines are usually operated at maximum power output, and centrifugal force and pressure against bearing surfaces leave the bearing surfaces unlubricated. Because small engines are lightweight, they may be subjected to a large amount of vibration, which increases bearing loads, which breaks down the viscosity of the engine oil.

Crankcase oils come in various types, and adding the wrong kind of oil to a small engine can be just as disastrous as operating an engine that is low on oil. The wrong kind of oil may severely damage the engine and greatly reduce its service and life. The manufacturer usually recommends a specific kind of oil to use under different operating conditions. The oil may be listed on the engine nameplate, in the operator's manual, or in lubrication guides produced by major oil manufacturers. Always follow the manufacturer's recommendations when selecting oil for your machine. Specifications always show the oil type as a Society of American Engineers (SAE) rating. SAE viscosity rating indicates the viscosity grade. Viscosity is a term used to measure an oil's resistance to flow. The SAE number on the top of an oil container indicates how thick the oil is. As a rule, lower-viscosity oils are used in cold weather, and higher-viscosity oils are used in warm weather. Examples of viscosity numbers might include SAE 5W (the "W" indicates winter use), which is a very thin oil, or SAE 50, which is a very thick oil used in hot operating conditions. Other SAE viscosity numbers include 10W, 20W, 20, 30, and 40.

Also available today are multiviscosity grade oils that can be used under a variety of operating conditions. An example of a multiviscosity oil is SAE 10W-50 oil. The numbers indicate that this oil can exhibit the viscosity characteristic of an SAE-10W single-viscosity oil, an SAE-50 single-viscosity oil, and any other single-viscosity oils that fall between these two numbers. The American Petroleum Institute (A.P.I.) Service specifications rating is often called the "type" of oil and describes the conditions for which the oil is best suited. The following table explains the various conditions that determine the choice of oil type:

A.P.I. classification	Service conditions
SA	Use only under light and favorable operating conditions; not recommended for farm tractors.
SB	Use under moderate to severe operating conditions where special lubrication problems, such as deposit or bearing corrosion, are present under high crankcase oil temperatures.
SC, SD, SE	Use under severe or unfavorable operating conditions and where special lubrication problems, such as deposit, wear, or bearing corrosion, are present.

Sometimes oils have multiple A.P.I. classifications listed on the container. The oil would then be satisfactory for use under any of the conditions indicated by the codes. For example, an oil coded SA would be suitable for use only under light and favorable operating conditions, while an oil coded SE, SC, and SD would be suitable for use on moderate to unfavorable operating conditions. Most manufacturers of 4-cycle engines recommend using an oil that contains special additives or chemicals for controlling corrosion, scuffing, and wear and to aid in cleaning. Because this oil is mixed with the gasoline in a 2-cycle engine, special additives must be present in the oil. Additives in regular crankcase oil, if added to a 2-cycle engine, would not completely burn. Residues left by this incomplete burning would foul spark plugs and clog exhaust parts, causing severe damage. Many of the oils containing these special additives for 2-cycle engines are marketed by the manufacturer of the engine.

Remember, *always* add the kind of oil (viscosity and type) suggested by the original manufacturer. Selecting and using the proper oil is one of the most important decisions you make for maintaining your engine-driven equipment.

Air cleaners

Servicing air cleaners on small-engine carburetors needs to be part of your regularly scheduled equipment maintenance. A small engine operates most efficiently when it has an ample supply of air. A dirty air cleaner cuts down on the amount of air that can get into the carburetor and allows dirt and grime to enter the engine. This dirt, grime, and reduced air supply cause damage to small engines, drastically reduce the useful life of the engine, and also cause frequent and expensive repairs. Air cleaners are easily serviced given a screwdriver, containers for washing parts, filter lubricant, and clean rags. The filter must be cleaned, defective parts must be replaced, and the filter must be reinstalled according to instructions in the operator's manual.

The importance of maintaining clean air filters becomes clear when you figure that a 3-horsepower engine operating at 3600 rpm requires about 6.5 cubic feet of air per minute. This figures out to be about 2 cubic feet of air per horsepower per minute. Not only does the engine need this large amount of air, but the air that enters the engine must be clean. Dirt and other impurities must be screened or filtered from the air before it enters the engine and combustion chamber. This filtering is only achieved by the use of a clean carburetor intake air cleaner or filter. Correctly servicing air cleaners at the proper time is very important.

Most small engines operate under very bad conditions — near the ground and in the dust. When air cleaners are properly serviced, they are almost 100-percent effective in filtering dirt from the air. Most people either fail to service air cleaners properly or do not service them often enough. They do not realize how many problems can be caused by a dirty or clogged air filter.

If the air cleaner is not properly serviced, dirt and dust can enter the engine and mix with the lubricating oil, changing the oil into a grinding compound that scratches and wears parts instead of lubricating them. Dirt may build up on the air cleaner, causing it to become clogged. As a result, there will be far too much fuel for the amount of air going into the cylinder. Since all the gasoline doesn't burn, the excess fuel washes oil from the cylinder walls. Then the pistons and cylinder walls may become scuffed and scarred from lack of lubrication. Moreover, a fuel mixture that is too rich tends to cause loss of power, excessive smoking, and choking. This problem is common in mowers that are not serviced regularly.

If the air cleaner has been neglected, no manufacturer will honor the engine's warranty. The manufacturer's owner's manual fully explains the details and procedures for servicing air cleaners and filters. It is the business owner's responsibility to see that his or her employees follow these service recommendations in a regularly scheduled equipment-maintenance program. It is virtually impossible to say when an air cleaner should be serviced. Most manufacturers recommend servicing the air cleaner every 25 hours if an engine is operated under ideal conditions; however, ideal conditions very seldom exist. There may be times when the air cleaner should be serviced two or three times per day if it is operated in a very dusty area. To be safe, check the air cleaner before each use or at least once per day.

Procedures for cleaning air cleaners vary with the type of air cleaner your small engine has. There are three main types of air cleaners. One of these will be used on your engine:

- The saturated element (oiled filter).
- The dry filter.
- The oil-bath filter.

To service these filters, the worker needs the following tools:

- Slot-head screwdrivers, 4 and 6 inches
- Phillips #2 head screwdrivers, 4 and 6 inches
- Container for washing parts
- Crankcase oil or special filter lubricant for polyurethane filter
- Clean rags
- Wooden scraper (metal scrapers will scar the motor)
- Old paintbrush
- Petroleum solvent (mineral spirits, kerosene, or diesel fuel)

Caution! Do not use gasoline, naphtha, or benzene. They are extremely flammable.

The worker must observe these safety precautions when servicing an air cleaner:

- Shut the engine off before removing the filter.
- Disconnect the engine's spark plug wire.
- NEVER SMOKE when working around small gasoline engines, especially when servicing the air filter. Gasoline in the engine and petroleum solvents used in cleaning the filter are highly flammable.

The two main types of saturated-element air cleaners are the flexible polyurethane filter and the wire mesh filter. To service the saturated element types of air cleaners, first disconnect the spark plug wire to prevent the engine from accidentally starting.

Caution! Never work on the engine while it is running.

Clean the area around the air cleaner to prevent loose dirt from entering the carburetor air duct. Remove the filter element cover, and then remove the filter element. Be sure to note the order in which the parts are disassembled. Cover the carburetor air intake with a clean rag or a plastic cover. Check the condition of the filter element and air filter cover assembly. Some polyurethane filters become brittle and crumble. When they do, they should be replaced. If the mesh breaks in a wire mesh filter, replace the filter. A strong solution of household detergent and water is best for cleaning polyurethane filters.

Caution! Never use gasoline for cleaning.

Carbon tetrachloride and paint thinner dissolve glues in the filter. Clean metal mesh filters with an acceptable petroleum solvent (mineral spirits, kerosene, diesel fuel). Dry the filter element. If it is a polyurethane sponge, dry it by squeezing. If it is the metal mesh type, dry by hanging in the air or by using compressed air.

Remove the protective cover from the carburetor intake, and clean the carburetor intake using a clean cloth dampened with solvent. Oil the filter element. This step is important, but many people neglect it. SAE 30-type oil is acceptable for use in oiling. For polyurethane filters, use 2 or 3 tablespoons of oil, depending on the size of the filter element. Squeeze the filter in your hand to distribute the oil equally. If you have a metal mesh filter, dip it into the oil and swish out the excess oil. Oil that is too thick causes the engine to choke. Oil that is too thin is drawn into the engine. Too much oil fouls out the spark plugs. Install the filter element. Be sure that it is installed the same way as it was removed. Install the cover, reassembling in reverse order of disassembly. Tighten the wing nut finger-tight. Reconnect the spark plug wire. The engine is now ready for operation.

Observe the same safety precautions when servicing the dry-filter air cleaner as when servicing the saturated-element air cleaner. To clean the dry-filter air cleaner, first disconnect the spark plug wire. Clean the area around the air cleaner to prevent dirt from getting into the carburetor. Remove the filter element cover. Some filters are self-contained units and do not have a separate cover. Remove the air filter element. Cover the carburetor air intake with a clean cloth or a plastic cover. Check the condition of the filter element and the air filter cover assembly. Replace any broken or defective parts. If the element is paper, clean it by tapping it on a flat surface. Do not wash unless the manufacturer recommends it. Replace paper elements if dust does not drop off easily during tapping, or if it is bent, crushed, or damaged. Handle the paper element with care. Do not use compressed air—it may rupture the filter. If the element is moss or fiber, direct the compressed air from the inside to the outside. Do not put oil on a dry filter. It clogs the pores in the paper, moss, or fiber, and air cannot pass through. Replace the filter element. Be sure the filter fits snugly around the air cleaner base to prevent air from bypassing the filter element. Replace the cover and tighten the wing nut finger-tight. Reconnect the spark plug. Your engine is now ready for operation.

Observe the same safety precautions when servicing the oil-bath air cleaner as when servicing the saturated-element air cleaner. To clean the oil-bath air cleaner, first disconnect the spark plug wire. Clean the area around the air cleaner to prevent dirt from getting into the carburetor. Remove the air cleaner cover. Remove the air filter base. Cover the carburetor air intake with a clean cloth or a plastic cover to prevent foreign material from entering the engine. Pour the oil out of the base and check the condition of the cover assembly and base. Replace any broken or defective parts. Clean the base and cover assembly with an acceptable petroleum solvent (mineral spirits, kerosene, diesel fuel).

Caution! Never use gasoline for cleaning; it is very flammable.

Dry the base and cover assembly. If solvent is left in the base or cover assembly, it will thin the oil and allow dirt to get into the engine. Remove the protective cover from the carburetor intake. Install the cover, reassembling in reverse order of disassembly. Tighten the wing nut finger-tight. Reconnect the spark plug wire. The engine is now ready for operation.

Idle adjust

Small engines that operate inefficiently waste valuable time and fuel. Often a correction of the idle-speed adjustment screw, which is located on the carburetor, increases efficiency. While adjusting the idle speed is not a complicated procedure, it does require some preparation and effort. Given the manufacturer's manual and a screwdriver, the worker may have to adjust the engine idle speed on a small engine during routine maintenance. The adjustment must prevent overspeeding and underspeeding. An engine that runs inefficiently does not do its job. Breakdowns waste time in labor costs and require expensive repairs. To operate efficiently, the engine idle-speed screw must be properly set. Unless the idle-speed screw is correctly adjusted, the engine may either underspeed or overspeed, causing serious engine damage.

Adjusting idle speed is really a throttle stop adjustment. A spring on the throttle valve tends to keep it closed. A set screw is provided to act as a bumper to the throttle stop lever. This set screw is called a bumper stop screw or idle-speed stop screw. It can be adjusted to hold the throttle at the desired engine speed. In some small engines, idle speed is relatively fast, varying from 1200 to 3200 rpms. Check the specific machine's operator's manual to find the correct idle rpm. It is usually one-half maximum operating speed. Never think that you are taking care of your small engine by operating it at slow idle speeds. Since small engines are designed to operate at full throttle, the fuel-air mixture is too rich to operate at slow throttle speeds. Unburned fuel may foul the spark plugs. Adjust the idle speed when either of the following conditions occur:

- *Underspeeding*. A spring is usually installed on the idle screw to hold it in place. Over a period of time, this screw gradually works itself out, allowing the engine to idle too slowly and possibly causing it to stop when the speed-control lever is completely retarded.
- *Overspeeding*. This condition occurs when the idle screw is adjusted too far inward. The engine idles too fast, causing excessive fuel consumption and excessive wear of engine parts.

The idle speed may also need adjustment when changing from cold-weather operation to warm-weather operation or vice versa. A difference in altitude also affects carburetor adjustment. Observe all safety precautions when adjusting idle speed on a small engine. Keep away from moving engine parts. Never work on an engine that is operating in an enclosed area (carbon monoxide poisoning may result). Keep onlookers, children, and pets away from the engine.

The tools required to adjust idle speed are a 4- to 8-inch slot-head screwdriver and a tachometer, which is an instrument used to measure engine rpm. The two most common types of tachometers are a vibro-tachometer and a portable dial tachometer. To adjust the idle speed properly on a small engine, the operator must first read the manufacturer's manual to determine the correct idle speed. There are different recommendations for different types and makes of engines. Generally speaking, to adjust the idle speed on a small engine:

1. Locate the idle-speed screw. It is usually on the side of the carburetor and is easy to find.
2. Operate the engine at about one-half throttle for two minutes for warm-up.
3. Set the speed-control lever at the completely retarded position so the engine operates solely from the idle screw.
4. Check the idle speed with a tachometer. Hook up the tachometer according to the manufacturer's instructions. Interpret the reading on the calibrated scale on the tachometer according to the manufacturer's instructions.
5. Adjust the idle speed to the recommended rpm.

Turning the adjusting screw clockwise usually increases engine speed. Turning it counterclockwise usually decreases it. If after adjusting idle speed the engine runs rough or misses, check for carburetor damage or malfunction. Disconnect and store the tachometer.

Maintenance schedule

All your small-engine equipment should be serviced regularly per a scheduled maintenance calendar of normal usage. This calendar is made up of the various manufacturers' service recommendations of each of your various pieces of equipment. Each undoubtedly is different and requires different servicing intervals. However, it pays to build and follow such a maintenance schedule because, in the long run, your equipment will run longer and make more profit ratio with less associated maintenance cost. I've supplied you with a sample in Fig. 10-2, but it would be impossible, given the wide variety of small-engine equipment out there today, to make it complete. So you're on your own here. My advice is to dig out all those owner's manuals you tossed back into the box so very long ago, and build each tool's maintenance schedule right from the manufacturer's specifications. Then add all your equipment together on a spreadsheet. Make a current timeline to see how badly your equipment needs servicing. Also use mileage and materials logs, as shown in Figures 10-1 through 10-4.

WORK ORDER NO. _____   DATE AND TIME REQUESTED_____/_____

REQUESTED BY _____   DATE AND TIME NEEDED_____/_____

STOCK NUMBER	DESCRIPTION	QUANTITY

10-1 *Stock request.*

VEHICLE MAINTENANCE CARD

Vehicle No: _____   Week of: _____

DAILY SERVICE & LOG:

Day	Operator	Gasoline	Oil	Battery Checked	Mileage Out	Mileage In
Mon.		gal.	qts.			
Tues.		gal.	qts.			
Wed.		gal.	qts.			
Thurs.		gal.	qts.			
Fri.		gal.	qts.			
Sat.		gal.	qts.			

TOTAL MILES DRIVEN FOR WEEK: _____

WEEKLY SERVICE: Tire Pressure   Check by _____   Date _____

REPAIRS NEEDED: _____

_____

EQUIPMENT USE AND SERVICE CARD

Equipment No: _____

Date	Operator	Job No. Equip. Used On	CHECK SERVICE PERFORMED						Hrs. Used On Job	Repairs Needed and/or Remarks
			LUB	ENG. OIL		TRANS. OIL		FILTER		
				Checked	Changed	Checked	Changed	Checked	Changed	

10-2 *Equipment maintenance records.*

For Vehicle # _____

Date	Time	Customer	Beginning Mileage	Ending Mileage	Driver

10-3 *Mileage log.*

☐ Confirming Order
 Order No. _____
☐ Routine

Account to be Charged _____   Date _____

Work Order Number _____   Requested By _____

Location _____   Wanted Date _____

☐ Estimated   ☐ Quoted   Quoted By _____

ITEM #	QUANTITY	DESCRIPTION	UNIT COST	TOTAL

VENDOR	SPECIAL INSTRUCTIONS
Name _____	
Address _____	
City _____ State ____ Zip _____	

10-4 *Materials/service request.*

11

Landscape design and planning

Basic landscape design principles

The main advantages of having a landscape design plan is that it serves as a guide for long-range development of the building's grounds, and it saves time, money, and effort. See Figures 11-1 and 11-2. The best time to develop a landscape plan is after a careful survey of the area and surrounding properties is made. The designer must also take into account the desires and purposes of the building's occupants. The following sections discuss the main areas to be developed in a landscape plan.

Private area

The private area refers mainly to the recreation area of the family. It includes such features as the barbecue pit, children's playground, flower landscape, specimen shrubs, birdbath, or rock landscape. Enclose the area to ensure privacy and to form a background for landscape features. Arrange flower beds, rock landscape, or other features around the perimeter. Allow the center to remain open. Make the area accessible to the house and to other parts of the property.

Service area

The service area should contain the garage and turning area. It should also contain the vegetable landscape, greenhouse, propagating frames, compost pile, and potting bench, if used. Tools, lawn mowers, and other equipment can be stored in a shed that is easily screened from view with fencing or plant material. A back or side door could have access to this area.

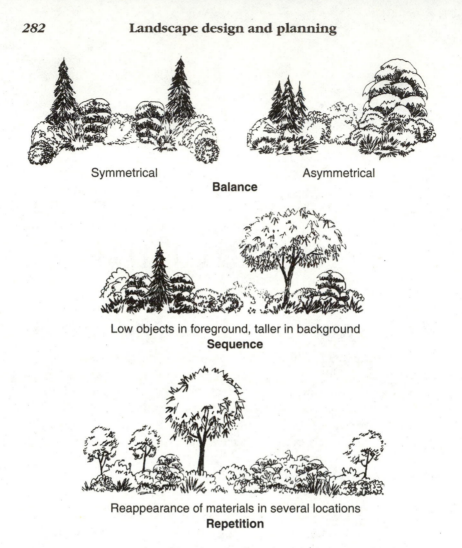

Symmetrical   Asymmetrical
Balance

Low objects in foreground, taller in background
Sequence

Reappearance of materials in several locations
Repetition

11-1 *Basic principles of landscape design include balance, sequence, and repetition.*

Public area

To establish a public area, make the lawn open and spacious in proper proportion to the area available. Balance the plantings, both trees and shrubs, about an imaginary line through the entrance of the house or property. Use only those trees and shrubs that complement the house to the best advantage.

Basic planting groups found in the public area are designed for their position. Entrance planting should emphasize the entrance and make it more inviting. Both evergreen and deciduous plants should appear here. Corner planting should grow taller than those at the entrance. It should soften the sharp angles of the corners of the house by using naturally rounded plant forms. Corner planting should be about two-thirds of the distance between the eaves and the ground and should be placed according to the style of the house and size of the lot. Foundation plantings should break the monotony of a wide expanse of blank wall or draw attention to a window. Keep in mind the rate of growth as well as the final size of the plant when mature. Accent the textures and colors of the building materials of the house by using plants for their shape, fruit, flower, and foliage effects. Common mistakes made in foundation plantings are overplanting (too many plants), planting too close to buildings, spacing plants too close together, using plants not suited to the building, and using plants not adapted for the local climate.

The general objectives for developing a landscape plan are to secure attractive grounds by harmonizing the home, buildings, various areas, walks, drives, and landscape into one complete unit; to

Contrast in form   Contrast in texture

Contrast

Proportion (Scale)

11-2 *Basic principles of landscape design also include contrast and proportion.*

provide natural, easy, and safe approaches; to provide privacy or recreational needs for the occupants; and to provide a convenient, well-arranged, attractive service area. The terms and definitions used in landscape design follow:

asymmetrical Uneven number of items on each side of a point.

balance Even distribution of mass on each side of an axis.

blueprint Reproduction of a scaled drawing (map, landscape plan, house plan, etc.) using special paper and machines (blueprinter or diazo copier) to produce a white background print with lines or a blue background print with white lines, both of which are commonly referred to as blueprints.

focal point Center of interest, such as a front door, statue, or fountain.

foundation plantings Plants at the base of a building.

landscaping design Selection and placement of plants to develop spaces around buildings and houses for a maximum of beauty and utility with a minimum of maintenance.

legend A list of the symbols on a map explaining what they represent.

materials list A list of all plant materials and other supplies necessary to install a landscape plan.

scale Making a drawing representative of the area of which it is a picture by letting a certain measurement, usually 1 inch, on paper represent a definite number of feet on the ground.

symmetrical Same number of items on each side of a point.

The guiding principles of landscape design are

- Simplicity
- Beauty
- Convenience
- Function
- Maintenance

The elements in a landscape design are *space* (which is the area you are allowed to work with, since the size of the space often prohibits certain designs), *line* (which moves the viewer's eye from one point to another; lines may be straight, curved, or angled), *form* (which gives the element shape; forms may be square, rectangular, circular, triangular, or irregular), *texture* (visual and tactile surface characteristics and appearance, like fine- or coarse-textured plants, rough-textured stucco walls, or a smooth-textured steel statue), and *color* (which attracts the eye and provides contrast as well as sets the mood of a design). Red, yellow, and orange are lively, warm colors, and tend to "jump" out of a setting. Blue, green, and purple are calming, cool colors, and tend to recede into a setting.

   The basic principles of landscape design begin with symmetrical *balance*. In symmetrical balance, landscape design on one side of a focal point is identical to the other side. Use of this type of balance creates a formal and planned look. This design element is most easily seen in a formal landscape. Asymmetrical balance is meant to be just the opposite. Landscape designs on each side of a focal point are not identical. Use of this type of balance creates a more informal, natural look. Design sequence refers to a logical order in the placement of plants based on their mature size and rate of growth. A logical order or sequence would be placing low plants in the foreground, followed by medium-sized plants in the middle ground, and taller plants in the background. To predict proper sequence, plant growth for each specimen must have a known growth rate, which is attained by knowing the cultivar.

   Contrast is desired to break what otherwise might be considered monotony. It is attained by using plants of different sizes, colors, and foliage characteristics. Flowers and fruits can offer contrast, but only part of the time. Foliage and bark are better and more harmonious sources of contrast. Contrast in plant forms and colors should be gradual and subtle. Too many contrasting forms and colors make the scene appear like a circus with too many elements vying for attention. However, in some designs, one may want *rhythm*. Repetition or rhythm means a reappearance of the same plant form throughout the landscape setting. It can be attained by varying and repeating forms, colors, and textures in an appealing and inviting way. Repetition can easily cross over to monotony. The master of good repetition is also a master of subtlety. Japanese-type landscapes are good examples of this design. They dramatize nature in perfect scale, line, and form and relate it all to the human element coexisting in the environment.

   Proportion or *scale* is the art of keeping all of the elements of the landscape in relation to one other. Proportion or scale is a relative term involving the artistic sense that one has been able to develop over the years, often with deliberate practice or training. The size of plant materials should be complementary to the size of other plant materials used nearby and to the size of the structure. For example, a 60- to 80-foot tall tree would overpower a one-story, flat-roofed home. A 15-foot tall tree would be lost next to a five-story hotel complex.

   Drafting of the plan is best done on a computer because of the ease of changes and fast calculations of numbers and data. Information on this process is found in Chapter 12. The basic drafting tools used in making a landscape plan by traditional hand methods are

- *T-square* or *parallel bar*, which is used to draw horizontal and vertical lines.
- *Triangles*, which are flat, plastic tools used to draw 30-degree, 45-degree, 60-degree, and 90-degree (perpendicular) lines when placed next to the T-square or parallel bar's horizontal plane.
- *Scales*, which are used for proportional reductions of actual (outdoor) dimensions to dimensions that fit on a drawing sheet. A scale has six edges, with each representing a different proportion such as $\frac{1}{4}$ inch equals 1 foot, $\frac{1}{2}$ inch equals 1 foot, etc.
- *Pencils* or *pens*, which are used for applying graphite or ink lines to a drawing.
- *Pointers*, which are used for sharpening pencils.
- *Erasers.*
- *Drafting media*, which are papers, vellums, and polyester films used as drawing bases.
- *Templates*, which are used for drawing common shapes, symbols, and letters.

In using a scale, drawing to scale means letting 1 inch on paper represent a definite number of feet on the ground. Some scales commonly used are 1 inch equals 4 feet, 1 inch equals 8 feet, 1 inch equals 10 feet, and 1 inch equals 20 feet. You need an engineering or architectural scale for manual (hand) drafting or cross-section paper to draw landscape features to scale.

Maintaining good manual drafting habits means keeping your instruments and equipment clean, keeping the leads on your pencils sharp for good line quality, and making sure your hands are clean before you start drafting. Always lift tools (triangles, templates, T-squares) when moving them across your drawing sheet. Sliding them can smear work underneath. Store drawings flat or rolled up. Do not fold drawings. Creases interfere in blueprinting or reproduction of the original. Use an appropriate straightedge (triangle, template, T-square, parallel bar) for drawing straight lines. Don't use your scale to draw straight lines. Use light pencil guidelines for uniform lettering. Pick one lettering style and stick with it throughout an entire drawing. Use all capital letters for standard landscape plans. Do not mix lowercase letters with uppercase letters.

In drawing a landscape plan, it is best to start by drawing a rough sketch of the area and its existing features, and then add possible locations for landscaping features. Time spent planning is well worth it—an eraser is much easier to use than a shovel. After making the sketch, you can then draw a finished landscape plan to scale. Draw the length and width of the selected site. Draw these dimensions to scale using an architect's or engineer's scale or graph paper. For the layout to have symmetry, you need to use a scale for all dimensions. Draw a north arrow to show the correct orientation of the site. Draw existing buildings using the exact dimensions and distances from property lines. Draw existing artificial features such as sidewalks, drives, patios, fences, planters, exposed utility lines, and sewer lateral lines, if known.

Draw existing natural features such as trees, shrubs, and borders or planting beds using appropriate symbols. These features should be drawn at their mature sizes to avoid overplanting. Draw the floor plan of the house. Also indicate doors, windows, porches, and steps. Indicate the height of the windows from the ground. Note any special features of the site such as good or bad views, drainage problems, and slopes. Draw proposed landscape plants and structures according to the principles of design discussed earlier, the planned use of the area, and your knowledge of plant characteristics. Label all materials neatly. Keep in mind the needs and wants of the homeowner, the plants adapted for your locale, the mature size of the plants, and any special requirements of plants, such as sun or shade, low or high maintenance, flowers or not, etc.

Take measurements of the physical features of the project site, including boundaries, existing buildings, other artificial features, and existing natural features, such as trees and water. Draw this layout to scale on the appropriate-size sheet of vellum or other paper that can be blueprinted. Complete a checklist of the site. Determine your client's needs. Draw a total landscape design for this area. Include a foundation planting for all sides of the house, corner plantings for the backyard, and entrance plantings for the main entry of the house. Label all materials used on the drawing. Create a materials list from the drawing. Have the drawing blueprinted at a copy store that has a blueprint copier.

Small turf sprinkler sample design

To properly design all the components of an irrigation system, it is necessary to follow a standard procedure. I have used this procedure to design a sample system for you that you can copy and use for your own project. This system could easily be labeled as any residential or commercial system as they both encounter nearly the same type of problems. The following is the basic procedure used to design the sample system:

1. Obtain all pertinent site information.
2. Determine the system irrigation requirement.
3. Determine water and power supply.
4. Select sprinklers and determine spacing ranges.
5. Circuit sprinklers and locate valves and mainlines.
6. Size pipe and valves, then calculate total system pressure requirement.
7. Estimate potential mainline surge pressure.
8. Locate controllers and size wire.
9. Prepare the final irrigation plan.
10. Prepare a bill of materials.

The actual irrigation plan is prepared in a step-by-step sequence that includes the turf-irrigation design criteria, followed by the actual design analysis, which is described in the irrigation system design analysis worksheet immediately following this section. It is important to note that not all of the items in the sample worksheet apply to each and every system design. The spacing of sprinkler heads is then computed by the formulas shown in Figure 6-8.

Step 1. Obtain site information. The important site information used to design the sprinkler system is shown and described in the irrigation system design analysis worksheet. Noted would be a specific condition of 55-psi minimum static water pressure. We might notice also the presence of galvanized iron pipe that connects the water meter to the structure. An available plot plan shows a standard scale of 1 inch equals 10 feet, which allows factoring for lengths of pipe and pressure runs.

Step 2. Determine the system irrigation requirement. From the design criteria, we know that a minimum of $1\frac{3}{4}$ inches per week of water needs to be added to the turf. This quantity of water represents approximately 0.25 inches per day. Notice the peak season temperature and its duration. If the temperature were significantly lower, say 80°F, perhaps the minimum water required might be $1\frac{1}{2}$ inches per week.

Step 3. Determine water and power supply. From design criteria, it may be shown that the supply of water for this system is provided by a domestic water meter 1 inch in size. The meter is fed from the city main through a $1\frac{1}{4}$-inch copper, Type M service line. The available minimum static water pressure in the city main is 55 psi. This is the design pressure you must use to estimate the eventual working capacity of the meter and service main. The irrigation system design analysis worksheet would show the approximation of the maximum usable (gpm) flow and pressure. Even though the total system pressure is calculated during a later step, calculating the available pressure and gpm allows you to allocate pressure to guarantee that you do not end up needing more than you have available. Calculation of the available usable gpm allows you to predict what the largest lateral circuit size can be without drawing too much water. Remember, this is extremely important if you have to irrigate and at the same time use additional water for some other need. The power supply is also noted in the irrigation system design analysis worksheet. It is important to locate the power source and to define how much voltage is available and when during the day as well.

Step 4. Select sprinklers and determine spacing ranges (see Fig. 11-1). The irrigation system design analysis worksheet feeds the plot plan, which depicts the selection of sprinklers and their placement in each individual area. The design criteria describes the calculation of the maximum spacing range. Here each sprinkler is selected for an operating pressure of approximately 20 psi. The 20-psi value was selected because of the following factors:

- The minimum available working pressure at the discharge port of the water meter is 45 psi at a maximum circuit flow of 25.4 gpm. Allowing for approximately 50-percent pressure loss due to pipe, valve, and fitting friction losses, 20 psi becomes a logical minimum operating pressure. The maximum operating pressure could be as high as 30 psi.
- The size and shape of the areas to be sprinkled are small, narrow, and irregular, requiring the use of small spray-head sprinklers with reduced radius of throw, and thus, lower operating pressures.
- The limited quantity of water (23 to 25 gpm) requires that low-flow rates from each sprinkler be used. With spray-head sprinklers, lower flow rates are obtained with lower operating pressures and by throttling the sprinkler. Throttling the sprinkler also reduces the diameter or radius of coverage. These types of sprinklers are shown in Figures 11-3 and 11-4.

An irrigation system design analysis worksheet describes the calculation of the typical sprinkler pattern precipitation rates and the approximate operating time for each type of pattern to achieve the required application of water defined in the design criteria. In our example in Chapter 6, we use pressure values for spray-head operation that are quite high, whereas the operating time values are relatively low.

Step 5. Circuit sprinklers and locate valves and mainlines. The division of the sprinkled areas into zones is shown on the plot

Integral rubber cover

Set of 12 standard or
7 low angle nozzles

Easy arc adjustment
(40° – 360°)

Ratcheting riser

Gear drive

Locking screw on
body cap

Heavy duty spring

Drain check valve for up
to 10' elevation change

11-3 *A spray-head sprinkler.*

plan layout. Zones are determined by the shape and size of the area with respect to the type of sprinklers required in that area. Another consideration is the type of planted material in the area. Shrubs or delicate flowers are placed in separate zones from large turf areas. The irrigation system design analysis worksheet depicts the analysis used to determine the actual number of individual control valves required and the maximum size of the largest lateral circuit. It further depicts the location of each lateral line, control valve, and mainline. Areas are noted for the grouping together of control valves. This grouping process in known as "manifolding" the control valves. Manifolding is done for two reasons. First, manifolding allows several valves to be located in the same valve box. Second, manifolding allows convenient access to the valves for adjustments, maintenance, and repair, if necessary.

Step 6. Size pipe and valves, then calculate total system pressure requirement. Shown in the irrigation system design analysis worksheet is the sizing of the pipe in lateral circuits and the sizing of the mainline extensions. The complete sizing of all pipe is noted, and the sizing of the control valves is shown in the analysis. If the maximum valve pressure loss is approximately 4 to 5 psi, this equals approximately 10 percent of available system pressure. The calculation of the total system pressure requirement for the largest actual circuit and the system should also be shown in the analysis.

Step 7. Estimate potential mainline surge pressure. The worksheet should also describe the estimate of the potential mainline surge pressure or water hammer due to a sudden closure of any gate valve. The maximum surge should occur in either the $1\frac{1}{4}$-inch plastic line adjacent to the valve or perhaps in the $11\frac{1}{4}$-inch existing galvanized iron line. It is wise to calculate approximate surge pressure conditions in any pipe that might present a problem. In this case, it is unlikely that the steel pipe would have any problems because of its strength.

Step 8. Locate controllers and size wire. The controller location is noted on plot plan layouts, and since only one control valve operates at a time, the actual wire lengths become the equivalent lengths. The wire sizes for the common ground and the individual control wires are read directly from the charts in the equipment catalog or the technical data section of the design manual. The worksheet should depict the selection of the wire sizes.

Captive solenoid plunger

Low-current solenoid

Adjustable flow control

Internal manual bleed

Captive bonnet screws

Fully supported diaphragm

Porting and filtering system

1" thread × thread or slip × slip

Globe or angle configuration

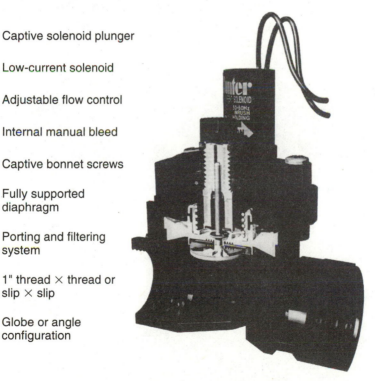

11-4 *Another example of a spray-head sprinkler.*

Step 9. Prepare the final irrigation plan. The final irrigation plan includes a set of typical installation detail drawings and special notes.

Step 10. Prepare a bill of materials. The bill of materials represents the invoice of materials for the system. Included in the bill are all approximate quantities of pipe, wire, fittings, sprinklers, valves, controllers, and any miscellaneous items. Any breakdown in greater detail as to specific quantities of components requires more evaluation by the landscape contractor or builder. A sample bill of materials is shown in Figure 11-5.

Botanical name	Quantity	Wholesale	Retail
Anemone coronaria	6	$ 12.00	$ 24.00
Aquilegia	10	$ 20.00	$ 40.00
Berberidaceae thunbergii	8	$ 80.00	$ 160.00
Cladrastis lutea	1	$ 50.00	$ 100.00
Convallaria majalis	6	$ 12.00	$ 24.00
Cotoneaster buxifolius	5	$ 50.00	$ 100.00
Elaeagnus angustifolia	1	$ 100.00	$ 200.00
Fraxinus pennsylvanica	1	$ 75.00	$ 150.00
Gleditsia triacanthos	1	$ 75.00	$ 150.00
Iris (yellow)	4	$ 4.00	$ 8.00
Petunia hybrida	80	$ 24.00	$ 40.00
Phlox	16	$ 24.00	$ 48.00
Picea pungens	1	$ 80.00	$ 160.00
Pinus cembroides	1	$ 95.00	$ 190.00
Pinus m. mugo	5	$ 250.00	$ 500.00
Poa pratensis	2952.50 sqft	$ 295.25	$ 442.88
Populus tremuloides	4	$ 200.00	$ 400.00
Potenilla rosaceae	11	$ 22.00	$ 44.00
Syringa oleaceae	4	$ 20.00	$ 40.00
Subtotal		**$ 1,488.25**	**$ 2,976.50**

HardScape items	Amount	Wholesale	Retail
Concrete	4.21 cuyd	$ 42.00	$ 84.00
Small Bench	3	$ 150.00	$ 300.00
Mulch	5.66 cuyd	$ 84.88	$ 141.47
Rock	11	$ 150.00	$ 300.00
Table	1	$ 50.00	$ 100.00
Garden edging	85.00 lnft	$ 21.25	$ 42.50
Subtotal		**$ 498.13**	**$ 996.26**

TOTALS

Wholesale	**$ 1,986.38**	
Retail		**$ 3,972.76**
LABOR (30% of retail cost):		**$ 1,191.83**
TOTAL Due from Customer:		**$ 5,164.58**

11-5 *A sample bill of materials.*

Turf irrigation design criteria

Use the following turf irrigation design criteria template (Figure 11-6) to assemble your project data and begin your irrigation system design analysis worksheet (which immediately follows this section).

The following information should be indicated on these plans: areas to be irrigated; location of buildings, walks, drives, trees, shrubs, flower beds; property lines; sprinkler overthrow limits; existing utilities; and available points of connection with utilities.

Project Name: Sample Small Turf System   Project No.:
Date Rec'd: Date Due:

Customer Name:
Project Address:
Contacts:

1. Required Material and Information:

Plot plan: Scale 1″ = 10′   Landscape plan: Scale   Utility plan: Scale
Topographic plan: Scale   Grading plan: Scale

2. Design Information:

Water source: Lake [ ]   Well [ ]   City main [X]   Reservoir [ ]

Available static pressure: 55 psi   Available gpm: 50 for 24 hrs.
Existing water meter: Size 1″   Mfg. by: Crescentworks
Model: MHF-1″   Age: 2 years
Existing feeder main size: 1-$\frac{1}{4}$″   Material: Copper type "M"
Existing pumping plant:
Number of pumps:
Age: Total GPM:
Pump ID:
Type: Mfg. By: Model: Size/gpm:
Motor HP: Volts, HZ:
    Pump #1:

    Pump #2:

    Pump #3:

3. Existing Power Sources:

Volts ac: HZ: Amps:
Available irrigation time: 12 am to 12 pm, 7 days/wk
    Source #1:
    Source #2:
Wind:

11-6

Direction: NE   Velocity: 2 mph   Time of day: 4 pm to 10 am
Temperature, peak season: 95°F   No. of days: 60   Water req'd: 1-¾ In/wk
Soil type: Clay loam   Growth types: Bluegrass, evergreen trees, hedge
Shaded areas: Areas around structure and hedge
Sun-filled Areas: All open turf areas

4. Material Requirements: (Pipe, Fittings, Valves, Wire, etc.)

Laterals: PVC class 200   Fittings: Sch 40 PVC
Main lines: PVC Class 200   Backflow: Brass/anti-siphon
Control valves: Brass/Solenoid   Isolation valves:
Check valves: Regulators:
Drain valves: Pressure relief valves:
Pressure reduction valve: Air/vacuum valve:
Wire: Direct burial-type UF   Valve boxes: Plastic with locking cover

5. System Design Specification:

Type of system: Manual   O/C:
Fully automatic: X   Semiautomatic:
Type of coverage: Full   Limited:

Type of Sprinkler	Model/ Nozzle	Min/max spacing Range	OP. Press Range	RAD/DIA. coverage:
Spray heads	2800 hp	55% max/50% min	20-25 PSI	As adjusted
	2600 B	10 ft max	20 psi	O' radius

Impacts
Rotors

Type of valves: (model & no.)
Lateral control: 100 EF   Manual drain:
Isolation gate: Auto drain:
Manual angle: Air/vacuum relief:
Mainline control: Pump control:
Pressure reducing: Check:
Pressure relief: Special:

Type of controllers: (Model)	Stations	Valves per station
Rainclox RC-8	8	1 valve per station

Type of wire: (size, color)
Underground low voltage: #14 AWG-Type UF, color optional
Controller power:
Wire connectors: 18 AWG to 14 AWG = Pentite-PT 102,103 and 104
Trench depths: Mains: 18 inches; Laterals 12 inches
24 VAC Wire: 18 Inches; 120 VAC Wire: 18 Inches

6. **Remarks:** Use separate sheet.

11-6 *Continued.*

Irrigation system design analysis worksheet

Project Name: Sample Small Turf System   Project No.:
Date Rec'd: Date Due:

Customer Name:
Project Address:
Contacts:

1.0 System specifications: (See design criteria sheet attached.)

2.0 Design assumptions:

    a. Maximum @P thru water meter should be less than 10% of available static water pressure at the P.O.C.
    b. Maximum usable flow thru 1" water meter should be less than 75% of the rated maximum safe flow.
    c. Maximum flow velocities in piping: city service line, 6 ft/sec; service main to building and control valves, 6 ft/sec; lateral piping, 7 ft/sec.
    d. Sprinkler operating pressure range: 20 to 30 psi.
    e. Maximum precipitation rate: 50% of average soil intake rate.
    f. Maximum sprinkler spacing: for 2 mph winds, use 55 to 60% of diameter of throw.

3.0 Available water supply:

Specification requirements	Calculated (@P) and flow	Adjusted (@P) pressure loss and flow:
1. *MAX* Meter @P to be less than 10% of available static pressure. Static pressure = 55 psi min.	55 psi × 1 = 5.5 psi @P at 31 gpm flow	At a flow of 27 gpm, the meter @P = 4.3 psi. Total pressure loss at avail. flow
2. *MAX* Meter flow to be less than 75% of "Max Safe Flow." MSF =50 gpm Meter = 1" Crescentworks	50 gpm × .75= 37.5 gpm at 8.1 @P to high psi	METER: 4.3 psi SERVICE LINE: 1.7 psi GATE VALVES 1.0 psi ELEVATION <u>1.21 psi</u> 8.2 psi
3. *MAX* Pipe velocity not to exceed 6 ft/sec. in 1-$\frac{1}{4}$" cu "M" tube Tube length = 28 ft.	V=6 ft/sec, @P/100' = 6.0 psi/100' for 27 gpm.	MIN STATIC PRESSURE = 55 psi (less) pressure loss= 8.2 psi
Actual pressure:	Loss: @P = 6.0 × 28'; 100' = 1.68 psi at 27 gpm flow	available working pressure =46.8 psi at 27 gpm

4.0 Sprinkler selection, spacing range calculation:

Model no.	Operating pressure (psi)	GPM	Rad/dia	Spacing range Max.	Min.
2800 HP-F	20	3.2	25' Dia	15'	12'
2800 HP-H	20	2.0	12½' Rad	15'	12'
2800 HP-Q	20	1.2	12½' Rad	15'	12'
2800 HP-TQ	20	2.6	12½' Rad	15'	12'
2800 HP-T	20	1.5	12½' Rad	15'	12'
2800 HP-HU	20	1.3	10½' Rad	13'	10'
2800 HP-QU	20	0.6	10½' Rad	13'	10'
2600-B	20	1.0	0' Rad	—	—

11-7

Controllers

Basically, all controllers are electric hydraulic converters that convert the electric output from sophisticated and flexible electronic controllers to the pressure-based signals in a hydraulic irrigation system. Controller features revolve around timing devices that can be set at a certain time to open and close the electric or hydraulic remote control valves. These are then coupled with pressure-compensating devices (PCDs) to ensure consistent, efficient performance without water waste in systems subject to varying pressures.

PCDs provide true matched precipitation rates with all sprinkler nozzles, effectively eliminating nozzle fogging and compensating for pressure variations within any system. Many can retrofit any nozzle to provide pressure compensating. PCDs maintain constant 30-psi performance at pressures exceeding 30 psi. Standard operating pressures are 30 to 75 psi, with a typical flow rate of 0.09 to 4 gpm.

A monitoring rain switch can be installed in the system controller. This switch is an innovative conservation device that shuts off sprinklers during rainfall. An additional option is a high-flow shut-off device that saves water and money by disrupting flow to damaged or vandalized sprinklers. These are ideal in controllers for commercial and municipal areas prone to foot traffic or vandalism.

Temporary electrical power

On many jobs, temporary power-distribution systems are established. Several companies manufacture temporary power systems. Most of the systems are similar, with the main differences being in the location of the electrical circuit breakers and the cord connection configuration. The following information is a reproduction of the instructional information regarding operation and safety procedures, relating to a temporary branch power-distribution unit with ground fault protection for personnel—ground fault circuit interrupter (GFCI) connector box power distribution units.

GFCI connector box power distribution units are equipped with circuit breaker guard products, that, when properly installed, protect your workers from dangerous currents leaking to ground from their intended paths. In such instances, the worker *becomes* the ground and is electrocuted. Such current leaks are called ground faults and can be deadly. Currents of only 60/1000 of an ampere can be fatal. GFCI connector box products, which are listed by Underwriters' Laboratories as Class A, Group I interrupters, respond to fault currents as low as 5 milliamperes and can shut off the current in as fast as 1/40th of a second, which greatly reduces shock hazard. At any location (especially on job sites where people work in close contact with water, mud, building steel, and ground), electricity can be hazardous. The GFCI connector box affords a high level of protection against line-to-ground faults. No attempt should ever be made to bypass the GFCI breaker and defeat its purpose.

The GFCI protects against ground faults only in those circuits to which it supplies power. It does not protect the circuit supplying it or other circuits that are not supplied from it. The GFCI connector box, like all differential ground fault interrupters, does not limit the magnitude of the ground fault current. It only limits the duration of the current that flows after the trip level is exceeded. During the brief period that it takes the GFCI to function, the current may rise considerably above the trip level, causing a momentary electric shock. This device does not guard against electrical shock hazard resulting from contact with more than one circuit conductor or disrespect for the dangers of electrical shocks or currents. The GFCI connector box using a circuit GFCI is designed to be used on a grounded electrical supply system. They do not operate when supplied from a portable generator whose circuit is not properly grounded. Overcurrent protection of the proper rating, according to the National Electrical Code, Article 240, must be used.

To test the GFCI, plug the GFCI connector box into the appropriate power supply and follow the testing procedure on the side of the box. If the unit does not trip after the testing procedure has been completed, do not use the GFCI and consult the manufacturer as soon as possible. When the GFCI trips, it has detected a ground fault current larger than the trip level. Try resetting the GFCI actuator, being careful to look for possible danger to personnel. If it remains on when reset, the fault was momentary and has cleared. If the GFCI actuator continues to trip after resetting, there is a ground fault present, and the GFCI is performing its safety function. To determine what is causing the fault, remove all plugs except the power supply plug and reset the GFCI actuator. Plug in the tools or appliances one at a time. If one is permanently faulted, it will trip the GFCI actuator again, indicating that the tool or appliance has ground leakage of a grounded neutral condition on the load slot of the GFCI connector box. The GFCI connector box will continue to trip when there is a continuing ground fault, the neutral has become grounded, there is an open neutral, the hot and neutral wires are reversed, or either hot wire is open.

The GFCI connector box typically consists of three basic boxes. Each box has six 20-amp, 125-volt and one 30-amp, 250-volt convenience outlets. Each outlet has its own circuit breaker overload protection and weatherproof cover with the rating of the outlet on the cover.

Because of the noninterchangeable nature of the GFCI connector box, all GFCI connector boxes have GFCI protection for personnel, either built-in or supplied from preceding connector boxes. It should be noted that should the GFCI connector box trip due to a ground fault, all succeeding units will also shut down. When shutting down the temporary power at the end of the day, do so by operating the test button on the actuator of the GFCI connector box. This will indicate that the device is functioning normally. Should power in one of the supply conductors be lost while the GFCI connector box is on, the unit still operates and continues to provide ground fault protection. If the neutral is lost while the GFCI connector box is on, it continues to operate and provide ground fault protection or shuts off when the load is sufficiently unbalanced due to loss of the neutral. If excessively high voltages (nominal 150V) occur, the unit shuts off.

Most units provide ground fault protection for personnel if the supply voltage drops below 102 volts after the GFCI connector box has been turned on. They continue to provide protection at all lower voltages until the GFCI connector box automatically turns off because of low voltage release (turn-off is a nominal 50 volts). All cable has some capacitive leakage, which can create nuisance tripping. In a 120V system, there is a limit to the length of cable that can be run before sufficient leakage to ground builds up, causing the GFCI to trip. However, capacitive leakage in the two feeder power lines flows in opposite directions. This design cancels the capacitive leakage effect, and there is no theoretical limit to the length of interconnecting cable runs. In regard to protection from electrical shock, the Construction Safety Orders refer builders to the Electrical Safety Orders. Excerpts from the Electrical Safety Orders that apply to construction equipment follow.

Electrical safety orders

Article 11. Grounding

2395.6 Portable and Vehicle-Mounted Generators.

(a) Under the following conditions, the frame of a portable or a vehicle-mounted generator need not be grounded and must be permitted to serve as the grounding electrode for a system supplied by the generator.

> *(1) The noncurrent-carrying metal parts of equipment located on the vehicle and the equipment grounding conductor terminals of the receptacles are bonded to the generator or vehicle frame, and*
>
> *(2) The generator supplies only equipment located on the vehicle or the generator and/or cord- and plug-connected equipment through receptacles mounted on the vehicle or on the generator, and*
>
> *(3) The frame of a vehicle-mounted generator is bonded to the vehicle frame, or*
>
> *(4) The generator is single-phase, portable, or vehicle-mounted, rated not more than 5KW and the circuit conductors of the generator are insulated from the generator frame and all other grounded surfaces.*

Title 24, Part 3, Section 250-23.

2395.45 Equipment Connected by Cord and Plug.

(a) The exposed noncurrent-carrying metal parts of the following cord- and plug-connected equipment must be grounded, where such exposed metal parts are likely to become energized:

> *(1) Refrigerators, freezers, and air conditioners.*
>
> *(2) Clothes-washing, clothes-drying, and dishwashing machines, sump pumps, and electrical aquarium equipment.*
>
> *(3) Portable hand-held, motor-operated tools and utilization equipment such as drills, hedge clippers, lawn mowers, wet scrubbers, sanders and saws.*
>
> *(4) Utilization equipment used in damp or wet locations or by persons standing on the ground or on metal or exposed concrete floors or working inside of metal tanks or boilers.*
>
> *(5) Utilization equipment used in hazardous locations.*
>
> *(6) Any electrical equipment which is operated at over 150 volts to ground.*
>
> *(7) Portable hand lamps.*

(8) Portable and mobile x-ray and associated equipment.
(b) The following equipment must not be required to be grounded:

>   *(1) Listed portable tools or utilization equipment supplied through an isolating transformer with an ungrounded secondary of not over 50 volts.*

>   *(2) Listed portable tools and utilization equipment protected by an approved system of double insulation. Where such a system is employed, the equipment must be distinctively marked.*

EXCEPTION: For replacement of nongrounding-type receptacles with grounding-type receptacles and for branch-circuit extensions only in existing installations which do not have a grounding conductor in the branch circuit, the grounding conductor of a grounding-type receptacle outlet must be permitted to be grounded to a grounded cold water pipe near the equipment. (Title 23, Part 3, Section 250-50.)

Site preparation

Grading

Grading involves changing the existing elevations of a site to provide surface drainage and allow for the construction and installation of landscape improvements. Grading work includes rough grading, import and export of soils, excavation and embankment fills, compacting, topsoil placement, surface drainage sloping, finish grading, and other related work. When required, testing of compacted fill and import soil should be done by a certified testing laboratory. Prior to commencement of grading operations, the landscaper should be aware of existing conditions and any hazards the grading operation may create for pedestrian or vehicular traffic and then implement proper precautionary measures. Existing structures, pavements, curbs and gutters, conduits, fences and walls, and other facilities (both above and below ground) should be properly protected and maintained in a satisfactory manner.

Legally, the landscape contractor must repair and restore damages caused by neglect or construction operations at the landscape contractor's own expense. There are also environmental conditions a contractor is responsible for, such as dust control during all grading operations, as required for health and safety. Wherever practical, water spray should be used to keep dust to a minimum. Any damage, such as compaction or rutting, caused to existing grades on the site during the grading operations should be immediately repaired and the damaged areas returned to their original grade and state of permeability. Settlement or erosion that occurs during the grading operations should be repaired and grades should be reestablished to the required elevations and slopes.

Fill soil material should be of comparable composition as existing soil on the site and should be free of rocks larger than 3 inches in diameter, vegetation, organic matter, and other debris. Where excavation areas yield material that is predominately rock or gravel, such material may be used as fill only in areas where it will be buried 3 or more feet deep. Under no circumstances should such material be used any closer to the surface, except with the approval of the owner or owner's representative. And my professional advice to you is to get it in writing. An on-site source of any additional soil required to balance the grading requirements may, when appropriate, be designed by the owner or owner's representative. All imported topsoil should be natural soil, graded to not larger than $\frac{3}{4}$ inch, and should be free of animal or vegetable matter, diseases, pests, and noxious weeds. The maximum slope ratio should be not more than 3:1 (3 feet horizontal to 1 foot vertical), unless otherwise approved by the owner or owner's representative and/or the grading inspector. Slopes, both cut and fill, should not be steeper than 3:1 unless a thorough geological and engineering analysis indicates that steeper slopes are safe and erosion-control measures are specified. Slopes should not be constructed so as to endanger or disturb adjoining property.

Rough grading grade tolerances are given in tenths of a foot, not inches, as engineers work in tenths and hundredths. All rough grading should be accurate to within $\frac{2}{10}$ (0.2) foot of designed elevation. Pockets or depressions that will not readily drain should not be allowed to remain. All grades should be prepared with a smooth, natural appearance, blending into the adjacent areas. Rough-graded areas should be free of large clods of dirt, rocks, sharp rises, unnatural mounds or ridges, and debris or foreign material. Temporary mulching, seeding, or other suitable slope surface stabilization measures should be used to protect exposed critical areas during construction. Ditches or dikes should be installed at the top of cut or fill slopes where surface runoff can flow down the slopes in contained channels.

Fill and compaction

All vegetative matter should be removed from the surface where any fill is to be placed. This process is called "clear and grub." Vegetation removed during the clearing operations should be disposed of as follows: All or some of the cleared vegetation may be chipped, if appropriate, for use as mulch or compost on the site. All other material should be disposed of in a manner and at a location approved by the local authorities. The soil surface is then ripped (scarified) to the depth specified and until the surface is free from ruts, hummocks, roots, or other uneven features that would prevent uniform compaction. Where fills are made on hillsides or slopes, the slope of the existing soil where fill is to be placed should be ripped or scarified to a depth of at least 8 inches. Where fill soil is to be placed on a slope with a slope ratio greater than 6 feet horizontal to 1 foot vertical, a licensed civil engineer must be employed to design appropriate methods of fill retention. Fill soil should be placed in layers that, when compacted, will not exceed 8 inches in depth. The first layer should be spread evenly and incorporated into the existing soil to an adequate depth to ensure uniform compaction.

Cut-and-fill areas should be kept shaped and drained during construction. Swales and drainage ways should be maintained in such a manner as to drain effectively at all times. Too much water turns dirt to mud in a hurry, and those of you who are tractor hands know that you cannot grade mud. Graded areas should be protected against the elements until completion and acceptance of the work. Compaction should be accomplished while the fill material has a moisture content sufficient to allow the necessary compaction to be obtained. This level varies per type of soil but averages 9- to 11-percent moisture before becoming unworkable. Engineers know this material is now uncompactable because of a high plasticity soil due to an overoptimum moisture level. The neighbor's kid knows it as mud. Same thing. Soil compaction should not be done when it is raining or when the soil contains excessive moisture. Minimum degrees of compaction should be achieved to meet the following requirements:

- Top 1 foot beneath walks or paving: 95-percent relative density
- Other fill beneath walks or paving: 90-percent relative density
- Fill in planting areas: 80-percent relative density
- Other nonstructural fill or backfill: 85-percent relative density

Fills should not encroach on natural watercourses or constructed channels. Fills placed adjacent to watercourses should have suitable protection against erosion during flooding. Grading equipment should not cross or disturb live stream channels without adequate temporary facilities to prevent sediment pollution. In most states, the

Department of Fish and Game will arrest you for making that mistake. Excavated material should not be deposited or stored in or alongside watercourses where the materials can be washed away by high water or storm runoff.

Finish grading

Placement of imported topsoil, if required, should be done prior to finish grading. Finish-graded surfaces should be smooth, uniform, and totally free of debris and rocks and soil lumps larger than 1 inch. All grades should blend into the adjacent areas in a smooth and natural-looking appearance. Finish grades abutting walks, drives, or structures should be even and uniform. All finish grades should slope away from improvements at a minimum 2-percent gradient. The national building codes mandate a minimum of 2-percent slope away from a building for runoff.

Standard grading practices are that all land within a development should be graded to drain and dispose of surface water without ponding, except where approved by the permit-issuing authority. Grading operations should be conducted so as to prevent damaging effects of sediment production and dust on the site and on adjoining properties. To prevent polluting discharges from occurring, erosion- and sediment-control devices should be employed for all grading and filling. Erosion-control devices and measures that may be required include, but are not limited to, energy-absorbing devices to reduce the velocity of runoff water and sedimentation controls, such as sediment debris basins and sediment traps. Sediment should be retained on the site. Sediment basins, sediment traps, or similar sediment control measures should be installed before extensive clearing and grading operations begin. Any trapped sediment that accumulates during construction should be removed to a disposal site as it accumulates. Dispersal of water runoff from developed areas over large, undisturbed areas requires multiple discharge points to reduce the volume of runoff over localized areas.

Provisions should be made to control the increased runoff caused by changed contours and surface conditions during and after development. To prevent excess runoff, the rate of surface water runoff should be structurally retarded. When making surface changes, be sure to do all of the following: Collect on-site surface runoff and dispose of it at nonerosive velocities to the point of discharge into the common watercourse of the drainage area. Direct existing and potential off-site runoff water into sediment basins, silt traps, or similar measures. Retain sediment being transported by runoff water on-site through the use of sediment basins, silt traps, or similar measures.

Concentration of surface water should be permitted only in protected swales or watercourses. Where drainage swales are used to divert surface waters, they should be vegetated or otherwise protected from the watercourse.

All or some of the topsoil on the site may be stockpiled for use on areas of revegetation. Stockpiled soil should be located so it cannot become a source of off-site sediment damage if erosion occurs, and it should be far enough from streams or drainage ways so that surface runoff cannot carry sediment downstream. Material from trenches and pits should be stockpiled on the upslope side of excavations. Trenches and pits should be promptly backfilled and compacted to reduce the risk of erosion. Mulch or other protective coverings should be applied on stockpiled material that will be exposed through the winter season or will face a high risk of summer rains. Seeds should be planted in time for the first germination-causing rains. Most regions with rainy seasons require that seeding be done before October 31st. If seeding is done long before the rainy season, loss caused by birds and insects may be significant. Seeds should be planted while temperatures are mild and daylight is relatively long (before the end of November) so plants can establish top growth and establish a root mat capable of resisting the erosive force of major storms by 30 days after the first rain.

Irrigation is expensive and not necessary unless the area is particularly critical. Once begun, it must be continued until plant cover is fully matured. Ceasing irrigation after germination results in seedlings being killed by drought before producing seeds. The surface to be seeded should be rough and broken up so that it can hold seeds and retard runoff. As an area is graded, it should not be smoothed to a hard, slick surface by grading equipment but left in a rough or serrated condition.

Whenever slope, soil, or timing factors allow, the seeds should be covered with soil or mulch. Small areas can be hand-seeded to provide uniform coverage. A seed drill works well on level areas but should not be used on slopes greater than 3:1. When seeds are drilled, seed and fertilizer quantities may be reduced compared to broadcast application. Hydroseeding or hydromulching is most efficient for seeding slopes steeper than 3:1. The advantage of hydroseeding or hydromulching is the ability of seeds and mulch material to adhere to steep topography. Application of mulch increases plant establishment and protects a disturbed site from erosive forces. Mulch holds fertilizers, seeds, and soil in place in the presence of wind, rain, and runoff and maintains moisture near the soil surface. Straw is acceptable mulch material under the following conditions:

- Open areas accessible by straw-blowing equipment within 50 feet.

- Slopes flatter than 1½:1.
- Fill slopes.
- Non-windy areas.
- Downhill or downwind applications.
- Hand-spread in very small locations.

Hydromulching is preferred under the following conditions:

- Areas far from road access that can be reached with hoses.
- Slopes steeper than 3:1.
- Slopes with shallow soil covers.
- Windy areas.
- Areas where fire hazard or weed growth is undesirable.

12

Plant identification

Plant classification

Botanists have classified the world's plants into an orderly, ranked system reflecting similarities among them. The plant kingdom is broken down into groups that are less and less inclusive; division, class, order, and then other groups, to be described next, which are the ones of most significance to landscapers.

Family

Each plant belongs to a family, members of which share certain broad characteristics that are not always immediately evident. The rose family, for instance, includes such diverse plants as the rose, the apple tree, and the familiar perennial Geum. Many family names end in *-aceae* (Orchidaceae, Asteraceae, Liliaceae).

Genus

A plant family is divided into groups of more closely related plants; each group is called a *genus* (the plural is *genera*). Sometimes a family contains only one genus: For example, Ginkgoaceae contains only the genus Ginkgo. At the other extreme, the composite family (Compositae) contains around 950 genera. The first word in a plant's botanical name is the name of the genus to which it belongs: for example, Ginkgo, Liquid amber, Primula.

Species

Each genus is subdivided into groups of individuals called *species*. The second word in a plant's botanical name designates the species. Each species is a generally distinct entity, reproducing from seed with only a small amount of variation. Species in a genus share many common features but differ in at least one characteristic.

Subspecies and varieties
A third word in a botanical name indicates a subspecies or variety. In the strictest sense, a subspecies is more inclusive than a variety. *Subspecies* is often used to denote a geographical variant of a species, but in general usage, *subspecies* and *variety* have become virtually interchangeable. Subspecies or varieties retain most characteristics of their species while differing in some particular way, such as flower color or leaf size. The name may appear in either of two ways: *Juniperus chinensis sargentii* (a subspecies) or *Juniperus chinensis 'San Jose'* (a variety).

Horticultural variety (clone or cultivar)
Varieties often are of hybrid origin. They are usually listed by genus name followed by cultivar name, as in Rosa 'Chrysler Imperial.' Some have been found as wild plants but have been perpetuated by cuttings or other means of vegetative propagation.

Hybrid
A hybrid is a distinct plant resulting from a cross between two species, subspecies, varieties, cultivars, strains, or any combination of these, or even between two plants from different genera. Some occur in the wild, but more often hybrids are deliberate crosses.

Strain
Many popular annuals and some perennials are sold as strains, such as State Fair zinnias. Plants in a strain usually share similar growth characteristics but are variable in some way, usually in flower color.

Trees

Trees are important to the planet and our continued existence as a species on this planet, so let me first begin the tree section by reviewing the modern practice of *tree topping*. This practice has been proven to be harmful to the tree, increases diseases, and is to be avoided unless absolutely necessary, as in power lines clearance. Tree topping is the shortening of branches to stubs and the removal of tree tops to reduce tree height and spread. Many past landscapers believed that the profuse growth of foliage and branches associated with severe topping indicated increased tree vigor. In reality, the tree is attempting to replace lost leaves needed to make the food that supports the entire tree. Heavy pruning removes much of the wood and buds that contain stored energy for new growth. New buds must form for the tree to continue growing. In some trees, buds are slow to form, and die-back or tree death results. All new growth is made by using stored energy. Topping can deplete a tree's energy reserves, increasing susceptibility to some insects and disease. Topping shifts a tree's priority from growth to survival and repair.

Topping actually disfigures trees, leaving unsightly branch stubs and large, conspicuous pruning cuts that stimulate dense, broom-like branch growth. Many professional arborists no longer include tree topping as a service, and in fact, most consider it malpractice. Experience and research has shown that tree topping destroys natural shape, causes branch die-back, encourages decay, and stimulates the growth of dense, closely spaced and weakly attached shoots just below the pruning cut. It often causes bark damage from sudden exposure to direct sunlight, weakens the structure, and reduces its useful lifespan. Large trees are often topped because people consider them to be unsafe. They fear branches may drop off or blow down. Although topping may initially reduce a tree's hazard, it seldom corrects existing structural problems. Unless resolved, these problems worsen with time, jeopardizing tree safety. Additionally, the new shoots that form near the pruning cut are weakly attached and prone to breakage as they grow larger and heavier. This fact often makes topped trees more hazardous than before pruning.

Proper pruning, on the other hand, is seldom noticed because it preserves the tree's natural shape, leaving it improved yet visually unchanged. Proper pruning of trees improves natural form and appearance, improves branch spacing, strengthens branch attachment, invigorates or slows branch growth rate, improves stability by reducing wind resistance, removes dead or diseased branches from the tree, and, if the tree is next to a structure, increases lighting to the interior. The fundamental concept of proper pruning is to remove an unwanted branch at its attachment point to the trunk or another branch without leaving a stub or damaging the branch collar and branch bark ridge (BBR). In this manner, unnecessary injury to the trunk or remaining branch is avoided. *Flush cutting*, the practice of cutting behind the BBR or removing the branch collar, destroys the natural protective zone, allowing decay-causing pathogens to invade the trunk or remaining branch wood.

A *heading cut* removes a branch to a stub, a bud, or a branch too small to assume a terminal role. Heading cuts stimulate vigorous, upright, poorly spaced, and weakly attached shoots just below the pruning cut. Wood decay often develops below such cuts, especially larger ones, further weakening branch structure. In some cases, "headed" branches die back several feet before shoots develop. Stubs that don't produce new foliage gradually die back. They steadily deplete their remaining energy supply, becoming defenseless to pathogens, which can proliferate in the dying branch remnant. Because the tree is unable to close over a stub, the tree's natural defenses eventually weaken and fail, allowing pathogens to invade the trunk or branch. Heading or, more commonly, "topping," is used to describe the removal of the upper portion of a tree's canopy to a desired height. This method involves shortening most or all branches to stubs or lateral branches too small to become leaders. Heading destroys natural shape, weakens the structure, and reduces health and useful life span. It is usually inappropriate for shade and ornamental trees.

A *thinning cut* removes a branch at its attachment point to another branch or to the trunk or shortens it to a lateral branch large enough to become a leader. The term *thinning* refers to the selective removal of branches, using thinning cuts to improve structure, reduce height, spread, branch weight, and wind resistance. Thinning can also be used to suppress or stimulate branch growth, depending on need. Thinning preserves natural shape and improves branch spacing and attachment while protecting the tree's natural defenses.

Excessive pruning removes needed leaves, branches, buds, and stored energy. Additional stored energy is used to replace the lost foliage and branches. Depending on severity, this practice can kill the tree, increase susceptibility to pests, reduce growth and health, stimulate epicormic sprouting, and result in sunburned bark. As a general rule, remove no more than 20 percent of a tree's foliage. Young trees can tolerate more severe pruning. Aging trees, on the other hand, are less tolerant of pruning. Such trees should be pruned only as necessary. Restrict pruning to remove dead, suppressed, structurally weak, diseased, and insect-injured branches or to lighten heavy horizontal branches.

Trees resist the entrance and spread of pathogens by forming protective barriers to isolate injured, diseased, and decayed wood. Contained within the flared base (branch collar) of most branches is an important barrier zone that prevents the spread of decay into the trunk or parent branch. The branch collar and the raised strip of bark (branch bark ridge), typically seen in the branch crotch, mark the boundary between the branch and trunk. Contrary to what their names imply, they are actually part of the trunk or parent branch. The trunk or parent branch envelops (overlaps) the branch base after it forms new wood each spring. Although the branch core extends into the branch collar, it is surrounded by trunk/parent branch tissue. Loss of the branch collar or branch bark ridge due to pruning or other means eliminates the protective zone within, leaving the trunk or parent branch relatively defenseless to decay.

Branch collars may be inconspicuous, sunken, slightly protruding, or bulging. Often they extend beyond the BBR, and sometimes even the BBR is indistinct. Thus the BBR is not always a reliable marker for making pruning cuts. If the branch collar is indistinct, the position and angle of the cut can be easily approximated. A number of methods to determine the location of the proper cut are discussed here; however, none are consistently accurate. Use the method that best protects the branch collar without leaving a branch stub. To remove a live branch, make the final cut just outside the BBR and the branch collar. Use an undercut, then a throughcut system to remove heavy branches that might split during removal, damaging the branch collar or tearing the bark. Make the final cut smooth without loosening or tearing the bark. Wound dressings have not been shown to prevent or reduce decay and therefore are not recommended. If the BBR is not clearly visible, approximate its position by bisecting the angle formed within the crotch. Make sure to cut outside the branch collar if it is well developed. You may also bisect the angle formed by the branch and the trunk below the crotch to approximate the final cut when the branch collar is indistinct.

To remove a limb with no apparent branch collar, make the angle of the final cut approximate the angle formed between the BBR and an imaginary line intersecting the top of the BBR parallel to the trunk. The angle formed between the BBR and an imaginary line intersecting the top of the BBR parallel to the limb being removed may also be used to approximate the final cut. Use the method that appears to best protect the branch collar without leaving a stub. Occasionally either method can be inaccurate. For some trees, the branch collar is well developed and extends beyond the BBR. The branch collar of a few trees, e.g., alder, redwood, dawn redwood, cypress, poplar, etc., are sunken. The final cut on such trees may be nearly vertical, resembling a flush cut. To remove a dead branch, make the final cut outside the collar of living tissue surrounding the dead wood, called *callus* (wound wood). Even if the collar has grown out along the branch stub, remove only the dead stub, leaving the live collar intact.

To reduce the length of a branch or the height of a leader, cut back to a lower lateral at least half the diameter of the trunk or branch being removed. Make the final cut from a point just outside the top of the BBR to a point directly opposite the bottom of the BBR. Another method to approximate the correct angle is to make the final cut bisect the angle formed by the BBR and an imaginary line intersecting the top of the BBR perpendicular to the axis of the limb being removed.

One goal of structural pruning is to maintain the size of lateral branches to less than three-fourths the diameter of the branch or trunk from which they originate. When a branch exceeds this limit, thin the foliage along the branch by 15 to 25 percent, particularly near the terminal. Thin the parent branch less, if at all. Growth will slow in the thinned branch and increase in the other, ultimately improving the strength of the branch attachment. Another option is to shorten the branch back (up to 25 percent) to a lower lateral at least half the diameter of the branch being removed. Either method serves to suppress a codominant stem (forking branches of nearly equal size). Codominant stems are inherently weak and should be eliminated while trees are young, particularly if they form the tree's scaffold branches. To remove a codominant stem, make the final cut just beyond the BBR to a point directly opposite the bottom of the BBR. A line intersecting the top of the BBR perpendicular to the axis of the limb being removed also approximates the angle of the cut.

Included bark, indicated by an inverted (ingrowing) BBR or bark pinched between the branch and trunk, often occurs in narrow-angled branch crotches. Typically, as such branches grow, the branch and the trunk above the inverted BBR begin to squeeze together. When this occurs, the actual union is lower than the apparent union. Although there is contact between the branch and trunk, there is no union. Such branches are inherently weak and should be removed. Some arborists recommend cutting upward at a 45-degree angle from the branch collar to the actual branch/trunk union. Others recommend cutting upward from a point directly opposite the base of the inverted BBR to the actual branch/trunk union BBR. Sometimes it's more practical to cut upward to the top of the apparent union, especially when the trunk has begun to envelop the branch. In either case, avoid cutting into the trunk or remaining branch. When there is included bark between two wide-angled or codominant branches, but no stem contact, cut from the branch collar to the top of the inverted BBR. Remove vigorous, upright branches that compete with the leader of excurrent trees. Try to maintain a single leader in trees with decurrent growth form for as long as practical to avoid codominant stems in the main scaffold branches.

Approximately one-half of a tree's foliage should originate in the lower two-thirds of the tree. On young trees, leave the branches along the lower trunk at least temporarily. These branches help shade and nourish the trunk. Space these temporary branches 4 to 8 inches apart, and shorten them to 12- to 18-inch spurs. Reprune as necessary to keep in bounds. Gradually remove them as they increase in size (exceed ¾ inch in diameter). Remove about one-third of the temporary branches each year, leaving the remainder well-spaced. Perhaps the most important reason to prune is to improve branch spacing. This process is best done gradually, over time. Select permanent branches that are radially arranged and vertically spaced 18 to 24 inches or more apart for large growing trees. Whorled branched conifers are an exception and seldom need pruning. For smaller growing trees, space branches 4 to 12 inches apart. Continue to improve branching as the tree matures. Some branches die or become suppressed as other branches dominate.

Proper pruning is also a matter of timing. Wounds made in the spring and early summer close more rapidly than those made later in the growing season, especially those made in the fall and early winter. The rate of wound closure is greatest during peak cambial activity (wood formation). Pruning wounds made in the fall and early winter typically close slowly and are subject to tissue die-back beyond the original wound. Most arborists discourage fall pruning when decay-causing pathogens are sporulating. They also caution about pruning during leaf flush when the bark can be easily damaged. Depending on the final objective, the following pruning guidelines are typical for most trees:

- Late dormant season pruning promotes vigorous growth.
- Maximum dwarfing is achieved by early to mid-summer pruning.
- Summer pruning minimizes sprouting and reduces bleeding (sap flow), common in maples, elms, birches, fruitless mulberry, etc.

Training procedures for young trees

- Don't top newly planted trees; the resulting structure is difficult to correct.
- Try to reestablish a leader in trees that have been topped by commercial growers by thinning-out crowded laterals. Better yet, avoid purchasing topped trees.
- Improve structure at the time of planting, but don't top-prune to enhance the root-to-shoot ratio.
- Start developing strong structure when trees are young (two to five years old). Establish the basic framework (scaffold branches).
- Maintain a single leader for as long as possible. Remove any upright shoots that compete with it. Round-headed trees eventually develop multiple leaders.

- Conifers seldom need pruning except to raise the canopy for clearance.
- Correct weak structure, such as crowded branches, multiple leaders, codominant stems (V crotches), included bark (ingrowing branch bark ridge), and dead and diseased branches.
- Maintain natural growth form.
- If present, leave branches temporarily along the lower trunk to shade and nourish the trunk.
- Remove the larger branches that are too low to be permanent or temporary.
- Remove vigorous, upright shoots (water sprouts).
- Prune out weak, poorly formed, crowded, and heavily shaded branches in the leafy canopy. Keep select well-spaced, strongly attached, and wide-angled branches.
- Keep lateral branches less than three-quarters the diameter of the trunk or parent branch on which they grow by shortening the branch or thinning its foliage by up to 25 percent in either case. Branches requiring greater suppression can be pruned more severely.
- When shortening a branch, cut back to a lateral that is at least half the diameter of the branch being removed. Small branches less than ¾ inch in diameter can be headed-back (stubbed) to a well-oriented bud.
- Select permanent branches that are radially arranged around the trunk and vertically spaced 18 to 24 inches apart for large growing trees and 4 to 12 inches apart for smaller growing trees.
- Correct severe problems over several years to avoid over-pruning.

Pleaching is a term in tree pruning that refers to a method of training plant growth in which the tree's branches are interwoven and plaited together to form a hedge or an arbor. Subsequent pruning merely maintains a neat and rather formal pattern. Trees that can be pleached include beech, apple, peach, and pear. *Pollarding* is another term for a style of pruning in which the main limbs of a young tree are drastically cut back to short lengths. Each dormant season following, the growth from these branch stubs is cut back to one or two buds. In time, branch ends become large and knobby. The result is a compact, leafy dome during the growing season and a somewhat grotesque branch structure during the dormant months. London plane tree (*Platanus acerifolia*) is most often subjected to this treatment.

When a conifer has been damaged by cold or breakage, you may have to remove entire limbs. It's almost impossible to restore the natural shape, but you can often make the most of the situation by trimming or training the damaged plant into an unusual sculptural form. If the central leader has been damaged, you can stake one of the next lower branches vertically and train it as a new leader.

Tree identification

Both deciduous and evergreen trees fall into two criteria for tree layout in the landscape design: shade trees and ornamental trees.

Shade trees

Common name: River birch
Botanical name: *Betula nigra*
Hardiness zone: 2
Form: Typically multiple-stemmed, oval, deciduous
Leaves: Simple, alternate, egg-shaped with point at the tip; double-toothed margin, veins generally on underneath side of leaf
Size: Large
Exposure: Sun to part shade
Texture: Medium
Flowers: Not showy
Fruit: 1-inch long cone-like containing small winged seeds
Color: Foliage is dark green, turning bright yellow in fall. Bark is copper-colored and papery.
Cultural notes: Transplant in very late winter to a location with abundant moisture. Needs supplemental watering during drought unless planted next to water. Ideal for soggy locations in the landscape.
Cultivars: 'Gulf Stream' has larger leaves and lighter, showier bark.

Common name: Lacebark elm
Botanical name: *Ulmus parvifolia*
Hardiness zone: 4
Form: Round to oval crown.
Size: Large
Exposure: Sun to part shade
Texture: Fine
Leaves: Simple, alternate, lopsided with a serrated margin
Flowers: Not showy
Fruit: Showy, borne in multiple clusters among the leaves during October
Color: Medium to dark green; yellow fall color; bark peels, leaving salmon-colored patches
Cultural notes: This tree is extremely tough and durable and grows almost anywhere. It tolerates many adverse conditions and is highly

resistant to disease and insect attacks. It responds vigorously to good cultural practices. It is susceptible to leaf spot in the spring.

Cultivars: 'Sempervirens' has greater retention of foliage. 'Drake' is like 'Sempervirens,' except it grows more upright. It is generally an inferior variety in moist, humid areas of the country because of leaf-spot diseases.

Common name: Northern red oak
Botanical name: *Quercus rubra*
Hardiness zone: 3
Form: Round to oval head
Size: Large
Exposure: Sun
Texture: Coarse
Leaves: Simple, alternate, 5 to 8 inches long, 4 to 6 inches wide, usually has 7 to 11 lobes with one to three bristle tips
Flowers: Not showy
Fruit: Mature in fall of second year; 1 to 1¼ inches long and ½ to 1 inch wide
Color: Foliage is deep dark green on top of the leaf with a lighter green underside; petiole is usually red; red-orange fall color.
Cultural notes: This tree grows well in fairly good soils. It grows west about as far as Oklahoma City and Wichita. It transplants well in fall, winter, or early spring.

Common name: Pin oak
Botanical name: *Quercus palustris*
Hardiness zone: 3
Form: Pyramidal with drooping lower branches
Size: Large
Exposure: Sun
Texture: Medium
Leaves: Simple, alternate, 4 to 6 inches long, 2 to 5 inches wide with five to nine variable lobes. Like most of the red oak group, the leaves are generally forked with bristles on the tips.
Flowers: Not showy
Fruit: Small acorn matures in early fall, is rounded and light brown, and bitter to taste.
Color: Dark green, with good fall color—either red or red-orange
Cultural notes: The pin oak does well in most conditions except areas where the soils are extremely poor and the pH of the soil is high. It sometimes develops chlorosis, usually due to an iron and manganese deficiency. It responds well under good cultural practices if the pH is kept below 6. This tree is more of a specimen tree because the growth habit requires the lower branches to be removed if it is to be used for shade. Once these lower branches are removed, only the narrow top of the tree remains, casting no shade. Do not plant this tree next to drives or sidewalks as the downward angle of the branches are stiff and hazardous.

Cultivars: 'Sovereign' has only horizontal or upright branches, which makes it more desirable for street and other uses. 'Clownright' is similar to 'Sovereign,' but is more narrow and upright.

Common name: Live oak
Botanical name: *Quercus virginiana*
Hardiness zone: 7
Form: Broad, oval-crowned
Size: Medium to large
Exposure: Sun
Texture: Fine
Leaves: Simple, alternate, leathery, elliptical shaped; leaf margins are usually smooth and unlobed, but new growth may have rounded lobes with serrated margins.
Flowers: Female flowers not showy; males are long and slender yellowish clusters in the early spring.
Fruit: Football-shaped acorn about 1 inch long
Color: Dark green foliage
Cultural notes: Growth is very slow in most areas. It is extremely tough and tolerant of poor soils and compaction but susceptible to cold weather. It also grows slower if the climate is colder. Transplant in spring.

Common name: Fruitless mulberry
Botanical name: *Morus alba 'Fruitless.'*
Hardiness zone: 3
Form: Spreading round-headed
Leaves: Simple, alternate, oval, or lopsided; usually has 3 lobes with a serrated margin
Flowers: None
Fruit: None
Color: Bright green leaves
Cultural notes: Grows rapidly in most soils with proper care. Dense shade makes growing anything except a ground cover very difficult.
Cultivars: *Morus alba 'Fruitless'* is the cultivar recommended because the common mulberry produces a lot of fruit, which creates a litter problem.

Common name: Water oak
Botanical name: *Quercus nigra*
Hardiness zone: 6
Form: Broad, oval, or round-topped
Size: Large
Exposure: Sun to part shade
Texture: Medium
Leaves: Simple, alternate, narrow with a club-shaped end; margin is smooth or wavy with a bristle tip.
Flowers: Not showy
Fruit: Small round acorn, which is ripe in early fall

Color: Deep green foliage; brown in the winter; tends to hold its leaves well into the winter

Cultural notes: It grows rapidly under very wet conditions, but this produces an undesirable tree. In more northern and western areas, it grows slower and produces a good landscape tree that tolerates most soil conditions and compacted soils. It is one of the best oak shade trees.

Common name: Chinese pistache
Botanical name: *Pistacia chinensis*
Hardiness zone: 6
Form: Low, vase-shaped
Size: Medium
Exposure: Sun
Texture: Fine
Leaves: Compound, alternate, 8 to 10 inches long, 4 to 5 inches wide, generally 10 to 14 leaflets
Flowers: Not showy
Fruit: Small, round berries about ¼ inch in diameter; green to purple-red in the fall
Color: Medium to dark green, with orange to red-orange fall color
Cultural notes: A very tough, durable, small tree that grows best in well-drained soil but tolerates other conditions, this tree transplants well in the spring.

Common name: Sweetgum
Botanical name: *Liquidambar styraciflag*
Hardiness zone: 4
Form: Oval-crowned
Size: Large
Exposure: Sun
Texture: Medium
Leaves: Simple, alternate, 3 to 6 inches long; star-shaped with a saw-toothed edge
Flowers: Not showy
Fruit: Golf-ball size, round, spiny fruit
Color: Deep green; yellow to red-orange fall color
Cultural notes: Sweetgum requires an abundance of water to grow well and needs a good soil. Fruit creates quite a litter problem. It should not be transplanted in the fall.
Cultivars: 'Autumn Glow' has better fall color.

Common name: Sycamore
Botanical name: *Platanus occidentalis*
Hardiness zone: 3
Form: Huge, pyramidal
Size: Very large
Exposure: Sun
Texture: Coarse

Leaves: Simple, alternate, 10 to 12 inches long, 6 to 8 inches wide, five main lobes that are coarsely toothed or lobed a second time
Flowers: Not showy
Fruit: Golf-ball-sized round ball made up of many seeds
Color: Medium-green foliage turning light orange-brown in the fall
Cultural notes: Sycamore is fairly tolerant to a wide variety of soils as long as extra water is present. It is very susceptible to anthracnose and lacebug problems. It creates a litter problem with large leaves and seed balls. They are easy to transplant in spring, fall, winter, and early summer if dug while dormant.

Common name: Weeping willow
Botanical name: *Salix babylonica*
Hardiness zone: 3
Form: Round-headed with drooping branches
Size: Medium to large
Exposure: Sun
Texture: Fine
Leaves: Simple, alternate, very narrow
Flowers: Not showy
Fruit: Not showy
Color: Medium to olive green; yellow fall color
Cultural notes: It does well all over the United States if an abundance of water is present. It is mostly a short-lived tree with only about 15 to 30 years expected. Borers and willow leaf beetles are major pests. The wood is extremely brittle.
Cultivars: 'Golden' has yellow stems.

Common name: Southern magnolia
Botanical name: *Magnolia grandiflora*
Hardiness zone: 7
Form: Pyramidal
Size: Medium to large
Exposure: Sun to part shade
Texture: Coarse
Leaves: Simple, alternate, thick, leathery, oval with smooth margin
Flowers: Single, cup-shaped, 6 to 16 round petals, usually white, and very fragrant
Fruit: Looks like a pine cone 2 to 4 inches long, $1\frac{1}{2}$ inches wide, splits open to expose red seeds (about 40 to 60 per cone)
Color: Shiny dark-green foliage
Cultural notes: It grows mostly in southeastern states with adequate moisture and fairly fertile soil. It is difficult to transplant but should be done in early spring. Magnolia is susceptible to magnesium deficiency, as evidenced by yellow band around the margin of the leaf. Winter damage turns leaves brown; protect it from the north winter wind. Even mature trees need supplemental irrigation during drought, which causes leaf drop.

Common name: Common hackberry
Botanical name: *Celtis occidentalis*
Hardiness zone: 2
Form: In youth, weakly pyramidal; in maturity, the crown is a broad top of ascending, arching branches, often with drooping branchlets
Leaves: Alternate, simple, ovate to oblong ovate, acute to acuminate, rounded at base, serrated except at base
Flowers: Not showy; solitary in axils of the leaves during April and May
Fruit: Fleshy, orange-red to dark purple rounded drupe; flavored like dates and relished by birds and wildlife
Color: Dull light to medium green in summer and yellow or yellow-green in fall
Cultural notes: The hackberry prefers rich, moist soils but grows in dry, heavy or sandy, rocky soils. It withstands acid or alkaline conditions and tolerates wind.
Cultivars: 'Prairie Pride' is selected for glossy green foliage and uniform compact crown.

Common name: Green ash
Botanical name: *Fraxinus pennsylvanica*
Hardiness zone: 3
Form: Pyramidal when young and developing an upright spreading habit at maturity
Size: Large
Exposure: Full sun
Texture: Medium in leaf; coarse in winter
Leaves: Opposite, pinnately compound, and serrate
Flowers: Not ornamentally important; dioecious, both sexes appearing in panicles before or with the leaves
Fruit: Samara, 1 to 2 inches long. Not of ornamental significance
Color: Shiny, medium to dark green in summer, changing to yellow in the fall
Cultural notes: Green ash is found native in most bottomlands and along streambanks. It transplants readily, and once established, it tolerates high pH, salt, and drought.
Cultivars: 'Kindred,' 'Marmust Seedless,' 'Bergeson,' 'Patmore,' and 'Summit'

Ornamental trees

Common name: Flowering crabapple
Botanical name: *Malus spp*
Hardiness zone: 3
Form: Low branches, rounded head
Leaves: Simple, alternate, oval, 2 to 4 inches long with serrated margin
Flowers: White, pink, or red, fragrant, clustered, end blossoms open

first and progress backward, producing a longer show of flowers than most trees.

Fruit: Small, tart, apple-like fruits, which are edible

Color: Dark green

Cultural notes: Crabapple tolerates most soils, needs some corrective pruning, and is somewhat susceptible to fire blight, cedar apple rust, powdery mildew, and scab.

Cultivars: 'Snowdrift' has white flowers; 'Hopa' has pink ones. There are many others.

Common name: Dogwood

Botanical name: *Cornus florida*

Hardiness zone: 4

Form: Rounded head

Leaves: Simple, opposite, egg-shaped, 3 to 5 inches long, smooth margin, short petiole

Flowers: Four petal-like bracts (white or pink) surrounding a cluster of small yellow or white flowers

Fruit: Clustered, egg-shaped, about ½ inch long, red

Color: Foliage is bright green on top with a pale green underside.

Cultural notes: Dogwood is an understory tree that grows best in fairly good soils that are moist but not wet. It does not tolerate wet feet, full sun, hot, dry, or exposed locations. It does not tolerate compacted soils.

Cultivars: 'Cherokee Chief' has dark pink flowers that are very showy.

Common name: Goldenrain tree

Botanical name: *Koelreuteria paniculata*

Hardiness zone: 5

Form: Broad, round head

Size: Small to medium

Exposure: Sun

Texture: Medium

Leaves: Alternate, twice compound, 16 to 22 inches long, ovate leaflets with irregularly toothed margins

Flowers: Bright yellow clusters on top of tree, 15 to 20 inches long; very attractive

Fruit: Thin-walled, round, pod-like capsules with two or three round black seeds inside; capsules are pink and are retained until late summer or fall, when they fall off.

Color: Foliage medium green; yellow fall color

Cultural notes: This is a fairly tough plant that grows in heavy clay as well as sandy soils. It needs some corrective pruning and responds well to good cultural practices. It attracts box elder bugs, which may become a nuisance since they move indoors in the fall. Leave adequate distance between tree and dwellings.

Cultivars: None

Common name: Yaupon holly
Botanical name: *Llex vomitoria*
Hardiness zone: 7
Form: Irregular
Size: Small to medium
Exposure: Sun to shade
Texture: Fine
Leaves: Simple, alternate, evergreen, flat elliptical or oval, usually small, ½ inch, serrated margins
Flowers: Not showy
Fruit: Red, showy, ³⁄₁₆ inch
Color: Foliage is glossy green
Cultural notes: Yaupon holly is very tough; it tolerates heat, drought, full sun, and poor soil. It also grows in swampy areas. Multitrunk specimens are very showy and decorative as ornamentals.
Cultivars: Dwarf cultivars are available; they reach 4 to 5 feet high.

Common name: Saucer magnolia
Botanical name: *Magnolia soulangiana*
Hardiness zone: 5
Form: Broad, spreading
Size: Small to medium
Exposure: Sun to part shade
Texture: Coarse
Leaves: Simple, alternate, 4 to 7 inches long, 2 to 4 inches wide, thick, smooth margin with a point at the tip
Flowers: White with purple center; 4 to 6 inches in diameter
Fruit: Not showy
Color: Foliage is light to medium green with pale yellow fall color.
Cultural notes: It prefers rich, well-drained soil and is difficult to transplant.
Cultivars: 'Alexandrina' has purplish-pink flowers that bloom later.

Common name: Bradford pear
Botanical name: *Pyrus calleryana 'Bradfordi'*

Hardiness zone: 4
Form: Pyramidal
Size: Medium
Exposure: Sun
Texture: Medium
Leaves: Simple, opposite, 2 to 3 inches long, rounded at base with irregular serrated margin
Flowers: White, spectacular show in early spring
Fruit: Generally fruitless
Color: Foliage is deep green with orange fall color.
Cultural notes: Bradford pear grows well in many locations, especially poor soil and urban situations. It is a very spectacular tree that grows well with minimum care. It is resistant to fire blight.

Cultivars: 'Bradford' is a cultivar.

Common name: Purpleleaf plum
Botanical name: *Prunus cerasifera*
Hardiness zone: 3
Form: Pyramidal
Size: Small to medium
Exposure: Sun
Texture: Medium
Leaves: Simple, ovate, 1½ inches long, ½ inch wide, round at base, tapering to tip, serrated edge
Flowers: Showy pink flowers in April
Fruit: Small plum about 1 inch in diameter, edible, but not very tasty
Color: Purple or purple-red foliage
Cultural notes: Plum is easy to grow and tolerates a wide variety of soils and conditions. It needs to grow in full sun for best color. Borers are a major problem and will kill these trees.
Cultivars: 'Thunderbond' has intense purple foliage. There are many others.

Common name: Redbud
Botanical name: *Cercis canadensis*
Hardiness zone: 4
Form: Flat-topped, widely spreading
Leaves: Simple, alternate, heart-shaped, 2 to 3 inches long and wide with smooth margins and long petioles
Flowers: Very showy with purple or white flowers grouped in clusters along the stem in early spring
Fruit: Oblong, flattened pod, 2 to 3 inches long, brown
Color: Foliage is dark green with yellow fall color.
Cultural notes: Redbud grows well in very poor soils but responds well to good culture. It needs some corrective pruning and is difficult to transplant. It is very susceptible to borers, leaf rollers, and tiers.
Cultivars: 'Alba' has white flowers. 'Oklahoma' has deep purple flowers and very shiny leaves that resist leaf rollers and tiers. The best variety, 'Forest Pansy,' has purple foliage.

Common name: Purpleleaf sand cherry
Botanical name: *Prunus cistena* (cross between P. pumila and P. cerasifera)
Hardiness zone: 2
Form: Upright and somewhat spreading
Size: Reaches 7 to 10 feet with slightly smaller spread
Exposure: Full sun
Texture: Medium in leaf and in winter
Leaves: Alternate, simple, and moderately serrate
Flowers: Single, pink, fragrant, and borne after leaves have developed in late April and May

Fruit: Blackish purple; desirable for wildlife
Color: Intensely reddish purple throughout the summer
Cultural notes: This tree is one of the hardiest purple-leaf plants.
Cultivars: None

Common name: Amur maple
Botanical name: *Acer ginnala*
Hardiness zone: 2
Form: Irregular to oval to rounded; can be successfully tailored to specific landscape requirements
Size: Reaches 15 to 18 feet, small tree, single or multiple stem
Exposure: Full to part sun
Texture: Medium-fine in leaf, medium in winter
Leaves: Opposite, simple, three-lobed, with middle lobe much longer than the lateral lobes, doubly serrate, and dark green
Flowers: Yellowish white, fragrant, borne in small panicles
Fruit: Samara, ¾ to 1 inch long, red to brown in September and October
Color: Bark, grayish brown; leaves, dark glossy green, changing to yellow and red in the fall; best color in full sun
Cultural notes: This maple performs best in moist, well-drained soils. It is very easy to transplant and is adaptable to a wide range of soils and pH ranges.
Cultivars: 'Compactum,' 'Durand Dwarf,' and 'Red Fruit'

Nursery plant selection for trees

Follow these guidelines for choosing which trees to purchase at a nursery.

Container-grown trees
- Trunk in center of container
- Straight trunk or meets design criteria
- Symmetrical branching
- No evidence of borers or insects
- No evidence of disease
- No damage to trunk or branches
- Container not crushed
- Root system fills container adequately
- Tree fully leafed out or green showing in dormant stems
- Roots not growing out through drain holes excessively

Balled-and-burlapped (B&B) trees
- Trunk in center of ball
- Straight trunk or meets design criteria
- Symmetrical branching

- No evidence of borers or insects
- No evidence of disease
- No damage to trunk or branches
- Base of trunk not loose in soil root ball
- Firm root ball
- Burlap not excessively rotted

Bare-root trees
- Straight trunk or meets design criteria
- Symmetrical branching
- No evidence of borers or insects
- No evidence of disease
- No damage to trunk or branches
- Roots are firm and well-developed
- Root system moist (not wet) and protected from drying

Deciduous shrubs

Common name: 'Crimson Pygmy' barberry
Botanical name: *Berberis thunbergi 'Crimson Pigmy'*
Hardiness zone: 3
Form: Dwarf, rounded
Size: Small shrub
Exposure: Sun to part shade
Texture: Medium
Leaves: Simple, alternate, oval with pointed tip, borne on clusters
Flowers: Inconspicuous
Fruit: Not showy
Color: Purple
Cultural notes: This shrub is tough and durable but not very tolerant of drought.
Cultivars: There are many cultivars of barberry from evergreen to deciduous, from dwarf to 8 feet tall.

Common name: Pampas grass
Botanical name: *Cortaderia selloana*
Hardiness zone: 7
Form: Grass clump
Size: Medium to large
Exposure: Sun to part shade
Texture: Fine
Leaves: Grassy clump often 5 to 7 feet tall
Flowers: Long 12- to 24-inch plumes on top of stalks are usually white and emerge in August, remain until January or February; good for dried-flower arrangements

Fruit: Not showy, like grass seed
Color: Foliage is dark green, flowers are white or pink
Cultural notes: Pampas grass is tough and drought-resistant, doesn't like shade or very wet conditions, turns brown in fall, but foliage must be left on until March. Leaves are serrated and will cut anyone who grabs the leaves. Use caution around children.
Cultivars: 'Rosea' has pink flower plumes but is not as winter hardy.

Common name: Forsythia
Botanical name: *Forsythia spp*
Hardiness zone: 5
Form: Mostly upright
Size: Large shrub
Exposure: Sun
Texture: Medium
Leaves: Opposite, simple, 3 to 4 inches long, oval, serrated margin
Flowers: Bell-shaped, yellow, very early spring, very showy
Fruit: Not showy
Color: Foliage medium to light green
Cultural notes: Forsythia is easy to grow in many soil types but is susceptible to drought damage.
Cultivars: Forsythia suspensa is a weeping or cascading variety. 'Linwood Gold' is the best upright variety.

Common name: Crape myrtle
Botanical name: *Lagerstroemia indica*
Hardiness zone: 7
Form: Multi-stemmed; can be tree form
Size: Large shrub or small tree
Exposure: Sun
Texture: Medium
Leaves: Simple, opposite, elliptical, 2 to 4 inches long, 1 to 2 inches wide, rounded at base and tip with a smooth margin
Flowers: Many different colors, including variegated; very showy
Fruit: Round, tan capsule
Color: Medium green foliage; shows variable full color
Cultural notes: Crape myrtle is a low-maintenance plant, easy to grow and transplant, and tolerates drought and poor soil, but it needs to be planted in an area with good air circulation because of susceptibility to powdery mildew.
Cultivars: There are many cultivars with different-colored blooms and many dwarf varieties, which grow up to 3 or 4 feet tall.

Common name: Common lilac
Botanical name: *Syringa vulgaris*
Hardiness zone: 3
Form: Multiple-stemmed, rounded head

Leaves: Opposite, heart-shaped with long point and smooth margin
Flowers: Terminal clusters in a variety of colors (white, violet); known for fragrance
Fruit: Not showy
Color: Deep green on top, paler green underneath
Cultural notes: Lilac is extremely tough and durable, but it is susceptible to powdery mildew in shade and areas with poor air circulation.
Cultivars: There are many cultivars with different flower colors. Persian lilac (Syringa persica) is more compact and smaller with smaller flower clusters.

Common name: Flowering quince
Botanical name: *Chaenomeles speciosa*
Hardiness zone: 4
Form: Round, dense shrub
Size: Large shrub
Exposure: Sun to part shade
Texture: Medium
Leaves: Simple, alternate, 1 to 3 inches long, oval with a sharply serrated margin, may be clustered on short stalks or spurs, has thorns
Flowers: Red, pink, or white, 1 to 2 inches across, very showy in early spring
Fruit: Small, 1 to 2 inches across, apple-like green or yellow
Color: Foliage glossy green
Cultural notes: Quince is very tough and durable and tolerates a wide range of soils except for very high pH. It is a low-maintenance plant and is susceptible to fire blight.
Cultivars: There are many cultivars with various colors of flowers.

Common name: Vanhoutte spirea or bridalwreath spirea
Botanical name: *Spirea x 'Vanhouttei'*
Hardiness zone: 3
Form: Upright to spreading, fountain-like with rounded top, arching branches curving to the ground
Size: Reaches 6 to 8 feet high with 6- to 10-foot spread
Exposure: Full sun
Texture: Fine texture when in leaf and in winter
Leaves: Alternate, simple, toothed, often incised, three to five lobes
Flowers: Flowers are white, appearing in late April or May; borne in many flowered umbels; very showy when in bloom
Fruit: Small and insignificant
Color: Stems are slender, brown, and rounded. Leaves are a light green with no significant fall color change.
Cultural notes: This plant is adapted to a wide range of soil conditions.
Cultivars: Vanhoutte is a hybrid between S. trilobata and S. cantoniensis. There are no cultivars.

Common name: Shrubby or bush cinquefoil
Botanical name: *Potentilla fruticosa*
Hardiness zone: 2
Form: A very bushy shrub with a rounded to bread-rounded outline
Leaves: Alternate, compound pinnate with three to seven leaflets, dark green, and more or less silky
Flowers: Perfect, bright yellow, June through frost; excellent color
Fruit: Not showy, persistently retained on plant
Color: Leaf emergence is silky gray-green changing to bright to dark green. Fall color is green to yellow to brown.
Cultural notes: Cinquefoil transplants well and withstands poor dry soils and extreme cold.
Cultivars: 'Abbotswood' is the best of the white bloomers; other cultivars are also 'Dakota Sunrise,' 'Goldfinger,' 'Hurstborne,' and 'Jackmanii.'

Broadleaf evergreens

Common name: Glossy abelia
Botanical name: *Abelia grandiflora*
Hardiness zone: 6
Form: Oval
Leaves: Simple, opposite, oval 1½ inches long and ½ inch wide, tapering to a point; turns green-bronze during cold weather
Flowers: White to pink, bell-shaped 1-inch-long flowers, very showy, blooms from May through August on new growth.
Fruit: None
Color: Deep green to purple-green
Cultural notes: Glossy abelia grows under almost any condition—wet or dry, good or poor soil. It can be hedged, yet still flowers profusely. Compact varieties are less durable.
Cultivars: 'Edward Goucher' is 3 to 4 feet tall with pink flowers. 'Francis Mason' has yellow variegated leaves and is a dwarf.

Common name: Aucuba
Botanical name: *Aucuba japonica*
Hardiness zone: 7
Form: Oval shrub
Leaves: Opposite, elliptical, 3 to 7 inches long, 1 to 3 inches wide, leaf margin smooth at base, coarse teeth on outer half of leaf
Flowers: Male and female plants; inconspicuous
Fruit: Not important criteria for selection; football shaped, 1-inch-long red berries
Color: Green to speckled with yellow to yellow blotched
Cultural notes: Aucuba must be protected from high heat, persistent winds, and direct hot sunlight. It can get blackened leaves during severe winters with inadequate soil moisture.

Cultivars: 'Picturata' has bright yellow gold centers and is slow-growing and compact. 'Variegata' is gold-speckled. 'Seratalfolia' has dark green leaves.

Common name: Azalea
Botanical name: *Rhododendron spp*
Hardiness zone: 6
Form: Dense mound
Size: Small to medium, 3 to 4 feet tall
Exposure: Shade to part shade
Texture: Medium
Leaves: Simple, alternate, 1 inch long, ½ inch wide, oval-shaped
Flowers: Very showy in many different colors
Fruit: Not usually seen
Color: Dark and glossy above, dull pale green below
Cultural notes: The soil must be well-drained, fertile, moist, and acidic. Use slow-release fertilizer and an organic mulch. Leaves are mildly toxic. Azaleas require yearly mulching, pruning, fertilization, and irrigation during the summer. Iron chlorosis is a problem with high pH. Florist types are usually unsuitable for exterior landscaping.
Cultivars: 'Snow' has pure white flowers, 'Hino-crimson' has deep dark red flowers, and 'Coral Bell' has clear pink flowers. There are more than 100 named varieties along with genetic crosses with rhododendrons.

Common name: Evergreen euonymus
Botanical name: *Euonymus japonica*
Hardiness zone: 7
Form: Oval
Leaves: Opposite, simple, 1½ to 3 inches long, 1 to 1½ inches wide; slightly serrate oval leaves; always attached to stems at a 45-degree angle
Flowers: Inconspicuous, small white clusters at leaf axes
Fruit: Low number, not an important consideration
Color: Green to cultivars with silver or gold variegation
Cultural notes: Evergreen euonymus is an extremely tough durable plant that grows almost anywhere and adds a definite splash of color to the landscape. It is very susceptible to euonymus scale, which is a major weakness of this plant. All plant parts are mildly poisonous.
Cultivars: Golden euonymus has gold margins with green centers. 'Gold spot' has golden-yellow blotches. 'Silver King' has creamy white blotches.

Common name: Burford holly
Botanical name: *Llex cornuta 'Burfordi'*
Hardiness zone: 7
Form: Compact and round-headed shrub
Size: Small to large; 4 to 20 feet high and 4 to 10 feet wide
Exposure: Sun to part shade
Texture: Coarse

Leaves: Glossy, plastic-like, oval-shaped; brittle with one terminal spire
Flowers: Clusters of small yellow-green flowers at the leaf axes; not showy
Fruit: Bright red, ¼ to ½ inch in diameter, in clusters of five to eight;
very showy
Color: Dark shiny green above, pale dull green below
Cultural notes: Burford holly tolerates almost any soil but performs
better in rich well-drained types. It gets spindly and fruits poorly in
dense shade. Avoid high-heat areas. It is susceptible to grasshoppers
in rural areas and occasionally to scale. It can be sheared to almost any
form and makes an unusual small broad-headed tree after many years.
It is a good foundation plant and a widely used sturdy plant.
Cultivars: 'Dwarf Burford' is a slow grower, eventually reaching 6 to 10
feet without pruning; it has smaller, very shiny leaves. 'Chinese or
horned holly' has three terminal, very sharp spines and is very vandal
resistant. There are many other cultivars.

Common name: 'Nellie R. Stevens' holly
Botanical name: *Llex X. 'Nellie R. Stevens'*
Hardiness zone: 7
Form: Round-headed shrub
Leaves: Alternate; typical holly leaf, but with three terminal spines
Flowers: Male and female are on separate plants of llex cornuta. 'Nellie
R. Stevens' is a female plant. The flowers, which appear at the leaf
axils, are not showy.
Fruit: Large amounts of bright-red berries
Color: Deep green
Cultural notes: 'Nellie R. Stevens' is a very tough holly that can grow
under almost any conditions. The male plant of llex cornuta must be
nearby for pollination and berry protection. It is one of the most
winter-hardy of the hollies, and, as with all hollies, it is very sensitive to
water-soluble fertilizers
Cultivars: 'Nellie R. Stevens' is a hybrid between English holly and
Chinese holly. Many cultivars of these species are available and are
worthy of their popularity.

Common name: Foster holly
Botanical name: *Llex X. 'Foster'*
Hardiness zone: 6
Form: Pyramidal
Size: Moderately large (20 feet)
Exposure: Sun to part shade
Texture: Coarse
Leaves: Alternate, leaves 1½ inches wide and 2 to 3 inches long; serrate
at tip with oval shape
Flowers: On female plants, borne at leaf axes; not showy
Fruit: Prolific producer of bright-red fruit approximately ¼ inch in diameter
Color: Deep blue-green with red berries in winter

Cultural notes: Foster holly is tolerant to varied amounts of light, exposure, moisture, and soil conditions. It is probably the best of the upright pyramidal-shaped hollies.

Cultivars: Foster holly is a hybrid between American holly (llex opaca) and llex attenuata. There are numerous cultivars of llex opaca that deserve attention as a landscape plant.

Common name: Nandina
Botanical name: *Nandina domestica*
Hardiness zone: 6
Form: Mounding, layered
Size: Small to large, 2 to 7 feet tall
Exposure: Sun to shade
Texture: Fine
Leaves: Alternate, two to three compound leaflets opposite on stems of leaves
Flowers: White terminal clusters; showy in spring
Fruit: Berries ¼ inch in diameter turn red in fall. They grow in spectacular grape-like clusters.
Color: Blue-green in shade; red-purple in fall
Cultural notes: Nandina grows under any conditions but does not like hot areas caused by structures or concrete. Avoid parking lots. A vigorous grower, it is a good foundation plant. Prune by removing the tallest canes at ground level.
Cultivars: 'Compacta' is a smaller version of parent, easily maintained at 3 to 4 feet. 'Dwarf' or 'Nana' has soft foliage and dense dwarf oval form. 'Harbour Dwarf' has smaller, darker leaflets.

Common name: Fraser's photinia
Botanical name: *Photinia X. 'Fraseri'*
Hardiness zone: 7
Form: Large, upright oval shrub
Size: Large; 12 to 15 feet high and 8 to 10 feet wide
Exposure: Sun to part shade
Texture: Medium
Leaves: Alternate, simple, 1½ inches wide, 3 inches long, serrated with a point at the tip
Flowers: Usually none
Fruit: Usually none
Color: Dark green upon maturity of leaf; new growth is bright red.
Cultural notes: This plant grows in most locations but does not tolerate wet feet. It requires repeated pruning to achieve dense growth. It gets leaf spots and powdery mildew during the spring when cool, wet, and humid. Allow for growth! It overgrows some locations, so plant no closer than 6 feet from buildings. Fraser's photinia makes good screens and specimen plants and good sound barrier
Cultivars: None

Common name: Atlas cedar
Botanical name: *Cedrus atlantica*
Hardiness zone: 6
Form: Pyramidal
Size: Large tree
Exposure: Sun
Texture: Fine
Leaves: Needles 1 inch long in clusters on spurs or short shoots
Flowers: Not showy
Fruit: Cone, 2 to 3 inches long, rarely seen in United States
Color: Green or blue depending on cultivar
Cultural notes: Atlas cedar is difficult to transplant and slow-growing. It does well in soils with good drainage and moderate nutritional conditions. Bagworms may be a problem.
Cultivars: 'Glauca' is a blue atlas cedar.

Common name: Eastern red cedar
Botanical name: *Juniperus virginiana*
Hardiness zone: 2
Form: Upright
Size: Medium tree
Exposure: Sun
Texture: Fine
Leaves: Scale-like foliage; new leaves have a distinct odor when crushed.
Flowers: Not showy
Fruit: Blue or purple, smooth, round, about ¼ inch in diameter
Color: Green or blue-green
Cultural notes: Eastern red cedar prefers a good, well-drained soil but adapts fairly well to others. It is very susceptible to bagworms and cedar apple rust.
Cultivars: 'Canaert' has sharp angular branching and pyramidal growth; it is one of the best. Others are 'Kosteri' and 'Manhattan Blue.'

Common name: Chinese juniper
Botanical name: *Juniperus chinensis*
Hardiness zone: 3
Form: Variable
Size: Medium shrub
Exposure: Sun
Texture: Fine
Leaves: Scale-like juniper with new growth being needle-like
Flowers: Not showy
Fruit: Smooth, round, blue, about ¼ inch in diameter
Color: Blue-green or green
Cultural notes: Chinese juniper is tough and durable but does not take very wet conditions. Branches layer and spread to outgrow a site if used incorrectly. Bagworms can be a serious problem.

Cultivars: There are many cultivars, including blues, compacts, and dwarfs; 'Blue Vase,' 'Pfitzeriana,' 'Pfitzeriana compacta.'

Common name: Austrian pine
Botanical name: *Pinus nigra*
Hardiness zone: 4
Form: Pyramidal
Size: Large tree
Exposure: Sun
Texture: Medium
Leaves: Stiff needles, 3 to 6 inches long, in bundles of two, often twisted
Flowers: Not showy
Fruit: Oval cones 2 to 4 inches long, mature every year
Color: Dark green
Cultural notes: Austrian pine is very durable and tough after established. It tolerates salt, wind, and drought, but it is susceptible to pine twig blight and needle blight during spring and summer.
Cultivars: None

Common name: Japanese black pine
Botanical name: *Pinus thunburgi*
Hardiness zone: 6
Form: Pyramidal
Size: Large tree
Exposure: Sun
Texture: Medium
Leaves: Straight needles, 3 to 4 inches long, in bundles of two, fairly stiff and harsh to touch
Flowers: Not showy
Fruit: Cone 1 to 2½ inches long, light brown, with prickly scales
Color: Dark green
Cultural notes: Japanese black pine is tough, grows rapidly, and transplants easily. It grows informally and is not for the formal landscape. It gets open and unsightly if grown too rapidly. It is susceptible to pine tip moth.
Cultivars: None

Common name: Scotch pine
Botanical name: *Pinus sylvestris*
Hardiness zone: 2
Form: Pyramidal
Size: Large tree
Exposure: Sun
Texture: Medium
Leaves: Needles 1 to 3 inches long in bundles of two, twisted and stiff
Flowers: Not showy
Fruit: Spineless cone 1 to 2 inches long, rounded, brown

Color: Light green
Cultural notes: Scotch pine is used in commercial Christmas tree production. It grows best in Midwest and Northeast. This tree gets very large and asymmetrical with age. Allow room for growth.
Cultivars: Many different cultivars

Common name: Colorado blue spruce
Botanical name: *Picea pungens*
Hardiness zone: 2
Form: Pyramidal
Size: Large tree
Exposure: Sun to part shade
Texture: Fine
Leaves: Stiff, sharp-pointed single needles 1½ inches long
Flowers: Not showy
Fruit: Drooping cone, 2 to 4 inches long
Color: Green to blue-green
Cultural notes: Colorado blue spruce needs cool soil and night temperatures and protection from drying southwest winds. It is difficult to transplant and establish. The addition of heavy mulch helps keep the soil and root systems cool. It is very slow growing.
Cultivars: 'Glauca' is more blue in color. 'Koster' is a very deep, powdery, blue spruce cultivar with dense pyramidal growth.

Common name: Mugo pine
Botanical name: *Pinus mugo 'Mughus'*
Hardiness zone: 3
Form: Round
Size: Small shrub
Exposure: Sun
Texture: Medium
Leaves: Straight needles in bundles of two, about 1½ inches long
Flowers: Not showy
Fruit: Small (1½ inch) oval cone
Color: Dark green
Cultural notes: Mugo pine can't take extreme heat. It grows best in zone 7 and northward. It needs well-drained soil, but it is not drought-resistant. Mugo pine is very susceptible to pine tip moth. Shearing the new growth lightly helps maintain a tight symmetrical shrub.

Common name: Yew
Botanical name: *Taxus media 'Densiformis'*
Hardiness zone: 4
Form: Irregular
Size: Large shrub or small tree
Exposure: Part sun to shade
Texture: Fine
Leaves: Long and slender, often 1½ inches long, ⅛ inch wide, spirally

arranged on stem

Flowers: Not showy

Fruit: Pinkins red, fleshy cup, open at one end, containing a seed; showy

Color: Dark green

Cultural notes: All plant parts are very poisonous. The yew needs adequate moisture but well-drained soil; it can't withstand hot exposure. It is a very slow grower. Make sure the location is very well drained as waterlogged soil kills the plant, even after a short time.

Cultivars: There are many different cultivars; some are upright growers while some are shrub and hedge types.

Common name: Purpleleaf honeysuckle

Botanical name: *Lonicera japonica 'purpurea'*

Hardiness zone: 4

Form: Spreading vine

Size: Ground cover

Exposure: Sun or shade

Texture: Medium

Leaves: Opposite, oval with a pointed tip

Flowers: Red turning yellow, very fragrant

Fruit: Not showy

Color: Dark green to purple with sunlight intensifying the purple color

Cultural notes: This plant grows in nearly any soil; it grows best in full sun. Transplant early spring to early fall. 'Purpurea' is one of the easiest to contain, as the others are ambitious in growth habit.

Cultivars: There are many different cultivars from vine to shrub-like; most vines tend to overgrow location and cover anything in their path.

Common name: English ivy

Botanical name: *Hedera helix*

Hardiness zone: 5

Form: Spreading vine

Size: Ground cover

Exposure: Shade

Texture: Medium

Leaves: Alternate, with three to five rounded lobes, with smooth margins

Flowers: Not showy

Fruit: Not showy

Color: Foliage shiny green

Cultural notes: English ivy is hardy ground cover for shady locations that are not too wet or exposed to extremely bright and hot sunlight. It is susceptible to spider mites in dry locations and leaf spot in humid locations.

Cultivars: Many; some are used for houseplants

Common name: Monkey grass, Liriope, lily tuft

Botanical name: *Liriope muscari*

Hardiness zone: 6
Form: Dense grass clump
Size: Ground cover
Exposure: Part shade to shade
Texture: Medium
Leaves: Grass-like blades about ½ inch wide, 8 to 20 inches long, many leaves coming from central crown
Flowers: Purple or white rising above foliage, very showy, mid to late spring
Fruit: Small, black berries
Color: Deep green on top, light green underneath
Cultural notes: Monkey grass doesn't like extreme heat and must be kept in shade or very little sun; otherwise, it grows well in fair soil with little care. Mow back to 3 to 4 inches in early spring before new flush of growth. Propagate by dividing clumps.
Cultivars: 'Variegata' leaves have a yellow stripe on outer margin. 'Big Blue' has taller, blue-green leaves.

Common name: Compact andorra creeping juniper
Botanical name: *Juniperus horizontalis 'Youngstown'*
Hardiness zone: 2
Form: Irregular
Size: Small compact shrub
Exposure: Sun
Texture: Fine
Leaves: Scale-like typical juniper
Flowers: Inconspicuous
Fruit: Not showy
Color: Medium green, turning plum purple in winter
Cultural notes: It does not tolerate water-logged soils but grows well in moderately dry conditions. It grows well in a variety of soils.
Cultivars: There are standard varieties available, but 'Youngstown' is preferred because it remains compact, while standard varieties open up in the center with age, allowing weed growth.

Common name: Common littleleaf periwinkle
Botanical name: *Vinca minor*
Hardiness zone: 3
Form: Dense ground cover
Size: Ground cover 4 to 6 inches tall
Exposure: Shade
Texture: Fine
Leaves: Opposite, ½ to 1 inch long, ½ inch wide, elliptical with a smooth margin
Flowers: Vary in color, small, not very showy
Fruit: None

Color: Glossy green upper surface
Cultural notes: This plant does best in a moist, shady location; it is not for hot, dry locations. It is one of the best ground covers because it grows into a dense mat, keeping out most weed infiltration.
Cultivars: 'Major Bowles' has slightly larger leaves and flowers, beautiful dark glossy foliage, and bright bluish-purple flowers.

Common name: Japanese landscape juniper
Botanical name: *Juniperus procumbens*
Hardiness zone: 4
Form: Ground cover
Size: Small ground cover 6 to 8 inches
Exposure: Sun
Texture: Fine
Leaves: Needle-like, grouped in irregular clusters about ¼ inch long
Flowers: Not showy
Fruit: Not showy
Color: Foliage is blue-green
Cultural notes: This juniper does not tolerate wet conditions but generally grows well in most soil types. It needs full sun to develop compact form. Spider mites can be a problem in late summer. The wood is somewhat brittle, so watch using this plant near foot traffic. It makes a good patio tub or planter specimen. It is one of the best, most beautiful junipers as long as spider mites are controlled.
Cultivars: 'Nana' is very dwarf and compact.

Nursery plant selection for shrubs and ground covers

Follow these guidelines for choosing which plants to purchase at a nursery.

- Inspect plants to ensure they are symmetrical in shape.
- Check for good branching (full with damaged branches removed).
- They should have no evidence of disease, borers, or insects.
- Make sure that the container has not been crushed.
- Check that the root system fills the container adequately.
- The plant should be fully leafed out or have green showing in dormant stems.
- Roots growing through drain holes excessively indicates a root-bound plant; pick another.
- Turfgrasses are adapted to the regions shown in Figure 12-1. Be sure to choose an appropriate grass for your area.

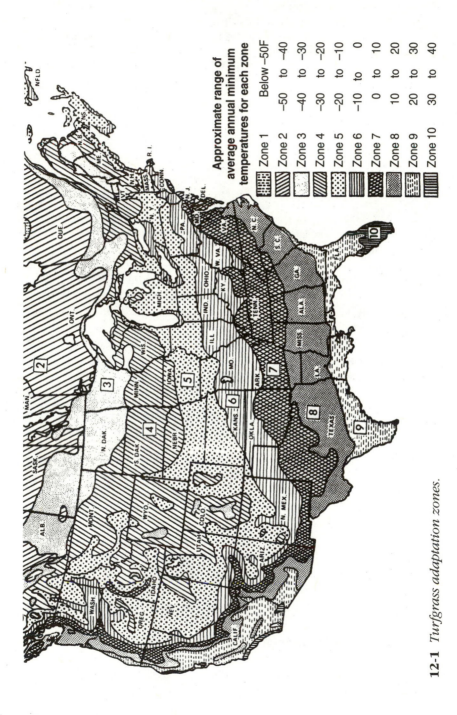

12-1 *Turfgrass adaptation zones.*

Approximate range of
average annual minimum
temperatures for each zone

Zone 1	Below −50F
Zone 2	−50 to −40
Zone 3	−40 to −30
Zone 4	−30 to −20
Zone 5	−20 to −10
Zone 6	−10 to 0
Zone 7	0 to 10
Zone 8	10 to 20
Zone 9	20 to 30
Zone 10	30 to 40

- Select ground cover grasses for warm and cool seasons, as shown in Figures 12-2 and 12-3.

Bermuda grass

Zoysia grass

St. Augustine grass

Centipede grass

12-2 *Warm-season grasses.*

Fescue

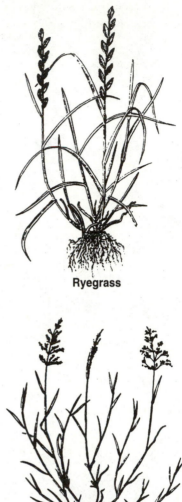

Ryegrass

Bluegrass

Bent grass

12-3 *Cool-season grasses.*

- Check grasses for the common disease and weed problems shown in Figures 12-4 through 12-6.

Brown patch

Rust

Leaf spot

Powdery mildew

Dollar spot

Snow mold

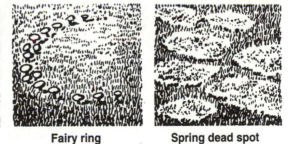
Pythium   **Fairy ring**   **Spring dead spot**

12-4 *Common turf diseases.*

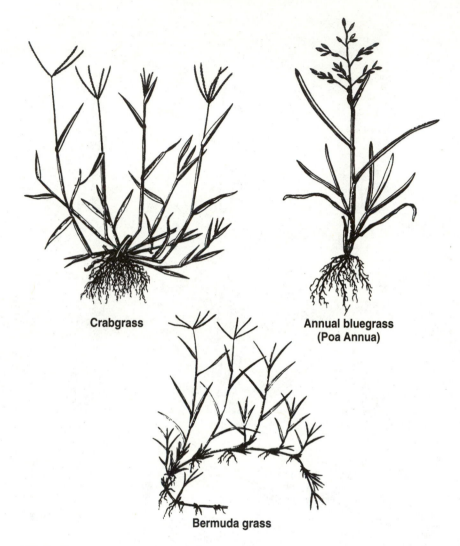

Crabgrass

Annual bluegrass
(Poa Annua)

Bermuda grass

12-5 *Common monocot weeds.*

{

Dandelion

Henbit

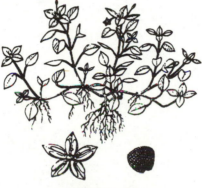

Chickweed

12-6 *Common dicot weeds.*

13

Conclusion

Future builder's guide to landscaping

How will the computer affect the landscape industry in the next century? Can you imagine a future time when blueprints are unheard of, having been replaced with a single compact disc (CD) loaded with an abundance of refined information for both builder and client? It is conceivable that landscape contractors will use a console built into the dash of their vehicle wherein the same compact disc could display every detail of a design. Also on the disc would be a library of photographs describing all the plants in a mature state specified for the design. The design would be accessible in plan view or video image just the way a design might look when completed. A landscaper could call up a photo of *Betula pendula* to determine whether the designer wanted to use a multi- or single-trunk specimen. Then, with only a couple of additional key strokes on his or her dash-mounted computer, the contractor could display the staking detail. The client might wander up and ask, "Are you sure you are installing this walkway following the same curve we planned?" The landscaper could take the property owner over to the display console and show him or her a video rendering of the completed walkway as designed by the landscape architect to assure the client that it is being installed correctly. Pretty wild, huh?

This is a current technology called *program extrapolation*. It is here now.

The computer has revolutionized many industries in the past decade, and it is important to remember that the personal computer has actually only been in existence since the early 1980s. Yet in this brief period of time, the computer has changed our work life more than the telephone. Imagine the banking industry without computers.

Or the accounting field without computers. And beyond the year 2000, it will be hard to imagine the landscaping industry without the computer. Nursery workers will employ handheld wand-scanners to read bar codes on potted plants with a single pass. The data will be transmitted into an accounting system to print out an invoice for the total. For physical counting of plant inventory, metallic disks could be applied to pots or to strip labels. Something akin to a radar gun can sweep the lot and produce a number count. A handheld computer will display the number. The inventory taker will finesse the number by subtracting the number of unhealthy plants to make it more accurate. The handheld computer will later be plugged into the main office computer, where the entire inventory will be logged into an accounting system which, in turn, subtracts from these numbers as sales are made each day. Because of the ease of this operation, physical counts will be done as frequently as once a week rather than four times a year.

Lest we forget, the computer is nothing more than a machine to manipulate information. As I said, the real age of technology exists between our ears. The computer is intended to make repetitive tasks, formulas, and computations easier, giving users time for more creative and imaginative tasks, thus making work more fulfilling and challenging. Skill in managing and presenting information clearly, quickly, and accurately will be at a premium as we enter the twenty-first century. Computers within the landscape industry must manage inventories, present pricing information, gather horticultural data, estimate costs, calculate slopes, select appropriate plant specimens, and perform countless other tasks. Though they assist us in many ways, computers are no substitute for sound judgment. Professionals in any business in 2010 will succeed or fail based on their ability to clearly evaluate, organize, use, and present information. The computer is the primary tool in this process, but let us remember that it remains a tool and nothing more.

Landscape designers will be able to easily create multimedia presentations of their projects. These multimedia productions will be transferable to VCR tape for TV viewing or storable in CD-ROM format for possible interactive applications. Designers will be able to accurately communicate their ideas in forms that can be viewed at odd hours, in distant places, or on the spur of the moment. The landscape industry, as a whole, is experiencing substantial apprehension in relation to the computer. So many choices, so many systems, so many programs, so many prices exist that the computer novice scarcely knows where to begin. People are concerned that if they purchase something today, it will be outdated or obsolete tomorrow (and that in fact, is what will probably happen). Most landscapers are quite naturally disoriented by computer technology. Landscape architects and designers, by and large, have an artistic bent. Contractors typically prefer work in the field to work in an office. Such inhibitions discourage some of today's processional builders from plunging into the world of the computer, yet as we know, our children use these machines almost daily and run programs with the ease we use to operate the telephone and TV. (You know this is true because your kid is the only one in the family who can program the VCR.) What is futuristic to one generation is commonplace to the next.

However, the writing on the wall is becoming increasingly clear to landscape professionals. Computer-aided design (CAD), computer-assisted manufacturing (CAM), bar codes, fax machines, and cellular phones have already revolutionized the construction industry in the past few years. Many builders have proudly purchased computers and software programs, but how many use them to their full potential? Retail nursery outlets in the twenty-first century might very well place kiosks where customers, either alone or with a salesperson, can access a touch screen computer that might ask, "What kind of plant are you looking for—tree, shrub, ground cover, vine, perennial, bedding plant, or indoor plant?" After the customer responds with the appropriate selection, it might query further, "Describe the lighting conditions for this plant—full sun, half sun/shade, full shade, indoor?" Questions will continue as required until finally the customer touches the search button. On the screen will pop not a list of plants, but rather a collection of color photographs of the plants available that same day at the nursery, all shown side by side. The client can point to one of the pictures with its accompanying botanical and common names and bring to the screen a complete, easy-to-read profile of the selected plant containing descriptive information, suggested plant combinations, and maintenance instructions for that community and, perhaps, even an address where a mature specimen of the plant may be seen. Finally, a printout, complete with pictures of the relevant plants, might be provided to the customer for little or no fee. An incidental code within the list can indicate the location in the nursery where these selections may be found.

Builders will be able to use digitizers to scan landscape plans to quickly access areas and volumes for their cost analysis. They may have created their own software routines to make use of unit costs that are specific to their own company's experience, even with built-in factors for access, material availability, and unreliable labor. Estimates will be performed in the field with the aid of small handheld computers. A career's worth of experience could be loaded into such a machine. Knowledge garnered from all past projects will come to bear on the present so that each succeeding estimate is more accurate and professional than the one before. The builder will walk back to the truck and plug the handheld computer into the console on the dash and type out a cover letter to accompany the proposal. All this will be printed on the spot from a portable printer the size of a present-day VCR hidden under the dash. The contractor will hand the potential customer the proposal and drive off. There could be a computer program to prompt the contractor to make a follow-up phone call every seven days for three weeks to keep the company name in front of the potential client.

Any technology devised by humans will either enhance life or complicate it. Computers are notorious for creating nearly as many problems as they solve. I have many times threatened mine with a new life as a microwave toaster. Some people, obtaining libraries of information and the ability to access it with great speed, mistake this information for knowledge. You see this a lot on the Internet. Unfortunately, such access to information is falsely ego-inflating. In the landscape industry, experience is most highly valued. Landscape professionals in the next century will be able to use a plant list to access a database that, in turn, will produce a report of all wholesale nursery sources for the plants specified. Via modem, the architect or contractor will be able to upload the desired plant list to the appropriate nurseries selected. The information will interact with the nursery computer and a report will be returned, or perhaps a phone call, specifying which plants the nursery is prepared to supply, the price offered, and time of delivery. The plants not obtainable from a first pass will be rechanneled back into the computer program, and a new list of nursery references will appear, again reinitiating a new round of phone/fax/modem transmissions to a different set of wholesale nurseries.

Perhaps, one day far in the future, landscape professionals will have the equivalent of a Star Trek "holodeck" (maybe a virtual-reality kiosk). The designer will simulate a Mediterranean land–scape . . . in blues and whites . . . with a water feature, Greco-Roman statuary, and a canopy of Italian stone pines. Any trees you like. Like these? We walk right in and experience it through virtual reality . . . before it even exists! Sound too fantastic? You'd be surprised—some of that stuff is here already. The future is like a big, happy dog with a long, slobbering tongue—ready or not, here it comes!

Marketing by computer

Landscape professionals have historically been notoriously poor at marketing. The ratio value of landscape work to property value has scarcely been researched, with the consequence that landscaping usually receives the short end of the stick when it comes to property development. In the building industry, landscaping is a low priority. Why is this? The answer is simple: marketing. The landscaping trade simply does not promote itself effectively. Landscape architects, for one example, have an unwritten prohibition from placing yellow-page ads. I have no idea why. Landscape contractors somehow overlook the fact that people read newspapers. And nurseries are as silent as country mice when compared with merchandising giants like Wal-Mart and Home Depot. The landscaping trade sorely needs a boost of professionalism to enhance its image, and the computer can play a fundamental role in this enhancement. Until quite recently, it was common for a landscape professional to present an estimate scribbled on the back of a business card.

Compare this to the professional presentation of a set of color photographs simulating a completed landscape, including a laser-printed cover letter introducing the company, documenting its quality work and past successes, along with a reference list of contented past customers who can vouch for the integrity of this professional's work. The list could be prepared with eye-catching landscape-related graphics to stylize the document. Perhaps a sketch or working drawing might be provided, dramatically laying out the project. A series of plant lists, solving key landscape problems, like erosion control, shady areas, or clay soil, might be included as well. The estimate itself could give a detailed breakdown of costs on a phase-by-phase basis. Unit costs for key elements of the job might be broken out for the client to consider. In summary, potential clients would be given a complete brochure filled with professional-looking documents, convincing them that they were dealing with a fully qualified, computer-savvy, skillful, and knowledgeable professional. Like P.T. Barnum said, sell the sizzle, not the steak. Image is important to sales.

As part of a design project by a landscape architect or as part of an installation project by a landscape contractor, a detailed diagram of the property in question with valve locations and emergency-maintenance instructions could be provided. A maintenance schedule for pruning, fertilization, integrated pest management, and watering instructions on a month-by-month basis could also be included. Furthermore, using irrigation-management software, the landscape professional could provide a client with a month-by-month timer schedule, maximizing water-usage efficiency. In short, the professional of the future can manage information, educate, and communicate far more completely than we do today. This new level of professionalism becomes a marketing tool. Rather than being shovel-and-broom landscapers working for dirt wages and development tidbits, the landscapers of the future will be skilled and knowledgeable professionals with a command of, perhaps, the most crucial technology of our time: computers. The use of computers must be demonstrated to the client not only at the estimating and design stages, but additionally as an information source for consulting and education at the conclusion of the project.

A remarkable marketing function of a computer is in keeping your company's name before prospective clients. In the real estate field, agents have made a science of communicating consistently with would-be home buyers and sellers. Consider the volume of junk mail arriving from realtors on a weekly basis, and think about the number of times a realtor comes to your door or calls concerning your property. Your patience may be taxed, but face it, it is effective. Good salesmanship involves proper timing. You can deliver a great sales pitch for a design project or installation project, but if it is presented too early or too late, the deal is off. You must be visible to the client when the timing is right, and this requires attention and persistence. Enter the computer once again. Set up a simple database of all key leads in any integrated software program. Include name, address, phone number, and any extra characteristics you would like to use to sort names (i.e., commercial, residential, etc.). Enter into the database all those you wish to communicate with—developers, homeowner associations, contractors, architects, past clients, current and past estimate people, etc. Try to assemble a couple of hundred names if you can. Then, perhaps once a month, every two months, once a season, or whenever you feel is appropriate, write them a general letter extolling the virtues of your company and inviting them to consult with you about any upcoming projects.

By incorporating a mail-merge feature (integrated into most word processors), you can send each company a personalized letter. Used in conjunction with window envelopes, you will have addressing already done, or you can use the same database program to create mailing labels. In the time it takes you to write a single letter and stuff and stamp an envelope, you have effectively corresponded with a couple hundred key leads. It is also helpful to carefully prepare the message you are presenting in this manner, since we are all inundated with uninteresting, unintelligent, and just plain boring trash mail almost daily. Try to keep your effort out of that category. Get help from a professional, perhaps only for a first letter, just to get the idea of how things can be done.

It is often helpful to include in your database a "notes" area to keep track of little idiosyncrasies and details of a project or client. These notes might include particular information (say, from another state). In another area, make space for a "callback" section. Have you ever given an estimate or had a consultation, followed up once, and never called back again? We builders are known worldwide for not returning phone calls.

The name of the game in marketing is persistence and attention to detail. Ideally, you want your company name to ring from each and every rooftop. Assuming you are doing good work, you want your reputation to proceed you. This doesn't happen by passively waiting around for work to arrive. The computer can be used to create flyers, brochures, and promotional pieces to be handed out whenever the opportunity arises. Simple pieces can be done with a word-processing program, or more elaborate brochures or flyers can be created with sophisticated page-layout programs. You may not feel that you have the budget to purchase nor time or inclination to learn these programs, but your competition very well might! Take a night class, hire a college student to come in to assist, or turn it over to a professional to work out.

Another effective marketing vehicle is a newsletter. A number of landscape and design firms are creating their own newsletters to keep their company name prominent among potential and current customers. Newsletters for our trade are printed on nice recycled paper, with full color, lots of graphics, and articles of pertinent interest.

It seems that the landscape industry has generally survived off those clients occupying the top 10-percent income bracket in our communities. Residential landscape contractors basically service the well-to-do. It seems reasonable to suggest that landscapers expand beyond this group and address the landscape and environmental needs of middle-income clients. Perhaps many cannot afford major projects, but enterprising landscape professionals might be able to turn a significant profit executing smaller property enhancements, front-yard facelifts, and consultations for do-it-yourselfers. I am personally convinced that there is money to be made in this arena. As America tightens the belt on luxuries, we simultaneously look for escapes from the doldrums. Entertainment is the typical release. Why not a beautiful environment to lift one's spirits? Go sell them on it!

Professional landscape imaging

Every landscape-design professional has struggled at one time or another to try to communicate design ideas to a client. Describing the curve of a walk, citing botanical names of plants, or presenting an overhead-view landscape drawing often leaves a client scratching his or her head in confusion. Still, it is our job as builders and designers to enable clients to visualize a landscape for which they are paying us to design and install. The traditional methods of achieving this end are various. For example, we can outline the lawn area with a landscape hose, or we can haul out voluminous photo collections in manila folders accompanied by our favorite plant books marked with sticky notes all laid in a heap on the client's coffee table. Some pros sketch a drawing of the landscape freehand. Some draft a plan using CAD programs. All of these approaches pale in effectiveness compared to professional landscape imaging.

Landscape imaging describes a process whereby a photograph is taken of a job site with a video or still camera. That image is then digitized (imported into a computer) and manipulated within the computer. The end result is a more or less photorealistic image of how the finished landscape will appear prior to any actual work being done to it. This technology has long been used within the movie industry. The salon business has picked up on it by showing clients prospective hair styles before they go under the scissors. The dental industry illustrates to their clients what orthodontic work would do for their smiles. Likewise, the plastic surgery field previews to potential subjects the hoped-for results of surgical alterations. Following these examples, what could be more persuasive to potential clients than viewing full-color photographs of their would-be landscape? Imaging applied to the landscape industry is called—ta da!—landscape imaging.

In addition to software development creating a software package specifically for the landscape professional, clip art of a wide variety of landscape elements, such as decks, pools, trellises, fences, paving, etc., are available to be used in the imaging process. Clipped images are pictures of features (decks, fences, walls) separated from any surrounding background or foreground elements. Once a clipped image is created, it can be copied and pasted into a larger picture, moved, shaped, sized, and shadowed so that it combines naturally with the larger picture. Possessing a large library of these clipped images is crucial to creating successful landscape images. The library, of course, must include a selection of plant materials. It would be impractical to have pictures of every plant commercially available, so one must exercise imagination and creativity.

Landscape imaging requires powerful computer equipment. Full-color photographic images are being displayed, resized, and embellished. The task of working with such memory-intensive images is slow and laborious with any PC less than a 486. The more RAM (random access memory), the better. You'll probably need at least 8 megabytes (MB) of RAM. Hard-disk storage space is also an issue. The bigger, the better. It is suggested to purchase 100MB capacity or more. A tape backup system or a large external hard disk is recommended as well.

The same applies to Macintosh users. The more power, the better you will work. Because of color requirements, older machines and the Apple Classic lines are pretty much ruled out. You need a Mac II machine or later. If you are buying new equipment, it would be advisable to acquire a PowerPC with greater clock speed and expansion slots. A complete Mac set-up with software can be had for less than $4000, while additional bells and whistles can bring the price to $15,000 or more. The PC setup is the same, with the high end being about $1000 to $3000 less than the Mac.

The alternatives to laser-printer output are usually not effective. It is difficult to get high-quality output with inexpensive printing devices. High quality in this context refers to book-quality photography, which is what your clients expect. Color printers for less than a thousand dollars can be found, such as the Apple Color Pro and the HP inkjets, but the printing quality is generally marginal, and printed pictures are usually very unconvincing. A couple of printers now coming onto the market, an Epson 720-dot-per-inch color inkjet (for around $600) and a soon-to-be-released Hewlett Packard color laser printer at a reasonable cost, might conceivably change the picture, but at present, for a commercial presentation or large-scale project where you charge for your imaging work, a service bureau with a high-end Canon or Iris printer is probably your best bet. You may also opt for outputting to slides, and creating a slide presentation of the images you create. The other option is using the color screen of a laptop color computer to display images to a client.

Make no mistake, landscape imaging is the wave of the future. It is becoming increasingly crucial to communicate design ideas to clients with clarity and persuasion. Color photography remains a persuasive method to convey your design ideas. Clients are certain to take note of your professionalism and technical savvy; however, this technology will not make a poor company good. Some companies bought into the imaging process early, expecting dramatic results. Those companies reaping great results were already great companies. The companies making little headway in imaging were ones previously struggling with marketing and client satisfaction. The moral of the story is: Imaging is no panacea, but it can be a fantastic tool.

It must also be noted that imaging, as nearly everything else worthwhile, takes practice and skill. There is little automatic about it. You must acquire a number of skills similar to those learned in the art field: shadowing, perspective, and proportion, for example. At the time of this writing, there are but two companies currently selling hardware and software for imaging within the landscape industry: IDP in the Midwest and Design Imaging Group in California.

Postscript

Stories of corporate downsizing and failures of small construction companies are all around us. If you haven't been affected yet, you probably know someone who has. Even if you have a good business now, you may be looking over your shoulder, wondering when your turn will come. While current studies reflect that most Americans are nervous about the future, in the construction industry the survival fear hangs like the fog rolling in on quiet cat feet. And it's making a profound change in our national economy and in our lives, whether we're aware of it yet or not.

It's hard to make a statistical case that big-business downsizing has changed American construction dramatically. The industry is making a slow recovery from the latest recession, but some people are still buying new homes. Economists say downsizing has forced a lot of people out of jobs, but the worst is over. "The wave of mass layoffs at American corporations is subsiding," the *Wall Street Journal* recently proclaimed. So if things are getting better, why don't we feel more bullish on America? Because, despite what the statistics say, life is tougher than it used to be for middle- and upper-middle-class Americans.

The construction industry has been no exception, and there have been some hard times in the last decade. The new technologies have changed everything, from design to production to project execution. But this change has also helped define and create demand for the professional builder, not only in the construction industry but also in other businesses that use landscaping maintenance in their facilities operations. This wave of change can work to your benefit if you are sharp enough to climb aboard now. Take advantage of the modern landscaping techniques contained within this reference manual. The companies that will build the projects of the future are looking for modern builders like you.

It has been my intent to produce a comprehensive builder's landscaping manual in conjunction with a parallel landscaping-layout and materials-takeoff software program. I hope I've been successful. I've tried to inject humor and real-world applications to demystify landscaping, because I've learned in my years as a teacher that one must put the student at ease. Only when one is relaxed does attention fully turn to the lesson at hand, allowing knowledge to truly flow. My "frontier colloquiums" style of writing (as my editor calls it) is undoubtedly too loose for some looking for a spit-and-polish reference manual. But I come from the trades, and I've learned from experience that people learn and retain more from working professionals than from isolated academics, so I make no apologies.

As one builder to another, it has been my great pleasure to serve as your author of this bookware product. When the knowledge contained herein becomes yours and begins to pay off in your career, it will be my great honor to have been your instructor. May the fair winds of success always fill your sails.

Index

Illustrations are shown in **boldface**.

WAKE TECHNICAL COMMUNITY COLLEGE LIBRARY
RALEIGH, NORTH CAROLINA 27603

About the Author

Jonathan F. Hutchings is one of the nation's premier authors in construction technologies books and bookware products (reference books with integrated software programs). He holds a Baccalaureate Degree in Construction Management, is a licensed building contractor, and certified construction technologies consultant. He also serves on the California State Legal Advisory Board as an Expert Witness and consultant to the insurance industry.

He is the author of:

- *CPM Construction Scheduler's Manual* (McGraw-Hill 1995)
- *McGraw-Hill's National Building Codes* (McGraw-Hill 1997)
- *Builders' Guide To Modular Construction* (McGraw-Hill 1996)
- *Builders' Guide To Landscaping* (McGraw-Hill 1996)

Written expressly for contractors and subcontractors, this easy-to-use, well-illustrated reference in McGraw-Hill's popular **Builder's Guide** series gives you all the information you need to handle every aspect of landscaping professionally and economically. Featuring complete methods for both traditional and innovative landscaping, this first-of-its-kind guide is your all-in-one key to success in every aspect of the landscaping business, from marketing your services to maintaining plants and putting in patios. A volume in the Builder's Guide Series.